REVEALING ANTIQUITY 20

G. W. BOWERSOCK, GENERAL EDITOR

KYLE HARPER

From Shame to Sin

The Christian Transformation of Sexual Morality in Late Antiquity

HARVARD UNIVERSITY PRESS Cambridge, Massachusetts and London, England

Printed in the United States of America

First Harvard University Press paperback edition, 2016
Fifth Printing

Library of Congress Cataloging-in-Publication Data

Harper, Kyle, 1979–
From shame to sin : the Christian transformation of sexual morality in late antiquity / by Kyle Harper.
pages cm
Includes bibliographical references and index.
ISBN 978-0-674-07277-0 (cloth: alk. paper)
ISBN 978-0-674-66001-4 (pbk.)
1. Sex—History—To 1500. 2. Sexual ethics—History—To 1500.
3. Sex—Religious aspects—Christianity. 4. Civilization, Classical.
5. Rome—Moral conditions. I. Title.
HQ13.H37 2013
306.7—dc23 2012043484

For Michelle,

my amazing wife

Contents

Preface

This book presents an effort to summarize, between two covers, what difference Christianity made in the history of sexual morality. It does so by exploring the late classical world out of which Christianity emerged and following the story of the religion's expansion down to the age of the emperor Justinian. That is an enormous topic and this is a short book, which can only claim to draw out some of the main lines of such a complex development. This project arises out of my previous work on slavery, which left me with the sense that there was still something worthwhile to be said on a theme that has evoked some of the most exciting work of the last thirty years. *From Shame to Sin* tries to speak to readers generally interested in antiquity, early Christianity, and the history of sexuality, while simultaneously offering something useful to specialists, who may find more attention devoted to topics like status, demography, and law than is customarily found in narratives of intellectual history. Therein lies the essence of the argument presented in these pages: by placing the rules and regulations, and their moral assumptions, into their material context, we might emerge with a richer understanding of what the transition to a Christian sexual culture meant.

From Shame to Sin

Introduction

From City to Cosmos

THE SEXUAL CULTURES of the classical world have been the object of unfailing interest, scholarly and otherwise. The reason for this fascination is not far to seek. Surely here, it might seem, in an age without doubt about simple pleasures, where desire was unchanneled by the narrows of sexual orientation, before guilt and penance, was an essentially different way of thinking about the morality of desire. In short, the sexual cultures of the Greeks and Romans have proven endlessly fascinating because they lie *before* the great watershed of Christianization. The Christian revolution in sexual morality, so the story goes, ushered in a style of sexual regulation that is less alien, more familiar. This book tries to identify and assess the changes wrought by the advent and triumph of Christianity. It moves across the late classical world, beginning in the high empire, when Christianity was no more than a faint voice in the vibrant, cacophonous world of the Roman Mediterranean, and ending in the haze of ruin and violent puritanism that characterized the reign of Justinian. Few periods of premodern history have witnessed such brisk and consequential ideological change. Sex was at the center of it all.

Over the last generation, as the history of sexuality became one of the great scholarly enterprises, the popular story in which Christianity put an end to pagan freedom with the body was exposed as a caricature, at best. In 1978 Sir Kenneth Dover published *Greek Homosexuality,* opening a new era in the study of ancient culture by arguing that the Greeks did not recognize permanent sexual orientation as a core feature of individual identity. In that same year, an article by Paul Veyne exploded the myth that pre-Christian sexual culture was an uninhibited garden; in his strong reformulation, the Romans were already, long before Constantine's celestial vision, pent-up pagan prudes who had sex timorously, at night, with their clothes on and the lamps off. The insights of Dover and Veyne were refined and greatly popularized in the late works of Michel Foucault, who showed that the history of sex could be about more than the changing balance of permissiveness and constraint; it could be about the categories of desire and morality, about the cultures that sustained differing visions of the human person as a sexual being. Above all, our understanding of early Christian sexuality has been revolutionized by the work of Peter Brown, whose *Body and Society* restored to Christian asceticism its original symbolic energy and human urgency. Brown's book inspired a whole generation of scholars by showing that the act of sexual renunciation was at the heart of a debate over the very meaning of Christianity's place in the world. The pioneers of Christian virginity, in denying the material demands the social order placed on their sexual capacity, transformed themselves into intermediaries of an otherworldly order. Acts of the flesh were burdened with a symbolism they had never known before.[1]

From Shame to Sin builds on the remarkable work of the last generation to reflect on the Christianization of sexual morality. It is an attempt to gather what has been learned about this great transformation, to take stock of what truly changed, and to offer an interpretation that grounds sexual morality firmly in the mechanics of ancient society. The reconstruction presented in these pages rests on four, mutually interdependent claims. The first maneuver of this book is to displace the Christianization of sex to a time rather later than it is normally thought to have taken place. The second century, it will be argued, was not careening toward a repressive future. The victory of a stern conjugal morality was not an inevitable triumph, over which Christianity simply happened to be holding the banner. The fourth century witnessed a fierce struggle, driven by the sudden advance of specifically Christian norms and prohibitions, and only toward the beginning of the fifth century did Christian values obtain a vice grip on public sexual culture. The ratification of this victory in public law was halting and, until the sixth century, incomplete and uncertain. This is a history of sex that begins by trying to sketch the specific quality of sexual life in the second-century empire and then chart the tumultuous changes of succeeding centuries down to the age of Justinian, by which time anything resembling classical eros had lost its pulse and a new order of relationships between sexual morality, public culture, and the legal regime was consolidated.

Second, despite the steady progress of the last decades, there remain specific topics that have not received adequate treatment in accounts of transformation. For example, although same-sex eros has attracted a lion's share of the attention from historians, there is, astonishingly, just one reliable treatment of the legal regime governing same-sex love in the Roman period; it has had no discernible influence on the major studies of ancient sex. We will depart from it in certain details, but the greater imperative is to integrate a credible account of structure and change in the legal system into a broader narrative of the history of sex. Equally urgent is the need to reckon with prostitution. This book will try to convince the reader that prostitution is important, even central, to the history of sex. "Prostitution" is not quite the right word, and for us it might evoke a host of marginalizing connotations: furtive vice, sanitary blight, guerilla warfare between the desperate and the forces of order. In the ancient world, the flesh trade was a dominant institution, flourishing in the light of day. The sex industry was integral to the moral economy of the classical world. The circulation of pleasures, outside the nexus of matrimony, must occupy the foreground, if there is to be any hope of recapturing the texture of life in the late classical world and of experiencing the jarring gospel of Christian sexuality. Christianity gave a name to the array of sensual opportunities beyond the marriage bed: *porneia,* fornication. Christian spokesmen for a time promoted the belief that the dominance of *porneia* was the sign of a world in disorder, and then, as they accumulated power, they set out, with some diligence, to repress it. The coordinated assault on the extramarital sexual economy marks one of the more consequential revolutions in the history of sex.[2]

Third, the passage from classical to Christian sexual culture required new conceptions of moral agency, and the idea (and the very formula) of "free will" was born in the struggle to define the meaning of Christian sexual morality. Greco-Roman culture, in the high empire, became profoundly aware of the embeddedness of its sexual norms in society and the consequent tensions between objective and subjective factors in the judgment of sexual acts. The early church, by contrast, developed a radical notion of individual freedom, centered around a libertarian paradigm of complete sexual agency. The Christians of the second century invent the notion of free will. In its original form, Christian "free will" was a cosmological claim—an argument about the relationship between God's justice and the individual. The Christian invention of free will was a radical innovation, and yet it cannot be understood apart from the main currents of contemporary intellectual culture. Questions of volition and force are also a privileged index to the progress of Christian sexuality in the later centuries, as Christian triumph undid naive, absolutist models of moral agency. The concern with free will remained central, but as Christianity became intermeshed with society, the discussion shifted, in revealing ways, to the actual psychology of volition and the material constraints on sexual action. The suddenness with which Augustine's distinctive understandings of divine election and human flesh could push back against centuries of Christian voluntarism reflect the new position of the church as a powerful social institution, part of rather than apart from the world. This book argues that sex was integral to the development of the concept of free will, and that the changing conceptions of the will as a moral problem trace the transformation of a rigorously austere dissent movement into the dominant culture of the Mediterranean world.

Fourth, *From Shame to Sin* will situate sexual morality within the material frameworks governing which erotic experiences were permissible. By insisting that the hard facts of social life actively created and constrained beliefs about the morality of bodily acts, the book departs, conceptually, from the way in which the history of ancient sexuality is often written. The study of Christianization has been colored by the widely shared view that culture is the active agent that creates sexual meaning out of inert physical material, that culture accounts for the extraordinary diversity of human behavior, and that culture is what we, as historians, find it our primary task to interpret. When sexuality is flattened into a web of meanings, a symbolic system that resides in cultural artifacts and creates moral subjects, fundamental changes introduced by Christianity are rendered invisible. Instead, culture ought to be treated as a set of values and representations of the world that impinge on behavior, that strike real human flesh in various ways, especially by cutting across hard, structural patterns in the experience of eros. Particularly in societies that lived in the unforgiving grind of high-mortality cycles, with limited technologies of reproduction, sexual morality existed within networks of power defined by law, demography, and the control of resources. Sexual morality must be seen as part of the circuitry of a sexual economy constituted by real human bodies. This book is through and through focused on *society,* on its machinery for regulating reproduction and dispensing pleasures, and on the place of sexual morality within the fabric of the social order. Seen in this light, the triumph of Christianity not only drove profound cultural change. It created a new relationship between sexual morality and society.

The book's title, *From Shame to Sin,* reflects the argument that Christianity transformed the very order of relationships between sexual morality and social reproduction. It is worth pausing to reflect on what is meant and, just as importantly, *not* meant by this frame. The claim advanced here is not that there was a sea change in the language of sexual morality. Shame and sin, to be sure, both have a real grounding in the classical tongues. The language of sin is narrowly confined—*peccare* and its derivatives in Latin, *hamartein* and its relatives in Greek. The idiom of shame, by contrast, and the closely related concept of honor, is more diffuse but no less powerful, in both Latin and Greek. In Latin, the notion of shame was centered around a cluster of words including *pudicitia* (sexual modesty) and its opposite *impudicitia* (sexual immodesty), as well as the more concretized states of being, *honestas* (social respectability) and *infamia* (dishonor). In Greek, *sōphrosynē* was used to denote both a virtue (self-control) and the possession of sexual respectability. Shame was expressed as *aischynē*—an act which brought dishonor on the actor, or the emotional experience of moral failure. *Aidōs* drew closer to the individual's "sense of shame," both positively, in the proper respect for others' opinions that evoked honorable behavior (similar to the Latin *pudor*), or negatively as the embarrassment that follows upon misconduct. In Greek the more concrete states of honor and dishonor were expressed by *timē* and *atimia,* respectively. The triumph of Christian sexual morality was, as far as these terms are concerned, linguistically neutral. The vocabulary of sin was as familiar to pre-Christian moralities (especially Stoicism) as it was to ecclesiastical authorities. Dio Chrysostom, for instance, could refer to the unlawful violation of women and boys as "sins." And

Christian authors will exuberantly deploy the language, and sanctions, of "shame" in their campaign to repress sin.[3]

If the argument suggested by the title, *From Shame to Sin,* is not about linguistic transformation, neither is it about a shift from external social judgment to an internal, psychologizing morality (such a book might be called *From Shame to Guilt*). It is true that, by our period, "sin," in both Latin and Greek, has the full sense of "moral transgression," with a strong sense of culpability that must necessarily look inward for a blameworthy faculty. But the mistake would be to imagine that the cluster of terms governing the idea of "shame" was somehow exclusively external. Shame, in the Greco-Roman culture of the high empire, shuttled between external judgment and internal affect; its very nature lay in the inseparable *connection* between the two. Robert Kaster's definition of *pudor* perfectly captures its essence: "a displeasure with oneself caused by vulnerability to just criticism of a socially diminishing sort." In other words, shame was an emotion or emotional state experienced by an individual because of the potentially valid disapproval of the moral community. For instance, a Latin encyclopedist of the high empire recorded a philosopher's definition of *pudor* and *aischynē* alike as "fear of justified reproach." Shame, in the Roman Empire, was necessarily an interpersonal concept, dependent on the potential judgment of the moral community.[4]

The demands of honor and shame also varied in the expectations they placed on the individual, according to the individual's place within the moral community. Herein lies the internal logic of shame as a moral sanction. Shame is not only a regulative emotion that mediates between the individual's self-surveillance and the community's power to render moral judgment; shame governs the moral expectations immanent in the structure of the moral community itself. Shame was a profoundly social concept, mediated always by gender and status. In the sexual life of the Roman Empire, it would be impossible to overstate the decisive influence of social position in the determination of sexual boundaries. Slavery, absolutely fundamental to the social and moral order of Roman life, gave sharp meaning to the concepts of honor and shame; slavery is an inherently degrading institution, which by its very nature deprives the slave of direct, individual access to social honor. "Slaves had no sense of *pudor* at all, perhaps because they were not usually conceived as having an interior ethical life, and certainly because they could not suffer social diminution." The free, by contrast, and especially the wellborn, were thought to embody social honor and to exhibit a finely wrought sense of shame proper to their station in life.[5]

The moral expectations inhering in the dynamics of shame were generated by the social order. As a result, the real tension in the moral world of the Romans was not between the internal and the external dimensions of shame, but rather between the subjective and the objective qualities of shame. Honor and shame were both states of mind and states of being—moral qualities and social conditions. Nowhere is this clearer than in the sexual field. *Pudicitia,* derived from *pudor,* described the quality of sexual modesty. It meant something different in the case of men and women, free persons and slaves (for whom it had virtually no meaning). As we will explore in Chapter 1, it implied, simultaneously, *both* the intentional, mental state of sexual propriety *and* the objective state of bodily sexual integrity. *Sōphrosynē* covered a similar range in Greek, differing in the case of men and women, and pointing both to a mentally virtuous condition and an objective state. What is notable about the moralizing literature of the Roman period is a heightened awareness of this duality. Greek and Roman authors will contrive elaborate scenarios testing the fundamental assumption that status and behavior cohere. The culture of the high empire, in short, became acutely sensitive to the deep interconnection of external and internal dimensions of moral behavior; the literate classes became sensible to the fact that what we are—our desires, our limits, our moral awareness—is given to us by the world.[6]

From Shame to Sin, then, reconstructs a transformation in the deep logic of sexual morality, in which the theological conception of sin came to override and to reshape an ancient sexual culture rooted in power and social reproduction. The specific prohibitions introduced by Christianity—such as the proscription of all same-sex love and the flat condemnation of prostitution—were part of this transformation. But even where the rules of conduct remained the same (such as the nearly unchanging expectations placed on respectable women), the sanctions of morality decisively shifted. The legacy of Christianity lies in the dissolution of an ancient system where status and social reproduction scripted the terms of sexual morality. The concept of sin, and its twin, free will, entailed what Nietzsche called "eine Metaphysik des Henkers," a metaphysics of the hangman, which is foundationally distinct from the social metaphysics of pre-Christian sexual morality. Shame is a social concept, instantiated in human emotions; sin is a theological concept. They represent different categories of moral sanction. That is the point: the transition from a late classical to a Christian sexual morality marked a paradigm shift, a quantum leap to a new foundational logic of sexual ethics, in which the cosmos replaced the city as the framework of morality.[7]

The logic, rather than the language, of sexual morality changed in the period we are exploring. A signal example of this change underlies a legal reform that might be taken as an inflection point in the transition described in this book (and which is explored in great detail in Chapter 3). In AD 428 the Christian emperor Theodosius II enacted a law banning the use of coercion in the sex industry. The law wished to repress the prostitution of slaves, daughters, and other vulnerable members of society, which was anything but a marginal part of the classical sexual order. The moral foundations of the law were, there can be no doubt, Christian. The law advertised the will to prevent "the necessity of sinning." The language of sexual sin is totally alien to Roman law and symbolizes the diffusion of a new pattern of moral reasoning. The complete, violent exploitation of women without any claim to civic protection was simply, as a problem in its own right, invisible in a culture whose moral foundations were immanent in the logic of social reproduction. The law of 428 was the first salvo in an enduring crusade against coercive procurement that the Christian emperors of the next century would carry out. Yet only ten years after the initial enactment, the laws returned immediately to the venerable language of shame, claiming to defend the *pudicitia* of women who, in the more ancient logic of sexual shame, had no claim to such a quality. In other words, the new logic could prevail even within an old language. So, throughout, we must try to peer behind language—whether the Greek novelists' clever manipulation of words like shame or virginity, or the efforts of Christian lawyers and litterateurs to convey radical ideas in traditional dialects—into the logic of moral command.

Chapter 1 sketches a portrait of sexual life in the heyday of Roman power, from the later first to the early third century. As in any portrait, the angles are carefully chosen, and necessarily selective. We must try, insofar as possible, to recapture the erotic values of the second century as a period in its own right. Here was a Mediterranean society, huddled into little towns that were at once primitive and unusually wealthy. It was a society whose moral lineaments were sculpted by the omnipresence of slaves and by the rigid stratifications of law. A particular feature of the frame used here must be noted: one canvas suffices for both the Latin and the Greek parts of the empire. This choice is a calculated gambit, not just dictated by the necessity of space but more deliberately by the belief that the institutions of army, the webs of commerce, the intimate ties of intermarriage, the syncretism of law, and a shared intellectual culture melded the Greek and Latin elements of the empire into a whole that is not homogeneous but at least capable of representation as a single, complex organism. As far as possible, the authorities of the second century are asked to present themselves. In part this is done because they are so rich and vivid. In part it is done to counterbalance the widespread idea that the Roman Empire was on a trajectory away from sexual freedom and erotic frankness. Above all, the aim in Chapter 1 is to describe the world in which Christian sexual morality took shape, to recapture something of its richness, its chaos, its vitality.

This presentation employs an eclectic armory of sources: law and literature, scientific treatises and moralizing tracts, even a glance at the ubiquitous erotic art of the Roman Empire. The mélange is deliberate, for it helps us resist the temptation to ascribe supremacy to any one witness or class of witnesses. There will be no doubting, however, which type of informant is accorded a measure of favoritism: the novelist. The history of the ancient novel is effectively coterminous with the four centuries of Roman Empire. Rarely in history are great genres of literature born, and when they are, it surely signals a significant cultural juncture. The novels are tales of eros; they are dedicated to the power of eros and celebrate its divine power. A heady synthesis of comedy, love poetry, travel literature, and philosophy, the novels are the quintessential cultural expression of a civilization with a mature tradition of speculation on human sexual experience. At the same time, the novels are breathtakingly unique creations whose narrative intricacy allowed their authors to explore, slowly and with a new sympathy, the contours of the soul experiencing eros. On the whole, the romances strike a tone of wry conservatism. These stories are the product of a confident and assertive aristocracy, capable of believing that the world could be redeemed through social reproduction. But it is too much to declare the novels simple propaganda. Their authors are too alert to the unruly power of eros, too eager to portray the sinuous routes to conjugal love to be trying to put over something as bland as a point. In particular, Chapter 1 lets *Leucippe and Clitophon*, a romance written in the second century by an author named

Achilles Tatius, act as a guide as we trek across the landscape of imperial sexual culture. Among the surviving romances, *Leucippe and Clitophon* is probably the most sensational and certainly the most canny. The whole work is marked by a sly, if not subversive, sympathy for the inevitable disjuncture between the inarticulate mysteries of human sexuality and the artificial constraints of any erotic code. Achilles Tatius makes an ideal tour guide, one who knows all the traditional details but gleefully spills unauthorized truths.[8]

Many scholars have treated the romances as a privileged source for the history of sexuality, so that we could simply invoke tradition in foregrounding the novels. But a more substantive justification is in order, particularly because it might seem outwardly contradictory that an interpretation that professes to respect the hard facts of social life also takes some of the most fantastic products of the imagination so seriously. The assumption underlying this strategy is not that ancient literature is realistic, nor even that it allows us to breach the impregnable unknowability of what people really did. Moreover, the fictional works that we will explore have no more claim to representativeness than the visual, legal, or philosophical sources with which they are juxtaposed throughout these pages. Indeed, built into the methodology of this book is a conviction that no one ideology had monopolistic control of Greco-Roman culture—not the Stoics, not the Platonists, not the erotic novelists, not even, in the later period, the church, though its totalizing ambitions were considerable. What makes literature valuable to the historian of sex is not its representativeness but its expressiveness. Fiction offers a vital complement to moralizing texts because stories were a medium for conveying something more than bare commandments about how people ought to behave; narrative fiction portrayed the place of moral commandments within the patterns of social life. The literature of the Roman Empire explored how sexual morality was generated, how it was experienced, where its tensions and its silences lay. The very artists who best understood the techniques of artifice—Achilles Tatius, Heliodorus—created playful complexity not for its own sake but because it allowed them to meditate on the power of literature and its relationship to life. We begin with stories that represent humanity, in its moral dimensions, within the organic world and its cycles of reproduction, and we arrive by the end at stories where the human being is a transcendent moral subject who stands apart from the world and all its demands, isolated before the divine judge.

If prose fiction was the great literary legacy of later classical antiquity, then it should be no surprise that the stories that are considered in this book trace the deep transformation in the logic of sexual morality.[9]

Within the channels allowed by social dictates, eros flourished in the high empire. The history of sex in antiquity is not a linear story of gradual repression. The Roman moralists did not act as forerunners, preparing the way for the Christian revolution. The gloomy tribe of Stoic brethren have been allotted too much say. In a confident, prosperous, urban empire, old patterns of lassitude prevailed, and even intensified within an economy that delivered pleasures with unusual efficiency. Yes, the sexual culture of the Roman Empire had its own complexion. Erotic life was caught up in the great sciences of the day—medicine, astrology, physiognomics—to a new extent; the body's sexual capacity became part of broader conversations about fate, free will, and the physical constitution of the self. But eros thrived. If there was a new anxiety, it was the anxiety of affluence, and the anxiety of an existentially serious culture, not a morbid or world-weary anxiety. The visual record alone is a stark correction to the odd stern moralist who groused about the power of the *aphrodisia.* Consider just the culture of erotic lamps. The use of erotic art on this humble domestic instrument reaches its pitch of expressiveness, variety, and popularity in second and third centuries, and only withers in the late fourth or very early fifth century. *Pace* Veyne, the Romans not only had sex with the lamps on—they had sex by the flickering light of lamps that had images of them having sex by lamplight on them![10]

The development of a Christian packet of sexual norms and a distinctive sexual program is the focus of Chapter 2. The goal is to understand the shape of Christian sexual morality as it was presented to the cast of literate, second-century philosophers and artists featured in the first chapter. In particular, the focus is on Clement of Alexandria, a profoundly important Christian voice of the later second and early third centuries. To understand Clement, it is necessary to understand the Christian apostle Paul (and it must be confessed that this book is more interested in Clement's Paul than in the actual mission of the first century). At the level of specific prohibitions, two strands of Paul's thought would come to occupy the foreground: the injunction against *porneia* and a radical opposition to all same-sex intercourse. The central Christian prohibition on *porneia* collided with deeply entrenched patterns of sexual permissiveness. With the lighthearted tolerance of male wandering to be found in imperial sources like *Leucippe and Clitophon* we can contrast the adamantine prohibitions of early Christian sexual morality. Among the earliest Christians, fornication quickly became the bright axis around which sexual morality turned. "Fornication," of course, is an unsatisfactory word, because it is churchy and has no clear referent in English beyond "sex forbidden by the New Testament." At some level, the word means "extramarital sex," but much is lost in translation when the word is removed from an ancient context where the legitimacy of sexual contact was determined primarily by the status of the woman. The significance of *porneia,* in historical terms, was precisely that it gave a single name to an array of extramarital sexual configurations not limited to but especially including prostitution. Asking what *porneia* means is like asking how a fumigation bomb is shaped: the word was destined to diffuse and poison all the air in the zone of free access between male laxity and female honor, which in antiquity occupied such an important place in the sexual economy.[11]

In the matter of same-sex eros, the Roman world knew its own intricate tessellation of rigid limits and extreme permissiveness. Christian norms simply ate through the fabric of late classical morality like an acid, without the least consideration for the well-worn contours of the old ways. As with *porneia,* Christian hostility to venery involving members of the same sex was nurtured in Hellenistic Judaism, imported to the gentile mission, sharpened in its application and expression. Paul's letters again provided an incomplete but, really, unambiguous template for the blanket condemnation of same-sex love in early Christianity. Nowhere is this clearer than in the first chapter of his letter to the Romans. There we find the apostle claiming that among the gentiles, "women exchanged natural relations for unnatural, and the men likewise gave up natural relations with women and were consumed with passion for one another." For Paul, a little unexpectedly, same-sex attraction symbolized the estrangement of men and women, at the very level of their inmost desires, from the creator. Paul's overriding sense of gender—rather than age or status—as the prime determinant in the propriety of a sexual act was nurtured by contemporary Jewish attitudes. But the analogy between male and female same-sex attraction was strikingly novel, and truly momentous. By boiling the sex act down to the most basic constituents of male and female, Paul was able to redescribe the sexual culture surrounding him in transformative terms.[12]

Beyond the moral rules, which varied so sharply from contemporary habits, two features of Christian sexual ideology deserve emphasis. First, in the early centuries the Christian leadership spoke in an apologetic key. This fact shaped the entire tonal arrangement of early Christian moralizing. For instance, one of the most notable and puzzling features of a sexual morality rooted in Pauline authority is just how much the apostle left unsaid. The silences of Paul are nearly as interesting, and just as important, as the flashes of thunderous moralizing that do survive. Paul says precious little about the requirements of female sexuality. He hardly needed to, so great was the overlap with contemporary norms. But the grounds were very different. And distinctive, too, are Paul's assumptions about the boundaries of the moral community. It is revealing that in the first letter to the Corinthians, Paul warns the Christians against letting sinners abide in their midst. For centuries the posture of the church, as an assembly of the holy set apart from the world, would insulate the Christian leadership from the need to worry about the social etiology of sin. It has been asked how Paul, or later generations of Christians with a scroll of First Corinthians in their hands, might have handled slaves who lacked control over their bodies but wished to join the church. The glaring fact is precisely that we do not know. For centuries the church avoided any visible confrontation with this problem, precisely because it was an institution set apart from society. Its sexual morality, through and through, is the sexual morality of a persecuted minority in strident dissent from mainstream society.[13]

Second, early Christian sexual morality was inextricable from incipient notions of free will. In part the Christian interest in models of human agency was generated by the struggle within the movement for the legacy of Paul; gnostic theologies (in various guises) tended to pull out the strands of Paul's writings that spoke to a providential elect; orthodox theologies, in the early church, tended to suppress the notion of divine election, insofar as it threatened to impair individual autonomy. The internal struggle gave sharpness, and venom, to the debates over human agency, but it must be emphasized that this fierce controversy was no parochial affair. The church's acute concern with volition places Christian philosophy in the liveliest currents of imperial Greco-Roman philosophy. Against both the high philosophical debates over the nature of voluntary action and the simultaneous diffusion of vulgar astrology, the orthodox Christians offered a radically distinctive notion of individual freedom. Perhaps inevitably, impossibly strong models of freedom found their starkest testing ground in the area of human behavior where motivation is most muddled, subconscious, indeterminate: sex. In the same period when Greco-Roman philosophy and literature became notably more conscious than ever before that our deepest, constitutive moralities, especially sexual, depended so inscrutably on the lottery of fate, Christians preached a liberating message of freedom—from the cosmos, from the sweeping cycles of social reproduction alike. Indeed, the absolutist model of free will was the doctrine of a persecuted minority, capable of rejecting the world and, more importantly, imagining itself and its morality apart from the world.

The discussion of early Christian sexuality is, in its way, as selective as the sketch of Greco-Roman sexuality as a whole, and some of the choices might arouse disagreement. The focus is on the development of orthodox, Pauline sexuality, because it is the style of Christian thought that ultimately triumphed. There is legitimate debate about when, and to what extent, it attained dominance even within the diffuse galaxy of little groups who identified with the gospel of Jesus. We have come to appreciate that early Christian sexuality developed not just through friction with the outside world but through the internal strife among Christians, and the victory of Paul's authority, much less the meaning of his message, was not a foregone conclusion. That strife is perhaps given short shrift in this book, but the limits are both necessary and defensible. We have had to mute the competing noises in favor of the specific harmonies that are later worked into the full arrangement of ecclesiastical sexuality.[14]

Chapter 3 turns to the age of Christian triumph and the gradual transformation of sexual preaching within the context of an expansionary church. Remonstrance, step by step, became regulation. Far from receiving a world prepared for its dream of austerity, the Christian leadership in late antiquity found itself at the helm of a hostile takeover. It was an eventuality for which there was no prepared script. The two pillars of the church's power were the threats of its penitential regime and the megaphone of its public preaching. These were limited and uncertain sources of power, and only gradually did Christian values prevail as shared public culture. Even more slow and piecemeal was the process by which these values became the inspiration for public law. But prevail Christian norms eventually did. The tradition of frank eroticism withers, and the visual depictions of lovemaking slowly recede. Gone is the warm eroticism of the Pompeian fresco, vanished is the charmed sensuality of the Greek romance. The protean energy of human desire resisted being corralled, but marriage, inexorably, became the only legitimate venue of erotic fulfillment. Freudian intuitions, or simple experience, may lead us to expect that if Christianity was a signal victory for the superego, the id endured, driven underground, searching for its own quiet quarters out of ecclesiastical view, or sublimated into religious ecstasy. But the transformation was epochal.

The story of same-sex love in the centuries between Constantine and Justinian unfolds with fierce predictability. Vituperative attacks on same-sex love are strewn across the late antique homiletic literature. Notable is the direct influence of a Pauline conception, in which same-sex love per se is an encompassing category, inclusive of all forms of erotic contact between males *and* females. At a rhythm that mimicked the deeper diffusion of Christian norms, the late antique state gradually turned its attention to the repression of same-sex encounters. The Theodosian age (ca. AD 379–450) was still marked by the predominance of old categories of masculinity as a regulatory platform, but there is a new, hostile energy in the air that it is not unsafe to attribute to religious fervor. The assimilation of Christian ideology and sexual policing culminates in the reign of Justinian (AD 527–565), whose *Institutes* for the first time classified sex between males as a crime without distinguishing between active and passive partners. Justinian also passed a law against pederasty and enforced it ex post facto in spectacular fashion. Most remarkably, if Procopius is to be believed, men could be accused of sexual crime even by slaves, signaling a total breakdown of the ancient sexual order.[15]

The ecclesiastical campaign against same-sex love was vicious but highly sporadic. By contrast, the struggle against fornication, *porneia,* was a full-fledged war, which saw the church muster its forces in deliberate array against an ancient style of sexual life. The preaching was endless, the penitential enforcement real. But the sex industry was too entrenched for the Christian state even to compass its repression. Instead, the Christian emperors focused on an aspect of the sex trade whose moral and material significance should not be underestimated: they banned forced prostitution. The brutal exposure of vulnerable women rested on a public indifference so vast that it lay invisibly at the very foundations of the ancient sexual order. As Christianity progressively absorbed society, and could ever less comfortably present itself as a dissent movement apart from the world, it was forced to reckon with the silences in its own sexual program. Because prostitution was at the center of an ancient sexual culture, an order of relationships between state and society built on the concept of shame, the progressive realization of its injustice is a privileged index of Christianization. The aggressive campaign of Justinian against compulsion in the flesh industry marks the end of a distinctly ancient sexual order, one whose distant origins lie at the very beginnings of the archaic Mediterranean city-state and finally crumble in the midst of his rule.[16]

Chapter 4 follows the Christian revolution in sexual morality through the medium of imaginative literature. The fictional word is an essential complement to the injunctions of the moralists and the dictates of law. Literature is capable of expressing, in a way more intimate than mere commands, the shape of sexual morality, when actually projected onto the furrowed plane of human life. Pagans, Christians, and Jews alike used stories as vehicles to express their deepest beliefs about the relationships between the sexual body, the mechanics of society, and the nature of the cosmos. The Christian transformation of sex can be retraced in the history of literature, which mirrors quite sensitively the passage from a public sexual ideology organized around the imperatives of social reproduction to a mentality founded in ecclesiastical norms. In short, the history of literature recapitulates the passage from shame to sin.

Chapter 4 is focused on one of the central preoccupations of ancient fiction, female chastity. Feminine purity was a transcendent symbol, capable of bearing the most consequential meanings. The authors of the imperial romances invested no small part of their talents in contriving elaborate threats to the chastity of their heroines. These scenes, looked at across the genre, provide direct access to the ideological code of romance. The romances are stories in which essence precedes existence. What is most remarkable about the imperial romances is the extent to which they are explicitly built on an acute awareness that forces beyond the individual's control shape his or her life. Fate furnishes us with moral ends, and more instrumentally, society constitutes us as selves. The romances make their most daring approaches to the inscrutable mysteries of fate in the image of the heroine's endangered chastity. The romances flirt with the possibility of her violation, because the transgression of her body would mark a visceral contravention of the social and cosmic order. These typological scenes are very near the deep theology of the romance. In the end, she is *always* rescued, and the deeper order of the cosmos prevails against the flux and frustration that is experienced in human time. The heroine is reserved, by the will of the gods, for marriage. There is salvation in the cycle of nature, which imparts to us the gift of eros within its mysterious order.

Christians and Jews would rework these very scenes of feminine imperilment to express their deepest reservations about the world and the place of eros in the constitution of the self. Already in the primitive phases of the religion, Christian authors were adept at reformulating the fictional tropes of Greco-Roman literature. A whole body of legend grew up around the heroes of Christianity, the apostles. In the apocryphal acts, we find the sexual mechanics of the romance deliberately inverted. The ruling Roman order provides the villains, while the apostles, intermediaries of a higher power, furnish the heroes. In these legends, sexual rejection functions as an expression of dissent from the dominant order. By reading the parallel scenes of female endangerment, we glimpse the theological imagination of a movement set apart from mainstream society and convinced in its belief in a separate, spiritual order.[17]

In the centuries after Christian triumph, the Christian literary imagination was transformed, as the church itself stood less as an alternative to society than an institution permeated by the world. Fiction still proved a vital medium for the expression of sexual morality and its relation to life. *From Shame to Sin* ends with the popular late antique tales of penitent prostitutes, stories of fallen women who repent of their sins and pursue spiritual rehabilitation. These lives are antiromances of some literary sophistication. The authors of the lives of the penitent prostitutes intentionally evoke the heroines of romance, all the more dramatically to violate the single, central rule of romance: the heroine's corporal inviolability. The genius of this new archetype was that it allowed the authors to create allegories of sin, as a paradigm in which sexual morality has been freed from the requirements of society. These are tales of abundant moral autonomy, which dramatize the severance of sexual morality from its social moorings and place the individual eternally before the judgment of God. The stories of penitent prostitutes are the fictional analogue to the social and legal program of late antiquity, epitomized by the reforms of Justinian. The ideological correspondence between law and literature is telling of a deep transformation. Indeed, even as Christian authors perfected their new archetype, of the free sinner who repented, Justinian attacked coerced prostitution and built a monastery to serve as a refuge for reformed prostitutes. It was named, of course, Repentance.

This book tries to tell the story of the passage across one of the great thresholds in the history of private morality. Like any such passage, it knew its limits, and no one should be surprised to find pieces of the old in the new, or the new in the old. There are patent risks in overestimating the extent to which immemorial patterns of erotic experience, shaped by the primitive dictates of power, desire, and reproduction, actually changed. But there are risks, too, in underestimating Christianization as a watershed, or reducing it to something so abstract as a cultural substitution. At the beginning of our story, the Mediterranean was home to a society where an emperor's male beloved, victim of an untimely death, would be worshipped around the empire as a god; in this same society, the routine exploitation of slaves and poor women was a foundation of the sexual order. By the end, we are in a world where the emperor will command the gory mutilation of men caught in same-sex affairs, even as he affirmed the moral dignity of women without any civic claim to honor. Paradoxically, these realignments were effected by the same, deep earthquake in human morality. Society and its needs had lost some measure of command over the sexual honor of men and women, and instead the individual, in his or her moral ends, was imagined as an isolate—free, frail, and awesomely responsible for all corporal stirrings. The triumph of Christianity within the public order was not the displacement of one self-deluding superego by another. It was a revolution in the rules of behavior and in the very image of the human as a sexual being. More profoundly, it was a revolution in the nature of society's claims on the moral agent, and in the place imagined for the sexual self within the cosmos.

CHAPTER ONE

The Moralities of Sex in the Roman Empire

LEUCIPPE'S SHIELD AND THE PHILOSOPHY OF ROMANCE

In the last of a long series of threats to her chastity, the heroine of a second-century Greek novel, Leucippe, stood in imminent danger of suffering sexual violence at the hands of a man claiming to be her master. The romantic novel, the characteristic literary invention of the Roman Empire, was a genre built out of such theatrical endangerments to feminine chastity. In the scene of her attempted rape, Leucippe is threatened by Thersander, a caricature of a villain whose very name means "Savage Man." Leucippe, a freeborn girl of unparalleled beauty, has been enslaved by pirates and sold to this stereotypical brute. It was "fate's wish" that she be a slave for a time, but her true status is never really in doubt, and the problematic relationship between status and behavior runs as a thread throughout the entire confrontation between Thersander and Leucippe. When Thersander puts his hands beneath Leucippe's chin and lifts her face upward for a kiss, she resists and reproaches him, "You are not acting as a free man, nor as a well-born one." While his hopes were still high, Thersander remained "wholly enthralled" by Leucippe, but the disappointment of rebuff lets loose his fury. He resorts to physical and psychological violence, striking Leucippe across the face and calling her a "miserable slaveling." "You should be grateful that I speak to you, and count your lucky stars that you seem worthy of my kisses. . . . I know that you're just a little whore, and the man you love is an adulterer. Since you don't want to accept me as your lover, you will experience me as your master." In the slave society of the Roman Empire, where the routine sexual exploitation of slaves was an integral part of the sexual economy, the narration of such pedestrian violence was highly unusual, and surely jarring. But the author builds up the uncomfortable potential of the scene, only to let it dissipate in arch melodrama.[1]

We are never really in suspense about Leucippe's fate, and—what makes the scene so revealing—neither is she. At the tension grows, Leucippe tells Thersander to "bring the lash, bring the rack, bring the fire, bring the sword. . . . For though I be naked, for though I be alone, for though I be a woman, my one shield is my freedom [*eleutheria*], and not blows, nor blade, nor blaze shall prevail against it!" Leucippe is protected by her freedom, her *eleutheria,* at the very moment when her control over her body seemed most elusive. Her rhetoric speaks on two levels. Most directly, Leucippe means that she will be saved from her imminent distress because she is, in reality, free. She is the knowing heroine, confident her objective status will somehow ensure that she is not the victim in this tale. *Eleutheria* was a powerful word, conjuring not only free status but sexual respectability; for the Greeks and Romans, the two were inseparably fused. The *eleuthera* was the sexually honest woman, a virgin until marriage, chaste within marriage. The opposite of the *eleuthera* was the prostitute, and Leucippe is consoled in the midst of apparently insuperable danger by the truth of her nature and by the rules of romance, which, she seems to know, will not allow her to be violated. Her faith depends on her knowledge that the narrative logic of the Greek romance will ultimately obey the expectations of the social order.[2]

At the same time, Leucippe's grand speech positions this novel within a matrix of cultural reflection on the perennial problem of free will and fate. Few cultures have been so pervasively fixated on the limits of human agency within a vast, impersonal cosmos as the inhabitants of the high Roman Empire. The Greek novels, on questions of sexuality and cosmology alike, were in direct dialogue with the homiletic and philosophical literature of the age. The novels explore the very themes that occupied sages and sophists across the Mediterranean. Freedom in the face of an overwhelming fate was the byword of Stoicism, and Achilles Tatius is, surely, manipulating the Stoic idea of an internal faculty, independent from any external cause, that Leucippe can exercise regardless of her circumstance. But the allusion to the problem of fate is hardly an endorsement of Stoicism—quite the opposite. Whereas the Stoics advised a carefully studied indifference to eros in a universe so vast that mankind's pleasures were dwarfed by the unfathomable enormity of the heavens, the novels present a world keenly knit by the gods so that mankind might find in erotic fulfillment nothing short of salvation. Like the Stoic, Achilles appreciates the limited range of motion allotted to the individual by the cosmos; unlike the Stoic, he would locate selfhood and salvation in the movement of erotic energy through the heated clay of the human body. The novelist had the discretion to let art speak for itself, but his romance stands as an intricate rebuttal to the gloomy fastidiousness of his philosophical contemporaries.[3]

Leucippe's freedom is a key to the way the novels work and the way they can guide us through the sexual landscape of the high Roman Empire. Her freedom referred at once to her social status and her subjective agency. Of course, the fact that she invokes her freedom at the exact moment when she seems most constrained underscores the extent to which the individual's agency was limited. The novels are fatalistic romances, stories of the overpowering, divine force of erotic love. They are unusually aware of the external forces—nature and society—bearing on the individual and determining his or her fate. Here is the novels' most authentic level of representation, and the greatest opportunity they afford to explore the relationship between erotic ideologies and social structure in the late classical period. They preserve for us something of the vitality, complexity, and chaos of sexual life in the second-century empire. Because *Leucippe and Clitophon* deliberately offers a panoramic vision of eros and its place in the world, we follow Achilles Tatius and consider the sexual experience of the high empire from various angles—same-sex eroticism, the expectations placed on women, the sexual life-course of men, the dynamics of marriage, the attitudes of the philosophers. Throughout, our goal is to find the interface between sexual energy and prevailing morality, the points of contact between the circulation of pleasures and the regulatory force of sexual norms. In the age of the romance, eros flourished unawares, serenely confident in its eternal powers, and if we did not know that Christianity was stirring in the hills, we might never have believed that the first icy gusts of denial could be felt sweeping across the ancient valleys.

THE CURRENT FASHION: SAME-SEX EROS IN THE HIGH EMPIRE

Around the age of nineteen, Clitophon's cousin Leucippe came to live with him and his family in Tyre. He fell in love with her at first sight. Paralyzed by his infatuation, he took his troubles to his cousin Clinias, only two years his elder but already "an initiate of eros." Clinias quickly became his trusty counselor. The passions of Clinias were for a *meirakion,* a boy somewhere in his later teens, and his coaching is meant to be understood in terms of pederastic norms. The ancient novels are, both superficially and in their deep structure, stories of heterosexual love, but same-sex amours still find an important place. In fact, the first two books of *Leucippe and Clitophon* are framed by the traditional assumptions of classical Greek pederasty, transposed onto a heterosexual plot. Clinias claimed that "boy and maiden" alike shared a sense of shame; seduction, he argued, required the lover to draw out the beloved's consent by the most delicate rituals of courtship, slowly wearing down the beloved's guard without making startling moves. Then, Clinias advised, "when you have a tacit understanding that the next step is the big deed, even those who are ready to surrender prefer the appearance of compulsion, to let the façade of force deflect the shame of consent." Couched in terms of a plot to seduce Leucippe, Clinias lays bare the central contradiction of classical pederastic norms: it required from the younger partner forms of consent that were intrinsically disgraceful.[4]

One of the more unlikely misprisions to have prevailed among historians of antiquity is the view that modes and practices of same-sex contact withered in the high empire. In Veyne's words, ancient bisexuality disappeared. But reports of same-sex love's demise have been much exaggerated. Clinias is presented as a sympathetic figure, even if his lessons nearly lead Clitophon and Leucippe into irreversible trouble. His erotic style looms over the first two books of the romance, culminating in a famous rhetorical set-piece on a boat that Leucippe and Clitophon have taken to elope. After noting that "male-love has somehow become the current fashion," Clitophon and one of the passengers, Menelaus, debate the relative merits of loving women and loving boys. Clitophon professes that his sexual experience has been limited to "the women who sell Aphrodite," but, as Menelaus notes, he certainly sounds like no novice. In fact, Clitophon delivers the most elaborate encomium on the female orgasm that the ancient world has left to us. The frantic, gasping delight of the woman is integral to his case for the superiority of female lovers. Like other advocates of women, such as Plutarch, Clitophon emphasizes the promise of mutual pleasure in heterosexual *aphrodisia* to contrast it with the presumptive one-way pleasure of pederasty. But where Plutarch focused on the warm companionship that could arise from sexual familiarity, the erotic novel describes the transport of sexual ecstasy experienced by men and women—even, if Clitophon has not been misled, by the vendors of Aphrodite.[5]

Menelaus, by contrast, marshals a highly conventional case against women, centered on their softness and artificiality. He extols the sharp, if brief, pleasures of loving boys, "whose very evanescence makes the pleasure so much greater." He develops a contrast between feminine contrivance and the "naturalness" of male kisses. Unlike other "contests of the loves," no winner is declared aboard the boat in the novel of Achilles. Nevertheless, the author's position is implicit, both in the narrative placement of the contest and in the fate of the same-sex amours. The first two books are full of failed love, most notably Clitophon's disastrous near-seduction of Leucippe, carried out under the advisement of Clinias. More revealing, both Clinias and Menelaus, the lovers of boys, experience the early death of their beloveds in tragic accidents for which they are indirectly responsible. In *Leucippe and Clitophon,* same-sex love can bring pleasure, but only mutual eros culminating in marriage receives the protection of the gods. Same-sex love is perishable, whereas the universe was built so that the rapturous delights of heterosexual *aphrodisia* would have a place. The love of boys, in the romance, was not sinful or abnormal, but it was transitory and tragic, for it had no happy resolution in a story destined to end with marriage.[6]

The ancient reader of Achilles Tatius would have noticed a conspicuous absence in the apology for pederasty. Nowhere do we find the soaring, spiritualized defense of an elevated form of mentorship that harnessed the power of erotic attraction for virtuous ends. In part the absence of any such defense is explained by the setting of the debate within an erotic novel, whose generic conventions accept and insist on the frankly sexual nature of human companionship. But in a deeper sense *Leucippe and Clitophon* is a cipher for attitudes toward pederasty in the Roman Empire. It is telling that Foucault sees pederasty in the novel as "episodic and marginal." Central to Foucault's presentation of Roman sexual culture is the claim that in the high empire, "reflection on the love of boys lost some of its intensity, its seriousness, its vitality." The decline of pederasty, or at least its diminished place in the moral economy of sex, is treated as the counterpart of the conjugalization of pleasure. Foucault finds in the high empire a "philosophical disinvestment" from the institution of pederasty.[7]

The claim rests entirely on a comparison with "the lofty formulations of the classical period," notably Plato's. If comparison with classical Greece seems inevitable in any discussion of pederasty, such a benchmark is nevertheless bound to lead to a stilted measure of Roman sexual culture. Seen in broader perspective, the story of Roman-era pederasty is not its decline but its liveliness. Foucault's judgments are simply misguided. The place of pederasty in *Leucippe and Clitophon,* which is important enough to frame the first quarter of the novel, helps us to situate contemporary attitudes to pederasty in terms of high imperial culture, rather than in comparison to classical Greece. A heightened and almost impolitic insistence on the physical essence of love, an awareness that the beloved's consent could not be squared with social honor, and narratives of eros that sought to understand the place of mankind's sexual instincts within the cosmos: these, rather than disapproval or disinvestment, make up the story of pederasty in the Roman Empire.[8]

The Greeks and Romans of this period believed that beauty resided in the male as well as the female body, and they were never surprised when the sight of a beautiful body aroused sexual desire. "Did you never feel eros for someone, for a boy or girl, slave or free?" A farcical tale of travel to the afterlife imagined that on the Isle of the Blessed, "all the wives are shared in common without jealousy . . . and the boys all submit to their pursuers without resistance." Pastoral poetry, meant to evoke an idealized harmony between man and nature, made boys the object of erotic attraction, from Virgil (who was said to be more fond of boys than of women) to Nemesianus, a court poet of the late third century. Marcus Aurelius, who learned from his adoptive grandfather to "cease all things concerned with the love of youths," thanked the gods that he had touched "neither Theodotus nor Benedicta"—the casual indifference to the gender of the erotic object is what is telling. The traditional myths still held that even the gods were sexually indiscriminate: Zeus became a swan for Leda, but an eagle for Ganymede: "some think one or the other is greater, but they're equal to me."[9]

Age dynamics were at the core of acceptable same-sex love in the Roman world. The "short season of rejoicing" was the span of time between early adolescence and the growth of the first beard. In the wry words of a witty courtesan, "boys are beautiful so long as they look like females." The physiological boundaries of pederasty were flexible, if inexorable, indeed a symbol of evanescence: "time, which lays waste to beauty." Sixteen to eighteen were the canonically acceptable years, propriety decreasing by degrees with distance from this window, without firm breaks. A mischievous poet from the age of Hadrian was indiscreetly precise: the age of seventeen marked a sort of perfection reserved for Zeus himself; after that, he said, there was a risk the boy might turn the tables. It was a traditional charge: by twenty, when the boy had a bristling chin, there was too much suspicion of alternating sexual roles. But in Lucian's satirical account of an all-male society on the moon, the boys played the part of wives until twenty-five, then entered the ranks of the husbands.[10]

The notion of "Greek love" is misleading on two counts. In the first place, practices and attitudes varied across the Greek world, and classical Athenian culture was hardly standard. Even in Athens, pederasty could not be washed of its aristocratic connotations, and the law was ambiguous enough that the adult partner might find himself liable for criminal violation. It is an even greater error, though, to insinuate that Greek love was not an indigenous Roman practice. This charge goes back to late republican moralists, who, in chauvinistic terms, decried the effects of underlying social change as the by-product of Hellenization. In reality, Greek and Roman codes of sexual behavior shared profound structural similarities: a sexual act was composed of an active and a passive partner, and masculinity required the insertive role. Roman pederasty was distinct in small but decisive ways. The Romans had an absolute abhorrence for the violation of freeborn boys; the body of the Roman man was impenetrable, and there was no twilight of indeterminacy between boyhood and manhood. This prohibition was backed by the fearsome power of public law. The severity of the rule eliminated the zone of ambiguity that had proven such fertile ground in the Greek philosophical tradition for celebrating the mentorship of the lover and beloved.[11]

The great chasm separating Roman pederastic practice from earlier models was the omnipresence of slaves. Classical Greece had seen an unprecedented expansion of the slave trade, which laid the institutional and commercial foundations for the Roman slave system. Slaves, already in Greek culture, were subjected to untrammeled sexual abuse. But the Romans built one of history's most enduring and extensive slave systems, and the ownership of slaves would gradually shape virtually every social institution in Roman life, including pederasty. The laws deflected lust away from the freeborn body, and slaves provided a ready outlet. In Roman pederasty, elaborate courtship before the act was replaced by the master's authority, and intentional obscurity about the nature of the act gave way to a coarse simplicity about the physical mechanics of pleasure. The most striking physical artifact of Roman pederasty, the Warren Cup, simultaneously celebrates love between males and explores the dependence of the practice on the institution of slavery. A silver goblet of the early first century, the Warren Cup juxtaposes two panels. On one side a young master, wearing a wreath, penetrates an even younger slave. On the reverse, the two figures are many years older. The slave lowers himself onto the master, who is again wearing a wreath. But this time another slave, a small boy, peeks through the door, observing the scene. Though opinions differ, the most compelling interpretation of the cup suggests that the same couple is depicted on both sides; on the reverse, the master's sexual partner has outgrown his role, and the younger slave watching the scene is catching a glimpse of his future life course. In the Roman context, the moral economy of pederasty was recentered around the bare fact of dominance.[12]

The sexual use of slaves is prominent from the very beginnings of Roman literature, and it is simply pervasive across the long tradition of amorous poetry at Rome. Only the idiosyncratic Ovid dissents, and even then as a matter of taste rather than scruple. "I hate amorous endeavors which do not end happily for both alike, and so I am less interested in the love of boys." The slave system was an entrenched part of Roman society throughout the imperial period. In an empire of some seventy million souls, perhaps seven to ten million were enslaved, a proportion with few parallels in premodern history. The Romans were promiscuous slavers. Rich households teemed with unfree bodies; decurions, equestrians, and senators owned scores, hundreds, in some cases thousands of slaves. The abundance of fungible sex objects in the rich household might turn the anxious paradox of the "brief bloom" into a mere economic inconvenience: we hear of a wealthy master keeping slave boys in the house until their first beard, then relegating them to the farms. Slave ownership was not just the preserve of such super-rich aristocrats, though; the sheer extent of slave owning meant that the mechanics of Roman sexuality were shaped by the presence of unfree bodies across the social spectrum. One in ten families in the empire owned slaves; the number in the towns was probably twice that. The ubiquity of slaves meant pervasive sexual availability. "If your loins are swollen, and there's some homeborn slave boy or girl around where you can quickly stick it, would you rather burst with tension? Not I—I like an easy lay." Slaves played something like the part that masturbation has played in most cultures: we learn in a book on dream interpretation that if a man dreams "he is stroking his genitals with his hands, he will obtain a slave or slave-woman."[13]

The stories of the Roman emperors, such a garish mélange of rumor and reality, have contributed not a little to the reputation of Roman sexual culture. The proclivities of the Roman emperors have been notorious; in the words of the inimitable Gibbon, "of the first fifteen emperors, Claudius was the only one whose taste in love was entirely correct." Their sexual profiles can provide some index of the erotic style of the empire, insofar as we remind ourselves that an emperor's sexual behavior acted as a cipher for his style of rulership. Nothing summarized the abject depravity of Tiberius as his use of young slave children on Capri. Nero's reputation for philhellenism and debauchery fused in his three reputed marriages to eastern eunuchs. Eunuchs did in fact come to occupy an ever more important place in pederastic practices of the Roman Empire; Domitian, whose favorite was a eunuch cupbearer named Earinus, banned castration within the empire, but the transfrontier trade was able to pump eunuchs into the empire at a sufficient level that their prominence continued to gain into late antiquity. The outsized villainy of Commodus could be seen in his incest and voyeurism, his three hundred concubines, and his infamous behavior, in which he "polluted every part of his body and his mouth, with both sexes."[14]

If reports about typologically "bad" emperors are hopelessly clouded by salacious invective, the biographies of successful imperial rulers may reveal more. Nothing belies the claim that pederastic discourse lost its vitality like the relationship between Hadrian and his Bithynian favorite, Antinous. Possibly a slave, Hadrian's beloved died on the Nile under clouded circumstances. Hadrian's sorrow was demonstrative, but what still defies easy comprehension is the paroxysm of empire-wide mourning that ensued. A city was founded at the site of his death; Hadrian believed reports that a new star had appeared in the sky, and Antinous was worshipped as a god or hero; statues of Antinous proliferated until his face was a universal image, known "across the inhabited world." Indeed, the haunting image of Antinous ranks behind only Augustus and Hadrian in the number of sculptures extant today. Dozens of cities issued coinage in his honor; games were being founded in his memory decades after Hadrian was in the grave. Provincial sycophancy and credulous paganism do not suffice to explain such an uncontrolled efflux of grief. The image and story of Antinous resonated in powerful and unexpected ways.[15]

Hadrian's sexual persona cannot be dismissed as a side effect of his energetic philhellenism. His predecessor Trajan, the masculine warrior, was "an enthusiast for wine and boys." The sexual culture of the high empire does not parse neatly into eastern and western styles; as with so much else, the pederastic mores of the imperial period fused Greek and Roman elements, and by the second century this synthesis was well established. Though the love of boys in the east could always be described in the fashionably antiquarian language of Platonic eros, in reality Greek pederasty reveals the creeping influences of the slave trade and of harder legal norms. Pederasty in imperial Greece was presumptively practiced with unfree partners. Herodes Atticus, the "tongue of the Greeks," was publicly enamored with his *trophimoi,* his fosterlings. One, Polydeucion, apparently was free, and Herodes treated him as a son, but the other two, Achilles and Memnon, were manifestly slaves. A recent assertion that they "no doubt acquiesced to his desires, whatever they were," may well be true, but we must admit that the nature of the relationships between them and Herodes is, in traditional Athenian style, perfectly obscure. The verse of Hadrian's court, as technically accomplished as any poetry in the anthologies, focuses with verve on the beauty of servile wine-pourers. Lucian's fiercest satires assume the love of slave boys. In the dream manual of Artemidorus, it was natural and auspicious to have sex with one's slaves—male or female.[16]

While the advance of the slave trade tended to align pederastic eros with the master's power, the law protected freeborn boys in ever starker terms. Violation of a freeborn boy was illegal in Roman law. What is underappreciated, though, is the extent to which freeborn boys in the east were gradually fenced off by public force. Dio considered sex with a freeborn boy "an assault" and "an even more lawless violation" than the corruption of women. The law "so far exceeds all else in modesty and faith that to it has been vouchsafed the matrimonial bond, the beauty of the virgin, the bloom of boys." Seduction of freeborn boys became conspicuously dangerous, but the statutory basis of the crime is a little unclear. In the early empire the Romans gave the towns under their sway considerable control over private law, so that the empire was a patchwork of jurisdictions and legal regimes. But Roman rules had an irresistible influence. Roman law applied to the growing number of provincials who earned Roman citizenship, and Roman governors played an ever larger role in the resolution of disputes. Through whatever channels, Roman officials came to preside over the sexual honor of free provincial boys. Lucian reports that the charlatan Peregrinus, having "corrupted a pretty lad," paid three thousand drachmas to the boy's parents, "who were poor, to avoid being hauled before the governor of Asia." In the early second century, a Roman prefect of Egypt, a member of the most genteel social circles in the empire, was himself undone after seducing the seventeen-year-old scion of a respectable Alexandrian family; the scandal became a cause célèbre in a culture with a ready taste for judicial drama, and stylized transcripts of the trial, before what judge we do not know, still remain.[17]

Whatever the law commanded, sex with freeborn boys went on. Fathers were endlessly anxious about the sexual dangers that lurked in the schools. The "lover of boys," it was conventional to believe, only had to bribe the pedagogue or attendant and entice his beloved with a little gift. Philosophers, whose position gave them opportunity, were regularly accused of taking improper liberties with their charges; "in sum all their doctrines are mere words and they are enslaved to pleasure, some cavorting with concubines, others with prostitutes, most of them with boys." One sign that older patterns endured is the intense reflection on the protocols of consent. The ideal partner was one who knew "the art of assenting and refusing at the same time." Poets, anyway, could profess to believe that the life cycle still afforded a brief window of indeterminacy: it was wrong to lure a boy into sin in the years before his moral reason was developed, and twice as shameful once the young man was too old, "but between not yet and nevermore you and I have the now."[18]

The impossibility of honorable consent is at the heart of Plutarch's *Erotikos,* by any measure a crucial document of sexual life in the high empire.

The *Erotikos* is a dialogue set within the frame story of a young widow's efforts to lure a handsome young man into marriage. The backdrop is essential, for Plutarch construes the woman as a sort of female lover pursuing her beloved according to the rules of classical pederasty. The story occasions an extended discussion of the relative merits of marriage and the love of boys. The defenders of pederasty give an apology as dramatic as any classical antecedent. True eros, claim its defenders, has nothing to do with women. Marriage is a domestic arrangement, more about keeping accounts and enjoying enervating pleasures between daily squabbling than the soul's ascent; bonding between males, they argue, is the true way to nurture virtue. The "form, complexion, and image of the boy's beauty" was just a powerful reminder, sent by the gods, of heavenly beauty, a sensible impression of the incorruptible reality. The true lover of wisdom experienced a chaste desire and would never indulge in base pleasures. Hence, sex with slaves must be explicitly renounced. "So too it is not gentlemanly or cultivated to lust after slave boys, which is nothing more than physical coitus." Sex with slaves was so insalubrious that it had nothing more to recommend it than did "sex with women."[19]

Plutarch, in response, defends marriage as an institution capable of gently pacifying the force of physical pleasure; the benevolent authority of the husband might be used to cultivate the same sort of virtuous friendship that the love of boys falsely promises. The *Erotikos* is indeed a grandiloquent expression of the conjugal values of the early empire. But the attack on pederasty is so devastating because Plutarch does not treat it as merely a debased reflection of a higher love. Instead, the amiable Plutarch uses the social facts of his age to cut through the cultured obfuscations of the pederast. The love of boys *either* requires consent on the part of the beloved, which makes him soft and womanish, *or* it requires violence on the part of the lover, which makes him a criminal. The claim to be free of physical consummation is so much specious misdirection, done out of simple shame and fear for the law. There can be no Eros without Aphrodite. Even in the classical period, pederasty danced on the head of a pin. In an empire saturated with the bodies of slaves, where the law was unequivocal, there was no room for maneuver: the pleasures could not be sublimated, the matter of volition could not be clouded. Plutarch's logical precision was merciless, its assumptions firmly rooted in the world around him. He did not denounce pederasty; he pronounced that it was, in reality, long since dead.

The *Erotikos* is a salvage operation, an attempt to rescue the most hallowed ideals of classical Greek eros by transplanting them into the vital institution of marriage.[20]

The *Erotikos* of Plutarch is a quintessential product of its age in another way; it gives lucid expression to the traditional bifurcation of same-sex eros into two types: pederasty and passivity. For Plutarch, while the love of boys was structurally impossible, the nature of the attraction itself was unexceptional. But the *Erotikos* was simply giving voice to mainstream attitudes in its pronouncement that "we place men who take pleasure from the passive role in the category of the most wicked and allot them no faith, no honor, no friendship." Acceptable homoeroticism was strictly limited to the offerings of youth. Desires for adult men flaunted gender norms and incurred broad hatred. Something of its raw viciousness is preserved in surviving invectives, such as those of the satirist Lucian. When a scholar refused to lend Lucian a book, it elicited a torrent of hatred that might seem disproportionate. The ignorant book collector was accused of having two passions: overpriced books and "muscular lads past their prime." Lucian advised him to keep his nocturnal affairs within the household; just yesterday "a male prostitute came around and told the most shameful stories about you, showing the bite marks to prove it." When another enemy criticized Lucian's misuse of a Greek word, his reply included a full-scale assault on this pseudosophist's manliness. He accused his adversary of being penetrated, and nothing was left to innuendo in Lucian's account of a revel in Italy, where his adversary had staged an obscene interpretation of the blinding of Polyphemus with a hired prostitute. While it is startling that cultivated men trafficked in such scabrous diatribes, these were products of an agonistic intellectual culture and a public sexual ideology in which codes of masculinity were paramount. The charges differ in eloquence, but not in substance, from many a graffito scrawled by the less genteel inhabitants of Pompeii.[21]

Whereas pederasty was a type of passion, in the Roman world the man who wished to be loved by men was a type of person. Nothing brings this out quite so clearly as the astrological literature of the high empire. The Roman era was the first great age of popular astrology in the west. Study of the stars was a serious science; Ptolemy was, after Galen, the greatest scientist of his century. His handbook of astrology was meant for learned practitioners of the craft. Astrology was a predictive science not because it provided a mystical insight into the future but rather because it could account for the individual's physical and mental constitution. Sexual traits were determined by the composition of the soul. Ptolemy imagines an extraordinary array of sexual phenotypes; the stars could make people erotic, frigid, passionate for women, passionate for boys, aggressive, pathic, impotent, incestuous, adulterous, and so on. Desire for boys was an expression of the same underlying passion for girls, and it could exist in normal or excessive quantities. The bewildering logic of Ptolemy's sexual schema becomes a little clearer in a chapter on "diseases of the soul." Most afflictions were said to be matters of excess or deficiency in ordinary qualities. Sometimes, however, the imbalances were of such extreme degree that the person's "whole nature" was "diseased." Deformations in the passive part of the soul were manifested in abnormal sexual morphologies. Two commonplaces of ancient thought underlie Ptolemy's doctrine. First, men are naturally active, women naturally passive. Second, the difference between men and women is one of degree rather than kind; masculinity and femininity stood on a single sliding scale. Thus, the pull of planetary forces might draw men and women alike toward either the masculine or the feminine end of the spectrum.[22]

If the planets completely disrupted the proper quantum of passivity, a monster was born. When sun and moon stood together unattended in masculine signs of the zodiac, the soul was made more virile; men would experience natural passions to an extreme degree, and women too would be somewhat manly. If Venus or Mars joined the luminaries in a masculine sign, the effects were further intensified. Men became hypermasculine, experiencing natural passions to such a degree that they were unrestrained and even unlawful. Women became monstrously masculine figures who played the role of men with other women. (It is worth pausing briefly to note that Ptolemy is the rare source who even reflects on lesbianism; a combination of young age at marriage for women, patriarchal regimes of control, especially in the upper classes, and the lack of a richly developed moral discourse about lesbianism created a zone of silence around love between women in the ancient world.) When, by contrast, sun and moon stood together unattended in feminine signs of the zodiac, the individual was disproportionately feminized. Women became especially womanly, and men became delicate and effeminate. If Venus intensified the effects, women became lustful and unlawful in their natural passions, while men became "soft," incapable of having sex with women; they became closet pathics. If

Mars was also in a feminine sign, the man's shamelessness was flagrant, like that of a common male prostitute. Thus, the pathic was a creature formed by the stars when a change in the quantities of masculinity and femininity triggered a change in the quality of his whole nature.[23]

There was little that was novel in these assumptions. Folk belief had long held that women were underheated and incompletely formed men; moist, clammy, the female body had been contrived by nature to play its role in the continuous regeneration of the species, "born to be penetrated." For men, too, manliness was a matter of degree, and the insufficiently masculinized male became damp, soft, in extreme cases an "androgyne." If a man was womanly in constitution, it was sure to manifest itself in sexual deviance. By the second century a heap of traditional abuses had piled around the stereotypes of sexual deviance, and the social tool kit of the Greco-Roman man taught him how to recognize clandestine sexual malfeasance. Lucian quotes an old saw, that you could sooner conceal five elephants in your armpit than one *kinaidos* – the monstrous gender deviant of ancient sexual culture. There were "ten thousand giveaways: his gait, his gaze, and his voice, the angle of his neck." Ancient techniques of discerning character from appearance found expression in the theoretical science of physiognomy, which flourished in the high empire as never before. "Knowledge of the internal constitution of the feminine and the masculine" was, tellingly, one of the three foundations of the science. We learn that androgynes might try to project a deceptive appearance, but "they are easily outed. For though they try to mimic the gait, speech, and glance of a real man, if they are ever startled or distressed, they instantly return to their true nature."[24]

Both Ptolemy and the physiognomists adopt a scientific idiom and studiously refrain from using the vernacular slur *kinaidos.* But we risk mismeasuring the import of their *scientia sexualis* if we do not recognize the utterly conventional social logic undergirding both astral and physiognomic doctrine. The conviction that society harbored individuals with monstrous imbalances of gender characteristics was imponderably ancient. The ex-slave Phaedrus, writing in the early first century, records a fable in which Prometheus, after too much to drink, made mistakes in assembling certain humans, placing male generative organs on women and vice versa, creating *tribades* (a word meaning "women who rub") and "softies." Both Ptolemy and the physiognomic treatises speak of a degree of gender deviance that bore on the individual's "whole nature," and the language of "nature" marks a subtle innovation. There was nothing new about the ascription of certain patterns of desire to a definite social type, but the placement of the traditional type, with all of the stereotypical qualities attached, into a scientific matrix, purportedly capable of explaining the natural mechanics of sexual deviance, was a step beyond the amorphous stereotypes of traditional prejudice. In short, what was new was the scientific framework and the types of sexual etiology it created.[25]

The codes of masculinity that suffuse the ancient literature belong to the millennia; the systems of knowledge that flourished in the Roman Empire provided a new medium for exploring the old stereotypes. But it is worth asking whether perhaps, beneath the placid ideological continuity and the crisper scientific paradigms, there was not a more profound movement under way. Our knowledge of Roman attitudes toward men whose sexual behavior violated prevailing norms comes exclusively from sources that are incandescently hostile; most of the evidence exists because, in the viciously competitive public sphere of the late classical world, it was a canon of invective to insult a man's sexual honor. Through such a haze of malevolence any speculation on reality is perilous. But there is surely enough testimony from the imperial era to posit the existence of men who openly flaunted dominant sexual norms. A scientist like Ptolemy set out to explain the patterns of social life around him, and what we have here is not an encyclopedist summoning his marvels into existence. There is, in fact, more evidence for frank sexual dissidence in the Roman Empire than for any other period before early modernity.[26]

Ptolemy distinguished between men who kept their behavior private and those who "straightforwardly and openly lack shame." That men indulged in deviant behavior behind closed doors was the inexhaustible stuff of invective. More interesting is the second type, those who self-identified as noncompliant sexual beings. This sort, Ptolemy said, occupied a role that was like "that of a vulgar prostitute, exposed to all shame and abuse." The assimilation of the public pathic and the prostitute may well reflect both material and legal reality. There was certainly a male brothel scene in Rome and presumably in most towns of any scale in the empire. More profoundly, willful sexual submission by a male entailed *infamia*, literally a lack of respectable reputation, which brought impairment of civil rights. In this atmosphere, it has been suggested, a subculture flourished.[27]

The notion of a "subculture" may be anachronistic, and it may too easily smooth over the brutal realities of social stratification in a world where slavery and prostitution played a fundamental role in many same-sex pairings. But the most intriguing novelty, by far, is the evidence for male-male marriage in the early empire. If we had only the extravagant reports about Nero or Heliogabulus marrying their favorites, we might ascribe it to conventional senatorial animus, although the extreme and unnecessary level of detail about the ceremonies would be striking. But there is plenty of evidence besides. The "adoption" of a young male beloved by his elder lover at the conclusion of the novel *The Ephesian Tale* is not quite a marriage, but it is clearly a happy resolution to parallel the other unions. The epigrams of Martial and the satires of Juvenal are insistent. While the mockery and the hostility are unrelenting, the descriptions are without parallel. Martial describes a man, Galla, who had married six or seven *cinaedi*. In another case he describes a marriage complete with the torch-lit procession, a wedding veil, a dowry, and the usual cheers of good luck. Juvenal's second satire, written sometime in the early second century, is even more compelling. Juvenal claims that recently a man of wealth and status was given away in marriage to a man; he imagines that the day is near when male-male marriages will take place publicly and be recorded in the state's registers. Amid a pastiche of the usual slurs, an adulteress threatens the *cinaedi* with the dangers of public law and laments, "Great is the concord among the effeminates." *Concordia* was the bedrock value of Roman conjugal morality, and beneath Juvenal's malicious irony lurks a reference to the solidarities of a community endangered by public norms.[28]

Similar patterns are evident in the way love between women was represented in the high empire. The experience of women amorously attracted to other women is a desperately murky issue. There is all the same hostility without nearly the same volume of material, but again Ptolemy's discussion is rich and revealing. Women who were excessively virilized would lust for unnatural unions with other women, becoming *tribades*. The satirical sources assume that during sex a woman would "strap on an artificial instrument of lust." It was assumed that even in female-female pairs, there was a dominant partner; precious little is heard about women who wished to "submit" to women. In Ptolemy's mind these relationships sometimes remained covert, but at other times women would "openly declare that their partners were their wedded wives." Clement of Alexandria, too, denounces with righteous indignation marriages between women. A vignette in Lucian's satirical "Dialogue of the Courtesans," meant to amuse and titillate, describes a marriage between women; it is hardly less vituperative than Clement's preaching. Perhaps the only testimony we have that does not come from the pen of a hostile informant is a funerary relief of the Augustan period depicting two women holding hands in a *dextrarum iunctio,* the prime symbol of marriage. It scarcely needs saying that same-sex marriages between women, or men, had no standing or consequence in public law, but that fact hardly diminishes the extraordinary testimony we do have for durable forms of same-sex companionship. In a peaceful and prosperous society, amid a highly urbanized and remarkably interconnected empire where marriage was valorized as an institution of the greatest moral and emotional fulfillment, same-sex pairs openly claimed, and ritually enacted, their own conjugal rights.[29]

It is beyond our ken to say how people truly behaved in any period of history. But at the very least it is time to lay to rest the bizarre notion, which is still sometimes expressed, that same-sex eros was, materially and ideologically, on the wane by the second century. This was the age when an emperor's favorite could become an object of worldwide veneration. When a novelist could claim that male-love was "becoming the current fashion." When a satirist could claim that marriage between men would soon be officially recognized. The question posed in the debates between marriage and pederasty, which figure so prominently in the literature of the era, was not an idle one. Indeed, same-sex eros was of greater interest to the Latin writers on either side of AD 100 than ever before; and as the Greek sources come to preponderance in the second century, there is no sign of abatement.

The Greeks and Romans of the high empire still conceived of sexual desire as an appetite that was basically indiscriminate in its choice of object. For a man to play the insertive role in coital encounters was normative, so long as the passive flesh was smooth. At the same time, the Roman male was impenetrable, even during the temporary indeterminacy of adolescence. In the imperial period, this norm, which was always one element among others in the Greek cultural atmosphere, if not always the dominant one, drove out the competing alternatives. Of course, such an attitude rests on a bedrock of slavery. To read closely the famous "contests of loves" in the imperial period is to see how deeply insinuated slavery had become in the nexus of erotic practice. Yet despite the vitality of various forms of same-sex erotics in the high empire, it would be a grave mistake to say that the Romans had anything resembling tolerance for homosexuality. The code of manliness that governed the access to pleasures in the classical world was severe and unforgiving, and deviance from it was socially mortal. The viciousness of mainstream attitudes toward passivity is startling for anyone who approaches the ancient sources with the false anticipation that pre-Christian cultures were somehow reliably civilized toward sexual minorities.

CHASTITY: THE SEXUAL LIFE COURSE FOR WOMEN

In a scene worthy of a modern action film, Achilles Tatius described a boat chase in which Clitophon and his comrades race after a band of pirates who have abducted Leucippe. As the pursuers bear down on the pirates, the villains expose Leucippe on deck and ostentatiously decapitate her, casting the headless body into the sea. Clitophon is despondent. He was so convinced of her death that he would reluctantly agree to marry the young widow Melite. Only at the very end of the novel, after Leucippe has passed a frightening test confirming her virginity, is "the enigma of the severed head" explained. In Leucippe's words, the pirates had also taken on board an "ill-starred woman who earned her living from selling the acts of Aphrodite," and they "sacrificed her in my stead." Although the drama of this revelation is deliberately heightened by the long delay, Achilles is not simply relishing the art of his own special effects. Apparent deaths and failed identifications are essential to the Greek romances. The decapitated prostitute was Leucippe's doppelgänger. Leucippe called her an "ill-starred" woman, just as Thersander called Leucippe an "ill-starred slave" during his crucial misrecognition scene. Leucippe described the prostitute's substitutional death in the language of animal sacrifice; it was a resonant statement in a culture that still very much believed in the mysterious powers of propitiation. While Leucippe's *eleutheria,* her freedom and sexual respectability, kept her body inviolate through the most extreme tribulations, fate was not so kind to her opposite, the unfortunate prostitute.[30]

Achilles Tatius has transformed mundane social prejudice into high art. That there were two fates for women was a fundamental and unchanging tenet of ancient sexual ideologies. Down one path lay promiscuity and shame, personified in the prostitute; down the other lay chastity and honor, personified in the virgin and the matron. These two fates were deeply embedded in patterns of social reproduction, loosely codified in public law, and actively reinforced by the social technology of honor and shame. It is an achievement of *Leucippe and Clitophon* that the story has so openly contemplated the inscrutable economy of fortune, in the stunning contrast between its beneficiary and its victim. The fate of the prostitute seems only more capricious and unjust in a novelistic universe where there is no redemption beyond life, only the prospect of salvation through conjugal eros. In the cosmos created by the author, the prostitute's grotesque demise serves only to exhibit the good fortune of Leucippe in even greater contrast.

The norms attaching to male sexual behavior inevitably attract the lion's share of the attention from historians. It is an obvious and insurmountable fact that our informants are almost exclusively male. More subtly, expectations of female sexual behavior can seem uniform and immobile: good girls remain pure until marriage, faithful within marriage. The imposition of these limits is as unsurprising as the dawn. The effort to control female sexuality is precultural, a permanent fixture of sexual competition. The regulation of female sexuality in the ancient Mediterranean shared all the predictable features of a patriarchal culture. Nevertheless, the actual mechanics and specific inflections of feminine sexual norms in the pre-Christian world merit closer inspection. The peculiar complexion of classical sexual culture derived from the institutionalization of a stark, binary opposition between women who possessed and women who lacked sexual honor. The great polarization of feminine types not only animated a whole code of signs and gestures, it actively gave structure to the material formation of classical societies. And in the Roman period, the reliance of female sexual ethics on patterns of socialization even became the object of philosophical reflection, though not a matter for reform, as the author of *Leucippe and Clitophon* well knew.[31]

The great dichotomization of female sexuality was embedded—materially, culturally, and legally—in the very foundations of the ancient city. Its assumptions are fully apparent in the earliest Roman literature. The contrast between the *matrona* and the *meretrix,* the respectable woman and the whore, runs throughout the entire oeuvre of Plautus. It animates the social thought of Cicero. Most consequentially, it undergirds the moral legislation of the first emperor, Augustus. The domestic reforms of Augustus were the cornerstone of his social policy, whose precise mixture of conservatism and laxity were to set the moral tone of the high empire. The adultery legislation of Augustus was, in the judgment of no less than Mommsen, one of the most intrusive and enduring creations in the history of criminal law. *Adulterium* meant the violation of a respectable woman. The true significance of the Augustan law against *adulterium* lay not in the imposition of repressive norms on a libertine society, but in the assumption by the state of an ever greater role in the regulation of sexual morality, along solidly traditional lines. The *lex Iulia* actually limited the role of private violence in the punishment of adultery, and in place of hoary threats of private death it established a standing court to hear charges of adultery; third-party accusation was even, within certain boundaries, permitted. With the Augustan legislation, the state got in the business of protecting feminine chastity. At the same time the state was required to define, or at least establish guidelines allowing judges to define, which women were beyond its purview: implicitly slaves and explicitly women who made a profit with their bodies. By insinuating the state into the traditional networks of violence controlling access to female bodies, the Augustan laws ratified the distinction between women with, and without, sexual honor.[32]

The *lex Iulia* was a momentous success, and one measure of its profound influence is that it subtly reshaped the vernacular of sexual honor. The Augustan laws protected the sexual honor of the *mater familias,* and the word became the Latin term for a woman with an all-encompassing sexual respectability, the equivalent of the Greek *eleuthera,* which had long denoted the married or marriageable woman. "We ought to accept as a *mater familias* she who has not lived dishonorably. For it is behavior that distinguishes and separates the *mater familias* from other women. So it matters not at all whether she is a married woman or a widow, a freeborn or freed woman, since neither marriages nor births make a *mater familias,* but good morals." Social status and sexual behavior were inseparably fused, and the *mater familias* was defined by a mode of being, visibly projected in her comportment and appearance. It was assumed that a *mater familias* could be distinguished, in the way she dressed, from women without sexual honor, whose "servile" or "whorish" vestments advertised their social condition.[33]

The sexual life course of free women was dominated by the imperatives of marriage. In a society that was never freed from the relentless grip of a high-mortality regime, the burden of reproduction weighed heavily on the female population. The demographic explosion of the Roman Empire, which pushed human settlement into every hill and vale, testifies to a society that was constitutionally geared for reproduction and technologically incapable of putting brakes on its own fertility. The age structure of Greco-Roman marriage was an expression of the need to exploit female reproductive potential to the full, from menarche to menopause. For girls, marriage came early and inexorably. The legal age for marriage was twelve. Most girls married in their mid-teens. The higher classes may have married off their daughters latest of all, sometime in their late teens. Marriage was universal for women; there were no spinsters in antiquity. In a world where death rates were grievously high and unpredictable, early widowhood was common. Although the *univira,* the woman with only one husband, was idealized, in reality society could not afford to be too fastidious about remarriage, and serial marriage was widespread and unproblematic.[34]

It would not be hyperbolic to claim that ancient sexual morality, for men and women alike, was immanent in the age structure of marriage. Virginity at marriage was paramount for girls, an ideal rendered practical by early marriage. Though rituals confirming defloration turn up mostly in Jewish sources, it is clear that Greeks and Romans of every station wished to be sure that their wives were pure on the *prima nox.* Medical texts reveal no sound consensus about the physical proofs of maidenhood. Male anxiety was fueled by rumors of nurses or midwives, the usual carriers of feminine arcana, who knew how to conceal the premarital loss of virginity. Reliable paternal surveillance and pristine reputation were the best forms of insurance. For most free girls in the ancient world, the wedding night may well have been a sexual initiation. Across the Roman Empire, marriage was the single, great rite of passage for women. Whereas the male life course was marked by fine and subtle gradations, the female life course knew only the stark before and after of the wedding. It was *the* rite of passage, whose timeless core was the procession from the father's house to the husband's. The attendants of the bride and groom escorted the pair by torchlight, bellowing out the traditional, bawdy songs about the girl's impending loss of maidenhood. Several writers of the high empire poignantly write of the woman's initial experience as a "wounding" or "injury," and they counsel sensitivity toward any confusion or timidity a young bride might experience. But it was not all timorous quavering: an extraordinary sequence of paintings that decorated a bedroom in a lavish villa from the age of Augustus depicts the bride's metamorphosis from demure and reluctant creature into a sensual enthusiast.[35]

The code of female sexual morality was summarized by one word, modesty—*pudicitia* in Latin, *sōphrosynē* in Greek. For a woman, the "single ornament, the noblest beauty, unravaged by age, the highest honor," was *pudicitia.* A man perfectly blessed by the gods was given a wife with fertility and *pudicitia.* If sexual modesty was a monopolistic virtue, it was nevertheless one that allowed surprising nuance and refinement. For women, *pudicitia* or *sōphrosynē* implied both an objective fact and a subjective mode of being; it was a state of body and a state of mind. Fundamentally, *pudicitia* was the corporal integrity of the free woman, untouched until marriage, vouchsafed for one man within marriage. Sexual modesty was inextricably fused with status, and *pudicitia* often appears alongside *libertas* as its inseparable adjunct. Nevertheless, *pudicitia* was a social rather than a strictly legal concept, and it could, exceptionally, even be predicated of slaves. In a vast and highly stratified slave system, where slaves were delicately intertwined with the life of the free family, *pudicitia* was a powerful and imprecise enough concept that some of its mystique might devolve even on the lowest members of the household; but the deeper truth was that, for slaves, access to honor depended on the discretion of the master.[36]

An ancient woman lived every moment engaged in a high-stakes game of suspicious observation. "The one glory of woman is *pudicitia,* and therefore it is incumbent upon her to be, and to seem, chaste." In the words of a Christian author, "A woman's reputation for sexual modesty is a fragile thing, like a precious flower that breaks in the soft breeze and is ruined by the light wind." There were "so many" potential signs of immodesty; her dress, her gait, her voice, her face all acted as external projections of her internal state. The woman's "only protection" was never to become the cause of any gossip. To guard against the attentions of other men, the Roman matron should dress only so nice as to avoid uncleanness, she should always be chaperoned in public, she should walk with her eyes down and risk rudeness rather than immodesty in her greetings, and she should blush when addressed.[37]

The sharpest of these patriarchal prescriptions come from rhetorical school exercises, sources that no doubt caricature contemporary male bombast and must be taken with healthful caution. Undoubtedly the scripts of female modesty could be stifling. In most quarters women wore their hair veiled from the time they reached sexual maturity. Coins of the high empire advertise *pudicitia* as a chief imperial virtue, and its image is a Roman matron, hair veiled, hand drawn partly across her face to shield it from full view. Conventional limits on visibility and movement were truly constricting. Even the gentle Plutarch counsels a woman to be most visible in her husband's presence and to hide when he is away. A woman without a man was "like a city without a wall"; fathers and husbands offered protection, and protection brings its own types of dependence. But it would be a mistake to underestimate the room for maneuver left to women. Debates over the appearance of modesty could be so intense because the lines were contestable—how much hair could be seen, when the skin of an arm could be exposed. Limits on movement were relaxed for women chaperoned by slaves, a considerable concession in Mediterranean towns where maybe the top fifth of all households owned servants. Moreover, the zone between the permissible and the forbidden carries its own erotic charge, and in a society where sex was always cheaply available, men and women alike were well aware that danger amplifies pleasure. We are considering a society that practiced public bathing, at times even mixed bathing, so we can feel certain that the striations of the forbidden and the permitted were densely compressed.[38]

Societies tolerate, or pretend not to detect, female infidelity in varying ways and degrees, and reports of wifely misconduct in Roman society are such a concoction of satire, invective, and bluster that nothing like the general sensibility can be ascertained. A belief in contemporary moral decline was practically a requisite part of Roman vigilance. "A modest matron is a rare thing." The satirist could claim that sexual modesty belonged to the age of Saturn, a mythical golden age. A Stoic philosopher believed that the women of Rome kept Plato's *Republic* in their hands because its utopian community of women justified their sins. In quite a different tone, Lucian imagined the frustrations of being a philosopher attached to a wealthy household: the matron would make him pause his discourse on *sōphrosynē* while she penned a note to her lover. In a slaveholding society, the specter of sex between the mistress and the slaves was a stock theme of ribald folk comedy. The timeless weapon of the seducer is reasonable suspicion about the secret behavior of others: "All women do it, my child. . . . But bolt the door so we don't get caught!" Many were too indiscrete: the historian Cassius Dio, during his consulate in the early third century, discovered a backlog of three thousand adultery trials in the dockets![39]

Dio's report is revealing in an unexpected way. The uncontrollable surge of adultery cases came from a swiftly imposed imperial crackdown that caught society off guard. But "[when] hardly anyone prosecuted these cases, the emperor himself ceased to meddle." Adultery was, from its origins, a crime against man, not God, and it never lost this sense in Roman society. Even the mature Christian church of late antiquity will struggle, mostly without success, to break away from this residual belief. Adultery was an act of theft, violation of another man's legitimate control of female sexuality. It was horrific, but principally as an affront to society. Adultery was a public crime because the state was charged to maintain good order, not because it was the steward of sexual morality per se. At least in the more developed corridors of the empire, women convicted of adultery were not stoned in fits of righteous vengeance. Rather, a condemned adulteress was forced by law to renounce the *stola*, the garment of feminine modesty, and don the *toga*, the traditional dress of the Roman man . . . and the Roman prostitute.[40]

The strict code of honor and shame was used to scare girls into submission, but it was not as retrograde as many later iterations of the Mediterranean syndrome. It was a disgrace to suffer sexual violation, but Roman society did not blame rape victims. Although sexual crimes were legally formulated in terms of status, at least from the age of Augustus, consent was fundamental. Certain signs of refusal—screams, physical resistance—might be required. Some worried that this allowance opened the floodgates by providing a disguise for sin. Lucretia's extraordinary virtue was revealed by the fact that she had the excuse of violence and refused to tender it. When Leucippe's mother discovered her daughter on the brink of losing her virginity to Clitophon, she lamented that her daughter was ruined, especially because it was a voluntary encounter: "at least a disaster which comes about through force is not shameful."[41]

When sex with a decent woman was not an open provocation of another man, attitudes might be less exacting. One of the finest representations of quiet indulgence occurs at the end of the fifth book of *Leucippe and Clitophon*. The young "widow" Melite falls passionately in love with Clitophon, yet he artfully avoids physical consummation of their engagement. When Melite's husband turns up alive, she makes one last effort to take Clitophon to bed. The seduction scene was the deliberate inverse of Leucippe's heroic resistance against Thersander, Melite's husband. Melite's speech is the *cri de coeur* of a desperate young wife infatuated with another man. Clitophon's response is tender. "Something human moved me, and I truly feared the god Eros too. . . . This would have to be reckoned not so much intercourse as a cure for an ailing soul. . . . Everything happened by the will of Eros." In the dramatic final act, Melite would indeed find herself charged with adultery. The prosecutors note that one who corrupts a wedded wife steals what belongs to another man. Nevertheless, Achilles Tatius is humane, or subversive, enough to let Melite escape on a technicality, by vowing that she did not violate her marriage *so long as* she thought her husband was dead, when in fact she hurriedly cheated on him as soon as she learned that his return was imminent![42]

The satisfaction of Melite demonstrates that sometimes eros transcended human rules, not that the rules were changing. Despite the episode's undoubted charm, it cannot count as a winking acknowledgment of women's liberation. Sometimes the Roman Empire is construed as a progressive moment in women's history, rolled back in late antiquity by the regressive alliance of religion and patriarchy. The vociferous, if satirical, complaints about powerful wives, the frank depiction of feminine sexual pleasure in the visual arts, the greater presence of women in the public sphere—all of these are signs that point to a wider range of motion for the Roman matron. As with any such caricature, this one has only a certain admixture of truth. A number of structural factors worked in a woman's favor. By the imperial era, older forms of marriage that placed the woman in the legal power of her husband had long fallen into desuetude. Roman rules that kept spousal property in separate funds meant that the woman's dowry was, as men complained, a subtle source of leverage. The woman's—or, more realistically, the girl's—consent was formally required for the marriage, and liberal laws of divorce allowed women to end marriages, unilaterally and virtually without cause. The Augustan social legislation created a path for women to achieve an exceptional legal competence, the ability to act without a male tutor, by bearing three children. The Roman woman is hardly a naive and feeble creature hopelessly under her husband's thumb.[43]

At the same time, none of the basic rules had changed. The double standard reigned almost universally. Even Plutarch, whose sensible advice for husbands included not provoking their wives by smelling like other women, ultimately expected the wife to find a way to cope with inevitable infidelities. "If he makes some little slip with a slave girl or hired lady, do not bear it too gravely, and consider that he wishes to spare you from his debauchery." A woman's range of motion remained always defined by her position among men. In a world with few informal and fewer formal constraints on domestic violence, the dynamics of physical force always loomed ominously in the background. In the Roman Empire, the norms of female sexuality were static, and even the fields of tension that gave women the capacity to maneuver were relatively unchanging. The real novelty was the extraordinary prosperity of Mediterranean society under Roman rule and a highly articulated class system in which women played an essential role in the maintenance and transmission of an aristocratic and bourgeois ethos.[44]

The danger of speaking of women's liberation in the Roman context is that it attributes to antiquity a concept that was intellectually unavailable. We risk misunderstanding the sexual culture of the Roman Mediterranean if we believe that repressive sexual norms were imposed on women by men. The relation between life and sexual culture is never so simple. Many women seized on the values of *pudicitia* and *sōphrosynē* and promoted them with verve. It would be surprising if it were otherwise. Women made their lives, they fashioned their sense of self-respect, out of traditional norms. Perhaps the most realistic character in *Leucippe and Clitophon* is Leucippe's mother, distraught at the prospect of her daughter's loss of chastity. After lamenting Leucippe's willingness to surrender her modesty, the mother added, with what has been called "bathetic class consciousness," that hopefully Leucippe was, at the very least, not sleeping with a slave. Adherence to the old ways ensured a woman's position in society. Chastity was a badge of honor, separating the Roman matron from the slaves whose bodies she ostentatiously controlled. The wealthy Roman woman could stroll through the forum, accompanied by her slaves, and point to the statues of her ancestors. Sexual liberation was not on the agenda of the woman who had thoroughly appropriated the values that made her what she was.[45]

If there was authentic dissent, it surely resided among those whose life condition exposed them to systemic exploitation. The high Roman Empire was a genuine slave society, consuming slaves as ferociously as any previous period, and perhaps on a wider, Mediterranean scale. Women accounted for at least half of the slave population, and they bore the brunt of sexual abuse. Without legal or social protection, they were devastatingly vulnerable. Sexual abuse was simply presumptive, and many slave girls probably experienced sexual initiation traumatically early. The slave woman's life course was undifferentiated by the great threshold between childhood and marriage that marked the stages of a free woman's development. Slaves in the house may have been more integrated into the rhythms of the free family's life, but at the same time proximity meant vulnerability and close control. The slave's public behavior could be seen as a reflection of the free family's honor; "the morals of the mistress are judged by those of the slave girls." Many slaves were owned in small numbers and surreptitiously sought companionship outside the home. In larger households, the slave staff may have offered its own opportunities. Rural slaves might have had the greatest chance of stability and privacy, but our ignorance of their lives is profound. When Leucippe was made a field slave, she was viciously threatened by the sexual advances of her overseer. Although slave marriages were afforded virtually no legal protections, slaves married nonetheless. We hear casually of "slave weddings." Plutarch knew that a slave girl who was married would suddenly become more resistant to her master's advances, but slave marriages were not protected under the adultery laws. Slaves were entirely cut off from their male relatives, and the surviving documents of sale are a chilling reminder that the slave family existed only at the master's will.[46]

As blurry as our perception of the slave's life is, the realities of prostitution are possibly even more obscure. Slaves haphazardly appear in our upper-class sources because they inhabited the same walls, because they inevitably intruded upon the daily affairs of their masters. Prostitutes, by contrast, represented "the most impure part of humankind," and hence real consideration of their existence has been exiled from all literature with pretension to gentility. When prostitutes do appear in the sources, it is thus usually as a cipher for pure sexual indecency. Like the miserable creature whose unfortunate destiny is lost in the brilliant glare of Leucippe's invincible sexual modesty, the prostitutes we know are mostly nameless, faceless distortions of an inconceivably brutal existence. But like slaves, prostitutes were in reality ubiquitous, and the sexual economy of the Roman Empire directly depended on the exploitation of their available bodies.[47]

Roman policy toward prostitution has been aptly described as a volatile mixture of "toleration and degradation." Prostitution was legal. It was taxed by the state and broadly supervised by the public officials in charge of keeping urban peace. Far from an institution that festered implacably in shadowy corners, prostitution in the Roman Empire was purposefully conspicuous. It played a well-established role in the sexual order. The idea that prostitution prevented adultery, that the prostitute's body acted as a safety valve for male lust, was already, by the high empire, very ancient, and it remained a vital notion across Roman history. The very model of ancestral Roman manliness, Cato the Censor, was reputed to have congratulated a young man exiting a brothel for avoiding other men's wives. Male sexual energy was a definite quantity that had to be expended, somewhere; a nickname for the penis was "the necessity." Dio Chrysostom, in his Stoic attack on prostitution, admitted that many believed that prostitution deflected desire away from respectable women. Wives belonged to the private sphere, but prostitutes were, like the baths, a public good. Folklore held that after Corinth expelled the legendary beauty Lais, the city was depopulated when the young men turned their attentions to free women and a cycle of honor killings ensued. It is a Christian bishop, though, trained in Roman law, who has left the pithiest description of Roman sexual policy: forbidding adulteries, building brothels.[48]

Prostitution was a boom industry under Roman rule. In the densely urbanized and highly monetized economy of the Roman Empire, sex was a most basic and readily available commodity. Girls stalked the streets. Taverns, inns, and baths were notorious dens of venal sex. Brothels "were visible everywhere." Companions, trained in various forms of entertainment, could be rented for domestic symposia. Sex was big business, and although pimps and procurers suffered legal and social stigmas, Roman law allowed slave owners to profit from a slave's entrepreneurial activities, so that undoubtedly some rather illustrious households capitalized, discreetly, on the flesh trade. In the few surviving scraps of evidence for real working brothels, including a handful of papyri from Roman Egypt, what is most notable is the sheer sophistication of the financial instruments undergirding the sale of sex. Prostitution was an exuberant part of Roman capitalism.[49]

Prostitutes were imagined in impossibly contrasting ways. Throughout the Roman Empire persisted the classical ideal of the *hetaira,* a "lady friend." Her title, like her very existence, is a euphemism. Like the prostitute, she circulates among men outside the marriage market and for avowedly sensual purposes. Unlike the prostitute, she trades in gifts rather than vulgar cash exchanges; she is discriminate rather than promiscuous, her allure heightened by her elusiveness; she is witty, even sophisticated, rather than common. Truly, once, these women bestrode the Greek world, making playthings of kings and philosophers alike. In the Roman Empire their images could still be seen in the temples where classical statues of goddesses, modeled on the bodies of the most famous *hetairai*, stood hundreds of years later. But from the beginning the line between the *hetaira* and the common prostitute was blurry, and the distinction survived through a healthy dose of sexual fantasy. By the second century of our era, the figure of the *hetaira* was so clouded by the broader cultural nostalgia gripping the empire that the truth of her existence is unknowable. The most elaborate literary reflection on ancient prostitution is, fittingly, the *Sophists at Dinner:* an imaginary transcript of a late second-century conversation, set at the table of a Roman aristocrat, where the symposiasts debate the obscurer corners of Attic Greek and the relative merits of *hetairai* and common prostitutes. The fog of erudition is so heavy that we cannot draw any safe conclusions about the real world.[50]

In a supremely rich, sexually open, and astonishingly interconnected society that was poised to embrace the power of human beauty (a gorgeous woman offered "no trivial happiness"), it would be unwise to doubt the existence of the demimondaine. We know that actors and actresses suffered from legal discrimination, such as the inability to intermarry with the aristocracy, and there was a material connection between the theater and the sex industry. The Roman Empire had an insatiable taste for stage performance, and it is likely that theatrical culture nurtured stars of various talents. Too much amorous literature presumes the existence of the glamorous, independent prostitute for her to have been a mere figment of an overactive cultural memory. But even more than before, her power to enrapture derived from her rarity. The preponderance of the evidence, and all of the evidence that takes us away from fantasy and toward the mundane realities of prostitution, points to the overwhelming connection between the slave trade and the sex trade. There is, of course, no reason to doubt that droves of poor women were forced to become prostitutes in the Roman Empire. In an economy with relatively few respectable employments for women and no social safety net, sudden shocks could render women hopelessly vulnerable. But the defining feature of prostitution in the Roman era, which gives Roman prostitution its particular tincture, is the pervasive influence of slavery.[51]

Convincing testimony confirms the sinister link between the slave trade and prostitution. The most chilling evidence is an iron slave collar, a typical means of preventing or punishing slave flight, discovered at Bulla Regia in North Africa; found still clasped around the neck of a skeleton, the collar's inscription reads, "I am a slutty whore; retain me, I have fled Bulla Regia." A third-century papyrus shows a dispute that arose from the sale of a girl by pimps. The pimp was, presumptively, a man "who buys girls." Child exposure, a significant input to the Roman slave supply, was presumed to lead "to slavery or to the brothel," fates that were not distinct. One of the more interesting, if oblique, indices of the role of slavery in the sex industry is that Roman law developed a special covenant allowing masters to sell slaves with the binding restriction that the slave not be prostituted; whether these covenants indicate residual benevolence or the frequency of biological relations between master and slave, they demonstrate the real danger that, for a slave, prostitution lurked in the future.[52]

The desire to romanticize venal sex was perduring, and even the erotic art in brothels idealized the sexual encounter between professional and customer. But the critics object. The lingering stench, the atmosphere of violence, the cramped concrete cribs, the systemic abuse: these were the reality of the flesh trade. Disease and chemical dependence surely followed in the wake of such exploitative drudgery. The low price of sex is stunning. Sex seems to have cost maybe two *asses* in an ordinary town, "about the price of a loaf of bread." Fellatio cost less. The vile rate of the transaction is also a harrowing indication of the crushing amount of work women had to perform to survive and to profit their owners. The commodification of sex was carried out with all the ruthless efficiency of an industrial operation, the unfree body bearing the pressures of insatiable market demand. In the brothel the prostitute's body became, little by little, "like a corpse."[53]

The lower-class atmosphere of the brothel lies behind one of the more subtle but important changes in the moral economy of prostitution under the Roman Empire. To the respectable classes, prostitution was not immoral—it was squalid. The wealthy had slaves to serve their needs, and it was unnecessary to share sexual receptacles. Prostitution was the poor man's piece of the slave system. In his *City of God,* Augustine imagined the simple desires of the ordinary man; after military victory for the Roman army and economic prosperity, he would think, "let public prostitutes abound for any who want to use them, but especially for those who cannot afford private ones!" The brothel was even patronized by slaves. It raised the disturbing specter of sharing women with men of the lowest ranks. The brothel was irredeemably vulgar, and in a carefully and formally stratified society, nothing was more damning.[54]

Given the moral and material centrality of prostitution in Roman society, it is noteworthy that so little comment was aroused by the problem of how women became prostitutes. In part this silence is explained by the constant influx of slaves into the sex trade; slaves were social nonbeings whose exploitation was unremarkable. But the silence is more deafening than that. In comparison with other cultures, Roman ideology placed virtually no emphasis on the prostitute's lust. Prostitution was a *bios,* a condition of life, not necessarily a result of the woman's interior constitution. In parallel, the Roman ideology of slavery was equally underdeveloped. Aristotle's natural slave theory had little purchase in the Roman Empire. Slavery was a fact; it was "an economic and political necessity, and that was that." The prostitute, similarly, required no deep or elaborate psychopathology. She was an ill-starred creature, like the faceless victim sacrificed for Leucippe.[55]

What is notable about female sexual morality in the Roman Empire is its resolute constancy. Primitive expectations of the woman's body endured with little questioning. A woman's sexual behavior was an organic expression of the role she was assigned in the economy of desire and reproduction. The principal novelty in the imperial era is a heightened awareness of the deep association of social status and moral expectations. This awareness seeped into ordinary consciousness. It is evident, for instance, in an oft-quoted series of rhetorical exercises preserved by the elder Seneca. These ephemera of the Roman schools, such an important organ of socialization in the empire, transmit some of the most primitive *and* most progressive sentiments to have reached us from the ancient world. One elaborate series revolves around the imaginary dilemmas of a virgin enslaved in a brothel who escapes unstained and wishes to become a priestess. Some orators argued that the mere placement of the girl's body in the brothel shamed it; others argued that her invincible chastity was all the greater for having triumphed over bad fortune. It would be inadvisable to extract any of these *dicta* and treat them as the Roman attitude. The exercise was aimed, with pinpoint accuracy, at the fundamental but unstable assumption that status and behavior were aligned. The tension, and even more so a consciousness of the tension, is specifically Roman.[56]

The imagination that produced these rich socio-legal riddles is not far at all from the literary spirit that informs the romances. The contemplation of the possible disjuncture between essence and circumstance is identical. In

Leucippe and Clitophon, this disjuncture is a constant source of dramatic energy. In a touching scene near the end of the romance, a priest of Artemis tries to dissuade Leucippe from submitting to the harrowing, and fearfully inerrant, divine virginity test. He assumes that the girl, in professing her purity, has tried to save face out of necessity and pride, but he wants to spare her, quietly. She confidently persists in the protestations of her innocence, and he realizes that she is indeed uncorrupted. "I rejoice with you in your chastity and your fortune." Achilles Tatius could not have chosen more resonant words—*sōphrosynē,* female sexual modesty, and *tychē,* fortune. Leucippe's sexual honor and her fate were inseparable. The novel contemplates, but does not ultimately doubt, a salvation that will realign Leucippe's subjective modesty and her objective respectability. The inhabitants of the high empire were highly conscious that female sexual honor was dispensed just as much by the lottery of fate as by the force of the individual's will. This awareness of honor's origins did nothing to dim its power. If anything, it made sexual respectability all the more precious, more intimate, more numinous.[57]

Here the novel scrapes very close to the deepest recesses of belief in the high empire. In the same years when Achilles was conceiving his romance, a woman named Regilla was voted an honorific statue by the people of Corinth. Regilla was a descendant of the reigning imperial clan, wife to the most powerful and eloquent Greek aristocrat of the age, Herodes Atticus (whom she married when she was around fourteen, he forty). She would eventually die during the miscarriage of their sixth child, after being kicked in the stomach by a freedman acting on her husband's orders. But in brighter times the Corinthians sculpted her in the image of the goddess Tychē, "Fortune." Regilla was priestess of the goddess Tychē at Athens, and had in fact introduced her cult there and constructed a grand temple perched over the stadium that her husband built for the city. The dedicatory inscription from Corinth survives. "This is a portrait of Regilla. A sculptor carved the figure, endowing the stone with all her *sōphrosynē.* . . . Regilla: the Council, as if to call you 'Tychē' has erected this marble image in front of the sanctuary." Ordinary women may not have hoped to merge with the divine in the way that an imperial scion like Regilla could, but in the monuments and images that surrounded them they saw memorialized the sublime value of feminine chastity, as an ideal somewhere between a moral attribute and an endowment of fate. Regilla embodied, in a superlative form, the hopes, values, and sufferings out of which Roman women could make their lives.[58]

MODERATION: THE SEXUAL LIFE COURSE FOR MEN

The ancient novels have been hailed as messengers of a new erotic sensibility focused on "sexual symmetry." No literary genre had so valorized the mutual devotion and shared attraction between two young lovers, nearly equal in age, whose love triumphs in marriage. But symmetry of passion did not mean equality of experience, and Achilles Tatius exploits the distinction with his usual sardonic enthusiasm. When Leucippe reemerged after her apparent beheading to find her lover engaged to Melite, she furtively sent him a letter, scolding him in the most pathetic terms. Pierced by her accusations, Clitophon defends his sexual comportment as impeccable. "You will find that I have mimicked your maidenhood, if there is also a maidenhood for men." This precious claim preceded the "cure" that Clitophon offered Melite, but the reader remembers that Clitophon has already delivered a well-informed paean to the female orgasm. At the end of the novel, when recounting his adventures, Clitophon would omit details of the favor he performed for Melite, while to Leucippe's father he would boast, "Throughout our exile we have behaved like philosophers . . . If men have a maidenhead, I have kept it with Leucippe up to the present." With an artful turn of phrase, and a whole culture's indifference toward male chastity, Clitophon could stare past his inconsequential sexual dalliances into the exalted light of his love for Leucippe.[59]

There was no natural word for male virginity in Greek or Latin. *Parthenia* meant "maidenhead," and the ordinary sense of *parthenos* was "maiden." The continent men of the incipient Christian movement searched, awkwardly, for an expression adequate to their unusual ideal. On rare occasions authors would simply appropriate the language of maidenhood for men: the canonical *Revelation,* for example, or *Joseph and Aseneth,* in which both protagonists are called *parthenos. Virgo,* too, primarily meant "maiden" or "young, unmarried girl," though it would later be adapted by Christians and applied to males. More often Christians found circumlocutions for male sexual abstinence, such as *eunouchia.* What is telling is that Clitophon's brazen protestations of his purity are *intentionally* amusing because they are linguistically bumbling. (Do we have here another instance where Achilles Tatius glances at contemporary cultural currents, such as Christian encratism, in order to mock them?) Regardless, the absence of a symmetrical term for male virginity is eloquent. So, too, is the fact that the prime sexual virtue, *sōphrosynē,* carried different connotations for men and women. For women, *sōphrosynē* meant chastity, the unbending criterion of corporal integrity before marriage and fidelity during marriage. For men, *sōphrosynē* meant self-control, the mind's orderly management of the physical appetites. For women, *sōphrosynē* was absolute; for men, it was gradational. In between these shades of meaning lay a field of extensible space for men to exercise their moderation.[60]

In a society where "the work of Aphrodite" could always "be bought for a drachma," self-control was no trivial virtue. *Sōphrosynē* was "the first and most fitting virtue of young men, harmonizing and choreographing all qualities of excellence." "Nothing in excess" was the sacred inner code of Greek ethics. Moderation was for men what chastity was for women, in that it served, on a millennial time scale, as the unwavering fundament beneath mainstream sexual ethics. The classical ideal of moderation flourished in a moral universe where it was ultimately the only force of resistance against the easy satiety of sexual desire. The material environment of the Greco-Roman city was unusually adapted for stimulating the appetites. The high empire was the Indian summer of classical nudity, when prosperity carried the culture of public baths and gymnasia further than ever before and when frankly erotic art was ubiquitous in refined and popular media. The slave trade and its unruly outgrowth, the flesh trade, made pleasure cheap and unceremonious. Throughout the city, professionals cruised the streets in shoes that left behind the words "follow me" in the sand. Unsurprisingly, the second century generated a rich discussion on the physics of vision—conceived as the flow of particles into the eye, so that Achilles could unforgettably describe looking at a beautiful woman as a sort of "fondling from afar." The inhabitant of the Roman Empire was constantly bombarded with visual allurements, so moderation was a virtue called upon, constantly, to perform heroic feats of restraint.[61]

The need for internal regulation of impulses was felt with special keenness in a society that celebrated the pleasures of "wine, baths, and venus" and delivered them with unprecedented efficiency to the male consumer. Most of what passes for "sexual morality" is, implicitly or explicitly, advice for men. The "conjugalization of pleasure" and the intensely interior, self-regarding morality that have been identified as Rome's signal contributions to the history of sexuality weighed principally on men. For decent women, what licit pleasure might be found had always been confined to the marriage bed, and nearly all philosophical literature implicitly addresses a male sexual subject. Below we consider how the institutions of marriage and the philosophical cultures of the high empire shaped the sexual experiences of men, but first we should explore the ambient atmosphere in which male sexual desires developed. The male sexual life course, the shared cultural assumptions about masculinity, and the practices of sociability in the Roman Empire are the backdrop vivifying the more rarefied concerns of philosophers and moralists.[62]

For girls, the window of time between physical maturity and marriage was fleeting; by contrast, young men in the ancient Mediterranean spent a formless eternity between puberty and marriage. Male age at marriage varied widely, but the vast majority of young men married in their twenties, most of them in their late twenties. In both Greek and Roman tradition, boys crossed the threshold between puerility and manhood around the age of fourteen. The moment was recognized by ancient rites of passage and, in the Roman case, by the weighty assumption of the *toga virilis.* Sexual experience presumptively followed on the heels of nascent maturity. Philo of Alexandria has left the most indelicately precise description of this sexual initiation. His hero, the biblical Joseph, utters words that are aimed at contemporary Alexandria, a city famous for its ebullient eroticism. "We descendants of the Hebrews live according to a special set of customs and norms. Among other peoples, it is permitted for young men after their fourteenth year to use with complete shamelessness whores, brothel hags, and other women who make a profit with their body. . . . Indeed, before legitimate marriage, we [Jews] know no sexual intercourse with other women but enter marriage as pure men with pure virgins."[63]

Philo's tribal righteousness foreshadows a Christian moralism that will cut, with pitiless severity, across the soft zones of pagan indulgence. For the Greeks and Romans, any hard restrictions on male sexual exertion in the years after puberty were considered implausible; through subtle but decisive evasions, this stretch of life was left unregulated. In the first years after sexual maturity, the moral faculty was too light and porous even to act as the receptacle of ethical prescription. This was the age of Venus, when the seminal channels were formed and the impulse for sex began to course throughout a young man's whole being. "Something like frenzy arises in the soul, the will is powerless, there is lust for sex however it may be had, the guile of one who is on fire with passion and the blindness of one who is reckless." The most that could be hoped for was that the young man, in this frantic period, did nothing to impair his manhood; he needed to pass through "that slippery time" without doing permanent damage to his reputation. Marcus Aurelius, a little cryptically, was grateful that he had managed "to keep safe the bloom of youth and not to become a man before the right hour, in fact to wait a little." In other words, he had never submitted to a lover, nor did he rush headlong into the *aphrodisia* at puberty, though even this dreary Stoic had given way to "erotic passions" for a time, before returning to sound control of himself.[64]

Ethical strictures lay lightly on young men, who made use of the "mirth conceded to their age." There was an unwritten "law of youth." "An untimely severity is not moderation but gloominess." Sexual exploration was "practically required training," after which it was expected the young man would cool off and ease into a more respectable self-control and eventually marriage. The "natural violence of youth" was better indulged than repressed, for repression would inevitably fail. The sexual escapades of boys in their late teens and early twenties were almost completely inconsequential. By contrast, the more seasoned sexual prowess of youth in their later twenties was a social problem. The predatory sexuality of young, unmarried men was a dangerous presence in the ancient Mediterranean city; in a society where men were half a generation older than their wives, the threat of adultery was conceived in generational terms, as a threat emanating from below, from younger men with enough cunning to play the seducer. The solution was a high degree of tolerance toward sex with slaves and prostitutes. A father who sensed that his son was in love with a freeborn woman gravely counseled him to use "the *venus* which is public and permitted." This father, whose son was saved by "the gratification of licit sex," even ranks among the *exempla* of so stodgy a moralist as Valerius Maximus.[65]

The ready availability of licit sexual release gave adultery its dark tint in Roman society. The violation of a respectable wife is the paradigmatic form of sexual malfeasance in most human societies. In the Roman Empire, the prohibition on adultery and the imperative of avoiding sexual passivity were the two heavy rules weighing on men. There is little trace of those paradoxical values, familiar in later Mediterranean societies, that simultaneously lionized and vilified the adulterer. In the classical world, the adulterer was purely villainous. The idea of sexual pleasure as a finite commodity, the object of an intense, zero-sum competition, was distinctly alien to the classical spirit, so successfully had the brothel made sex a public good. Adultery was theft, an injury to another free man. In the ancient languages, the woman was the passive object of adultery, the violator the active agent. Because classical societies had resolved the problem of sexual competition through the democracy of the brothel, adultery was a heinous political sin, a transgression of the very order of civilized life. It was the characteristic act of the tyrant. The adulterer destroyed his own "sense of shame, orderly self-control, citizenship, neighborliness." In a papyrus an adulterer is accused of "breaking the order of the laws established for the public welfare."[66]

We might imagine that in every society there will be an element that, without tremendous refinement, equates virility with sheer capacity for sexual exertion. There is evidence that at least in some quarters there thrived a priapic scale of values. What is more noteworthy is the broad expectation, among all authors who exhibit any pretension to respectability, that manliness entailed self-control. Excessive pleasure, especially of the sexual kind, was feminine. Women lacked the physical constitution to control their appetition. But men were expected to be hard, capable of resisting the wiles of sensual satisfaction. Pleasure was enervating. By drugging the senses it threatened to undo men, to break down their manly hardness and induce a cascade of feminizing habits—too much bathing, a taste for soft clothing, submission to unspeakable obscenities. The opposite of the real man was the *kinaidos;* far from being an exclusive homosexual, the *kinaidos* could experience fierce cravings for women. It was his addiction to pleasure that led him to lose his sense of manly propriety and allow himself to be penetrated. The real man attained composure and mastery over all his impulses. "He who cannot bridle his anger, often over some trivial matter, who cannot cut off his lust for shameful pleasures, who cannot ignore physical pain, sometimes even when it is illusory, who cannot endure labor, even for the sake of pleasure . . . is he not surpassingly unmanly, less a man even than a woman or a eunuch?"[67]

Medical theory lent scientific authority to commonplace assumptions about the virtue of moderation. The high Roman Empire was the heyday of ancient medicine. For second-century experts, the human body was a warm, sentient mixture of the natural elements—earth and water, fire and air. Health, for doctors like Galen and his contemporaries, was the maintenance of equilibrium among the elements and their qualities of heat and cold, moisture and dryness. "Health is a form of harmony." The body's constitution changed over the course of life. The young were warm and moist, and the old were cold and dry. To age was to become desiccated, slowly; senescence was a sort of prolonged evaporation. For the doctors, the *aphrodisia* had to be considered in terms of the maintenance of balanced flux and the gradual loss of heat and moisture with age. Just as the proportionate intake of foods, in the right mixture and quantity, was necessary to regulate the body, so too sex was an act with distributional effects for the material economy of the whole organism.[68]

Far from being lodged in a subconscious realm teeming with abstract pressures, desire and pleasure were enmeshed in a thoroughly physical chain of cause and effect. Nature had contrived mankind, like other animals, to feel desire. It was a natural effect of heat in the young. But desire could be modulated by diet and environment. Hot and flatulent foods fed desire and led to the buildup of semen, considered a warm concoction of blood and spirit (pneuma) spread throughout the whole body. External stimulants to desire—a beautiful body at the spectacles, a memorable scene of erotic art—threatened to disturb a balanced regimen. Habit, too, mattered. Just as the individual could sculpt the body's exterior through exercise, so the gears of the body's internal system could be tuned at a higher or lower speed through practice. Rapid changes of sexual habit were likely to be harmful in and of themselves because they disrupted the body's established rhythms. Galen knew of a patient who "refrained from sexual intercourse out of grief for his late wife. He had previously enjoyed sexual activity quite regularly. Upon ceasing sex, he became nauseated, and could hardly digest the little food he consumed. . . . He was despondent. But these symptoms subsided when he resumed his old habits."[69]

Ancient beliefs about wine cast light on the place of sex within a thermal economy. The Roman Empire was a civilization of the vine. Without tobacco, coffee, or sugar, with little taste for beer or distilled spirits, the Romans chose wine as their utterly dominant psychotropic commodity. The sheer volume and variety of wine consumed in the Roman Empire testifies to its reach across all social classes. It was drunk by everyone, men and women, young and old, every day. Wine, like sex, was an immanent divine force, and the wash of its warm ecstasy was experienced as a communion with Dionysus. It is hard for us to appreciate the invisible but ubiquitous effects of wine in the Roman Empire. In his list of inputs and outputs that will have to be modulated to maintain a healthy equilibrium, Galen notably puts wine first and sex last. The Romans were alive to wine's effects on the body, attributing its disinhibiting qualities not to altered consciousness so much as to greater heat. Wine was an accelerant. Wine was especially healthy for older men, whose bodies were cold, and especially dangerous for younger ones, whose bodies were already hot. Wine was "Aphrodite's milk"; it was, in the words of Achilles Tatius, "sex fuel."[70]

Youth, gassy foods, wine, exposure to beauty: all precipitated the buildup of heat and the production of semen that spurred sexual desire. On the other side of the ledger, sex itself was an expenditure—a highly elaborate and particularly costly one. The sexual act set all the parts of the body to work simultaneously, "as in a dance," pulling semen through the body's channels. Seminal fluid was blood packed with pneuma culled from the entire body; the pneuma discharged during sex included the precious and especially fine psychic pneuma, the medium of the soul itself. Blood and pneuma were brought to boil in the testes. Then, the convulsive pleasure of orgasm was like a brief epilepsy that left the body depleted. Heat and moisture were expelled. For the Roman doctor, the most revealing part of sex was not the ecstasy but the aftermath—the immediate exhaustion, the languid body.[71]

Sex was a negative term on the body's energy balance sheet and, for some doctors, ipso facto deleterious. For most, though, sex was simply one output among others that could be integrated within a balanced regimen. The amount of sex to be prescribed varied case by case, with age and individual constitution. Especially for the young in the prime of life, whose bodies were warm and moist, sex was salubrious. At any age, excessive indulgence left the body cold, dry, and withered. But abstinence had its own dangers too. Lovesickness was a very real pathology in the Roman Empire, and no less a scientist than Galen was able to diagnose its symptoms. Too little sex might slow the body's natural cycles, leaving the person dull and melancholic. Unfulfilled desire could lead to nausea, fever, and poor digestion. The retention of seed was unhealthy. Modern historians have been fixated on the idea of sex as a loss of vital spirit, a notion that is certainly present in Roman medical literature. It is true that sex was a costly enterprise. Pneuma was a precious biological commodity. But it was not a finite one. It was continually regenerated. It was present in snot as in semen. What mattered, for the doctors, was an equilibrium that would not unduly accelerate the inexorable process of putrefaction. Roman medical advice was more interested in establishing healthy and balanced rhythms than in stemming the leak of vital fluids.[72]

The doctors were, to be sure, not erotic enthusiasts. Galen could recommend sex for its hygienic effects, but not for its pleasures. He put forward the Cynic philosopher Diogenes as a model. Diogenes engaged in sexual intercourse to expel sperm, and he retained the services of a courtesan for his regular evacuations. One day when she was tardy, he manually recalibrated his system. The lesson drawn for Galen was that the self-controlled man would view sex as the satisfaction of an urge, a necessary transaction in the maintenance of the body's flux. In his estimate sex was much like the evacuation of stool or urine—a purely natural act but nothing to sentimentalize. Unlike digestion, sex was discretionary, a voluntary process that, once started, triggered an autocatalytic chain reaction. From this perspective, sex, with its perfervid internal cycles, was a mildly hazardous necessity. The ideally healthy man would achieve a measured state of self-control by regulating the consumption system of the body, amorous expenditures included. Pleasure was a valueless term in the equation of health.[73]

Overall, the attitude toward sex in the Roman medical literature is one of attentive sufferance. But it would be a mistake to treat Roman medicine as a midway point between a classical cult of the healthy body and a later obsession with sensory deprivation. What is novel about Roman medicine is less its stance on sex than its popularity. It seems likely that in the age of Aelius Aristides and Marcus Aurelius more people than ever before looked upon themselves as life-term convalescents. But the pervasiveness of medical culture in the high empire is not to be ascribed to a public mood of weariness or even a new anxiety toward the body. The peculiar vigilance toward the body that we encounter in Roman medicine is the product of an affluent society. Medicine was a branch of learning that flourished with the support of public and private patrons in a wealthy empire. Abundance created the anxieties of imbalance that fueled an interest in medical knowledge. The medical literature addressed the concerns of a well-fed elite whose physical labors were few and artificial. The doctors spoke to the greying crowd, who could take comfort in hearing that wine was healthful and sexual deceleration was natural. Roman medicine was neither morbid nor ascetic; it was *bourgeois,* and a little geriatric.[74]

The eternal moderation expected of Roman men was, ultimately, a flexible demand. For most of the population, who lived along the edges of subsistence, moderation was imposed, without pity, by the unrelenting pressures of their material condition; destitution was the better part of virtue. Sex outside the house was limited to occasional moments of release, a day at the spectacles, a religious festival, or a visit to a tavern. It was the more privileged classes who had to navigate the choppy waters of sexual restraint by the strength of the will alone. The city and the school offered perpetual temptation. Rich youngbloods were characteristically pleasure seekers. The household itself was a haunt of allurements: private baths, spacious groves, shaded promenades, all attended by an army of servants. The dinner party remained the central venue of social intercourse in the Roman Empire, and unsurprisingly it is here that endless tales of erotic intrigue turn up. Though Roman men increasingly dined in the company of their wives, the all-male symposium—with trains of female as well as male servants and entertainers—was always a staple of sociability. "What happens to the boys when they're in their cups, and what the men dare when Pan has hold of them, would take a long time to tell," said the satirist. But to a philosopher, nowhere was the battle between desire and moderation so starkly fought. At the symposia, the quality of a man's character was revealed. In a telling contrast, the vast body of ancient moral and medical literature rests almost completely silent on the ethics of self-stimulation. So effectively had slavery, prostitution, and other forms of conviviality rendered pleasure available to men of means, so far beyond ethical surveillance was this most private sphere of all, that it simply did not enter formal moral conversation. Late classical sexual culture was, tellingly, as anxious about nighttime revels as it was indifferent to masturbation.[75]

The public sexual code of the second century was resolutely ancient. The association between masculinity and dominance, the benign neglect of youthful endeavors, the circulation of dishonored bodies, and the fluid restraints of self-control were all distinctly late classical. In material terms, the Roman Empire was the most complete and most refined expression of a sexual economy that had its origins in the very birth of the classical Mediterranean city-state. If the disciplines of sexual self-knowledge were more rigorous in the high empire, the delivery of sexual pleasures was more efficient than ever. The velocity of commerce was greater, and the self-reflectiveness of superannuated ideas was more apparent. Sex remained, as ever, a crucial element in the art of the self. "It is the pleasures, above all, by which a man's *gravitas,* his piety, and his self-control are judged."[76]

ENCHANTING FATE: MARRIAGE IN THE HIGH EMPIRE

A Byzantine reader of *Leucippe and Clitophon* could recommend the novel, so long as the moral of the story was constantly remembered: honorable matrimony is the final destiny of the erotic tale. If the protagonists of the romance were not always paragons of sexual restraint, marriage redeemed such indiscretions as might be encountered along the way. However much this mode of interpretation is inspired by prudery, it does stir profound critical questions. The novels are stories of adventure, trial, and intrigue that end happily in marriage. For some readers the resolution has been the key to the code: the romances celebrate the reproduction of the elite through honorable marriage. The novels are thus expressions of a confident, conservative provincial aristocracy. For others the journey is as important as the destination, and the authorial stance is too canny, too ironic, for these narratives to be solemn exhortations on behalf of a stable worldview. At issue ultimately is how the treatment of eros and marriage in the ancient romance fits into imperial culture, into a society that was preoccupied with sex and its place in the world.[77]

In the Roman Empire, marriage came to weigh more heavily, or at least more visibly, upon the individual's expectations from life. Yet the rules governing marriage changed relatively little, the reasons for marrying remained mostly the same—the dictates of necessity rather than the impulses of the heart led, as ever, to the formation of marriage. If the representation of marriage and its place in the moral economy has shifted by the high empire, it was nothing more than a subtle realignment: the belief that a procreative partnership and a domestic enterprise could also be the source of the most intense and meaningful erotic pleasures. Yet few alignments have been so momentous. The creeping emphasis on conjugal pleasure meant that the unruly dynamics of eros became slowly but irreversibly entangled in the art of the married life.[78]

Any claim that marriage was more important in one part of human history than in another is designed to guarantee its own debunking. Tracing the origins of the "sentimental" family has been a historian's sport over the last generation, and students of Roman culture have now detected traces of the sentimental ideal in the very earliest Latin literature. It can go no earlier. The sentimental ideal requires, as its foil, a primitive period, before the family was full of tender emotion. In the Roman case, this was conveniently provided by Roman antiquarians, for whom the belief in a tougher time, when men knew better than to care too much about women, became part of a Roman national mythology that always viewed the present as an unexampled nadir of corruption. The Romans believed that in the old days wives were kept properly under thumb and at an emotional distance. Women used not to drink wine at all, and Roman society went 520 years without a single divorce! In the late republic, men indifferently traded their wives as pawns of political convenience. The Roman man was a citizen and a soldier first, and there was simply little space left for the role of husband to animate his identity. Whatever mask of manly indifference the early Romans may have worn, such a broad caricature must fail. The mass of men led lives of humble domestication. It is dangerous to posit that a change in the representation of conjugal reality corresponds to a change in underlying patterns of emotional investment. What is remarkable about the prominence of conjugal values in high imperial culture is the extent to which an aristocracy—now an aristocracy of service under the autocratic rule of an emperor—embraced the private sphere as a domain of extreme emotional and moral fulfillment. After all, the morsels of domestic wisdom doled out by the moralists can be found centuries earlier. The Roman moralists cannot be accused of great creativity. What is new, and important, is the projection of these values in the public sphere.[79]

The marriage relationship in imperial Rome was immersed in the dynamics of social reproduction and social competition. The purpose of marriage was the production of legitimate offspring. In the language of the law, marriages were formed *causa procreandorum liberorum*. A complex of considerations, glimpsed mostly between the lines of an enormous moralizing literature, lay behind the formation of a conjugal union. The words of the doctor Soranus are well known: "Women are usually married for children and succession, and not for mere enjoyment, and it is utterly absurd to make inquiries about the excellence of their lineage and the abundance of their means but to leave unexamined whether they can conceive or not, and whether they are fit for childbearing or not." What distinguishes Soranus from his philosophical contemporaries is his clinical insistence on fertility as a criterion of suitability. Complaints about a marriage market where money and ancestry dominated became clichéd, surely because material concerns did dominate the formation of marriages for families with any pretensions. The couple was ideally a suitable match, and suitability depended on a suite of external factors, especially family reputation, wealth, and status. The groom was nearly a decade older than his bride, and ideally he was her slight social superior, a pattern that reinforced the patriarchal expectations of marriage. Of course, the abundant satire on men dominated by their powerful or wealthy wives suggests that the ideal was not universally achieved.[80]

It is accurate to speak of a marriage market in the Roman Empire, an arena of intense competition and high-stakes strategy where, in effect, families mobilized their resources to bid for partners. We know the workings of the marriage market mostly from its critics. Dio, for instance, vividly describes the prelude to the wedding between a rich pair. Professional matchmakers played much the role that real-estate agents play today. They identified prospects, carried out the negotiations, scrutinized property and birth. Promises were made, contracts were signed, and agreements were forged. According to Dio, the wrangling would continue right up to the ceremony itself. He offers a hostile description of an ordinary reality. In the letters of Pliny, in less caustic words, we can catch glimmers of this very same process at work. Pliny acted as a go-between, writing what amounts to a marital letter of recommendation on behalf of a young man. He extols the virtues of the potential groom and, with affected reluctance, passes along the vital information that the promising fellow was also rich.[81]

That material considerations were primary in the marriage market is unsurprising. The need to camouflage this obvious fact is more revealing. A transparently venal or ambitious engagement was unseemly. Moralists insisted that virtue should guide the choice of a partner. For a fifteen-year-old bride, a reputation for good character can have consisted in little more than the absence of a reputation for anything else. What is truly interesting about the moralizing literature—which, it must be said, is unusually vapid—is the absence of romance. The commentators have little to say, good or bad, about the place of love in the choice of marriage, so distant was the heart from the workings of the marriage market. And yet there are slight but significant signs that affection might pull two lovers toward marriage. After all, the novels are an entire genre of literature built on the idea that two superhumanly beautiful creatures might fall in love with each other at the sight of each other's body and eventually wed. Although the novels celebrate the reconciliation of the lovers' passion with the civic order of marriage, in reality the untamed love of young people could disturb the paternalist forces shaping the reproduction of society. In the Roman period we hear ever more of abduction marriages in which the girl engineered, or at least allowed, for her lover to take her without her father's approval. The great physiognomist Polemo, with his uncanny ability to read faces, crows that he had foreseen the abduction of a girl, contrived by her own design, on the very day of her wedding—twice![82]

By the time evidence for Roman marriage becomes meaningfully thick, around the age of Cicero, a revolution in material life had already turned a sleepy, agrarian economy into the most prosperous, urbanized civilization the premodern world would ever know. High mortality and a vigorous slave system ensured that the "Big House" style of habitation flourished. Domestic slaves, considered little more than breathing furniture, were often spectators in the conjugal bedroom; we hear of a rabbi who would ring a little bell when he was about to have sex with his wife, but he was a prude. With in-laws and parents, slaves and freedmen, nurses and children sharing a domestic space, the Romans had little notion of what we would consider privacy. But it is meaningful that the physical house in the Roman Empire was not a castle of the transgenerational *gens;* as time, circumstance, and resources allowed, the married couple sought residential independence for their domestic enterprise. Urbanization only encouraged young couples to set up their own stead. Material factors thus reinforced the model of affective, companionate marriage.[83]

It may seem paradoxical, but the legal advantages enjoyed by Roman wives—progressive by primitive standards—conduced to promote the affective nuclear family. In the Roman Empire, a husband took his wife *sine manu,* meaning that she remained in the legal power of her father, so long as he was alive, rather than passing into the *potestas* of the husband. A woman could transact legal business only with the representation of a tutor, who came from her father's family, not her husband or his family; after she bore three children, the woman earned the *ius trium liberorum* and could act on her own behalf. Created by Augustus, the *ius trium liberorum* was a badge of honor, and it became a wild success. The wife brought a dowry into the marriage, but it was not a gift to the husband; the property of husband and wife were, legally, distinct funds, and the married pair could not even make significant gifts to one another. All of these rules had the effect of making the wife a partner of her husband, not a ward. We might suspect that Roman women earned considerable legal rights because fathers cared to protect their daughters, and their property, and not because Roman legislators held progressive attitudes toward women. The pressures behind developments in family law are always complex, but whatever the cause, companionate marriage flourished in part because the Roman wife was perched, legally, between her old family and her new.[84]

Though the Romans did not marry for love, they hoped it would grow within marriage. Marriage in the Roman Empire was freighted with high emotional and spiritual promise. A Roman lawyer could define marriage as "the joining of a husband and a wife and a sharing of their whole life, a union of divine and human law." There was even a new openness to the potential for romance to germinate in the expectant period of the engagement. The grace of sexual familiarity in marriage would breed *philia,* a blend of friendship and love. In the letters of Pliny the Younger, we read almost with embarrassment the effusions of saccharine affection toward his wife (more than twenty years his junior), but the public nature of the letters reveals how far private emotional investment had become an acceptable element of the elite's self-projection. The highest ideal of marriage was harmony, *homonoia,* a charged term that located the peaceful partnership of husband and wife within the civic and cosmic order. The man who was going to harmonize the city, with its internecine squabbles and intense factionalism, was expected to have a harmonious house. Like the "ceaseless circling dance of the planets," companionate marriage was part of nature, "an image of order and harmony."[85]

Sex inevitably became enmeshed in the high ideals of conjugal harmony. "Where does eros more rightly belong than in the lawful marriage of man and wife?" It was a short step for Roman moralists to lay down rules of pleasure. Aphrodite, within the household, was to be subjected to "reason, harmony, and philosophy." Injunctions of mutual sexual fidelity easily arose from the high spirit of companionate marriage. For Plutarch, sexual fidelity was advised on pragmatic grounds. Plutarch reminded a bride not to lose her modesty with her clothes off; he counseled the groom to make the bedroom a "school of orderly behavior." But nothing is more likely to render a stilted view of Roman marriage than exclusive focus on the stern counsels of the moralists. Viewed in isolation, the moralizing literature on marital sex is too easily construed as a step toward a more repressed future, as though the conjugalization of sex might already achieve by boredom and grim routine half of what the preachers and prudes would later seek to control by religious command. Nothing could be further detached from the original soil of Roman marriage. The advice complex sprang from a culture where companionate marriage and erotic investment were intertwined as never before.[86]

A pessimistic view of the Roman marriage couch has become surprisingly entrenched. It is not impossible to find indications that sex was muddled, perfunctory, and embarrassed. In what age could a diligent search not return indications of the most varied sensual experiences? The truth is that many a Roman of the high empire would not recognize his experience in the pages of some modern treatments that deemphasize the charged eroticism of Mediterranean culture in the Roman world. Nothing gives the lie to the myth of the pent-up pagan couple like the artistic tastes of the imperial era. Erotic art flourished in the Roman Empire, in both commercial and domestic contexts. Indeed, the stark ubiquity of sex as a preferred aesthetic theme has even made the identification of ancient "brothels" a vexing challenge; what modern cultures might regard as obscene or pornographic was an ordinary part of bourgeois and elite domesticity. No one was shielded from the facts of life in Roman antiquity. Men, women, and children were surrounded by lush paintings of venereal acts in various stages of consummation. Truly elite villas, like the Villa Farnesina, often placed sensual art in bedrooms. At other times the placement was more public. Some of the most important specimens of Roman domestic art survive, of course, in the mural frescoes buried under the ashes of Vesuvius, long sequestered in the Pornographic Cabinet of the Naples Museum. Among the more striking examples of Roman erotic art is a beautiful painting from the house of a banker, Caecilius Iucundus, the son of a freed slave who built a successful enterprise offering financial services in the bustling port city. He commissioned the painting, in the portico of his villa's garden, of a man and woman nude in bed, attended by a slave. The painting's original placement was aimed at maximum visibility; it has been argued that Iucundus wanted to imitate the sort of luxuriant image prized by the high social elite to advertise his own refinement and experience of the good life.[87]

The stunning finds of Pompeii are *nonpareil,* but in the more scattered and exiguous evidence of the second and third centuries we find that the representation of eros remained a standard element of domestic presentation across the Roman period. An upper-class house of the third century in Ostia presents lovemaking in the most direct and frank fashion, depicting men and women in a range of conjunctions. In the view of an authority on erotic art, this house is valuable proof that the same ideology and sensibility so well preserved under the ash at Pompeii remained alive in a period for which well-preserved domestic paintings are much rarer. Literary evidence also suggests the continuity—and geographic reach—of erotic art. Clement of Alexandria fumes against the erotic aesthetics of the culture surrounding him in late second- or early third-century Roman Egypt. If we look beyond the walls of the ancient house, too, there are other indications that Roman visual culture was vibrantly sensual. In the Antonine era, it became fashionable among the respectable classes for a married couple to have themselves depicted as Ares and Aphrodite, borrowing the bodies and accoutrements of the gods beneath the recognizable visages of the married pair. The images are ludicrously disconsonant. More profoundly, we wonder why a married pair would wish to present themselves as the world's most discreditable adulterer and adulteress. Yes, the mythological veneer licensed the portrayal of decent women in the nude, but at a more symbolic level Ares and Aphrodite signified pure, ardent passion. In a society that believed in the mysterious, indwelling presence of the gods, there could hardly have been a more powerful evocation of the power of marital eroticism.[88]

Given the vagaries of survival, the most representative artifact of Roman eroticism is the humble lamp. Small, ceramic, and produced in truly innumerable quantities, lamps survive across the centuries. The culture where sex was supposedly reduced to sexual fumbling in the dark is the same culture that has left, in rather startling abundance, lamps decorated with the most uninhibited exertions. Lamps assure us that erotic art was not the preserve of the elite alone. The sheer numbers and archaeological findspots of erotic-themed lamps, furthermore, militate against the suggestion that these artifacts were anything other than a basic and broadly diffused domestic instrument. Sex—along with mythology, the animal kingdom, and the world of public entertainments—provided one of the most inexhaustible sources of decoration; the standard study of the huge collection of Italian lamps in the British Museum suggests that sex may have provided the very most common theme. The range and inclusiveness of the erotic repertoire suggests that myth, fantasy, and farce were exuberantly mingled. Modern studies conventionally divide the erotic lamps into two classes: Erotes (depictions of Eros) and symplegmata ("embracings"—a sort of learned prudery). This division does not adequately capture the range and meaning of different erotic motifs. The figure of Eros himself, symbol of joy and life, was unfailingly popular; though our eyes may be desensitized to the power of such a mythological commonplace, in Roman culture, where sexual passion was an immanent divine force, the blending of spirituality and sensuality ought not be discounted. The symplegmata lamps present the most varied images. Some are mythological, such as Zeus (qua swan) and Leda. Others are perhaps allegorical, such as the scenes of women with horses (which, maybe, refer to the Ass legend; the scenes of men with donkeys are probably not so easily rescued into decency). Some have a theme that is perhaps comic, perhaps poignant, perhaps mocking: the popular motif of the old man watching a couple perform feats of love. There are some same-sex pairings, and some elaborate sexual positions, but these are all rare. Mostly what the lamps depict is one man and one woman on a bed—sometimes beneath a canopy, sometimes with a lamp in the background—joined in carnal embrace.[89]

Of particular interest are the lamp workshops of the Greek world in the high and late empire. The lamps produced in Corinth and Athens have the advantages of being clearly dated, well published, and relatively closely studied (though a detailed study of the iconography, context, and chronology of erotic motifs on ancient lamps is a desideratum). What they reveal is a world of ebullient sensuality, deep into late antiquity. The shop of Pireithos in Athens, which started in the early third century and flourished for over half a century, specialized in sexual themes. Shops that were first established in the fourth century continued to offer their clientele a range of erotica. Only in the later fourth century do the erotic lamps of Athens begin to give way to abstract designs and Christian symbols; just one workshop seems to have produced both erotic and Christian lamps. By the early fifth century, Christian iconography prevails. In the fifth and sixth centuries erotic lamps can still be found, but they are vanishingly rare. It can be reasonably assumed that the lamp workshops produced for a market, a market broadly shaped by public culture; other than their ubiquity and durability, there is nothing particularly special about lamps, which in fact reflect artistic styles from other media. What the story of erotic lamps suggests is that the positive valence of eroticism endures across the high empire and recedes only behind the advancing tide of Christianization in later phases of the Roman Empire.[90]

If Roman marriage was an erotically charged institution, it is worth noting how firmly the actual practices of the Roman bedroom lay beyond explicit regulation, even among the moralists of the age. The fact is that authors like Plutarch, who goes so far as to advocate orderly sexual habits, retreat into pragmatic discretion before legislating on specific acts. So, notably, did the rabbis, who refrained from heavy-handed interference in the married couple's sexual life. In turn we are left to glean from a largely barren field. We find in different types of evidence a distinction between the sexual acts to be expected of a wife and those to be expected of a disreputable woman. A magical papyrus casts a spell on a woman in the hopes of achieving "whorish sex," as though that more or less summarizes a style, or intensity, of amorous encounter. Seneca, among others, counsels men not to love their wives as though they were mistresses. Fellatio is regularly assumed to be the domain of the prostitute. Still, Roman art depicts a wider range of positions and configurations than ever before, and not all of these have to involve paid professionals. Whereas late classical Greek art had tended to focus on the gratification of the man, Roman erotic art takes a far more variable perspective. Scenes of women on top, *mulier equitans,* focus on the reposed beauty of the woman's body. If the representation of male fulfillment was still predominant, there was undoubtedly a new visual emphasis in Roman art on the mutual pleasure of the partners.[91]

Still, it can only be wondered how well women fared in the bedroom. There was an abiding prejudice against acts that were considered to pollute the mouth. Visual evidence suggests that women could turn to male prostitutes to enjoy exotic pleasures, but this cannot have been an option to many women. There are signs that sometimes the possibilities were even unknown. More often there is simply blind disgust. Galen, who was not a prude, could claim as a matter of fact, "We find cunnilingus even more repulsive than fellatio." Cultural conventions of male dominance could be a powerful force. Or they could just act to draw a curtain around what really happened in the bedroom. The truth is that there is more discussion about female orgasms in the Roman Empire than ever before, and for a long time after. For

Ovid, mutual satisfaction was a vital part of his sexual code. For the author of the Lucianic *Amores,* it is what recommends heterosexual love. But nothing can match Clitophon's panegyric. For him, the climbing ecstasy of shared pleasure encapsulated the real meaning of eros. When the woman neared the "climax of Aphrodite," she became frenzied with pleasure, and at the peak of orgasm the woman's gasps even carried a little of her vital spirit into the mouth of her lover, where it mingled with his wandering kiss and returned to the heart.[92]

This description of the woman's pleasure, the reader of the romance remembers, is delivered by a young man whose experiences, on his own admission, have been limited to professional women. Part of us may wonder if Clitophon has not himself been sold a convincing act, but that is to bring a modern cynicism into the picture. Achilles is a sly author, to be sure, but his rendering of female pleasure is integral to the whole conception of eros in the novel. The novels embrace the physical power of eros and celebrate its potential to be reconciled within the order of married life and the city-state. The Greeks and Romans recognized eros as a wild, destructive force. The novels present a cosmos where the feral power of eros is harnessed by marriage, not dampened by it. For Achilles, marriage itself exists as part of nature, or at least on an indistinct border between wild nature and human civilization. The novels are about the ending, about marriage, but they are not sermons or political pamphlets on behalf of marriage. In the world of the novel, civilization does not repress eros. For the novelist, the fires of sexual love gave warmth and meaning to human life. Civilization is nourished by absorbing eros into its most vital institution.

THE GLOOMY ONES: THE PHILOSOPHERS AND SEXUALITY

In the very opening scene of *Leucippe and Clitophon,* the "author" sails to Sidon and meets Clitophon in a temple of the goddess Astarte. The topic of eros arises and the two descend to a nearby grove bordered by a clear cold stream; the rest of the novel is Clitophon's first-person account of his experiences. The story of Clitophon and Leucippe's romance is an afternoon conte in the cool shade of the plane trees. The ancient reader would have known immediately that we have been placed in the surroundings of Plato's *Phaedrus,* one of the Athenian's most celebrated dialogues on eros, in which

Socrates extols the power of love to draw humans toward the divine. It was by design an ambitious place to set an erotic story. From the beginning Achilles Tatius evokes the atmosphere of philosophy and the possibility of a rivalry between philosophy and art. The novel presents a narrative of eros that is permeated at every turn by the concerns of contemporary philosophy. *Leucippe and Clitophon* is a philosophical novel, though not a dogmatic one. Indeed, Achilles Tatius was one of those creative spirits whose prime conviction was the superiority of art over doctrine as a vehicle for representing deep human truths.[93]

The references to philosophers and philosophizing scattered throughout his novel are uniformly smirking. The word "philosophy" occurs six times in *Leucippe and Clitophon*. Three times "to philosophize" means "to abstain from sex," as when the villain Thersander incredulously asks Leucippe if the pirates who abducted her became philosophers. Twice it means "to wax eloquent for self-interested purposes," as when Melite makes her final proposition to Clitophon. One time it means "to suffer, passively," as when Clitophon takes a throttling from Thersander without resistance. Certainly these passages play on the mixed reputation of contemporary philosophy for sophism, complaisance, and fussy continence. Stoicism is clearly in view. The Stoic allusions of the novel are deliberate, but they are not flattering. Stoicism is evoked because it represented the closest thing to a philosophical *koinē* in the Roman Empire; more than a school, Stoicism seeped into public consciousness. Achilles Tatius is less concerned with its doctrines than with its stance toward the world. *Leucippe and Clitophon* is, in fact, a grand rejection of Stoicism, or of any philosophy that denies eros as a positive, constitutive source of the self.[94]

Stoicism in particular was a systematic philosophy, and its sexual ethics cannot be abstracted from the web of problems internal to Stoicism. The core ethical commitment of Stoicism was the principle that happiness, as the end of life, consisted in the possession of virtue. Virtue was sufficient for happiness. Stoic virtue was a thoroughly rationalist exercise, for virtue was the state of a soul in reasoned accord with nature. To live in agreement with nature was the highest ideal of the Stoic sage. Such serene rationality could be fully exercised only in a state of calm that was immune to the impulses of the passions. The Stoic sought *apatheia*, peace of mind, a reasoned indifference to things external. Hence, the true Stoic was impervious to misfortune; because he would "not for even the shortest time look away from reason," he could "remain ever the same, in the sharpest pain, at the loss of a child, through the worst disease." The Stoic achieved, through meditative self-discipline, a wisdom that brought freedom, in the highest sense that nothing external could truly affect the Stoic and his moral commitments.[95]

One of the central paradoxes of Stoicism was the simultaneous emphasis on fate and freedom. The Stoics believed in a deterministic cosmos where human behavior was locked in a materialist chain of causality. Destiny was an unbroken sequence of causes. At the same time the Stoics emphasized individual responsibility and moral freedom. Although nothing could have been otherwise, fate nevertheless worked through the individual human, his character and dispositions. For Stoics, fate operated through, not on, individual humans. In the Roman period especially, the problem of determinism became a central issue of Stoic thought. Epictetus, without reworking the cosmological assumptions of the old Stoa, places a much stronger accent on the freedom of the rational soul to act virtuously. He believed that reason allowed humans, unlike animals, to assent to impressions or to withhold assent, and thereby to achieve freedom from all external forces. To reconcile fate and freedom, the Stoics had to make enormous assumptions about god and providence that were not satisfying to many. Christianity did not so much unconsciously absorb Stoicism as provide radically new answers to some of its most difficult questions.[96]

For the Stoics, sexual morality was epiphenomenal to the deeper commitments of physics, logic, and cosmology. Nevertheless the Stoics recognized that sexual desire was one of the most essentially human experiences, and when the Stoics turned to practical ethics, sexuality was ever-present. Stoic attitudes toward sex, it can be said, agreed on core valuative principles but differed on the specific implications. First, pleasure was morally indifferent; second, passion, including sexual longing, was inimical to reason and led to false judgments of value. Sexual desire was inevitable, but not something to which the wise man would offer assent. For the Stoics, sexual morality was primarily about the internal regulation of desires. There is nothing terribly dramatic about the "internalization" of sexual morality in Stoicism; it was foreordained in the opening maneuver, which measured virtue by the activity of reason.[97]

The stern counsels of Musonius Rufus represent one logical outcome of Stoicism's starting principles. Musonius flourished under Nero and the Flavians, and he was the most respected public philosopher of his generation.

A member of the equestrian order, Musonius was a native of Etruria who lived in Rome and conducted his philosophizing in Greek. His words are preserved only third-hand, and assuming they yield an accurate impression, Musonius focused his intellectual energy on the practical implications of Stoic ethics. The famously rigorous sexual prescriptions of Musonius are detailed in a passage titled "On Sexual Pleasures." Throughout his argument, a dualism between "luxury" and "self-control" guides his logic. The life of luxury led men to lust after excessive and abnormal sexual pleasures with both women and men. The man with *sōphrosynē,* by contrast, would not compass sexual relations with a prostitute, a slave, or a respectable woman other than his wife. "Anyone who is not craven or evil must reckon that only sex within marriage and for the generation of children is just, for it is lawful. But sexual affairs that have in view the love of pleasure are unjust and unlawful, even within marriage."[98]

There is no denying the severity, and the novelty, of such austere prescriptions. Musonius would limit sexual intercourse not merely to marriage, but to procreative endeavors within marriage. The logic of his argument was impeccable, his view of "nature" highly restrictive. Within a system of values that placed no store in pleasure as such, sex had no positive measure. The procreative strictures of Musonius were not a "Pythagorean" code clothed in Stoic language; he was little preoccupied with the problem of wasted seed as a seepage of vital force or lost soul-matter. His conclusions and his logic were authentically Stoic. What is creative about the tantalizing passages of Musonius that survive is an instinct for finding powerful objective correlatives to his moral principles. He spoke with unprecedented clarity of the behavioral rules implied by the devaluation of pleasure. What made Musonius such a sensation was his stunning and provocative ability to legislate a code of personal behavior. His strictures on the use of slaves and prostitutes may have been no more effective than his (far less celebrated) disapproval of shoes, but they are in the same spirit and equally account for the spread of his legend.[99]

Musonius had an impact that continued to reverberate in lasting and unexpected ways through the work of his pupils. Musonius inspired the remarkable social thought of Dio Chrysostom, who carried his teacher's legacy into the world of grand public oratory. Dio's seventh opus, the "Euboean Oration," is a unique masterpiece of Greco-Roman rhetoric. The speech vividly narrates an encounter with two peasant families living in the idyllic hinterland of a Greek town. The natural virtue of their rustic life was contrasted, in the second half of the speech, with the vices of the contemporary Greek city. The fact that stares out at us from the speech is the utter centrality of prostitution in the social life of the high Roman Empire. Prostitution was the fixed point in Dio's roaring diatribe against contemporary society, and on it hung all the ills and disorders of the world. It was an established tenet of Stoic psychology that indulgence was self-reinforcing. Normally, though, these reflections focused on the individual. Dio turned to consider the circulation of pleasure through the social body, and his attention was locked on the vicious spiral of a society geared to deliver sexual satisfaction cheaply and easily. In the thought of Dio, Stoic skepticism toward pleasure is suddenly refracted through a panoramic vision of society.[100]

Prostitution was, for Dio, symptomatic of civilizational disorder. In the "Euboean Oration," Dio launched a frontal attack on the timeworn rationalization of prostitution as a safety valve for dangerous sexual energy. Stoic psychology gave Dio a powerful rejoinder to the assumption that male sexual energy was a determinate quantum. The rulers were wrong to think they had discovered "a sexual-restraint drug" in the "open, unlocked brothels" of the city. Dio argued that men would inevitably become bored with the pleasures that could be had "with permission, at a negligible rate," and turn their amatory energy to the "freeborn women," locked in inner chambers. Sexual lust was a self-accelerating force, and far from staving off the violation of respectable women, prostitution fueled the desires that would inevitably lead to adulteries. The "open, dishonorable violation," even of prostitutes, led straight to the corruption of "respectable women and boys." Once unbridled, sexual lust could ultimately only lead to sexual ruin—the corruption of wives and the submission of sons.[101]

In the "Euboean Oration," Dio proved himself willing to contemplate the social matrix of desire with a frankness and objectivity that was surpassingly rare. His train of reasoning led him to the precipice of an epochal moral insight. The sexual economy rested on the "women and boys taken captive or bought, prostituted for shameful purposes in sordid brothels, which are apparent everywhere in the city—at the governor's porch, in the marketplaces, by the buildings both civil and religious, right in the middle of what ought to be most revered." Dio recognized the mechanics of blunt force, of slavery, behind the flesh trade. The "Euboean Oration" reveals an inchoate legislative impulse; Dio would have had the magistrate forbid prostitution, like a doctor tending to the "disease" infecting the civic body. But having walked to the brink, Dio retreats. Dio stopped short of pondering the impossible, the sexual honor of the dishonored. He was concerned to cure the internal moral disorder of the civic body through Stoic therapy writ large. The civic body, rather than the mass of humanity, was the framework for his moral prescription.[102]

The former slave Epictetus also carried the thought of his teacher Musonius in new directions. If Dio brought a panoramic social perspective to Stoic thought, Epictetus stood in the internalizing, meditative tradition of Stoicism. For Epictetus, pleasure was a nullity. The wise man would place it in the scales and, realizing it had no weight, cast it completely aside as irrelevant. Marriage was a duty, rather than a partnership glued together with the bond of eros. Epictetus would allow for marriage as one of the primary duties: "citizenship, marriage, child production, piety to God, care of one's parents . . . all as one was born to do. And how are we born to live? As free men, as well-born men, as men with a sense of honor." Beyond the expectation of marriage, we find few explicit social correlates in the doctrines of Epictetus. He was concerned with the internal regulation of desire and, unlike Musonius, did not express his aversion to pleasure in external rules. Rather, the wise man needed to have reason to recognize the falsity of impressions that stirred desire. "If you see a pretty young lady, do you hold off the *phantasia?*" Sexual desire was something to be discounted by a rational faculty that had been keenly prepared through the contemplation of the truth. Conquering sexual desire was not unlike solving a logic problem. "If a girl is willing, beckoning, inviting me, grasping me and pulling me close, and I still resist and conquer, then I have solved a problem greater than the Liar or the Quiescent."[103]

The extant ruminations of Epictetus offer a clear image of the place of sex in the moral economy of Stoicism. Desire was human, and it was inevitable: a man could cut off his penis more easily than his desire. In consequence, the sage had to wean himself of pleasure through reason and self-discipline, but sex was only one category of pleasure and by no means a privileged one. "Learn to use wine with refinement . . . and to hold back from some little lass or a little flatcake." Stoicism, at least its more austere side, was no philosophy for young men; a passage surviving in the *Stoic Handbook* of Epictetus is particularly revealing. "Remain as pure as you can before marriage with regard to sexual pleasures, and insofar as they are engaged in, let them be lawful. Yet do not become oppressive or reproachful toward those who do indulge, and do not hold forth all the time on your own restraint." It would be harder to craft a statement more alien to the flamboyant renunciations and pellucid interdictions of Christianity.[104]

The quiet placability of Epictetus in his sexual morality is not far removed from the stance of the latest and most remarkable of the Roman Stoics, Marcus Aurelius. His Stoicism is known through the cheerless if not funereal collection of meditations preserved under the title *To Himself.* The pessimism of Marcus was not just the by-product of a sickly, world-weary emperor. His obsession with the cosmos was in the mainstream of Stoic thought. Indeed, it was only through the contemplation of the universe, and the place of human life within it, that man's reason could truly comprehend what a "cheap, contemptible, filthy, perishable, defunct" thing pleasure was. The life of man was a narrow point, crushed in on either side by eternity. Meditation on the cosmos put sex and marriage in true perspective. For Marcus, sex was "a commotion of the innards and a convulsive secretion of mucus." Marriage was a sign of perishability and meaninglessness: "meditate on the times of Vespasian, see all these things: people marrying, raising children, falling sick and dying, warring, reveling . . . and yet there is nowhere any trace of that life of theirs. Switch now to the times of Trajan, and again the same things, and that life too has perished." In time, all the deeds of the body passed away for eternity. Pleasure was an indifferent, not an evil; reason should conquer the false impressions arising from desire. Sexual morality hardly looms over the philosophy of Marcus. He reminds himself, in oblique language, that he had not rushed into sexual activity as a young man. We know, too, that his marriage to Faustina was exceptionally fertile, producing fourteen children, and that after his wife's death Marcus did what many Roman widowers did for solace, he took a freedwoman as a concubine. As Epictetus would have advised, the Stoic emperor's indulgences were lawful, and his restraint was not oppressively vaunted.[105]

The cosmology of Marcus, which is so important to his ethical outlook, was inseparable from orthodox Stoic determinism. "The peculiar quality of the good man is to love and to embrace whatever things have been bestowed and allotted to him." At its deepest spiritual core, Roman Stoicism assumed that moral action was made possible by a benevolent providence.

What is truly astonishing is how close Dio, Epictetus, and Marcus each come to realizing that this was materially not tenable, and how each retreats from more disturbing conclusions: Dio by focusing on the civic body rather than the dishonored, Epictetus by insisting on absolute internal freedom, and Marcus by the sheer assertion of divine justice. "The gods do exist, and human affairs are a concern to them. They have dispensed to man the power not to fall into anything that is truly evil." Theodicy is not a demonstration of Stoic philosophy, it is an assumption, perhaps its deepest assumption.[106]

The providence of Stoicism was part of the religious atmosphere of the high empire, and it is here that philosophy draws closest to literature. The fatalism of *Leucippe and Clitophon* was just as conscious and overt as that of the Stoic philosophers. For Achilles, as for the Stoics, the individual was the plaything of destiny, which made kings and slaves alike. Achilles is just as close as Dio—perhaps even closer—to realizing the dark side of fate. His nameless, faceless prostitute, the foil of Leucippe, is the corollary of Dio's searching examination of the social dynamics of sex, which cannot ultimately cross to consider the moral position of the enslaved. Yet the surface similarities between Stoicism and the romance are hardly a sign of influence or agreement. Stoicism and narrative fiction breathed the same air, and they addressed themselves to the deepest spiritual questions of the age. Stoicism and the erotic novel, in fact, give diametrically opposite answers to precisely the same questions. Marcus was a near contemporary of Achilles, and it would be hard to find more incompatible attitudes toward sex: for Marcus sex was a type of excretion, for Achilles it was an ecstatic communion with the "mystic fire" in the experience of erotic consummation. For Achilles, marriage is the end, the resolution; on an individual scale, it offered salvation and completion.[107]

Leucippe's very name, "the white horse," evokes the Socratic metaphor of the chariot from the *Phaedrus.* Like Plato, Achilles believes that eros can lift the human soul just high enough to glimpse the divine. Unlike Plato, Achilles describes eros for a girl. And yet *Leucippe and Clitophon* does not just present Platonic eros in heterosexual guise. For Plato, physical eros was a force sublimated in the intellectual search for wisdom, a mere image of the true form of love. It is epitomized by the pederastic mentorship. *Leucippe and Clitophon,* by contrast, begins with a series of failed courtships modeled on pederasty and ends with the marriage of the protagonists. The implied consummation of Leucippe and Clitophon is a deeply physical union. The ecstasy of sex is, in the imaginative universe of the novel, a profoundly embodied experience. For Achilles eros is not a force that has to be sublimated, because eros belongs to the cycle of nature. The cosmos is so contrived that the "white horse," Leucippe, the agent of salvation, is to be had in marriage, in the same institution that reproduces life. Achilles has no doctrine, other than eros and its compatibility with the narrative arc of human life. It is the genius of his art to raise romance to heights of self-awareness that allow it to compete with philosophy. Achilles does not argue for eros. He, unlike Plato, unlike the Stoics, embraces the world, with its ceaseless cycle of rebirth and death in which eros finds its natural place. And he laughs at anyone who believes it might be otherwise.

CONCLUSION: COSMOS AND EROS IN THE ROMAN EMPIRE

The sexual culture of the high Roman Empire was dominated by the imperatives of social reproduction. The symphony of sexual values, in all its various movements and complex harmonies, was set to the rhythms of the material world: early marriage for women, jealous guarding of honorable female sexuality, an expansive slave system, late marriage for men, and basically relaxed attitudes toward male sexual potential, so long as it was consonant with masculine protocols and social hierarchies. Moral expectations were in tune with social roles, and social roles strictly determined both the points of release and the rigid constraints in ancient sexual culture. The value of a sexual act derived, first and foremost, from its objective location within a matrix of social relationships.

The romances of the Roman Empire are such extraordinary witnesses to the experience of eros because they transform the exigencies of social reproduction into the workings of a cosmic destiny, they toy with the tensions between flux and order in the individual's coming-to-be in the world, and in the end, they spiritualize the mysterious erotic energies that connect man to nature. In the romances, these stirrings are a constitutive source of the self. When a romancer like Achilles Tatius looked out upon the gloomy counsels of the philosophers, it was not as a partisan of one ideology upon another, competing for supremacy in the public mind; it was, rather, as a spokesman for life, and the timeless patterns of sexual experience, upon a small reformation movement. But somewhere in the city where Achilles lived, there lurked the germ of a new ideology, one that could envision stilling the timeless patterns of life itself, and whose rules would reorder the experience of sexuality. Achilles at times seems aware of this radical movement, but he never deigns to mention it explicitly. It is in that context, as a dark horse in the chaotic, competitive atmosphere of the high empire, that the early Christians, with their highly distinctive sexual gospel, need to be imagined.[108]

CHAPTER TWO

The Will and the World in Early Christian Sexuality

TO SOAR CLOSE TO ANGELS

In the romance of Achilles Tatius, the heroine Leucippe personifies the white horse of Plato's chariot, capable of lifting the soul to the loftiest heights; it was an ambitious vision of conjugal eros, in which the most profound stirrings of the body not only connected man with the divine forces that replenished the earth but also offered personal transcendence. A little more than a century after Achilles Tatius wrote his novel, Plato's chariot of the soul reappears, now in a dialogue written by a Christian. Methodius, bishop of Olympus in Lycia, wrote the Christian answer to Plato's *Symposium,* in which the indulgent symposiasts of classical Athens have been replaced by ten female virgins. The Christian symposium of Methodius is a discussion circle on the surpassing merits on virginity, "something that is great, marvelous, wondrous, and exceedingly honorable." For Methodius, the chariot of the soul, far from being pulled by the power of erotic attraction, could soar above the horizon only by lifting over the swamp of physical pleasures. The pure body might carry the virgin's soul to the vault of heaven, where she could glimpse from afar "the vales of immortality." After such a revelation, she would come to regard as trifles the things of this life, "wealth, honor, birth, marriages." Marriage, on this view, is not sinful, but its merits shrink to invisibility in the blinding glory of sexual abstinence.[1]

The star of this Christian *Symposium* is Thecla, the semilegendary traveling companion of Paul, who makes an effective mouthpiece for the sexual teaching of her apostolic mentor. Behind the imagery and mystical hierarchy of a Platonic cosmos, the ideological framework on which the *Symposium* rests is thoroughly Pauline. The compressed words of Paul in his first epistle to the Christians of Corinth determine the boundaries between the ideal, the permissible, and the forbidden throughout the dialogue. Paul's passing endorsement of continence as an optimal state, so gently embodied in his own example, has been expanded into a thoroughgoing devaluation of physical pleasure. If virginity is a marvelous foretaste of salvation, Methodius holds, then what store could be set in the corporeal agitations of sex? The sleep of Adam during the creation of Eve prefigured the deadening trance perpetually reenacted in the marriage bed: during sex, so one of the virginal interlocutors had heard, the generative element in the husband's blood was boiled into a sort of liquefied bone and implanted by the vital organ into the living field of the wife. In the loving embraces of his wife, a man was overcome by "generative impulses." The gravest danger of the sex drive was, in fact, that it impelled a "yearning for offspring."[2]

The pleasure of the marriage couch was a distraction, an insidiously dangerous one. Like a torrential river, the delights of sex threatened to drag the soul into its raging currents and send it careening down the "rapids of incontinence." For the virgins of Methodius, pleasure lacked any positive value. Sex could not act as the warm bonding agent it is in Plutarch's marital counsels, nor could it be celebrated as the mysterious wash of ecstasy vouchsafed for man by nature and nature's gods. Sex, with its corporal gyrations, was a little putrid. But it was not, in itself, immoral. The virgins of Methodius knew it would be overbold to declare the generation of children sinful, when God himself had installed marriage and reproduction in the order of creation. Besides, marriage produced new generations of martyrs, soldiers of God ready to face the trials of persecution. Marital intercourse, even for these virginal symposiasts, also served another, less exalted purpose: it prevented worse uses of the body. For those too weak to pursue virginity, who smoldered with desire for sex, marriage was a safe harbor to prevent them from crashing on the rocks of fornication, *porneia.* The logic is distinctly that of Paul. Marital congress was a prophylactic against other, easily obtained satisfactions. In their alertness to the perils of fornication, the virgins at this symposium reveal the influence of a mental world, even a language, that would have been unrecognizable to Plato and his many followers in the Roman Empire. Fornication was one of the "horns of the devil," by which the evil one would cast down those who lacked self-control. It became for Christians a supremely depraved form of sin, embedded in the institutions and practices of the world around them. Even the virgins of Methodius, in their lofty acclamations of bodily purity, must pause to worry about the pollutions of fornication.[3]

Although the specific rigors and allowances of his sexual code flow from a reading of Paul's epistles, Methodius does reveal one preoccupation that would have been as unfamiliar to the apostle as to Plato. "Of all evils, the greatest that has taken root among the many is the notion that the movements of the stars cause our sins and that the necessities of fate steer our life." In his concern with astral determinism, Methodius marks himself as a man of his age. His tirade against determinism addressed one of the predominant themes of intellectual culture in the Roman Empire, one whose currents run through popular wonderment and formal philosophy alike. Methodius dedicated an entire tract, *On Free Will,* to the problem of fate. He revealed himself as an advocate of radical moral freedom. The Christian was possessed of a "self-ruling and autonomous" moral faculty, "free of all compulsion, its own master to choose what it wishes, slave neither to fate nor fortune." The problem of free will cut to the core of the most profound questions about the nature of the cosmos and man's place in it. Unsurprisingly, debates about moral autonomy gravitated toward sex. Sex became a privileged testing ground for doctrines of moral freedom. The authors of romance knew as much. For Achilles Tatius, Leucippe's "freedom" was a perfect alloy of her virtue, her social status, and her assurance that she was safe within the rules of the romantic narrative; Achilles Tatius playfully mocked Stoic ideals of freedom by revealing how little space for action was implied in the notion of voluntary assent to fate. For Christians, there could be no ambiguity about a matter so fundamental, and so eternally consequential, as the cause of sin. Nothing—not the stars, not physical violence, not even the quiet undertow of social expectation—could be held responsible for the individual's choice of good and evil. The Christians of the second and third centuries invented the notion of free will. Against the threat of gnostic determinism, amid a popular culture increasingly addicted to astrology, and in opposition to a philosophical culture with ever more sophisticated accounts of moral causation, the Christians entered the fray with a message that was jarringly simple and distinctive. The individual, whatever his or her condition, was a moral agent with unqualified capability and responsibility. These crystalline notions of freedom and responsibility came to focus on the realm of moral behavior whose wellsprings might seem most inscrutable: sex.[4]

The *Symposium* of Methodius can be regarded as the last text of early Christianity. It reflects the authority of Paul's words as a benchmark of Christian sexual morality. It gives poetic expression to an ascetic theology forced, begrudgingly, to accommodate marriage as an acceptable institution. It treats sexuality as a prime domain of moral exercise and sees humans as sufficiently equipped always to choose righteousness. But for Methodius, the freedom of the sexual will was still an intellectual problem rather than a social or psychological one. In this regard Methodius is much closer to the self-styled philosophers of second-century Christianity than to many of his own contemporaries, who would survive into the heady age of Christian triumph. In the work of Methodius, moral autonomy is a cosmological postulate, a statement about the place of man before the eyes of God. His *Symposium* is untroubled by the possibility of material constraints on human volition or even by dark undercurrents of the self that required external grace to enable moral freedom. Methodius is one of the last Christians to write in an apologetic voice, as the spokesman of a philosophy distinctly apart from the machinery of society. On June 20 of AD 312, that machinery turned against him. Methodius was tried—perhaps before the Roman emperor himself—and executed, in one of the very final spasms of state violence faced by the early Christians.[5]

This chapter attempts to summarize the sexual code which took shape in the unruly world of early Christianity and to take stock of how the new religion's outlook on sex differed from mainstream values and philosophical attitudes toward the body. It has been very much doubted that there was anything like a consensus within the early church on questions of sexual comportment. Indeed, the discovery of the fierce internal struggles that took place within the Christian movement has been a revelation, for it restores some of the urgency and depth to the ancient debates. We know the future of the early church. But the men and women of the first centuries did not imagine a future where the sexual protocols they formed would be placed in the hands of a powerful institutional church. Indeed, the strident tone of so much early Christian writing on sexuality was nurtured in an atmosphere where the advocates of the religion were a small, persecuted minority. Christian sexual morality of the second century has a shrill tone precisely because it is the urgent message of an embattled, if confident, group of dissenters.[6]

By nature a synthesis must concentrate on what is most important, and despite the astonishing diversity within the early church, what matters is the formation and triumph of a radical new orthodoxy of sexual propriety. Early Christian sexuality was like a great braided river, but one kept within certain boundaries by the geological features of the landscape. In an important sense, with Paul the landscape was formed, and any movement that was going to treat Paul's letters as authoritative was bound to gravitate around certain lines. Here we must focus on the contours and the destination of early Christian thought on sex, while resisting the pull of each winding channel. What such an account loses in passing over the contingency, and contentiousness, of early Christian sexuality, it hopes to gain by taking a long-range perspective. For three centuries, Christian sexual ideology was the property of a persecuted minority, and it was deeply stamped by the ability of Christians to stand apart from the world, to reject the world. From the fourth century on, Christian sexual morality would be ever more deeply enmeshed in the world. The break was not necessarily sharp: there were married Christian householders from the earliest days of the church, and the ascetic movement carried on the world-rejecting style of the early church. But the changing center of gravity was decisive.

The focal point of this chapter is the orthodox model of sexuality presented by the remarkable figure Clement of Alexandria. Clement was a slightly later contemporary of Achilles Tatius, and a fellow citizen of Alexandria. It is important to imagine the two inhabiting the same culture and the same cityscape. Clement is the first Christian whose sexual doctrines are known in depth. Nearly every interpretive problem in the study of early Christian sexual morality comes to a head in the question of how to situate Clement within the trajectory of the church's sexual mission. Was he an isolated voice for the "silent majority" of married Christians or a characteristic representative of an ever more powerful ecclesiastical establishment? Is he a spokesman of moderation or an impertinent meddler in erotic affairs? To Clement the society surrounding him was corrupted, root and branch: "the whole world is full of fornication and disorder." To understand how Clement came to this judgment, we must discover precisely how the doctrines embodied in the authoritative traditions of early Christianity intersected mainstream sexual expectations. The model of normative sexual behavior that developed principally out of Paul's reactions to the erotic culture surrounding him received fuller expression in the second and third centuries as a distinct alternative to the social order of the Roman Empire. Clement, writing just before more radical experiments in asceticism would begin to capture the Christian imagination, presents a sort of asceticism within the order of marriage and within the order of the ancient city. Ultimately Clement's principal achievement was exegetical; he was able to weave into a whole the disparate strands of authoritative tradition and give clear expression to the meaning of Christian norms in the midst of a world alienated from God.[7]

Clement, more than any other representative of the early church, presented his views in the language of the culture around him. Early Christian sexual morality can sound deceptively familiar. But the familiar echoes belie a radically new sensibility. The few and mostly feeble injunctions against prostitution and same-sex love in Roman culture have been deliberately preserved by Christian authors in search of classical pedigrees, and the pre-Christian dissenters loom larger in retrospect than they did in their own day. Regardless, in no sense should early Christian sexual morality be construed as an offshoot of Roman conservatism. The ideas about sex emanating from the new religion marked a discrete and categorical rupture. For the community of the faithful, the pleasures of the flesh became caught in a cosmic battle between good and evil. New rules, more interesting and less predictable than sometimes argued, formed. *Porneia,* fornication, went from being a cipher for sexual sin in general to a sign for all sex beyond the marriage bed, and it came to mark the great divide between Christians and the world. Same-sex love, regardless of age, status, or role, was forbidden without qualification and without remorse. Unexpectedly, sexual behavior came to occupy the foreground in the landscape of human morality, in a way that it simply never had in classical culture. "Above all else take thought for chastity; for fornication has been marked out as an exceedingly terrible thing in God's eyes."[8]

The code of sexual rules that came to prevail in the early Christian church was highly distinctive; its moral logic was more innovative still. For the Greeks and Romans, public sexual ideology was an organic expression of a social system. Sexual norms were in harmony with public law, the protocols of marriage, and the patterns of inheritance. Even pagan philosophy tended, at its deepest level, to offer a duty-based sexual ethics that accepted the logic of social reproduction while devaluing pleasure as such. But early Christianity showed itself prepared to abandon the traditional needs and expectations of society, if necessary in the most dramatic fashion. Christianity broke sexual morality free from its social moorings. The indifference toward secular life and the new model of moral agency—centered around an absolutely free individual whose actions bore an eternal and cosmic significance—were covalent propositions. The individual was morally responsible, and moral responsibility required freedom, from the stars and from social expectation alike. The chill severity of Christian sexuality was born not out of a pathological hatred of the body, nor out of a broad public anxiety about the material world. It emerged in an existentially serious culture, propelled to startling conclusions by the remorseless logic of a new moral cosmology. The discovery of the free will was not a circumstantial adjunct of early Christian sexual morality; it was an essential feature, determined by the deep logic of a moral order founded on sin and salvation.

FORNICATION: FROM HEBREW TO GREEK

Around the year AD 51 the apostle Paul arrived for the first time in Corinth, the bustling seat of Roman power in Achaea. The city, once razed by the Romans but long since resurrected by its destroyers, was an imposing sight. In Paul's own words, he came to Corinth "in weakness and in much fear and trembling." The Acrocorinth, the sheer escarpment housing Corinth's most archaic temples, dominated the views of the approaching visitor. Perched on its eastern summit was a temple of Aphrodite, looming over the town that sprawled toward the sea beneath her solicitous watch. As Paul entered the forum, he would have been confronted by the bewildering noise of power, commerce, and diffuse piety that characterized urban life in a vibrant provincial town of the Roman Empire. The sanctuaries of the gods—Tychē and Aphrodite, Artemis and Dionysus—ringed the crowded center of the town, hard by the merchants' stalls and public offices. The haphazard accretion of religious monuments, and the tessellation of the sacred and the profane, belied the reverent balance and careful rhythms that guaranteed the gods their due honor. Into this enveloping cityscape of tremulous paganism crept a missionary with a startling message. "Do you not know that your *body* is a temple of the Holy Spirit within you?"[9]

We meet the community of Christians Paul founded in Corinth through the tantalizing but imperfect prism of the letters he wrote, some six years after first visiting the city, when challenged by the unexpectedly fractious relations in a small apocalyptic movement. Word reached Paul in Ephesus that the Corinthian Christians were feuding, split on a range of mundane problems, from marriage and manumission to sacrificial meat. In the patient response of the apostle that has come to be known as First Corinthians, fierce disagreement over proper sexual behavior lurches to the surface. Such dissent was surely inevitable. Nowhere did the moral expectations of the Jesus movement stand in such stark contrast to the world in which its adherents moved. Corinth in particular was not famous for its sexual virtue. In recent decades the reputation of Roman Corinth has enjoyed the sort of undeserved rehabilitation that comes only when generations of gross exaggeration allow overcorrection to pass as healthy revision. It is true that Corinth had first earned its notoriety in centuries long past. But the laxity of the Corinthians in venereal affairs was not just hoary legend. In the words of a second-century admirer, Corinth was a city "more dear to Aphrodite than all cities that exist or have existed." The eroticized atmosphere of Corinth was the predictable attribute of a wealthy, imperial crossroads; even against the indulgent backdrop of late pagan sensuality, Corinth stood out as louche.[10]

It is unsurprising that the inchoate sexual code of the Christian gospel—terse yet austere—came to a head here. More surprising are the extremes around which members of the Corinthian community had polarized, in full belief that their radically divergent views were consistent with the demands of the messianic religion. Such fundamental conflict was to characterize Christian thinking on sex into the fourth century, even as Paul's views would exert a continuous and irresistible pull toward the compromise he forged in his fateful response to the crisis in Corinth. Paul's approach in First Corinthians was shaped by his decision to steer a middle course between an element within the Christian church who tended toward libertinism and another group who espoused strict continence as an urgent ideal. Between those who said "All things are lawful for me" and others who insisted "It is well for a man not to touch a woman," Paul sought a defensible middle ground.[11]

Paul's reply, because it is an epistolary intervention rather than a treatise on sexual ethics, assumes more than it reveals. In some sense the entire Christian conversation on sexuality has been a search for the unstated assumptions of Paul's delicate guidance in the three central chapters of First Corinthians. At the core of Paul's thought is the term *porneia,* fornication, a word packed with connotations less obvious to us than to his contemporary audience. *Porneia* is the cornerstone of the sexual ethics of First Corinthians. Paul's whole attitude toward sex—not to mention his place in Jewish tradition and his distinctiveness against the backdrop of the Roman Empire—is destined to remain opaque unless we demystify the word *porneia.* It is not easy to do so, and a cottage industry has been devoted to unlocking the meaning of this primary Christian term. To translate it as "fornication" is mere convenience. Fornication is ecclesiastical argot—and always has been. Even in the astonishingly rich sexual vernacular of Latin, there was no word ready to hand to translate *porneia,* and an equivalent had to be hastily contrived. *Fornicatio* was derived from *fornix,* literally an arch and figuratively a den of venal sex. No classical author used the term *fornicatio.* Likewise, *porneia* has no classical pedigree. In classical Greek, *porneia* is the activity of prostituting oneself, not the institution of commercial sex or any class of forbidden acts. Before its adoption by religiously inspired sexual activists, *porneia* referred squarely to the production, not the consumption, of venal sex. Likewise, in classical Greek the *pornos* was the male prostitute—the gigolo, not the john. Tellingly, for Paul it was the reverse, and it can be confidently asserted that the meaning of *porneia,* for Paul, was not derived from the classical heritage.[12]

The Christian understanding of *porneia* was inherited from Hellenistic Judaism. The word first entered the parlance of Hellenistic Judaism as a calque of the Hebrew *zenuth.* The core meaning of the Hebrew verb *znh* describes the activity of a woman who loses her sexual honor. This sense dominates the primitive strata of the Jewish Bible. Because legitimate female sexuality was strictly confined to marriage, a woman who engaged in any extramarital sex was guilty of *zenuth.* In the patriarchal logic of early Hebrew culture, she became a "whore," and the feminine participle, *zonah,* was the primary word for prostitute throughout the biblical period. The Hebrew Bible is decidedly tepid in its condemnation of males patronizing the brothel—there are practical, but not legal, warnings, and this same irresolution will echo down through the monuments of Hebraic literature in the Roman period. But crucial to the later expansion of the term's meaning, especially in Greek, was the introduction of a metaphorical sense of the word. From the time of the prophet Hosea, *zenuth* came to stand as a powerful metaphor for idolatry. Israel's religious promiscuity was compared to the sort of infidelity that was most likely to evoke a visceral reaction in a patriarchal society: feminine unchastity. The rhetoric was jarring, and was meant to be so. The prophets accused Israel of being a "spiritual slut."[13]

By the late Second Temple period, the metaphorical meaning had bled back into the literal meaning, so that spiritual whoring and sexual whoring were irreversibly blurred. Sexual misconduct could be construed as tantamount to idolatry. This equation was reinforced by the presumption that idolatrous people have whorish women; the prejudice that out-group females are less virtuous than the women of one's own family, clan, and tribe has often proven compelling to the human mind. Fatefully, the sense of *zenuth* as idolatry allowed for acts of male commission. This sense was destined to have a long future, but it is important to be precise about its place in Jewish tradition. The decisive expansion of the word's meaning, to include *sexual* acts committed by *men,* is not overt in the Septuagint, the Greek translations of the Hebrew scriptures. The Septuagint was the milk nurse of Paul and the early Christians, but in it they would have found *porneia* to mean female unchastity or religious idolatry. The decisive expansion of the term's meaning, to include male sexual error, occurred extrabiblically.[14]

A tectonic shift in Jewish sexual ethics, concerned with the moral regulation of male sexuality, is attested in texts staggered across the last centuries BC. Perhaps the earliest extant witness to the more encompassing meaning of *porneia* is *Sirach,* written in the first decades of the second century BC. The most intriguing witness to the spread of *porneia* as a regulative norm is a text known as the *Testament of the Twelve Patriarchs,* where *porneia* has become the "mother of all evils." The *Testament* is invaluable because its unusual detail confirms that *porneia* could be used to describe a whole array of improper sexual configurations: incest, prostitution, exogamy, homosexuality, and unchastity. But by far the most important witness to the sexual sensibilities of Hellenistic Judaism on the eve of the Pauline missions lies in the dossier of Philo. Philo is, to be sure, an idiosyncratic figure, his ethics a singular attempt to synthesize the Mosaic law and Platonic psychology. The key to Philo's sexual code is that it was a tribal code. The boundaries of the moral community were constitutive. Exogamy threatened to fray the cordons of the moral group. It led Jewish men away from their ancestral customs. The sexual purity of the Jewish people set them apart. The "polity of Moses," by its very nature, "excluded the prostitute from citizenship." As a "common *miasma,*" she was worthy of stoning. Adultery was punishable by death, while the seduction of a free citizen girl was a damnable violation. In a community without prostitutes, where honorable women were available only as wives, the limitation of sex to marriage would be built into the very borders of the sexual polity. In this, above all else, does Philo anticipate the early Christian church: the internal structure of the minority community, adrift in a sea of depravity, quietly forms the moral architecture of his sexual ideology.[15]

In Philo's voluminous commentaries on sexual propriety, *porneia* never becomes a central term. The idea of "fornication" was in the air of the Jewish communities strewn across the Mediterranean, but it was not a dominant element in their sexual outlook. In other words, fornication was not predestined to become the presiding term of Christian sexual morality. But in the middle decades of the first century, as missionaries poured out of Palestine with the message that the Jewish messiah had come as a universal savior, "fornication" was ready to serve as a shorthand for the culture of sexual indulgence that followers of the new cult were being asked to leave behind. In the first decades of the Christian mission, no single form of sinful sexual behavior stuck to the term with any greater force than others. In the texts that would become part of the Christian canon, *porneia* still means, variously, incest, exogamy, even idolatry. Nowhere is this extreme breadth and pliability of the word's meaning clearer than in the Apostolic Decree, the code of conduct laid down at the Council of Jerusalem to impose minimal standards of purity on gentile converts. The inclusion of *porneia* on the short list—the very short list—of moral imperatives signals the uncanny power of the term to condense a whole bundle of expectations about the use of the body.[16]

The inclusion of *porneia* in the Apostolic Decree is a signal that the word's adoption by Paul in First Corinthians was not circumstantial. The word was already a slogan of moral rectitude in Christian circles. But it is through the epistolary conversations between Paul and his eclectic assemblies of messianic believers that we watch the early and decisive development of the term. Paul was drawn into the topic of sexual comportment by a scandal within his Corinthian community that had shaken the small circle of the faithful. A man was living with his father's wife, "a kind of *porneia* that is not found even among pagans." A man had begun to cohabit with his stepmother, probably widowed. The two may not have been so far apart in age. Such scenarios were the material for much ribald comedy in Greek and Roman cultures. For Paul, the relationship was intolerable, and he sternly reminded the Corinthians, "I wrote to you in my letter not to associate with fornicators." The Christian community, an evangelical minority steeled for the end times, could not abide such impurity. As for Philo, so for Paul, sexual morality was a presumptive requirement of communal belonging.[17]

The backsliding believer in love with his stepmother was symptomatic of deeper and more complex antagonisms at Corinth. Paul was faced with an intellectually armored libertine wing within the incipient church. Some of the Corinthians were claiming that the emancipatory message of the gospel freed the body from petty moral demands: "All things are lawful for me." Paul's response was both sharp and ranging. The body, he insisted, was not made for fornication. The believer's body was a "member of Christ," and the member of Christ could not be made "a member of a prostitute." Paul's libertine interlocutors espoused a traditional upper-class attitude toward the male body, whose desires were to be balanced by vigilant control but not self-denial. Paul's response betrays an acute sensitivity to bodily purity. The sexual machinery of the body was something to be protected from contamination, not simply kept in proper balance. Coition was anything but a vacuous physical act without effects beyond the circulation of heat and moisture. "He who joins himself to a prostitute becomes one body with her." Paul's demand was simple: "flee fornication." The stakes were pitched deliberately high, and in an idiom of Mediterranean piety that gentile converts would immediately understand. "The fornicator sins into his own body. Do you not know that your body is a temple of the Holy Spirit within you?" Fornication was an act of pollution in the sacred space of the Christian body.[18]

Paul's reflections on fornication, like a stone on the river bottom that suddenly catches the light, reveals the unexpected depths of the term's meaning. Fornication was not just a marker of ethnic differentiation, providing a template of sexual rules setting God's faithful apart from the heathens. Paul's understanding of fornication made the body into a consecrated space, a point of mediation between the individual and the divine. When Paul heightened the term's meaning, he also foreshadowed a certain narrowing of the term *porneia* and its scope in gentile Christianity. The specter of sexual lassitude presented by the libertine faction immediately suggested not the establishment of a free love commune but the traditionally harmless and "lawful" outlet for male sexual energies: prostitution. The availability of dishonored women traced the profoundly different foundations of sexual morality in the outside world. It was almost inevitable that fornication would come to identify, ever more narrowly, the types of extramarital sexual license entrenched in gentile society, centered on bodies without access to sexual honor. In First Corinthians, Paul has set his sights not on heavy petting gone too far among young innocents in the congregation, nor on carnal bohemianism. Far more consequentially, Paul intended to dam the traditional canals long approved as spillways for the inevitable sexual heats of young men in the ancient world. Christian *porneia* would recast the harmless sexual novitiate that was an unobjectionable part of sexual life in antiquity as an unambiguous sin, a transgression against the will of God, echoing in eternity.

Despite the extraordinary weight Paul places on sexual purity, his missive to Corinth was a delicate act of triangulation. Word had reached Paul of a faction within the Christian community who declared that strict continence was the measure of holiness. Paul could not register unqualified disagreement. "I wish that all were as I myself am," he writes, foregrounding his own celibacy. For centuries Christians will elaborate on this most gentle of moral suggestions, usually with a stridency that contrasts with Paul's cautious sensibility. Paul was not willing to disenfranchise the reliable married householders who held together the fledgling church. Marriage was to be accommodated, "by way of concession, not of command." In fact, although marriage might tie down a man or woman to the dull distractions of everyday life, it was the surest bulwark against sexual sin. "Because of fornications, each man should have his own wife, and each woman her own husband." Paul imagines a sexual version of Pascal's wager: "It is better to marry than to be aflame with passion." Surrounded by the temptations of the Greek city, the Christians for whom continence was not a practicable goal were to find safe exercise in the licit amours of the marriage bed. Eros was an ominous threat hanging over the purity of the body, not a constitutive feature of human identity. The most that could be said for marriage was that it was not, at least, an act of desecration. Amid the ubiquitous lures of Aphrodite's city, that was not necessarily a trivial blessing.[19]

Paul's compromise between libertinism and continence was to reverberate throughout the rest of Christian history. It was a settlement forged in the compressed atmosphere of apocalyptic time. Paul offered a wisdom "not of this age or of the rulers of this age, who are doomed to pass away." Like any treaty, it would eventually show the marks of age, strained by the passage of time and subtle realignments in the balance of power. But it laid down the key terms that acted as the starting point for all future negotiations. At the same time, the urgency of the moment left much unsaid. There was much that simply did not need saying. The protocols of feminine respectability—virginity followed by fidelity—were so universal and obvious that their express declaration would have been otiose. Paul's focus was squarely on the quarrels that had arisen in the church. His letter was an intervention. But it was an intervention that would progressively attain canonical status within the diffuse network of tiny communities who viewed Paul as an authoritative messenger. Almost immediately Christians were scrambling to interpret what Paul meant, both in what he said and what he left unsaid. The prophets of virginity would latch on to the apostle's own celibacy, and the glaring absence of any enthusiasm for marriage, as sure signs that Paul had not allotted any grace to acts of the flesh. But the authors of the pastoral epistles would come nearer to the spirit of Paul, when they envisioned, in the unfolded expanse of continuous time, the moral viability of orderly Christian households. Paul may well not have endorsed the abrasive patriarchy of the pastoral letters, but their explicit affirmation, against those who would forbid marriage, that "everything created by God is good," is not alien to his thought. This strain of Paul's sexual ideology was destined to prevail. But what could not be credibly doubted, by any Christian claiming descent from the Pauline tradition, was the irredeemable depravity of fornication and the need to secede from the moral economy of the Roman sexual order.[20]

THE NATURAL USE: EARLY CHRISTIANITY AND SAME-SEX LOVE

Not long after the composition of his dispatch to the Corinthians, Paul authored his letter to the church in Rome. Written to a community he was yet to visit in person, the Letter to the Romans is different in character, and grander in vision, than any of his other writings. Like First Corinthians, Romans assumes far more than it explicitly reveals about Paul's sexual ideology. In this case, though, the visible surface, which juts above the horizon with sudden and unexpected violence, rests on foundations lying submerged in the depths of Paul's theology. In the thundering introit of the letter, it becomes evident that for Paul the sexual disorder of Roman society was the single most powerful symbol of the world's alienation from God. Paul draws on the deeply rooted association between idolatry and sexual immorality: sexual fidelity was the corollary of monotheism, while the worship of many gods was, in every way, promiscuous. But in Paul's hands the association was transfigured into a fearful comment on the human condition. When the nations substituted "images resembling mortal man or birds or animals or reptiles" for the "glory of the immortal God," God "gave them up to dishonorable passions." Paul was unusual in the degree to which he saw illicit desires as a metonym capable of standing for mankind's rebellion against monotheism. But the greater surprise that emerges in the first chapter of Paul's Letter to the Romans is the specific form of carnal decadence that encapsulated, for the apostle, the total depravity of the heathen world: same-sex love.[21]

It is worth pausing to take seriously the evidence of Romans as the statement of an earnest, if hostile, observer of Roman society. Moralists who extolled the married pair as the model of natural human sexuality were not inconspicuous in polite Roman circles. But the fervor of a religious enthusiast like Paul reveals how far removed those speculative ideologies were from the experience of sexual culture in the middle of the first century. Same-sex love stood out, incandescently, as a measure of the gulf between Paul's view of eros and the state of human affairs. Same-sex love served Paul's theological purposes well. A central proposition of Romans is that God's "power and deity" are "clearly perceived in the things that have been made." For Paul, God's moral will inheres in the order of creation and is manifest in it. Same-sex love was thus, for the apostle, a particularly egregious violation of the natural order. "Their women exchanged natural relations for unnatural, and the men likewise gave up natural relations with women and were consumed with passion for one another." For Paul, same-sex attraction symbolized the estrangement of men and women, at the very level of their inmost desires, from nature and from the creator of nature. And it was the creator's stark decree that "those who do such things deserve to die."[22]

For the historian, any hermeneutic roundabout that tries to sanitize or soften Paul's words is liable to obscure the inflection point around which attitudes toward same-sex erotics would be forever altered. It is precisely here. Paul's originality lay in the violence with which his thought shuttled between and then beyond both Greco-Roman and Jewish strictures to form an unambiguous and all-embracing denunciation of same-sex love. Paul's overriding sense of gender—rather than age or status—as the prime determinant in the propriety of a sexual act was nurtured by contemporary Jewish attitudes. The very language of "males" and "females" stood apart from the prevailing idiom of "men" and "boys," "women" and "slaves." By reducing the sex act down to the most basic constituents of male and female, Paul was able to redescribe the sexual culture surrounding him in transformative terms. Paul's view of Roman sexual culture captured patterns invisible through the lens of traditional Greco-Roman moralism. One sign of this recategorization, staring the reader squarely in the face, is the equivalence of same-sex love between men and between women. The bare mention of female same-sex desire was rare in the ancient sources, and it places Paul within the *nouvelle vague,* a broader culture of sexual observation in the Roman Empire that would call unprecedented attention to love between women. But the analogy between male and female same-sex attraction was strikingly novel, and truly momentous.

Paul's concern in his epistle was to take the diffuse and disorderly eroticism of a Mediterranean town as an expression, an unusually potent and jarring symbol, of the pulsing spiritual errors of ancient polytheism. One small lexical clue to the pedigree of Paul's thought is that nowhere in his letters do we find any mention of the *kinaidos,* the starkest figure of sexual deviance in mainstream Greco-Roman culture. The *kinaidos* was a permanent fixture on the ancient social scene, a stereotype of the monstrously dissolute and feminine male. The invisibility of the *kinaidos* in Paul points to a primary dependence on the moral armory of Hellenistic Judaism. Once again, comparison with Paul's near contemporary, Philo, offers instructive parallels. It is revealing that, in the voluminous remnants of Philo, the *kinaidos* is equally missing. Philo's attitudes toward same-sex love do not pose any mystery. Philo abhorred any manifestation of homoerotic desire or practice, though his loathing was pulled mainly toward the institution of pederasty. The ubiquity of Plato's writings in the mental world of Philo evoked the energetic critique of pederasty in the writings of the Alexandrian

Jew. But the attack on pederasty was not an attempt to slay some imaginary monster from the past and purge the Platonic kingdom of an unwanted intruder. For Philo, pederasty was a characteristic affliction of the society that surrounded him. It had become "something boasted of, and not just by those who indulge in it, but also those who suffer it." It was a damnable act, for both parties to the transaction. The deviance of pederasty, at its core, lay in the attraction of males for males. Philo contrasted the madness of men for women and women for men, "in which case the desires themselves are pursued according to the laws of nature," with the madness of men for other males "who differ only in age." The pederast sought a "pleasure" that was itself "against nature."[23]

Far more than Paul, Philo makes strategic use of the models of masculinity in the culture around him to bolster his own attack on same-sex erotics. Amorous encounters with free boys drew his special indignation. Philo argued that the victim of pederasty was constitutionally transformed by the experience of sexual passivity. The receptive role literally damped the circulation of warmth through the developing male body and turned it toward physical femininity. "Becoming accustomed to suffer the affliction of women, they waste in body and soul, so that not one ember of their manly nature is left flickering with heat." Similar conceptions may well have underlain Greco-Roman opposition to pederasty with free boys, though Philo has given fullest voice to the fear. Pederasty, he argued, might so disrupt the buildup of proper heat that turned a boy into a man that an irreversible cycle of tabescence would set in, rendering the boy cold, frail, moist: an effeminate. Manliness was such a fragile, indeterminate thing that it might be lost altogether. The *eromenos* might become an androgyne, a she-male, a physiological monster. The androgyne, thought Philo, for "debasing the coinage of his nature," should be killed with impunity, not allowed to live for one day, or one hour.[24]

The shrill tone never falters. There is a sense, in Philo's fevered attacks, that he is throwing the kitchen sink at a practice that he held in special disfavor. But beneath the vernacular assumptions about masculinity, Philo's attack on same-sex eros is governed by an irreducibly Jewish logic, a sense of blinding dread toward all forms of sexual contact between males. For Philo, no mitigating factors—not age, not status—could render male flesh an appropriately neutral object of sexual desire for men. His coruscating attack dispersed all the mists of ambiguity—the sympotic drunkenness, the close philosophical mentorship, the obfuscated exchanges of gifts and favors—that had, for centuries, sustained the institution of pederasty amid a culture of machismo. What is so striking about Philo's invective is the remorseless efficiency with which he unravels the contradictions of pederasty from the inside out, in native terms of masculinity, all in the service of his own exceptional opposition to venereal contact between members of the same sex. It is but a short step from Philo's logic to that which animates Paul's thought in the epistle to the Romans.

The unexpected outburst at the head of the Letter to the Romans was to prove absolutely decisive for Christian attitudes toward same-sex erotics. It would completely overshadow the even more fleeting and oblique condemnations in the vice lists of the New Testament. These rapid-fire rosters of iniquity regularly included adulterers and fornicators, as well as two types of sexual actors whose crimes are less obvious. Paul provides the first attested use of the term *arsenokoitēs.* Although it recurs sporadically across the centuries, *arsenokoitēs* was not destined to become a primary term of the Christian sexual vocabulary. It has perennially befuddled earnest translators. The term itself—"male-bedders"—points, ambiguously, to some form of sexual transgression, as does its placement next to other carnal vices. But as a sensitive observer has pointed out, *arsenokoitia* is usually located along the border between sexual deviance and economic exploitation. Perhaps the key to unlocking the meaning of the term is recognizing that in the Roman Empire the frontiers between sexual and economic exploitation were hazy and indistinct. The realities of eros, especially same-sex eros, were hopelessly enmeshed in the dynamics of power and status. At the time of Paul's mission, the sexual use of slave boys and male prostitutes was entrenched in the sexual economy. But Paul was not primarily concerned with the exploitation of vulnerable males, any more than his condemnation of fornication was rooted in sympathy for the prostitute. In a culture without a ready label for men who casually used the bodies of their dependents as sexual receptacles, Paul summoned a portmanteau to fill the lexical gap.[25]

The figure of the *malakos,* the "soft one," also appears in the Pauline vice lists. With *malakia,* though, Paul was not improvising on the spot but rather drawing from a familiar social typology. The *malakos* presents us with an ancient bogeyman who has no direct analogue in the modern social repertoire. The essence of *malakia* was softness, an interior disposition formed of luxuriance, effeminacy, and weakness. Sexual deviance was not the sole mark of softness, but it was a practically inevitable consequence of the inability to impose one's hard will on the enervating poison of desire. Excessive fondness for bathing, fine food, and soft clothing were characteristic of the *malakos,* but "above all and with the least self-control" he was possessed by "a sharp and scalding madness for sex, for coition with both women and with men, and even for inexpressible and unknown acts of shame." The *malakos* was as likely to surrender to the love of women as to the love of men. The desire underlying the sexual behavior of the *malakos* was not so much deviant as excessive, a surplus of lust dissolving the steely power over the self that was the surest guarantee of manliness in the ancient Mediterranean.[26]

Paul's words on same-sex love were few and oblique, but they were searing enough. A continental shelf of latent prejudice lies just beneath what we can see. There was much that Paul did not need to say. And as little as same-sex love occupies Paul's attention in his extant letters, the flashes of vitriol were enough for subsequent Christians to locate their apostle indubitably outside the practices of mainstream society. Within a few decades, the early Christians had contrived a new word to convey their unqualified disapprobation of practices that had subsisted across the centuries. A compound word, *paidophthoria,* "the violation of children," appears scattered throughout the earliest layers of Christian literature. It is utterly unattested before its appearance amid the literary debris of the primitive church. The word seems to be a deliberate transfiguration of pederasty, replacing eros, erotic love, with *phthoria,* violation, and thereby construing all sexual contact with the young as an act of corruption. The Christians reduced to a one-word slogan the more artful denunciations of Philo, but the sensibility was identical, as was the sense of where contemporary sexual culture strayed most egregiously from the divine will.[27]

As with *porneia,* the very novelty of Christian language mirrored the transformative logic of a distinctive sexual morality. The fact that the early Christians were forced to coin two terms—*arsenokoitia* and *paidophthoria*—merely to speak about same-sex eros is not a sign of cautious precision or hesitant reflection on the exact nature of sexual sin. Rather, it reflects the absence of an equivalent category in Greco-Roman culture and the grasping attempt to find a language adequate to the moral disapprobation conveyed by the early Christian authors. Their attitude is most evident in the eternal torments imagined for same-sex lovers in the early apocalyptic literature, especially the Apocalypse of Peter. Considered authentic by many in the early church, the Apocalypse of Peter envisions a curious hell where sinners are punished according to their crime. Men who "pollute their own bodies, conducting themselves like women" and women who "copulate with each other as a man with a woman" were cast off a cliff, only to reascend it in an eternal cycle of punishment. In treating male and female homoeroticism as a singular transgression, the Apocalypse belongs to that handful of imperial-period testimonies that reflect the first stirrings of a concept with a long future, a sort of "unnatural" sexuality based strictly on gender preference. The grid of sexual configurations underlying the Apocalypse is not structurally dissimilar from the *scientia sexualis* we encounter in contemporary astrological and medical texts. But in the Christian scales of value, the licitness of penetration depends on the gender of the receptive flesh. And instead of being relegated to a life on the margins of society, the sexual deviant in the Christian imagination would be relegated to an eternity of sensational torment.[28]

It scarcely needs saying that the early Christians inhabited a world vastly unlike our own. They moved in a society where same-sex eroticism between males was conceptualized *either* as pederasty *or* as passivity. Surely, not all amorous unions fit into one of these two clear channels, but the moral and medical discussion formed around these two poles of experience. What is significant about early Christian moralizing, from Paul onward, is that it drew so little from established modes of criticism. It is impossible to imagine a "contest of the loves," debating the relative merits of women and boys, in a Christian setting, and nowhere do we find the usual arguments that pederasty was simply inferior to conjugal love. Similarly, early Christian literature—with one exception—offers none of the vicious attacks on sexual passivity that can be found in Lucian or Achilles Tatius, because the precise synthesis of machismo and sexual moralism was wholly absent from Christian discourse. Yet none of this means that the Christian posture toward same-sex love was uncertain. From Paul onward, Christian sexual ideology collapsed all forms of same-sex contact, whether pederastic or companionate, into one category. This conceptualization incubated, quietly, in the early centuries; in late antiquity, when the Christianization of state and society gave these new moral preoccupations wider berth than ever before, the opposition to "unnatural vice" would hatch forms of repression that the ancient critic of pederasty or passivity could not have imagined.[29]

A COMMUNITY APART: PURITY, *PORNEIA*, AND THE APOLOGETIC VOICE

Already for Paul, sexual morality was a communal property; fornication and unnatural sex were inveterate habits—among the heathens. Paul's imputation of base immorality to his enemies was in the best Roman tradition. Sexual slander was standard practice in Roman public culture. As a result, much early Christian discourse about sex takes the form of self-defense against charges of a sensational kind, or, conversely, briefs against the dominant culture for lubricious misdeeds. So the African Christian Tertullian, with a rhetor's verve and a lawyer's instinct for the clinching detail, defended his religion against the charge of incest by prosecuting the Romans for exactly the same. The Christians, he averred, should be least suspected of all. "If any race is completely free of intercourse itself and from the necessities of sex and age, to say nothing of lust and luxury, that will be the race that is free of incest." The conspicuous chastity of the Christians meant the charges of sexual depravity could be summarily dismissed, with prejudice. The institution of Christian virginity recommended the Christian race, the *gens,* as a whole. In a culture crowded with competing public philosophies, the rejection of the implacable demands placed on the body cut through all the noisy posturing with an act whose radical tone was jarring. Virginity was a blaring advertisement for the religion. The virgin's body was a merit of the Christian community, which marked out Christian propriety from Roman debauchery.[30]

It would be hard to overestimate the extent to which Christian sexual moralizing, in its first three centuries, was shaped by the boundary between the righteousness of the Christian community and the seething depravity of the vast outside world. Classical paganism's enduring reputation for sexual decadence has its origins in the biting critique of Christian apologetic literature (with imperial biography supplying ample help). It has seemed easy enough to dismiss Christian accounts of Greco-Roman sexual practice as so much predictable exaggeration in the arms race of sexual invective. In need of shock value, amid a culture desensitized to any but the most unlikely configurations of venereal pleasure, the imagination was free to contrive extravagant forms of sexual villainy. Certainly Tertullian's countersuit against the Romans qualifies as immoderate. The Christian advocate alleges pervasive sexual irregularity: "With so many acts of adultery, so many shameful violations, so many vessels exposed to public lust both in stalls and in the street, how much mixing of blood, how much commingling within the clan, and thus how much general inducement to incest?" Promiscuity was, he noted, the inexhaustible raw material of low popular entertainments such as mime and comedy. But for Tertullian the decisive evidence for Roman lechery was not to be found in the appetite for vulgar theater. More concretely, it was witnessed in the public courts, including a recent tragedy that was no fiction of the stage but "an affair judged while Fuscianus was prefect of the city." The shock value of Tertullian's case against the Romans derives, quite intentionally, from an awful precision of time, place, and circumstance.[31]

Some years before the prefecture of Fuscianus, which can be dated to AD 187–189, a Roman boy of respectable birth had escaped the clutches of the small staff of attendants who actually did much of what we would consider parenting. He was, like so many others, pulled into the slave trade that lurked in even the most civilized corners of the Roman Empire. After some time he reappeared in Rome, in a slave market. Unwittingly, his own father bought him and "used him in the Greek fashion." Soon enough the slave was sent to perform chained labor in the fields. There he encountered his old pedagogue and nurse, and a sequence of disastrous recognitions ensued. The slave dealer was interrogated, the truth revealed. The masters were the parents, their slave in fact the son. The parents committed suicide, and the prefect awarded the estate to the poor son, "not so much as an inheritance as a recompense for incestuous violation." For Tertullian, the case was as clear a statement about the inner nature of Roman sexual culture as could possibly be needed. "The public revelation of such a crime is sufficient proof of what is hidden among you. Nothing happens just once in human affairs. That such a case could come to light even once says it all."[32]

Although it is not altogether impossible that this ghastly case was ripped from the headlines, the chance of unwitting incest in Roman society was, *pace* Tertullian, vanishingly remote. What is significant about Tertullian's apology is the overriding awareness that the vast gulf between Christian standards and contemporary sexual practice was shaped by an expansive slave trade and a flourishing sex industry. The important *comparandum,* for an apologist of the second century, was not Platonic or Stoic sexual ideology but public sexual culture. Tertullian's diatribe is shaped by its stark attribution of a sexual profile to two groups, "we" and "you." It is easy enough to accuse Tertullian of selecting his enemies wisely, in order to place the opposition in the worst possible light. But he has understood the foundations of Roman sexual culture rather accurately, and his case should not be too lightly dismissed as the salacious concoction of a zealot. Tertullian's address belongs to an important class of early Christian literature, apologetics. Apologetic literature marked the coming-of-age of Christianity as a self-aware movement within the pluralist landscape of Roman intellectual life. Christian apologies were part of a broader culture of public address, often aimed at the awesome figure of the emperor himself. We need not believe that most, or any, Christian speeches reached the ears of the prince, to recognize how powerfully the context of the official audience shaped the self-projection of the religion. Indeed, apology was not just a category of literature but also a stance, a style of perception and presentation. The apologetic literature of the second century was not only a crucial bridge between the compositions of the New Testament and the oeuvre of Clement—the greatest of the apologists. It offers us a chance to witness the development of orthodox Christian sexuality as a moral ideology that set Christians apart from the world.[33]

In the peaceful middle decades of the second century, a Greek speaker of Samaritan origin settled in Rome. He had, by his own account, passed through the hands of Stoics and Aristotelians, Pythagoreans and Platonists, during the course of his studies. He was impressed by the Platonic doctrine of an eternal soul. But this seeker, Justin, was unconvinced until he found Christian philosophy. Following baptism, he became a Christian teacher and the first of the apologists whose work survives. Justin studiously maintained the persona and trappings of a philosopher. His two apologies and his *Dialogue with Trypho* are usually mined as evidence for the gradual accommodation of Christian theology with Platonic metaphysics. But they are at least as interesting as statements of a second-century sexual ideology that parted quite as much from Plato as from the regnant norms of imperial society. For Justin the conversion to Christianity meant leaving behind a life of entrenched sexual indulgence. "Those who once reveled in fornications now cleave to chastity alone." The sexual propriety of the Christians was one of the chief recommendations for the new religion, and it stood in sharp contrast to the patterns of sexual conduct not just allowed but institutionalized in the ancient Mediterranean. "We see that nearly all of them are led into prostitution, not only the girls but also the males. In the way that those of old are said to have reared herds of sheep and cattle, goats and grazing horses, in these times children are reared, but for shameful use. So too an abundance of women, she-men, and ineffably wicked ones are set up for this sort of pollution. And you receive income, revenue, and taxes from those whom you ought to cast out of your civilization." The centrality of prostitution stood as a stain on the *oikoumenē,* the hard-won civilization of the Roman Empire.[34]

Justin's apology provides an important witness to Christian self-presentation in the middle of the second century. The Christians had created a way of life indifferent to the lures of pleasure. "It is our principle either to marry for the purpose of rearing children or to abstain from marriage and live in complete continence." Justin does not offer a strictly Pauline justification for marriage as a safeguard against sexual pollution. Instead, marriage is justified as a procreative project. In part Justin is appealing to the broadly accepted purpose of marriage in the ancient world. Marriage was understood, and structured, above all as a procreative relationship. Procreative intent distinguished marriage from all other relationships, and marriage contracts often included a purpose clause, *procreandorum liberorum causa.* But Justin is the earliest witness to the co-optation of this ideology for specifically Christian ends. For the Greeks and Romans, the procreative purpose of marriage located the relationship in a network of legal exchanges and transfers; it was certainly not seen as a palliative for the otherwise dubious exercise of sexual faculties. Justin, like so many Christians after him, turns the purpose of marriage into a mitigating factor, excusing the sexual use of the body. It is important, knowing the future, not to read too much into Justin's rationalization of marriage. Procreation justified marriage. Traditional discretion and conjugal privacy obviated the need to say more. Justin did not go so far as to say that procreation justified sex, though it would be a short, fateful step from Justin to such a view. In apologetic mode, Justin simply needed to point to the rectitude of the Christians, who either remained celibate or married with most scrupulous intentions.[35]

Within only a few decades the procreative purpose of marriage would gradually become a conceptual justification for sex. The shadowy figure of Athenagoras, a Christian philosopher writing in the reign of Marcus Aurelius, took this fateful step. His *Embassy* is among the finest of the second-century apologies. Athenagoras accused the Romans of a litany of formulaic sexual excesses. "They set up a marketplace for fornication and set up unholy stations offering every shameful pleasure to the young. They refrain not even from males, men practicing terrible things with men. . . . These adulterers and pederasts reproach us, who are eunuchs and monogamists." Athenagoras focuses his disdain for contemporary sexual practice not on any lurid rumor of imperial debauchery, nor on improbable tales of private debasement, but rather on the institutionalized dispensations of pleasure, visible in the light of day. He pointed out that Christians owned slaves, whose omnipresent eyes were the surest form of surveillance in the Roman world, and yet no plausible charges against Christian chastity could be alleged. The exceptional purity of the Christians was emphasized by the fact that they, in obedience to the words of Jesus, did not even look with lust upon women. In an empire full of cities that offered endless visual allurements, such restraint would have stood as no minor accomplishment. But ocular abstemiousness was not the end of Christian virtue. "Since we have a hope for eternal life, we hold in contempt the affairs of this life, up to and including the pleasures of the soul. We consider her a wife whom we have taken according to our own laws, exclusively for the purpose of procreation. Just as the farmer sows his seeds in the earth and waits for the harvest without sowing again, so for us procreation is the limit of our desire."[36]

The Christians were not the first moralists to invest the "seed" with ponderous moral associations. The Pythagoreans had long since staked out a procreationist model of sexual ethics, rooted in a fixation on the vital qualities of sperm and a science of reproduction based on Pythagorean harmonics. But the similarities with Christian procreationism are superficial. Procreationism was not a piece of found wisdom, picked up by Christians struggling to legitimize their faith in the competitive public arena of Roman philosophical culture. Neither inheritance nor osmosis can explain *why* certain specific resemblances between Christian and philosophical sexual norms appeared. Among the innumerable aspects of man's sexual life that the early Christians found occasion to moralize, the Pythagorean anxieties about wasted soul-force and eurhythmic coition were simply absent. Christian procreationism emerged from exegetical tensions specific to the diverse body of textual artifacts in which Christians, already by the generation of Athenagoras, vested authority. The Jesus of the canonical gospels had warned that lust itself was a sexual crime and hinted that "becoming a eunuch for the kingdom of God" was a supreme state. Paul allowed marriage to fend off temptation, but it was clearly a concession; he regarded his own celibacy as the ideal, if one not practicable for all. At the same time the Jewish scriptures revealed that marriage belonged to the order of creation and that God himself had commanded his creatures to be fruitful and multiply. The pastoral letters unambiguously allotted grace to the married life. Christian procreationism was a spontaneous generation out of this unstable stew of received teachings. But it was a nonrandom outcome for a sexual ideology that extolled virginity while allowing marriage. If timeworn metaphors and familiar language imparted a touch of urbanity to radical ideas, especially in the persuasive context of apology, all the better. But Christian procreationism was, at its core, purely Christian.[37]

Strict procreationism developed amid fierce internal struggles over the proper reception of the encratic flashes that are manifest in the textual artifacts of the early Christian mission. Already in the second century, as an underground religious movement that vaunted the glories of virginity, Christianity harbored within its fold some who came to doubt that sex, even sex within marriage, could find any redemption at all. Indeed, a former student of Justin, Tatian, stood as the most visible representative of this outlook. Most of Tatian's surviving apology, his *Oration to the Greeks,* fits comfortably within the traditions of second-century apologetics. The routine criticisms of Roman society are prominent. "Pederasty, which is condemned by the barbarians, is deemed a privilege among the Romans, who strive to gather herds of boys, like horses at pasture." The mystery cults of the Roman Mediterranean were hiding grounds for "effeminates and she-men." (This discovery, he relates, was the proximate cause of his rejection of Greco-Roman religion.) Most of this invective could pass for standard Christian fare. Tatian declares himself an enemy of fornication: "I hate fornication." Yet in one telling passage Tatian casually assimilated "those who marry, those who violate children, and those who commit adultery" in a list of sinners mired in worldly pursuits. Clement of Alexandria accused Tatian of regarding marriage as a form of corruption, of equating marriage and fornication. Tatian, apparently, reserved no grace for conjugal sex.[38]

There is much about Tatian that we simply cannot know. To call Tatian the "patriarch of the encratites," as Jerome would label him, may well be an overstatement, prompted by the need to give heresy a more definite form and face than in reality it possessed. Irenaeus and Clement, scourges of heresy, are not always the most informed, accurate, or generous guides to the diversity of early Christian thought. But they furnish indispensable testimony to the landscape of second-century Christianity. To say that Tatian lay outside the bounds of proto-orthodox Christian sexuality should not be doubted, nor even controversial. What is most interesting about Tatian's encratism is his apparent desire to anchor it in a defensible hermeneutics of Pauline scripture. Marriage was "fornication." Jerome relates that Tatian regarded several of Paul's letters as spurious, and Clement takes Tatian to task for his tortured interpretation of the crucial passages in First Corinthians 7. Nowhere in the extant fragments of Tatian's writings do we find any particularly graphic or gruesome denunciations of sex. (The perfectly orthodox *Symposium* of Methodius actually offers far more melodramatic condemnations of the flesh and its satisfactions.) For Tatian, the allowance of marriage was not a disgusting concession to the body. It was a misreading of Paul, bolstered by the unscrupulous production of fraudulent documentary evidence.[39]

Encratism was less a coherent movement than a recurrent tendency within a dispersed religious mission whose praises of virginity and devaluation of sex, at all times, threatened to choke out any remaining air for marriage. The true position of encratism in the early Christian centuries is reflected in its haphazard appearance in the diffuse body of legend known as the apocryphal acts. Sex is uniformly devalued throughout the stories of apostolic wandering, and encratic ideas surface forcefully in some of the texts (especially the Acts of Andrew and the Acts of Thomas, which may have originated in Tatian's Syriac milieu). Nevertheless, the complete renunciation of sex in the apocryphal literature functioned symbolically, as a dramatic gesture of withdrawal from the fallen order of this world. Continence, in the acts, is like martyrdom: a trait admired in heroes as an especially stark rejection of secular values. As in the formal apologetic literature, the attitude toward sex in the apocryphal acts is strongly colored by the urge to distinguish Christian life, with its commitment to an invisible order, from the corrupt structures of Roman society. The apocryphal acts have rightly been called an "open text," a sprawling, amorphous body of memories, constantly reshaped by Christian communities. The place of sex in the acts—generally devalued, at times veering toward strict renunciation, but above all deeply symbolic of the relationship between Christians and the world—reflects some of the formless energy of sexual austerity in a radical movement that was only gradually brought under the control of an orderly church. The institutional church, too, lodged its authority in the very apostles who so fired the Christian imagination, but in the place of the raw enthusiasm that animates apostolic legend, the church came to offer a disciplined and definite interpretation of the textual artifacts of the apostolic generation. That hermeneutic project was a collective effort, but nowhere is it more in evidence than in the literary output of that scourge of encratism, Clement of Alexandria.[40]

CLEMENT AND THE CORE OF ORTHODOX SEXUALITY

The apologists were Christians speaking in the vernacular of Greek philosophy. None of them was quite so striking, or as successful, as Clement. More than any other Christian of the age, he belongs alongside his learned polytheistic contemporaries. He was a figure of Mediterranean horizons, born perhaps in Greece, passing time in Italy, but settling in the polyglot metropolis of Alexandria. He was thus a contemporary, and neighbor, of Achilles Tatius. Like so many of his competitors, Clement wore his erudition heavily: his work quotes no fewer than 348 different classical authors and cites Plato some six hundred times. Clement has fully absorbed the eclectic Hellenic nostalgia that was characteristic of his age, mainly to reject it. He had little patience for the "great throng" of "accursed sophists" who loomed so large in the civic culture of the period, or for their "useless rivers of words, with scarcely a drop of sense." The scriptures, he believed, counseled the Christian "to use the wisdom of the world but not to abide in it." Clement would offer a guide to the Christian life that was not afraid to affirm the "doctrine of the Greeks as necessary, at the right moments."[41]

Clement's ostentatious mobilization of Greek *paideia* for a Christian purpose has occasioned endless debate over how successfully he has resisted the seductions of Hellenic thought. Clement himself had no doubt that he was passing on, untainted, "the true tradition of blessed teaching" handed down from the apostles to his teachers. Clement quotes the scriptures more than five thousand times, and he is one of the first known Christians to have produced commentaries on the sacred writings. Yet the prevailing view is that Clement's work bears the stamp of his secular erudition. The problem matters greatly for the history of sexuality, for no Christian before him has left such an extensive and minutely detailed record of his attitudes toward the proper use of the body. In Clement's writings, Stoic, Platonic, and Pythagorean language mingles with Christian tradition. The flip side of this coin is Clement's place in the Christian tradition, for Clement is perched at a crucial transition point in early Christianity. Some have seen Clement as the faded voice of a lost cause, others as a portent of gathering ecclesiastical powers eager to meddle in the bedroom. The problem of how to situate Clement is the problem of how to define the essence and trajectory of early Christian sexual morality altogether.[42]

It is tempting, of course, simply to retreat to the position that Clement's sexual ideology is a hybrid of mixed ancestry. But behind the language of contemporary philosophy, Clement's sexual ideology is purely Christian; again and again, Platonic concepts of appetition and Stoic attitudes toward desire are held responsible to the logic of Christian tradition. The embroidery of philosophical language obscures the fact that Clement's achievements were largely exegetical. Clement's sexual morality had to answer to a body of texts, bewilderingly diverse in origin and intention. For the Old Testament, Clement could make good use of the pioneering syntheses of Philo; for the New Testament, Clement had predecessors, but none who had so completely wrapped together the gospels and the Pauline letters into a single encompassing vision of man's sexual obligations. Clement's problem was not how to integrate *paideia* and revelation, Athens and Jerusalem. Rather, it was how to integrate the commands of Genesis and those of First Corinthians, how to square the Jesus who would speak elliptically about eunuchs for the kingdom of heaven with the Jesus who treated marriage as an indissoluble bond. Having reconciled the multifarious strands jostling for primacy within the Christian tradition, decorating it with beads carefully plucked from the rich jewel box of Greek philosophy was the simple part.

Clement's sexual philosophy is shaped by notions of sin, the flesh, and fornication that were simply alien to the classical intellectual tradition. Where Clement does try to graft his sexual ideology back onto the familiar inheritance of philosophical ethics—especially on the issue of desire—his conceptions differ so radically that on close inspection the fissures remain visible. For Clement, desire was the central problem of sexual ethics. He sought not its use nor its control, but its extirpation. "For Christ always has this remarkable capacity to cut out the very roots of sin. 'Do not commit adultery' is but an outgrowth of 'do not lust.' Adultery is the fruit of lust, its evil root." Clement taught an ethic of radical self-transformation. He belongs among the ascetic theologians, but he still inhabited the ancient city; his sexual morality was never overshadowed by the awesome prospect of its imminent vanishment. Within the city, and within marriage, Clement imagined a transcendence of physical desire that within only a few generations would inspire the great experiments of Christian asceticism. Clement envisioned a monasticism *avant la lettre,* one poised, a little uncertainly, within the *oikos* and the *polis.*[43]

Contests with other Christians consumed much of Clement's energy. To one side of him stood various modes of libertinism, whose reality is obscured by the intense glare of Clement's disdain. Far more serious was the threat on Clement's other flank, encratism. Advocates of virginity captured Clement's full attention and bore the brunt of his polemical acumen. These heretics "through their continence commit sacrilege against creation, against the holy creator and sole all-ruling God, teaching that marriage is not to be allowed." They taught that procreation was fuel for death; intercourse itself was "polluted." What most alarmed Clement was their claim to exegetical authority. Those who claimed that marriage was fornication "vaunt that they apprehend the gospel more deeply than others." They offered not only mystical readings of texts but argued that Paul had denigrated marriage in plain sight. It was too much for Clement. "It is not to be accepted, as some have interpreted it, that he means to say the binding of man and woman is a mixture of the flesh with corruption." Clement has Tatian specifically in mind. "In his exegesis of the apostle, he is engaged in sophistry rather than verity, fabricating falsehood from the very stuff of truth." Clement agreed that fornication and dissolution were "passions of the devil." But Tatian went too far in declaring marriage sinful in itself. "Indeed, the distance between marriage and fornication is as great as the gulf separating God and the devil."[44]

It must be admitted that as an exegete of First Corinthians, Clement routs Tatian. But he reserves his clinching evidence for last. For Clement, Paul was also the author of the pastoral epistles, which left no ambiguity about the licitness of marriage. "Taken *together,* all the letters of the apostle teach chastity and continence, offering up so many thousands of commands about marriage, procreation, and the arts of housecraft without anywhere rejecting self-controlled marriage." Clement's exegesis demanded the interpretation of a body of texts, read in light of each other; no strand of the tradition could be privileged at the expense of another. Clement's writings are filled with an uncompromising conviction that he had solved the encratite challenge, salvaging the virtues of both marriage and continence. "The harmonies of a self-controlled marriage offer a middle way, continence conducing to prayer and nuptial solemnity to procreation."[45]

Talk of a "middle way" is apt to obscure the fact that the actual distance between Clement and Tatian was less immense than either might have wished to admit. Their disagreement was something on the order of a technical argument over the salvageability of marriage. To keep marriage afloat, Clement was willing to jettison most of the lore accumulated to justify it. What survives this disencumbrance bears little resemblance to any contemporary ideals of marriage. In all his brooding over the problem of marriage, Clement once, and without great conviction, compasses the traditional reasons to marry. "Marriage is generally advisable, for the good of the fatherland, the succession of children, and the completion of the universe, as far as that is our concern." The voice is oblique, content to relay arguments that were unobjectionable and might advance a position, even if the reasoning carried little weight. Throughout Clement's corpus, marriage is reduced, almost completely, to nothing more than a scriptural injunction. "Scripture counsels us to marry." The order to marry was there, plain as day, in the opening of Genesis: "Be fruitful and multiply." The man taking his wife to bed shared a little of the awesome power of the creator of the universe. "In this man becomes a likeness of God—man, co-worker in the creation of man."[46]

The power of creation imposed grave responsibilities, and adamantine limits, on the use of sex. Clement emerges as a meticulous exponent of procreationist sex. "Procreation is the aim of those who have married, and fruitfulness is the aim of procreation." The continuance of the species depended on the "vital soil" of the woman's womb. But the man looking to farm his conjugal fields had to know that "the seed is not to be cast upon stony places, nor is it to be contemned, since it is the origin of generation and has the order of nature dispersed within it." Seed was to be sown "at the proper moments." Clement, following Philo, believed that the thicket of Mosaic purity regulations in reality pointed to a deeper procreationist ethic. Moses prohibited men from approaching their wives during menstruation, so that what was "shortly to be a human would not be polluted in a stream of filthy matter." Moses prohibited the violation of captive women, or the use of hired professionals, because they were not "exclusively for the production of children." Following Philo, Clement took the command not to eat the meat of the hare or hyena as a cryptic sexual command against fruitless intercourse. In one of those passages that sent Victorian translators scurrying to the decent obscurity of a learned language, the hyena was taken as a symbol of misused orifices. Various modes of same-sex intercourse are abused, but in a world with only the most primitive technologies of contraception, this tirade was no small infringement on conjugal liberty either. "Sex not intended to produce children is a rape of nature."[47]

This imaginative allegorization was ready to hand in the writings of the idiosyncratic Philo, who did the pioneering work of squaring Plato with Moses. But it is too easy to soften Clement's radicalism by ascribing it to the influence of Philo or, even more distantly, Plato and the Pythagoreans. Clement shares, or at least deploys, a certain reverence for human seed, but he is never overwhelmed by fears of spermatorrhea. The architecture of his thought is neither Philonic nor Pythagorean. Clement's procreationism is much closer to that of Athenagoras, and it was born out of the same exegetical tensions. The deepest principle of Clement's sexual ideology is not procreationism but rather the transcendence of desire.

For Clement, Christian marriage had received a special dispensation. "For the others, marriage achieves a concord through the shared experience of pleasure, but for the philosophers [Christians] it leads to a concord according to the Word." Christian marriage had as little to do with pleasure as possible. "A love of pleasure, even if pursued within marriage, is irregular, unjust, and irrational." Clement addressed those who argued that marriage, and its tame pleasures of the bed, were according to nature. His endorsement of the view was tepid. "Even if this is true, it is still shameful that man, created by God, should be more uncontrolled than the beasts." The furthest Clement would go was to admit that "nature, as in the case of food, so in the case of lawful marriage, allots to us what is proper, useful, and seemly, that is, to seek after procreation." Clement believed that in Christian marriage the couple's sexual intimacy would be aimed exclusively at procreation, so that it could even escape the nets of desire and pleasure. Marriage according to the Word was no sin because it offered a mysterious exemption from the normal pangs of desire that motivated sex. These sentiments appear most clearly in Clement's *Miscellanies,* which transmit his deepest teachings. "With marriage, food, and other things, let us do nothing from desire, but only will those things that are necessary. For we are not children of desire, but of will. And so the man who marries for procreation should practice continence, not even desiring his wife, whom he should love. Procreation should be sought with a reverent and controlled will." For Clement, proper sex was solemn, cool, ratiocinative. Marriage itself was encratic.[48]

The Christian could achieve the transformation of natural desire into rational will. Clement believed that Moses had prohibited an Israelite man from violating a captive woman for a period of thirty days so that the "physical impulse could be scrutinized and mastered into a rational appetite." The coming of Christ had "completely destroyed the works of desire—greed, striving, vainglory, lust for women, pederasty, gluttony, indulgence, and the like." Clement envisioned a sort of self-transformation that was alien to the philosophical tradition. "Man's capacity for continence, as far as the Greek philosophers regard it, is said to be a matter of striving against desire and not serving it in its deeds. The Christian ideal is not to experience desire at all. The aim is not for one to prove as strong as one's desires, but rather somehow to be continent *from* desire. There is no way to achieve this continence except through the grace of God." This is as lucid a self-perception as might be hoped for.[49]

Clement's sexual ideology is closer to the monastic desert than we might suppose. "Our antagonists are Olympian in stature and sting, as is said, more sharply than a wasp. Above all pleasure, which not only by day but also by night, in our dreams, bites us and aims to deceive us with its sorcery." But Clement's asceticism is lodged within marriage, within the city. The endless stream of minute directives for Christian living proffered by Clement amount to a monastic rule for the Christian household. Clement clasped enthusiastically to the Paul of the pastoral letters, who had offered "so many thousands of commands about marriage, procreation, and the arts of housecraft." Paul's commands are exuberantly expanded into a punctilious rubric for the Christian life. Time, place, and manner restrictions are unmercifully imposed on the sexual act. Sex was not for the daytime, but neither was the darkness of night to be a veil for hidden excess. Immemorial patterns of sociability are wrapped in new rules of Christian modesty: Clement could prescribe which sorts of dinners to attend and how to behave. If women had to attend social gatherings, they should be entirely covered; the "gravest calumny" that could be leveled against an unmarried woman was that she was present at a symposium. If young men were present, they were to sit motionless, look down, and keep their legs uncrossed. Men were to eat and drink moderately, but also slowly, with a cultivated air of self-control, pausing frequently, never reaching for food, sharing generously, and departing early. For Clement, the Christian sage could pass through life amid the city, but exposure to so many temptations required unfailing vigilance and supreme control of the will.[50]

Clement has what might seem an embarrassing amount of advice on the proper consumption of food and drink. His interest in dietetics and medical lore places him in the mainstream of imperial culture. Clement admired those who abstained from wine completely in the name of chastity and "thought it best if boys and girls are kept apart from this drug completely. It is not advisable to pour liquid heat on smouldering youth. . . . Ramped up by its influence, their privates expand and their breasts swell, so that their genitals are an omen, the image of fornication." Clement would harness conventional medical wisdom in the name of not just healthful balance, but also transformation. "Food is for hunger and drink is for thirst, but it calls for the most acute self-protection against any slip, for one step down the path of wine makes one apt to fall. With care we can keep our souls pure, dry, and luminous." The more extreme regimes of mortification, which will exploit the medical tradition with gusto, lie not far in the future.[51]

Clement's Christians find their will to transcend the lures of desire and pleasure threatened in every direction. His writings are an unmatched guide to the mundane dangers of modest wealth in a household of the Roman Empire. He is the first Christian to worry about the temptation that slaves, specifically eunuchs, posed to the *women* of a household. He is distressed by the built environment of the ancient city, aghast at a culture in which erotic art was a normal accoutrement of the domestic sphere. Clement's believers faced constant visual bombardment. They were surrounded by the vibrant erotic anarchy of ancient Alexandria. Clement was, like so many of his contemporaries, acutely sensitive to the ocular experience of living in a great Roman town. For him the words of Christ not to look with lust posed an overwhelming challenge. "He pulls up desire from its root." Inviting looks were "nothing other than adultery with the eyes, desire cast from afar through them. For the eyes are corrupted before the rest of the body." In his belief that vision was a sort of particulate intromission, it has been noted, Clement is not at all far from Achilles Tatius, who described the erotic gaze as "fondling from afar." What for Achilles was one of the harmless thrills of life was for Clement an environmental hazard, clogging the air with pollutants that threatened the purity of the body.[52]

Clement's attitude toward same-sex love is a predictable extension of his commitment to Pauline authority and his strict procreationism. Following Philo, Clement believed that the Mosaic prohibition on the consumption of hare, that "lewd beast," was really a ban on pederasty. Clement also believed that Moses had condemned same-sex relations literally, for he repeatedly cited the triune ban on "fornication, adultery, and the corruption of children," and, wrongly, attributed it to Moses. The injunction against pederasty has even snuck into the Ten Commandments, between adultery and theft! For Clement, Paul's condemnation of same-sex love in Romans was a straightforward continuation of the Mosaic law. Clement elaborates on the idea of "natural use" with unsparing literalism. Every orifice, every canal, every protuberance had a natural use, to which it was limited. Procreationism and the naturalization of heterosexuality went hand in hand.[53]

Though Clement's hostility to same-sex eros was inevitable, the specific complexion of his moralism marks him as a man of Hellenic erudition in the Roman Empire. Clement's erudition could plumb the depths of Greek mythology whenever it provided an opportunity to embarrass; the lusts and escapades of a Zeus or Dionysus were fodder for humiliating recital. Clement's sensibility of male prostitution as a "disease" would have been comfortable to Dio or Ptolemy, and it is an idea with an ominous ecclesiastical future. For Clement, open love between males was always closely associated with the flesh trade. Clement was an acute, if glowering, social observer. His image of manliness was a unique concoction of Christian ideals and contemporary assumptions, without precedent or successor. Clement took hair as the "mark of manhood." He describes, in gruesome detail, the hair-plucking shops of Alexandria; the habits of anal and genital depilation symbolized for him the entrenched disorder of civic life. There could be no doubt, he said, that a man who would submit to such violation "by day" played a woman "by night." The statement is perfectly at home in a culture where manliness was policed by competitive social surveillance. More than any other early Christian, Clement's understanding of masculinity has absorbed some of the machismo of his world. He thinks of "she-men" as soft voluptuaries, as likely to have sex with women as with men. The Christian was to avoid "all softness and daintiness." There is no clearer sign of Clement's cultural horizons than this: he is one of the vanishingly few Christians to use the vernacular term of abuse for a man who monstrously flaunted gender protocols—*kinaidos.* Clement's outlook on same-sex love is an unstable mixture of Moses, Paul, and Lucian.[54]

Of all the early Christians, Clement is most sensitively estranged from the civic fabric of the Roman Empire. This was a dizzying vantage from which to view the world. There is something of Dio Chrysostom's alienated perspective in Clement's lofty pronouncements. "Such complete lasciviousness has poured over the cities that it has become the law." Like Dio, Clement located the essence of the ancient sexual economy in the institution of venal sex. "Women are prostituted in brothels, selling the violation of their flesh for pleasure, and boys are led to reject their nature, taking on the role of women." Clement had the pulse of imperial sexual culture. No matter what any moralist said, "the whores are proof of what is actually done." Indulgence was not a matter of abuse or excess; it was embedded in the order of society. "The wise men of the laws allow this. They let them sin with the protection of law. They call unspeakable acts of pleasure contentment." In Alexandria Clement had a disturbing front-row seat to the most brutal machinery of the Roman sexual economy. He could watch the giant slave ships at dock, bringing "fornication like wine or grain," selling girls wholesale to procurers throughout the empire. Sexual moralism inspires Clement's discomfort, but he is one of the most striking observers of the realities of the Roman slave trade. The sale of sex was anything but marginal. "The whole earth is filled with fornication and disorder." This was something Dio could never have said. Fornication was not just a word; it was a worldview, in which the cosmos, the order of civilized life, appeared to be in the grip of sin.[55]

Clement's thought-world and modes of expression are still shaped by the vital civic backdrop and eclectic philosophical *koinē* of the high empire, but the logic of his sexual ideology is exclusively Christian—a highly rigid form of Christianity at that. Clement is not a voice of moderation. His attitudes toward sexuality are as rigorist, or more so, as much of what will become orthodoxy after him. Clement fended off encratism by strategically occupying as much of its ground—and appropriating as much of its language—as his interpretation of Paul would allow. Clement's defense of marriage bears utterly no resemblance to the warm ideals of conjugal affection or cheery romantic patriotism of the culture that surrounded him. Clement's sexual ethic is one of personal transformation and transcendence of desire, but it is still locked into the mold of an ancient way of life. For Clement, this transformation would be marked by a vastly new relationship between the Christian and the minutiae of ordinary social life. In short, the radical discovery of the desert, which would allow the transformational ethic to unfold against the open backdrop of empty space, had not yet happened.

Clement's sexual ideology was in many ways idiosyncratic, most of all in his belief that physical desire could be graciously metamorphosed into a rational will to participate in creation. The small but decisive differences between Clement and his greatest student, Origen, are highly telling. Origen is almost totally unconcerned with procreation as a justification for sex; he assumes that "holy procreation" is part of the married life, but it does not bear the same great moral weight that it does in Clement, as the prime justification for the reproductive act. Even more than Clement, Origen was content to tread wherever his exegesis led him: Paul had allowed marriage and considered it a gift of God, and that was that. Origen was thus much closer to the actual spirit of Paul in First Corinthians 7. Origen was cautious not to denigrate marriage: the call to purity and the call to marry were different forms of grace, each dispensed by the mysterious benevolence of God. Origen stands one step closer to the ascetic theologies of late antiquity. But it is less often appreciated that he anticipates the entanglements of pastoral leadership that will occupy the fourth-century church. Origen is anxious about the realities of sin. Fornication is not just a property of the outside world; it is a problem for the Christian community. "If someone is in fornication, they are not just in the flesh, but something worse . . . they are in the mud." "Sin corrupts the temple of God. Someone who brings a scandal upon the church corrupts the temple of God. Even more powerfully does the fornicator corrupt the temple of God." Origen believed that there were "different classes of fornication," some more grievous than others; each would be "judged according to its quantity and quality, its intent and duration." Sins were to be taken "to the bishop." "We have rulers in the church before whom we are to submit our disputes, so that we are not mocked in the courts of the heathens."[56]

For Origen, the possibility of personal transformation looms large. But for Origen it is virginity, and the complete dissociation from the grip of the world, rather than Christian housecraft, that offers the surest path to such transformation. This is the most subtle, and decisive, shift between Clement and Origen. Total sexual renunciation steadily came to occupy a larger place in the moral imagination of Christian theologians. Origen was the prophet of a type of cosmic spiritual warfare that would captivate the next generation of Christians and lead directly to the desert. Clement assumes, but rarely talks about, a Christian cosmology that for Origen was always near. Angels and demons lurk in the background of Clement's panorama, behind the statues of the pagan gods, in the lush erotic art of the ancient town. For Origen, otherworldly spirits crowd around the soul. Where Clement draws on an ancient philosophical vocabulary of "inclinations," Origen will imagine demonic "impulses" rushing through the finely tensed air making up the human soul. The ascetic movement of which Origen is the premonition was not a sudden wave that washed out the foundations of a moderate core of conjugal Christianity. Rather, it presages the development of a bifurcated church, in which virgins represented a spiritual elite. Clement imagined that somehow the marriage relationship could act as a venue for such transformation. The discovery of the desert would make that impossible. But it also left unsettled the exact relationship between virginity and marriage, which would become an ever more pressing demand in the fourth century as the church absorbed the machinery of social reproduction.[57]

THE PREREQUISITES OF SIN: A FREE WILL

In the midst of a long discussion on the Old Testament prophecies, Justin Martyr pauses to make the point that the foreknowledge demonstrated in successful prophecy did not imply a deterministic universe. "Judgments, retributions, and rewards are dispensed according to the worth of each one's actions. . . . If it were not thus, but everything occurred according to destiny, our control over the things up to us would not be complete. For if it were fated that this man be good, that one bad, it would not be possible to say that this one is worthy of commendation, that one worthy of condemnation." Justin's aside might have been no more than a curious digression, if he had not stumbled on an epoch-making formula. Justin Martyr has the signal distinction of being the first philosopher on record to make unambiguous use of the term "free will." "Indeed, if mankind were not endowed with the faculty to flee shameful deeds and choose excellent ones by their free will, they cannot be responsible for whatever deeds they commit." Free will was, for Justin, an essential quality of human life. "Not like plants or beasts, without the faculty of choice, did God create man." The motivation for this discovery is obvious: it was a prerequisite of divine justice. Man has moral freedom *because* the nature of existence is such that a divine judge will evaluate his moral actions; it is a thoroughly libertarian view of free will, defined by the capacity to act in a certain way. The passage of Justin's apology calls to mind the dictum of Nietzsche, that the purpose of the will is chiefly to find guilty.[58]

The sudden appearance of philosophical concepts that will endure for centuries is rare. Justin's discovery of the idea of free will was not haphazard or circumstantial. It lies at the heart of his understanding of the cosmos. It was a teaching that he bequeathed directly to his student Tatian. "The good is a purpose that man may accomplish through the freedom of his will, so that the evil man is justly punished, having become wicked through his own doing, while the just man is worthy of praise for his good deeds, not having transgressed the will of God in the exercise of his autonomy." It is equally prominent in Irenaeus and Clement. For Origen, and other Christians of the third century, it is central. The concept receives its finest expression in the writings of the Cappadocian fathers in the fourth century, before Augustine opens a distinctly new chapter in the history of the will by describing it as a precognitive, pre-emotional faculty, partly beyond the control and understanding of man's conscious self. This commitment to absolute autonomy is all the more remarkable because it required Christians down to Augustine to repress the strong moment of divine election in Pauline scripture. But the conception of radical moral freedom as an essential human quality was integral to the worldview of Christianity in precisely the period during which its sexual ideology received form and expression. The rise of the concept of free will and the sea change in the logic of sexual morality went hand in hand.[59]

The place of early Christianity has been underestimated in the principal treatments of the history of the will. In part this neglect is due to a tendency to confine the development of Christian attitudes toward volition—and the complex of ideas connecting cosmology, anthropology, and divine election—to the ghetto of gnostic-orthodox controversy. Clearly the meaning of individual freedom was an important part of second- and third-century theological debates. In their efforts to redescribe the origins and form of the universe, and the place of mankind within it, the gnostic Sethians may have developed a view of the "saved" as an elect seed whose redemption was predetermined. The Sethians, the group that most clearly deserves the label "gnostic," illustrate the primacy of cosmology to questions about human nature and individual autonomy. Even more importantly, the school of the Christian teacher Valentinus, a "heresy" that may have drawn from some gnostic teachings but was not itself gnostic, provoked orthodox Christians to articulate a model of free will and human equality. The threat of Valentinus was heightened by the claims that he was himself a student of Paul's disciple Theudas and by the fact that the Valentinians were formidable exegetes of Pauline scripture. The Valentinians developed a tripartite division of humanity: the spiritual, the animate, and the material. The spiritual natures were elected to salvation by grace; the material natures were destined for damnation. In between were the animate natures, whose fate was uncertain and depended on their own acts. It seems likely that the Valentinians viewed themselves as the spiritual ones and, in a sort of olive branch extended to their Christian brethren, construed the orthodox sect as the animate ones. Despite the talk of different "natures," Valentinian ethics and ritual seem to presuppose that the lines between these divisions are traversible. On the other hand, texts that describe salvation "through nature" suggest the influence of divine dispensation. It is much debated whether the Valentinian system was strongly determinist, but what matters in this context is that for orthodox Christians like Irenaeus, Clement, Origen, and Methodius, the view of humanity propounded by the Valentinians trampled the sacred inviolability of human freedom. "These heretics practically ruin the concept of free will by introducing some who are lost without the possibility of salvation and others who are saved without the possibility of being lost."[60]

To reduce the orthodox commitment to free will to an adjunct of zealous heresy hunting is to miss the fact that these conversations were part of a much wider fascination with cosmology and the essence of human freedom. Cosmological speculation was the formative crucible of a new concept of the will, and not just for Christians. It is also easy to miss the centrality of sexual ethics to the development of a novel model of moral agency. Sex represented a domain of action uncannily suited for debates over the causation of human behavior. Sexual morality not only became a standard paradigm, almost instantly evoked in debates over the will. The peculiar characteristics of sexuality—at once so externally determined and so existentially consequential—drove the terms of the discussion about human agency. In the process, the sex drive became the core feature of human identity, tensed between a robust sense of human freedom and our deep embeddedness in the world.

In a provocative recent study, Michael Frede attributes the invention of the concept of free will to the Stoic Epictetus. There is certainly a case to be made for the former slave who would become the most important thinker in the Stoic tradition during the Roman period. In the notes of Epictetus's teaching that have come down to us, questions about "what is in our control" and the freedom of our internal "will" loom larger than ever before. The tensions inherent in Stoic determinism—which held that the purely materialistic universe unfolded from the moment of its creation through an unbroken chain of causes—had been an open problem since the Hellenistic period. The compatibilist theories of the great Stoic Chrysippus held the field for nearly three centuries. Although Epictetus follows Chrysippus, the dynamics of freedom are far more pronounced in the Roman Stoic. On the one hand, man was a creature of fate. The threads of his being were spun by Zeus and the Fates. Thus, much of life consisted of things "not under our control: the body, the parts of the body, possessions, parents, brothers, children, country." Epictetus was far more interested in the one faculty absolutely "under our control": our "will and all the acts of the will." Man always retained the power of the will, *if he "cared" for it.* Epictetus's "chief care" was to make his will "free."[61]

In his insistence on a radically undetermined faculty with the capacity to make use of external impressions, Epictetus represented a watershed. The individual will was beyond all external causation, even the interference of God: "My leg you can fetter, my will not Zeus can overcome." But, crucially, for Epictetus the free will is an achieved state, a rational serenity attained by the Stoic sage. It could be obtained by the philosopher who "withdraws from external things, and turns to his will, cultivating and perfecting it to make it harmonious with nature." Submission to fate, acceptance of what was not under one's control, were preconditions for freedom. As Frede notes, Epictetus's conception of a free will makes massive assumptions about the order of the universe, which must be one in which "there is no power or force in the world which could prevent [the will] from making the choices one needs to make to live a good life." Free will inhered in the sage's ability to consent rationally to his fate, a fate that was in turn the instrument of a benevolent and rational providence.[62]

From Epictetus Frede turns to consider the prominence of free will in the thought of Origen, the sage of the third century whom Frede calls, wrongly, the first Christian to treat the problem of free will rigorously and systematically. Origen's commitment to free will does not derive neatly from Christian scriptures. In fact Origen is at pains to adduce clear scriptural support for his concept of the free will and must explain away a number of passages whose emphasis on providence, grace, and divine sovereignty cut against Origen's beliefs in a radically free will. The contrast with his sexual ideology, which hews dependably close to the body of authoritative texts, is instructive. The Christian investment in the notion of a free will was not an obvious outgrowth of the textual tradition. It thus all the more starkly requires explanation. Frede has no doubt where the Christians found the idea: in imperial Stoicism. What Epictetus created, the early Christian theologians popularized, if in slightly debased form. Free will is thus construed as one of the greatest intellectual heists in the annals of philosophy. Justin and Tatian were trained in the philosophical schools of the Roman Empire and openly admired Stoic ethics, so it can be inferred that they "got their notion of a free will" from the schools. Origen is alleged to have plundered contemporary philosophy for his theological ends; his account is "through and through Stoic." The Christians, in their theological squabbles, adopted "Stoic ideas" as expedience dictated.[63]

The role of Christianity in the development of the concept was not so derivative. The early Christians had an uncanny ability to provide decisive answers to precisely the same questions that endlessly floated in the air at the "schools of the philosophers," where there was "nothing at all but the assertion and controversy of stale dogma without end." Certainly Justin would have been startled to learn that he aped his notion of a free will from Stoicism. In his *Second Apology,* Justin explicitly takes aim at Stoic determinism. "The Stoics have declared that all things come about through the compulsion of Destiny. But in the beginning God created the race of men and angels with autonomy, so that it will be with justice that they undergo the punishment of the eternal flames for their transgressions. It is the very nature of all creation to be capable of evil or righteousness." For Epictetus, free will was an achieved state; for Justin, it was a native endowment. For Epictetus, free will was the carefully cultivated prize of the sage; for Justin it was a universal attribute of mankind. For Epictetus, free will was the serenity of resignation in the face of the smallness and finitude of existence: "Don't make your death into the material for a tragedy. It is just time for the material of which you are constituted to be restored to those elements from which it came." For Justin, free will was a corollary of God's solicitude for man's works and a precondition of eternal judgment. Justin's discovery of free will cannot, without severe injustice to both parties, be attributed to the influence of Epictetus.[64]

A better question to ask is, why did the Stoics become fixated on the problem of fate and free will at the same moment that Christians began preaching a radically new doctrine of human volition? Epictetus was not the only imperial Stoic to be drawn to the problem of freedom and determinism. Just a generation or two later, a Stoic named Philopator—the teacher of Galen's teacher—was making important advances in the Stoic concept of "what is under our control" within the framework of a causal universe. Selective preservation makes the Roman Stoa appear more concerned with ethics than physics or metaphysics. But the problem of fate permeated imperial Stoicism because it was a pervasive issue in the intellectual culture of the Roman Empire. "In the first two centuries AD every philosophical school and every sect of thinkers . . . had their say on fate, determinism, and freedom somewhere in their works." There are an astonishing number of tracts on fate, from gnostics and Christians, Platonists and Aristotelians, Stoics and Epicureans, dating to the high empire. Fate was a topic equally suited for public declamation or Lucianic satire. The tensions between destiny and autonomy lie at the foundation of the great literary creation of the Roman Empire, the novel. The Christians did not pilfer and debase a Stoic doctrine. Rather, both Christians and Stoics were responding to a broad and urgent fascination with the problem of man's place is the cosmos. Cosmology, and its moral ramifications, became a cultural problem in the Roman Empire as never before; the intellectual atmosphere in which Christian sexual morality took shape was deeply concerned about the nature of the cosmos and the place of humanity in it.[65]

The science of astronomy was part and parcel of this cultural fascination. The inhabitants of the Roman Empire had discovered the secrets of the stars. Their beautiful regularity was a sign of cosmic order. Astronomical science first spread into the Mediterranean world in the Hellenistic period. Under Roman rule, it reached new heights, and it became, in the form of astrology, a popular obsession. The scraps of papyri remaining today offer a highly suggestive proxy for popular interest in astrology. The earliest firm date for a horoscope on a papyrus is from 10 BC. Thereafter, growth rapidly ensues and peaks in the late second century. No less a scientist than Ptolemy composed a handbook for learned practitioners to be able to cast horoscopes with exactitude. His *Tetrabiblos* makes it obvious that sexual phenomena were an abiding preoccupation of astral prognostication. The stars exerted no random or arbitrary force. Life here beneath the moon was pushed and pulled by the heavenly bodies according to scrutable patterns. The basic constitution of the self was indelibly shaped by astral configurations; the warmth, the moisture, and thus the sexual proclivities of the body were produced by the elemental forces of the universe. Astrological science promised to submit something so mercurial and intimate as sexual desire to the possibility of firm understanding.[66]

The extent to which free will had become an urgent moral problem in the high Roman Empire is also reflected in the attention devoted to the dynamics of volition in the romantic literature of the period. Fate is central to the poetics of the romance. A popular fatalism is prominent already in Chariton's early novel and remains so down to the last of the romances, the *Ethiopian Tale* of Heliodorus. As usual, Achilles Tatius presents the most self-conscious and sardonic treatment of determinism in any of the romances. In book 1, Clitophon launches his first-person narrative with the report of a portentous dream. The nocturnal vision prompts a remarkably forthright reflection on the importance of dreams in a fatalistic universe. "The divine spirit loves to speak to men by night, not so that suffering may be forestalled (for Destiny cannot be overruled), but so that misfortune might be borne more lightly. The shock of the sudden and unforeseen stuns the soul, and overwhelms it, while the anticipation of misfortune allows us to brace ourselves and, by degrees, takes away the shock of suffering." After the premonitory dream, Clitophon claimed, Fortune initiated her drama. The conscious theorization of the tension between Destiny and Fortune, at the very outset of the narration, is remarkable. The romances are narratives driven by the dialectic between order and flux, displacement and resolution. Fortune authors the sufferings and misadventures that drive the plot, but Destiny prevails in the felicitous ending.[67]

This passage of *Leucippe and Clitophon* is remarkable, and revealing, for another reason. It closely mirrors a sentiment that appears in Ptolemy's astrological treatise. But in the case of Ptolemy, consolation is to be found in astral prognostication, rather than oneirological forewarning. "Events that come about from necessity, if they are unexpected, are especially likely to give rise to extreme disturbance or manic delight, but foreknowledge readies and attunes the soul by preparing the soul for what is not yet present as though it were." The similarity is so striking that it cannot be accidental. Ptolemy's *Tetrabiblos* probably belongs to the 150s or 160s; Achilles Tatius was writing at nearly the same time. We cannot be certain who has imitated whom. Regardless, the parallel with Ptolemy's programmatic justification for astrology locates the concern with destiny in *Leucippe and Clitophon* in the mainstream of second-century intellectual currents. We have already seen how Leucippe's dramatic insistence on her freedom at a pivotal moment in the narrative playfully mocks Stoic concepts of moral autonomy. Throughout the entire novel Achilles toys with the disjunctures between internal volition and external circumstance, between subjective intention and objective fact. The mockery culminates in the climactic scene of the novel, the double ordeal faced by Melite and Leucippe. Melite enters the waters of the river Styx as a test of her chastity, and she escapes on the most dubious technicality (she swears not to have had sex with Clitophon while she believed her husband was dead). Leucippe's virginity is tried in the cave of Pan; the reader recalls Leucippe's stated wish for a virginity test after her mother interrupted her on the brink of losing her purity to Clitophon. In that case, Leucippe's integrity was saved *against* her will, but now the test will vindicate her physical purity! The achievement of the novel resides in these brilliant juxtapositions, which suggest that internal will and external fate do not always align in the ways the world suspects or hopes.[68]

The romance *Leucippe and Clitophon* was a wry reflection on the moral preoccupations of contemporary society, carried on the same currents that swept Christian thinkers toward a new vision of freedom and fate. The novel's deep connection with contemporary culture is underscored by another intertextual connection, in fact with the Syrian Christian Bardaisan (AD 154–222). Bardaisan wrote a lost work, *On India,* fragments of which are preserved by the Neoplatonic philosopher Porphyry in his work *On the Styx.* Bardaisan describes the existence of two ordeals, one in a river and one in a cave, that were used as tests of intention—as a form of scrutiny for that which was otherwise inscrutable. The double ordeal in *Leucippe and Clitophon*, by river and cave, is an obvious appropriation of the same tradition. Bardaisan wrote some decades after Achilles, and on chronological grounds it is impossible that Bardaisan was the source for the romance; Bardaisan reportedly heard of the ordeals firsthand from Indian ambassadors, which if true makes it unlikely that he has borrowed from Achilles. They seem to have drawn, independently, on the same exotic legend. Still, the connection is instructive. Bardaisan was fascinated by the possibility of an ordeal that could peer into the soul and read its intentions. Achilles was clearly bemused by the fact that anyone could believe life, or eros, might be submissible to such knowledge.[69]

The connections between fatalism, astronomy, and romance continue right through to the latest of the novels, the *Ethiopian Tale.* In the novel of Heliodorus, the possibilities of astral science and the mysterious benevolence of Destiny receive their loftiest formulation. One of the main characters of the story is Kalasiris, an Egyptian priest who wanders to Greece and becomes the protector of the novel's hero and heroine. Kalasiris relates how he came to leave his home of Memphis where he was high priest. The "stars in heaven turned the circle of destiny" and brought misfortune on his house. His knowledge of the stars gave him foreknowledge but not escape from his calamities. Though the decrees of fate were immutable, foreknowledge of them could alleviate their tortures. The sentiment is precisely the one expressed by both Ptolemy and Achilles Tatius, but in *The Ethiopian Tale,* the power of foreknowledge has been removed from dreams and vested once again in the arts of astrology. Kalasiris, as a priest, would make a likely adept in astrology, as temples were the center of astrological knowledge in Roman Egypt. But the affliction that Kalasiris was destined to suffer is perhaps surprising. An irresistible courtesan, named Rhodopis, had arrived in Memphis. Afraid he will be unable to resist her erotic energy, Kalasiris exiles himself, a punishment for his sins, "not of commission but of desire." By leaving, Kalasiris was "resigning to the necessities of the fates," lest the "ruling star" prevail over him and compel him into "the more shameful sin of commission." Heliodorus firmly believes in the possibility of virtue, rooted in intention, and in the overwhelming power of a benevolent destiny. As his beautifully complex narrative resolves itself, the author makes sure the reader is aware of the gods' ultimate solicitude for mankind. When the heroine's father recognizes his daughter, he marvels at "fate's stage management" of the story; in the end, Charicleia and Theagenes are joined in marriage "by decree of the gods" who arranged their conjunction. Heliodorus offers a sort of high pagan fatalism, in which human destiny is closely overseen by the numinous management of the gods, a fact that does nothing to dim human moral responsibility.[70]

It is evident already in Justin that Christian doctrines of free will developed against these fatalist cosmologies. Justin's conception of free will lies at the beginning of a trajectory of specifically Christian thinking about freedom and determinism. Some half a century after Justin, Clement of Alexandria evinces an equally strong concern with the challenges of fatalism. He agreed with Justin that if evil were involuntary, it would be unjust to punish it. But he goes beyond Justin in imagining the complex causation of moral action. "For fever is involuntary, but when someone falls sick from his own lack of self-control, we blame him, and so too with involuntary evil. For no one chooses evil *qua* evil, but drawn by the pleasure of it and thinking it good, believes it to be acceptable. Thus, it lies in our control to deliver ourselves both from ignorance and from the choice of what is wicked and pleasurable and not to assent to these deceiving impressions." Clement seems closer to Stoic thought in holding that choice results from a state or condition of being, but Clement's aim was to locate freedom in the universal inheritance of nature rather than in an accomplished state of indifference to externals. Clement's work, which attacks astrology, pagan philosophy, and gnosticism alike, accurately reflects the broad and intermingled thought-world of these second-century debates.[71]

Stoicism, gnosticism, and popular fatalism all spurred the articulation of a libertarian notion of free will among orthodox Christians. These concerns converge in the remarkable work of Bardaisan, an almost exact contemporary of Clement. According to Eusebius, Bardaisan dedicated a work *On Fate* to the emperor Caracalla. It was not the only learned tract on fate the emperor received. The greatest Aristotelian of the high Roman Empire, Alexander of Aphrodisias, also penned a treatise *On Fate* dedicated to Caracalla and his father, Septimius Severus; Alexander's work attacked both astrology and Stoic determinism in staking out a strongly libertarian view of moral action. If the historian Cassius Dio is to be believed, all of this learned instruction failed to take, and Caracalla was so convinced of the veracity of astrology that he dispensed honors and punishments based simply on horoscopes. He might have found Bardaisan's outlook more congenial, because the dialogue preserved under the title *Book of the Laws of the Countries,* composed by a disciple of Bardaisan, reflects a Christian attempt to make strategic concessions to the power of astrology while preserving intact the core of moral freedom. The dialogue surveys the bewildering variety of human customs to argue that such vast differences must imply a wide scope for indeterminist views. Bardaisan developed a unique cosmology and anthropology. He distinguished between a realm of nature and a realm of liberty. "It is man's natural constitution to be born, grow up, become adult, procreate children, and grow old . . . this is the work of Nature, which does, creates and produces everything as it is ordained." These affairs of the body man shared with all living creatures. "As matters of their mind, however, they do what they will as free beings disposing of themselves and as God's image." One proof of moral freedom was the ability of individuals to change. "There are people who used to go to prostitutes and get drunk but who, when they received guidance from good advisors, became decent, continent men and despised the lust of the body." Bardaisan, like the apologists before him, was concerned to reconcile human freedom and divine justice. "We are justified and praised on account of those things we do of our own free-will, if they are good, but if they are bad, we become guilty thereby and are reproached with them."[72]

Bardaisan professes training in astronomy, and he admits he is willing to concede that "there exists something which the Chaldaeans call Fate." In the words of Bardaisan, "not everything happens according to our will." All people want wealth, but few achieve it. Together with nature, Fate determines the events outside the realm of liberty. But Bardaisan insisted that liberty could override Fate in all moral affairs. To demonstrate the power of liberty over Fate, Bardaisan launches into a world tour of various human cultures. "The Seres [the Chinese] have laws that they shall not kill, shall not commit fornication and shall not worship idols." Among the Seres one would find that poverty and wealth, sickness and health, power and dependence "are given into the power of the Guiding Signs." But the influence of the stars stopped at the threshold of moral action. "In the whole country of the Seres there is no idol, no prostitute, no murderer and no man murdered, although they too are born at all hours and on all days. . . . Nor does Venus, when in conjunction with Mars, force any of the Serian men to have intercourse with the wife of his neighbor or with any other woman." The force of law, far from limiting human agency, demonstrates the potency of freedom.[73]

Bardaisan's innovation was to allow astral sovereignty over externals while limiting the power of the stars to the boundaries of moral freedom. *The Book of the Laws of the Countries* reveals how uncannily, and inevitably, sex was drawn to the center of debates about human freedom. For Bardaisan, the inability of the stars to predict sexual phenomena was proof positive of the limits of astrology. The Brahmans of India committed no fornication, regardless of the stars under which they were born, because such was their custom. The Persians "take their sisters, daughters, and granddaughters to wife" because it is their law. The Gelian men dressed like women, not from "effeminacy," not because "Gelian men have Mars in Ares with Venus," but "because of the law that they have." In the lands east of the Euphrates, a man accused of having sex with a boy would revenge himself for the insult; among the Germans, by contrast, boys were treated as wives. "Yet it is impossible that all those in Gaul who are guilty of this infamy should have Mercury in their nativity together with Venus in the house of Saturn, in the field of Mars and in the Western signs of the Zodiac. For regarding the men who are born under this constellation, it is written that they shall be shamefully used, as if they were women." For Bardaisan, cultural plasticity was a concomitant of human freedom. Entire cultures might be guilty of shameful acts, but they were no less worthy of divine punishment, because their acts originated in moral liberty.[74]

Despite Bardaisan's influence in Syriac Christianity, his unique synthesis of moral freedom and astral determinism was not destined to prevail. Most Christians remained allergic to admissions of astral influence. At almost the same moment the *Book of the Laws of the Countries* was redacted, Origen published his great work of systematic theology, *On First Principles.* The third book of Origen's great work was an extensive essay dedicated to the meaning of free will. Origen was committed to absolute moral freedom. It was, in his words, "the problem of single greatest urgency." His account of free will rests on the cornerstone of divine justice—on the received "ecclesiastical preaching about the just judgment of the word of God." The first condition of just judgment was that "things worthy of praise and blame are in our control." Throughout his discussion Origen demonstrated a mastery of Stoic thought and vocabulary, even as he departed from Stoicism in subtle ways. Origen, unlike Epictetus, equated freedom with the ability to *do* the things that are "under your control." When Origen argued that humans natively possess moral freedom, sex immediately presented itself as a paradigm of action. "If a woman appeared to a man who had resolved to be continent and to keep himself apart from intercourse, and she entices him to act against his resolution, her temptation will not constitute a completely sufficient cause for the abandonment of his resolution." Regardless of external temptations, the moral agent always retained the ability to choose the right or wrong course of action. The man who surrendered to pleasure chose to commit a shameful act. But another man in these same circumstances, who maintained his resolve, whose reason was "made more firm and strengthened by care," would "resist the provocation and dispel his desire." Free will was not the absence of external causation, but the capacity to act morally regardless of circumstance. In a revealing passage, Epictetus also imagined a philosopher who encounters some handsome boy or woman. If the lady summoned him, drew close to him, tempted him, but the philosopher "conquered," this sage would have solved a logic problem of the greatest magnitude. This man was the "true athlete," whose prize was "freedom." For Origen, moral liberty inhered in the capacity to choose either of two paths, the freedom to do otherwise; Origen evoked both the sinner *and* the sage to demonstrate the properties of free will. For Epictetus, freedom was the prize won by the philosophical athlete who conquered the false impressions that bombarded him.[75]

Origen's beliefs about free will quickly became entangled in his account of the soul's preexistence. But his presentation of free will would survive the shipwreck of his unorthodox cosmology, and his exegetical prowess in overcoming problematic passages of scripture was indispensable. Even Methodius, who would adamantly oppose Origen's views on eternity, unapologetically absorbs his teaching on free will. It should be no surprise to find Methodius's staunch rebuttal of fatalism in a treatise on virginity: the complete abstention from sex was a radical expression of human freedom. In the *Symposium,* Thecla offers a speech on free will that is one of the most detailed ancient Christian attacks on astrology. Methodius believed that the stars had been created posterior to mankind, so that there had been a time when people existed who could not have had a horoscope. In *On Free Will,* too, we see the close connections between free will, the problem of evil, and the nature of God's creation worked out in a manner that vindicates God's justice by ascribing free will, and the origins of evil, to mankind.

Origen's views on free will continued to prove congenial to Christians throughout the fourth century. The crucial third book of his *First Principles* is preserved in Greek precisely because it was included in the *Philocalia,* the anthology of Origen's works redacted in the middle of the fourth century. As we will see in Chapter 3, the Cappadocians fully absorbed the Christian doctrine of free will, but in the context of Christian triumph, they were also brought face-to-face with the limits of a concept of moral freedom that turned on the ability to choose an act.[76]

The fascination with fate and individual autonomy retained its purchase across the centuries of ancient Christianity, in formal philosophical literature as well as fiction. The *Philocalia* was redacted around the time that Heliodorus wrote his *Ethiopian Tale,* with its strong affirmation of high pagan fatalism. In the same period, a Christian in Syria took up the same issues in fictional form in the unwieldy mélange known as the *Clementine Recognitions.* The *Recognitions* are a Christian family romance interspersed with a harsh dose of doctrinal lecturing; Bardaisan's *Book of the Laws of Countries* has been shamelessly raided for its attacks on the doctrine of astral determinism. In the background to the narrative is a family travesty that had separated the main character, Clement, from his parents and brothers. His mother had, once upon a time, received a foreboding vision and fled from Rome with her twin sons; they vanished; the father set off in search of them; he disappeared; the third son, Clement, was left alone in the world. Clement heard the gospel from Peter himself and became a Christian. Through a series of spectacular coincidences, the long-lost members of Clement's family were gathered around the apostle and, gradually, they recognized one another. The pattern of separation, endurance, and reunion is familiar; an enigmatic divine Providence has been neatly substituted for the mixture of destiny and fate that steered the course of the Greek romance. The author of the *Recognitions* has grasped the deep structure of the romance and managed, by recalibrating a minimum of core assumptions, to create a narrative that presents a wholly new vision of the relationship between the individual, society, and the order of the cosmos. Inevitably this realignment laid new expectations on the body and its sexual capacities.[77]

The significance of that realignment is explicit in the *Recognitions.* It emerges in a long debate between the apostle Peter and a poor, elderly dockworker. The embittered old man is an obdurate fatalist. "I have learned quite well that men become murderers, adulterers, or perpetrators of other sorts of wickedness because of stellar configurations, and in the same way women who are honorable and chaste behave well because they are compelled to do so." His own wife had been born under an evil horoscope, with a configuration of Mars and Venus that "leads women to be adulteresses and lovers of their own slaves, to perish in travels and in waters." When his wife mysteriously abandoned him, he concluded that the awful destiny had materialized. Peter, in reply, offers a lengthy defense of free will; Peter admits that external agents, such as demons, encourage and intensify sin, but he insists that every human is endowed with an internal faculty of choice, free of all external causation and ultimately responsible for sin. Only a friend of Satan would "attribute to the course of the stars his own sins, which he chose deliberately and willingly." It shortly emerges that the old man is Clement's father, and his deterministic philosophy collapses in the cascade of ensuing recognitions. His wife, far from succumbing to sexual lust, had fled to save her virtue from the nefarious designs of her brother-in-law. Like a romantic heroine, her chastity was imperiled but safeguarded by her virtue. Her example proves that "a chaste mind can prevail over irrational impulses . . . and horoscopes mean nothing." She was the author of her own destiny; her sexual honor stands as a rousing vindication of free will. Once again sexual action is the truest test of individual freedom.[78]

The *Recognitions* are unusual only for the extent to which the reworking of traditional literary mechanics becomes an explicit reflection on the order of the cosmos. Christian fiction, as we will explore in Chapter 4, consciously manipulated the conventions of Greek and Roman narrative. Stories of Christian sexual austerity turned the pagan romances inside out, right down to the fatalism that is built into the very structure of the ancient novel. Sexual austerity was a symbol of absolute human freedom. Unlike the protagonists of romance, the heroes of Christian fiction are the agents of their own destiny. Their "freedom," unlike Leucippe's, is not a passive attribute, not a mysterious dispensation of the stellar lottery, nor an adjunct of social position. Christian freedom meant the power to choose one's sexual fate. It was a choice with eternal ramifications. It was a model of human agency that would not long survive the mainstreaming of the religion, as Christian leaders came to encounter, at a more intimate level, the contours of the human will and the material complications of freedom and unfreedom. But, we might imagine, the power of Christian narrative, with its stark simplicities, contributed in some way to the diffusion and triumph of the religion. And in new circumstances, when called upon, the impresarios of the Christian imagination would summon a new world of fiction, adequate to the changed position of the church in society.

CONCLUSION: A WORLD IN DISORDER

Early Christian sexuality developed within and against a society where sexual culture was immanent in social reproduction; the strict controls and the points of release in Greco-Roman sexual culture were dictated by the imperatives of reproducing a monogamous, patriarchal society. Even when Christian authors mimic the language of contemporary sexual morality, the content of their rules, and the grounding of their moral logic, departed greatly from the world surrounding them. The prohibition on fornication and the revolutionary new conception of same-sex eros were destined to break apart, forever, the old coherence of social structure and sexual morality. Even more than the sheer embrace of virginity and the devaluation of eros, the prohibition of sex beyond marriage, precisely because it could be reconciled with a reproductive social order, would come to reshape ancient erotic culture. What Christianity did share with its competition in the high empire was not so much a broader push toward austerity, nor even a public mood conducive to anxiety about the body, but a willingness to address fundamental questions about man's agency in a vast cosmos. Where Christianity comes closest to its contemporary challengers is not in the answers it offers, but in the questions it asks. The answers it offered were resolutely extreme, preaching an image of man as a radically free being, with total control over his erotic experience. Early Christian sexuality, with its unusually austere code of ethics, was nurtured by the heady cosmological speculation that enjoyed such a place in the culture of the high Roman Empire. It was a rarefied environment for a sexual morality, with distinctive notions of freedom and responsibility, to take shape.

Christians would develop an alternative scale of values, organized around sin and righteousness, and then watch, almost unexpectedly, as the population-reproducing machinery whose moral program it had rejected gradually became reabsorbed into its sexual ideology. If we are watching only texts and not the interface between texts and populations, we risk missing the tectonic shifts that rearranged the order of western sexuality. Sin, for so long the property of the world outside, would become the problem of the church, as the church and the world became coextensive. Freedom, for so long a statement about man's place in the cosmos, was a slogan that, in the aftermath of triumph, quickly became bogged in the thicker realities of the world, with, as we will see, startling ramifications.

CHAPTER THREE

Church, Society, and Sex in the Age of Triumph

THE TWILIGHT OF APOLOGETICS

As Methodius, author of the Christian *Symposium,* was being tried and martyred at Patara in June of 312, the armies of an ambitious western emperor were marching south through Italy. That emperor, Constantine, had recently experienced a celestial vision that he soon came to understand as a message from the Christian God. By the end of October his troops, with crosses painted on their shields, had destroyed his western rival and left Constantine as the sole ruler of the western provinces. Tolerance for Christianity, and then official favoritism, soon followed. In the aftermath of Constantine's conversion, a small, increasingly articulate, and highly organized spiritual movement became a powerful institution, and, more gradually, a dominant social ideology in the territories ringing the Mediterranean. Among the most unusual traits of this movement was its core commitment to sexual austerity. The choice to mark out the body and its sexual potential as a domain of moral authenticity was savvy. In the cacophonous, polyglot world of the Roman Empire, the Christian message was unmistakable. Of all the competing religions and philosophies of the late classical world, this one, with its distinctive attitude toward erotic pleasure, prevailed. The anarchic pluralism of the ancient Mediterranean would gradually recede behind the universalizing orthodoxies of that extraordinary institution, the Christian church. The world would be very different if any of the alternatives had become the preferred religion of the emperors. But as it happened, Aphrodite was to be slain by the Christians—toppled "like some debauched slave-girl."[1]

The Christians were little prepared for this eventuality. There was, to be sure, a stable and standardized packet of sexual norms carried by the religion wherever it insinuated itself: virginity was ideal, marriage acceptable, sex beyond marriage sinful, same-sex eros categorically forbidden. Beyond this zone of consensus there were peripheral aspects of sexual life where Christian regulation lacked definition and sharpness—the validity of remarriages, the measure of virginity's superiority, the exact peccability of surplus marital congress. But the main drama of late antiquity was not the gradual resolution of questions outstanding. The main drama, rather, was the absorption of society by the church, the mainstreaming of the religion. The most astonishing development of late antiquity is the transformation of a radical sexual ideology, for centuries the possession of a small, strident band of vociferous dissenters, into a culture, a broadly shared public framework of values and meanings. The Christian vision of sexual humanity, incubated in the radical air of persecution, was forced, unexpectedly, into the mold of a regulatory system. Certainly Paul, who believed that the rulers of this age were "doomed to pass away," would not have dreamed that his terse missives would become the touchstone of an entire culture.[2]

The shift from an apologetic to an imperial mode was halting and not always predictable. In sum, it meant a deeper engagement with society and with the moral entanglements of the sexual agent as a part of society. This shift is detectible already in the *Divine Institutes* of Lactantius, an apology written against the backdrop of the great persecution but a work that nevertheless points toward the new, imperial sensibility of Christian sexual ethics. Lactantius is intensely aware of the moral agent's embeddedness in the world. When he turns to consider the libido, "which must be severely repressed, because it does the most severe harm," it is a faculty tempted and threatened by the habits of the Roman world. The devil had contrived ingenious tests of the moral will and institutionalized them in Roman society.

"So that no one would have to abstain from sex with another out of fear of punishment, he established brothels and exposed the sexual modesty of unfortunate women, to the ruin of the men who use them as much as the women who are forced to suffer." To the audience that Lactantius was addressing, the brothel presented an especially diabolical source of temptation, because it removed all material impediments to the fulfillment of desire. Still the devil was not finished with his tricks. "He also joined males with males and designed unholy coitus in violation of the laws of God and nature." What most disturbed Lactantius was a shared feature of same-sex eros and prostitution: they were socially acceptable. "Among them these outrages are a light matter, virtually respectable." Lactantius still spoke, in the apologetic tradition, of depraved sexual habits among "them," the mainstream non-Christians. But the line between the Christian and the outside world has started to grow decidedly thin, and within only a few generations it will have quietly vanished.[3]

It is highly telling that the passages of the *Divine Institutes* devoted to libido are followed immediately by the presentation of Christian notions of penance. A rigorous sexual morality, if it is genuinely ambitious, will have mechanisms ready for the contingency of errant behavior. "Let no one desert or despair of himself if, overtaken by passion, driven by lust, deceived by error, or coerced by violence, he has fallen down the path of injustice." Just a few years later, after the conversion of Constantine, Lactantius issued an abbreviated second edition of the *Divine Institutes.* Indulgence is given an even wider berth. "But in fact all of these things are difficult for man, nor in this state of frailty can any be without stain. Therefore the ultimate cure is that we may take refuge in penance." The distance traveled from the time of Paul—who counseled in such searing, urgent words that sinners should be cast from the midst of the Christian assembly—is measured by the triumph of pragmatism over puritanism in the church's management of sexual sin. The elaboration of a penitential discipline that could regulate the errors of the flesh is a sure sign of Christianity's coming-of-age as a mass movement. The famous canons of Elvira, one of the earliest Christian synods, are almost precisely contemporary with the *Divine Institutes.* At this summit of Christian leaders in Spain, it was apparent that sexual discipline would be a leading preoccupation for a church quickly gathering size and strength. The canons of Elvira, like the pages of Lactantius, reflect the first stirrings of a great revolution in the boundaries of the church, in which it was transformed from a puritanical minority into an immense sexual sanatorium for all the world's sinners.[4]

The subject of this chapter is the fate of Christian attitudes toward the *aphrodisia* in the period of triumph. The purpose of this exploration is to trace the contours of that profound transformation, between the reigns of Constantine (AD 306–337) and Justinian (AD 527–565), which saw the transition of Christianity from cult to culture, and in particular to search for the zones of tension and change as Christian sexual ideology was disseminated on an ever greater scale. An investigation of such a daunting topic must necessarily be selective, and what is sought after here is the place of sexual ethics within the shifting configuration of church, state, and society. The Christian model of sexual morality, with its specific prohibitions and allowances and its distinctive logic, came to overlay an ancient and deeply entrenched culture of sexual morality rooted in the machinery of social reproduction. The church gradually absorbed that machinery, with its considerable pluralism and inherent chaos, a process that had considerable feedback effects on the shape of Christian sexual morality itself. In short, as the church was forced to accommodate itself to the world, there were both frontiers of intense conflict and peaceful assimilation, and the church's sexual ideology was reshaped by protracted war against inveterate habits as much as gradual reconciliation with the order of state and society.

The grand ascetic experiments that are such a stunning feature of late antiquity have, naturally, attracted enormous interest. Here we will deliberately look away from the monks, partly in the name of a scholarly division of labor, in the belief that absolute sexual renunciation has garnered such considerable notice already that the marginal returns will be greater elsewhere. But more profoundly, the focus on ascetic extremism threatens to produce a stilted and partial view of the Christianization of sexual culture. The ascetic extremism that originated in the desert and then hurtled itself across the Mediterranean in late antiquity was certainly the most flamboyant, but not necessarily the most consequential, front in a broader assault on eros that swept up society as a whole. An imbalanced focus on the most radical practices and institutions of sexual renunciation is liable to suggest that "the rest," the ordinary baptized Christians, formed a "silent majority" who could more or less carry on life as normal, marrying and breeding without great inconvenience from any newfound religious scruples. Such a conception of sexual culture in late antiquity, often implicit, has been quietly underwritten by the unsustainable view that Greco-Roman society was already well on the path toward sexual prudery by the time of Constantine's vision. Not only does this narrative entirely misunderstand the high erotic charge of conjugal sex in pre-Christian culture, it simply ignores the vitality and anarchy of eros in a society where the hard sexual rules were essentially economic rather than repressive. The ostentatious deprivations of the desert draw our eyes away from the main drama in late antiquity, which occurs squarely in the middle of the ancient city.[5]

Instead of approaching the Christianization of sex in the generations after Constantine as the story of a committed ascetic minority and an accommodationist "silent majority" who muddled through, it will be revealing to treat the entire Christian revolution as ascetic in spirit and anti-erotic in its intentions. By redirecting attention toward the pastoral front, we can recapture some of the fierce and unforeseen struggles that followed in the trail of religious change. This focus forces us to question the actual instruments of cultural power—such as preaching, ritual, and law—that the church could wield or hope to wield in the remaking of public sexual culture. Here we will also put more focus on Roman law, partly because there is considerable room for expansion in our basic understanding of the nature and chronology of Christian influence on the law as it came to bear on same-sex love, the marriage relationship, and above all prostitution. Moreover, there is perhaps something to be gained by a synoptic approach, for deeper patterns seem to emerge when the question of Christian influence in these separate domains of sexual life is treated as a single problem. The shifts in the law reflect deeper realignments in the order of state, society, and Christian sexual morality. The law reflects no more than the Christianization of the state, and that is a considerable limit on what exactly it is capable of saying. The expression of Christian values in state action could not be neat, because Roman law was an entire institutional order of relationships between state and society, public and private, harmonizing the circulation of property, status, and honor. Coitus was not principally the object of Roman regulation in the classical period, except insofar as it existed within a network of social transfers. Hence, classical Roman law embodied specific patriarchal sexual values, but it regulated sex principally at the moments when sex manifested itself in social transfers, in matters of property, violence, and honor. Christian sexual prejudices could not be simply projected onto Roman law, like an image on a blank screen. But in late antiquity, sex itself, by degrees and up to certain limits, becomes the object of public regulation. The most profound shift may be that in late antiquity it becomes not totally anachronistic or overreaching to talk of sexual policy.[6]

The first object of our attention must be the fate of same-sex eros in late antiquity. Given the considerable diversity that prevailed in the high empire, the Christian assault on modes of same-sex contact was sudden, violent, and total. Several developments are notable. Under the influence of Paul, the discussion of what is "natural" looms large in the period, and even more profoundly the conception of "natural" sex is reorganized around the gender of the partner rather than the role of the sexual actor; the traditional bifurcation of love between males into pederasty and passivity gives way to a monolithic conception of unnatural sexual practice. The moral demands of nature displace (or overshadow) the ancient culture of machismo, which is, with a few notable exceptions, strikingly muted in the late antique record as a method of regulating sexual life. Gradually these Christian attitudes had an influence in public law. The classical law had punished violations of freeborn boys and imposed civil disabilities on openly passive men. The late antique legislative program became progressively more violent and aggressive toward practices deemed sexually deviant. Underlying the legal developments is not only blunt hostility, but more subtly a new sense of the populace itself as the framework of sexual regulation and of homosexual acts as a contamination that was a threat to public order. The legal reforms are highly contingent, and incompletely Christian, until the reign of Justinian, who mobilized the state's energies in a sweeping campaign to eradicate same-sex eros.

Regarding the Christianization of marriage, there was much that the church could find congenial in the valorization of marriage in Greco-Roman culture. But the effort to Christianize such a central social institution was inevitably turbulent. The attempted takeover of the institution was not simply the absorption of a preexistent idealism about the relationship between husbands and wives. There were considerable frictions generated by the place of marriage, and conjugal sex, within a broader socio-legal system. The legal and demographic structures of marriage presented formidable obstacles to the Christianization of marriage. Above all, Christian ideals of sexual exclusivity, including male fidelity, were radically discordant with the patterns of life and the expectations of public culture. The war against fornication was fought parish by parish in the late ancient Mediterranean.

Fornication, once the property of the impure outside world, was an object of pastoral reform, as sermons, penitential literature, and the deepening ecclesiastical awareness of its social basis make clear. Together with the demand for sexual exclusivity came rigid insistence on the singularity of the marriage relationship, which discouraged divorce and remarriage. The Christianization of marriage was a great revolution, but it was incomplete and uncertain in late antiquity. One measure of this incomplete transition was the inability of late antique Christianity to corral the marriage rite into the church itself. Similarly, the law of marriage is an index not just of change but of the limits of change.

Finally, the relationship between free will and sexual morality presents a privileged vantage on the deep relationship between social structure and Christian sexual ethics. The high notion of absolute freedom that is so deeply embedded in early Christian thinking about sex and sin enjoyed its fullest ascendance in the aftermath of Constantine's conversion. The fourth century was the golden age of free will. But triumph brought unforeseen challenges. The early Christian notion of free will was a cosmological assertion, forged in opposition to Stoic causality, popular astrology, and gnostic determinism. In its very structure this libertarian model was premised on the separation of the church and the world, and its highest symbol was virginity, as a rejection of all exterior demands on the body. By the later fourth century, with the progressive entanglement of church and society, this model of free will came to look grossly inadequate. In the very generations when Christianity became a majority religion, its leadership was awakened to the insufficiency of the old absolutisms. Discussion of free will changed key, the older cosmological mode giving way to debates over the nature of volition and the absence of material capacities to choose. Augustine came to expound a view of divine grace and original sin that cut against centuries of Christian voluntarism. Moreover, rather suddenly some Christian bishops came to realize that their pure notions of free will were simply incompatible with the realities of life, above all with the centrality of sexual coercion in the Roman sexual economy. The sudden recognition that Christian sexual morality would have to account for those without volition over their sexual fate is a sign of the church's broader social power from the later fourth century. Most remarkably, this new anxiety led directly to a program of legal reform in which Roman emperors, from Theodosius II to Justinian, attacked coerced prostitution. The campaign against violent sexual procurement is deeply symbolic of the triumph of a Christian logic of sexual morality, rooted in sin, in the order of imperial law and public culture.[7]

A DISEASE NOT JUST OF DESIRE: SAME-SEX EROS IN LATE ANTIQUITY

In the waning years of the fourth century, an anonymous Christian lawyer assembled a small handbook juxtaposing Mosaic and Roman law, with the evident purpose of emphasizing the commonalities between them. Although the governance of sex presented inauspicious prospects for such a comparison, the author was not deterred. He presented the Levitical prohibition on same-sex coupling (in an Old Latin translation), which dictated the death penalty for both partners when "a man lies with a man as with a woman." On the Roman side of the ledger, matters were far less clear. The author of the compilation could cite two rules preserved in the late legal collection known as the *Sentences of Paul.* "Anyone who will have corrupted a free male against his will is to suffer capital punishment. Anyone who will have submitted, of his own volition, to shameful and impure violation, will be deprived of half his property." The *Sentences of Paul,* composed around AD 300, accurately reflected the foundations of classical law, which still prevailed when the author wrote his comparison of Mosaic and Roman law in the 390s. The violation of free boys was fearsomely punished, and sexual passivity incurred severe public penalties. Roman law was inspired by norms of masculinity; it guarded the impenetrability of the Roman youth and debilitated the *pathicus.* The Mosaic law sits across a conceptual divide so vast from the aims of Roman policy, and derives from a juridical regime so alien from the techniques of Roman jurisprudence, that the Christian author of this tract has made the best of a very bad job.[8]

He must have sensed it. For this unflappable compiler appended a recent enactment of the emperor Theodosius I, the only contemporary inclusion in his handbook, a decree that, in his judgment, "followed the spirit of the Mosaic Law to the fullest." In 390, Theodosius had issued a law declaring, "We cannot allow the city of Rome, the mother of all virtues, any longer to be polluted by the contaminating emasculation of men's sexual honor, and the rude vigor handed down from the ancient founders to be depleted by a people weakened in softness, becoming an insult to ages past and present."

The law explicitly punished men who suffered their bodies to be used like the flesh of women, but the focus of imperial energy was specific and revealing. "Having dragged out all—it is embarrassing to say—from the male brothels, let the flames of vengeance expiate their crime with the populace watching, so everyone will know that the soul of a man is to be treated by all as an inviolable precinct." Such florid effusions are characteristic of late imperial statecraft. But the public incineration of the male prostitutes of Rome is almost totally unaccountable in terms of ordinary Roman policy.[9]

Opinion has been divided about the judgment of the author who included a copy of this law in his comparison of Mosaic and Roman jurisprudence. Was the spirit of the Theodosian constitution, indeed, akin to religious injunctions against same-sex love, or was the compiler overreaching in his effort to bend the law into a point of contact between the "spirit of Moses" and the Roman state? In other words, was the Theodosian measure inspired by religious homophobia, or by the immemorial ideals of Roman manhood? On the one hand, the attack came at a moment pregnant with change, as Theodosius I was transforming the Roman state into a Christian one, and the official conflagration of a whole class of sexual outcasts was uncharacteristic of Roman jurisprudence. On the other hand, the language of the law could not possibly be more emphatic about its roots in Roman tradition, and it would be a dodge to explain this rhetoric as a cloak for a clandestine Christian agenda. The official who actually drafted the language of the law was, in fact, one of the most visible pagans around the court. But most tellingly, the object of regulation was sexual passivity, and in the form of public prostitution. The categories of regulation are fundamentally, undeniably Roman.[10]

The chemistry of the Theodosian measure was complex, and it simply cannot be broken down into discrete proportions of the constituent elements, classical masculinity and unfamiliar malevolence. The law raises the most profound questions about the passage from an ancient legal and cultural regime, whose protocols required men to play the dominant role in sexual encounters, to a legal and cultural regime that treated the gender of the participants as the primary fact of any sexual conjunction. The gradual transition from a classical to a Christian regulatory system produced many complex harmonies along the way, of which the law of 390 is a signal example. It can only be explained by considering the maturation of Christian attitudes toward same-sex eros. In late antiquity Christian opposition to same-sex love developed far beyond the brief, violent injunctions of the scriptural tradition that ascribed the habits of same-sex eroticism to the fallen confusion of polytheistic cultures. The eradication of sexual sin became the object of a nascent penitential discipline; simultaneously, same-sex love became pathologized to an unprecedented degree, spoken of as a disease that threatened to contaminate the body politic. Indeed, a new concern for the sexual behavior of the populace as such grows up in the fourth century. At the same time, the process of legal change cannot be understood apart from the specific mechanisms and traditions of regulation in Roman law, the place of prostitution in the public order, and the subtle institutional shifts in late antiquity that enabled more aggressive attempts at the legal control of sexual morality. In short, a host of much broader changes within Christianity and within the state converged to ignite the awful blaze of 390.[11]

As the church was transformed from a persecuted minority into a triumphant majority, its preaching on same-sex eros found a broader audience than ever before. But the energy directed against same-sex love, so far as the surviving homiletic and penitential literature is representative, was minuscule compared to the massive mobilization of force against forms of illicit heterosexual contact. In the canons of Elvira, from the first decade of the fourth century, sexuality is the dominant theme of the church's regulatory impulses. Of the dozens of canons that in some way lay down definite prescriptions for sexual sin, adultery and fornication receive the lion's share of the attention. Love between males is addressed exactly once. "Any who shamefully violate boys are not to receive communion, even as they near their demise." This rule is a transcription of the older apostolic command against "the violation of children," *paidophthoria,* but now it is attached to a penitential regime—in fact, unlike most forms of sexual deviance, this sin is placed explicitly beyond the possibility of return to communion. Nowhere in the canons of Elvira is male sexual passivity or lesbianism compassed. The canons of Elvira in fact foreshadow the way that sexual passivity will be so far beyond the pale that it often did not require comment, even in the late antique church.[12]

The broadening of the penitential regime of the church in late antiquity is a sign of the mainstreaming of the religion. As the church became a sacramental dispenser on a mass scale, it generated a need to manage sinners like never before. Though no one will mistake the late antique church for its powerful late medieval successor, the elaboration of rules for the administration of baptism and communion reflects the nascent influence of ecclesiastical structures in private life. The *Apostolic Constitutions,* an important collection of church canons redacted in the later fourth century, reflect this expansion. The *Apostolic Constitutions* are especially revealing because the collection preserves multiple layers of canonical tradition. In book 7, we find a lightly reworked presentation of the primitive *Didache,* whose bare injunction against the corruption of children has been modestly elaborated. "Do not violate children, for contrary to nature is the evil born at Sodom, which was laid waste by the fire of God." A rule deriving from a slightly later tradition uses the "sin of the Sodomites" as a synecdoche for all same-sex intercourse, which is grouped with bestiality as a violation of nature. The latest stratum in the *Apostolic Constitutions* does not just prohibit various sexual practices but addresses how the bishop must react when confronted with sinners seeking entry to the church. "The doer of unspeakable deeds, the *kinaidos,* and the debauched," along with miscellaneous rogues like magicians and astrologers, might be admitted to baptism, but not at first. They were to be "scrutinized for some time." *Dokimasia,* "the Scrutiny," was the same word once used to describe the ethical inspection of ancient Athenian citizens, but it has now been adopted by the church, which was willing to rely on the moral espionage of rumor in a face-to-face society. The church's sexual expectations were far more strict, and its ambitions of control reached deeper into the soul, than the institutions of the ancient polis had ever imagined. Former sinners were to be watched so carefully because "such evil is so hard to wash out."[13]

Though the baptismal candidate was given a broad moral entry exam, the sins of the initiate were continually monitored, and over the fourth century a penitential regime began to achieve some measure of universal consistency. An accommodation with sin is noticeable. The canons from Elvira had denied communion to the violator of boys, even to the point of death. But by the second half of the fourth century, forgiveness was placed within reach. In his canonical letters, the bishop Basil of Caesarea prescribed fifteen years of excommunication for anyone guilty of adultery, bestiality, or "shameful acts with males." Gregory of Nyssa applied the same grid of punishment, subjecting those guilty of adultery, bestiality, or "pederasty" to eighteen years of excommunication, though he allotted the bishop discretion to shorten the punishment. Episcopal oversight was the lynchpin of a therapeutic regime for the sick sinner. Penance was "the common cure for the raging desire after such pleasures, to purify the man through repentance." Gregory's letter also offers a rare insight into the informal systems of surveillance behind the nascent penitential system. A man who became his own accuser might be treated leniently, because confession was a sign of contrition. But the sinner who was "detected in his wickedness, or unwillingly called out through some suspicion or accusation," was shown no mercy. The church was not yet a fully organized confessional machine, designed to reach inside the souls of its wards, but we might imagine that "suspicion" and "accusation" had, in their own ways, an insidious reach.[14]

Gregory's canonical letter hints at one of the principal developments in the church's understanding of same-sex desire in late antiquity. Pederasty and bestiality were grouped with adultery, Gregory explains, because these two sins were "an adulteration of nature." Same-sex love was a crime "against nature." It is hard to appreciate just how comprehensive was the triumph of a particular understanding of "nature" in the morality of sex. In late antiquity "natural" sex came to mean, exclusively, the one configuration of body parts that has generative potential. This transformation drove a profound shift in the idiom of sexual deviance. One casualty of this shift is the gradual obsolescence of the term *kinaidos/cinaedus,* a word that appears in a handful of fourth-century texts and thereafter declines. Once an indispensable monster of sexual deviance, who condensed a whole array of stereotypes rooted in ancient assumptions about manliness and the body, the *kinaidos* gradually became unnecessary, as the thought-world that called him into existence crumbled around him. Perhaps even more surprising, much of the Pauline idiom of sexuality simply vanishes too. The words connoting same-sex love in his vice lists quietly disappear. The term *arsenokoitēs* is virtually nonexistent in late antique texts, and even *malakia* has somewhat more limited traction in the post-Constantinian world.[15]

In place of these older vocabularies, Paul's Letter to the Romans would come to act as a land bridge between Christian ideologies and Greco-Roman discourses of sex. The language of "nature" displaced a preexisting idiom, gathering a fragmentary lexicon around its homogenizing force. It is easy to miss the radicalism of this revolution, because the idea of "nature" had for centuries already formed an important sanction of sexual moralizing. In pre-Christian sources, though, "natural" sex was sex that mirrored the social hierarchy, above all when the free male was the penetrator. In the dream interpretation of Artemidorus, to cite just one example, sex "according to nature" aligned the masculine partner with the insertive role: it was as natural to penetrate one's wife as one's male slaves. "Unnatural" sex included lesbianism, necrophilia, and bestiality. There is one strikingly important exception to this universal pattern, the first-century Stoic Musonius Rufus. In his discourse on the *aphrodisia,* he claimed that sex between "males" was as indulgent as adultery, because it was "a provocation against nature." His classification of sex according to the gender of the partners would have been at home in Christian moralizing. But the comments of Musonius stand alone in the world of Greco-Roman ethics, and even within his own diatribe the thought is fleeting. His opposition to same-sex love occupies exactly one line of text.[16]

In late antiquity the discourse of nature was harnessed by movement with a highly motivated opposition to same-sex love. The early stirrings of such a concept of nature should not be allowed to obscure the fact that in the late classical world this change in quantity becomes a change in quality. Setting matters. Musonius spoke to a circle of Young Turks, children of the establishment enchanted for a season by the eccentric philosopher's moral authenticity. In late antiquity we are in the basilica, where men and women of startlingly divergent status gathered to receive moral lectures. And rather than the passing glances of an eccentric philosopher, we find same-sex love the object of dedicated pastoral ire. Christian preachers like John Chrysostom might dilate on the sinfulness of same-sex desire, indifferent to any distinctions between pederasty, the exploitation of slaves, or even durable forms of companionship. Rooted in Pauline scripture, Chrysostom's own preaching on same-sex eros is such a spasm of hatred that its logic is not always recoverable. His caustic fourth homily on the Letter to the Romans, possibly a specimen of extemporaneous moralizing, evokes the atmosphere of intense hostility that prevailed in late antique churches. "Look how vividly he [Paul] chooses his words. He did not say they desired or lusted after one another, but burned in their longing for each other. Now, is not all desire born of greed which fails to adhere to its own limits? For all desire exceeding the laws set down by God is desire for what is strange, and not what has been allowed." The reach of Chrysostom's claims are startling. Musonius fixed on same-sex "intercourse" as an act against nature; so would most Christian moralists. But on occasion a sense of illicit, abnormal *desire* begins to find expression. Pre-Christian ideologies treated sexual deviance, even deviance involving same-sex attraction, as a matter of excessive desire and insufficient manliness; there was no "queer desire," only desire overflowing its proper bounds. In Chrysostom we see how the logic of excess begins to give way to a sense that this excessive desire was, in its very essence, strange.[17]

Chrysostom speaks of same-sex eros as a pathology. "All passions are without honor, but especially the madness for males. The soul suffers more in the disgrace of these sins than the body does in disease." The books of the philosophers are "full of this disease." But tellingly, for Chrysostom, same-sex love is not *only* a disease whose origins lie in deviant desires of the soul. "Do not think, because you have heard him say 'they burned,' that this is a disease of desire only. In fact it comes more from their state of dissolution, which kindled their lust." Chrysostom's etiology of same-sex love, then, is complex. It does not rest purely on an improper *kind* of lust, nor an *excessive* amount of it, but a virulent synthesis of the two. He compares the man who enjoys same-sex love with a person who is titillated by smearing himself with sewage and running naked through the streets: strange desire *and* lack of control combine to produce the deviant. In Chrysostom's harangues, there is no sense that sexual deviance is inborn, but it could certainly become physiologically embedded. If a virgin was sentenced to sexual debasement with animals, he said, but then came to enjoy it, she was lamentably in thrall to a "disease." In other words, Chrysostom's sexual pathology imagines an escalating feedback loop between act and desire, body and soul. "With this sin, the soul is ruined by the body. Whatever sin you might name, you can utter none equal to this in lawlessness. If those who suffer from it realized their sin, they would accept ten thousand deaths rather than suffer it."[18]

Just as important as the incipient pathology of desire is the primary term that has, quietly, dropped out of the equation in the late antique sources: masculinity. Dio Chrysostom, for example, compared "androgyny" to a progressive disease that gradually wasted a man's nature, leaving him effeminate in manner and sexual predilection. Pre-Christian concepts of erotic misuse were embedded in a well-established order of thought about manliness. Gender deviance and sexual deviance were an ideological pair, their causes and effects—and outward signs—deeply intermeshed. The Christian moralists have excised the concern with gender deviance to focus on sexual deviance. And their moral anxieties are inserted within a different scale of values, one more fundamentally concerned about sin and salvation than secular honor.[19]

It is unsurprising, then, that Christian hostility toward love between males could not be easily reconciled with an ancient regulatory system organized around masculinity. In classical Roman law, there were two points of intersection between public regulation and same-sex eros. First, the man who violated a freeborn boy was guilty of *stuprum*—criminal violation. Pederastic culture in the Roman Empire accordingly came to depend on the objectification of the slave's body as a zone of free access. Second, the man who voluntarily submitted his body to sexual penetration, to "womanly use," also faced dishonor, disability, and punishment. Both the violation of freeborn boys and male sexual passivity seem to have been criminalized by a shadowy enactment known as the *lex Scantinia,* a law in force at least by the age of Cicero. The law's obscurity—it is mentioned but a handful of times and left virtually no mark in the extant codifications of Roman law—is matched by its longevity, for it is described as a law in vigor from the first century BC to the fourth century AD. As a result, the law has occasioned no little controversy in modern scholarship. Its mysterious nature is not so much a problem to be overcome by sifting for just the right clues, as it is in and of itself the explanandum. In other words, the very obscurity of the classical rules is an important part of the story about the way the Romans regulated sex.[20]

The explanation for such obscurity lies in the nature and long-term development of Roman institutions. For most of republican history, *stuprum* was a private matter. The *lex Scantinia* first made *stuprum* committed against free boys into a public crime. The most unambiguous evidence is in fact late antique; the Christian poet Prudentius—a legal advocate, twice provincial governor, and presumably in the know as far as the law was concerned—noted that Zeus would have been culpable under the *lex Scantinia,* an allusion to his habit of abducting boys. The *lex Scantinia* was an early law that preceded by at least two generations the great *lex Iulia de adulteriis coercendis.* In some sense the *lex Scantinia* was to be swallowed up by the extraordinary creation of the *lex Iulia,* the pillar of the reforms enacted by the first emperor, Augustus. The *lex Iulia* was destined to become the bulwark of Roman sexual policy. The repression of adultery dominates the surviving legal commentaries, even clouding from view the regulation of same-sex intercourse. Adultery was clearly the focus of the *lex Iulia,* although *stuprum* committed against virgins and widows—in short, all respectable women—came under its purview. At some point in the empire, the criminalization of *stuprum* with a boy was integrated within its reach, and much of the extant commentary on the punishments for violating boys survives in commentaries on the *lex Iulia*.[21]

The magnetic force of the *lex Iulia,* as the centerpiece of Roman sexual regulation, partly accounts for the diminished role of the *lex Scantinia* in the protection of free boys. The more subtle, and perhaps more important, force driving the law toward obsolescence was the broad power of Roman magistrates and provincial governors to punish *iniuria,* private injuries. It is telling that, in the *Sentences of Paul,* the most detailed discussion of *stuprum* against boys appears in the section on injuries. The *Sentences of Paul* also provides the most important indication that the boy's age was part of the issue, for it specifically names the *puer praetextatus,* a boy up to fifteen or so, as the object of protection. The penalties envisioned by this late text are severe, clearly late classical if not postclassical. "If the flagitious deed is accomplished, the punishment is capital, if incomplete, deportation to an island." What is most significant about the progressive expansion of the governor's ability to punish *stuprum* against boys under the umbrella of *iniuria* is that it underscores the continued role of private protections in the regulation of sex. The punishment of *iniuria* provided public procedures and penalties for the redress of private wrongs. The most intense fields of force in the regulation of sex in the ancient world were, by technological necessity, private in nature. The punishment of *iniuria* was the intersection of public and private, reliant on self-help rather than surveillance and prosecution. The punishment of *iniuria* progressively crowded out the public criminalization of *stuprum* against free boys.[22]

Far more complex, however, is the treatment of sexual passivity in Roman law. The *lex Scantinia* had also laid down penalties for men who voluntarily submitted to penetration. A range of literary sources, in particular Juvenal and Ausonius, leave no doubt on this point. But again, lacking help from the legal corpora, we are largely in the dark about the law's scope and application. In this case obscurity is not to be ascribed to the large shadow of the *lex Iulia* and the creeping influence of *iniuria,* but rather to the inherent limits of Roman institutions. The *lex Scantinia*, the sources agree, was fearsome in the penalties it laid down. The *Sentences of Paul* describes the penalties for sexual passivity around AD 300. "Whoever of his own volition submits to flagitious and impure violation will be deprived of half of his property, nor is he allowed to make a testament disposing of a greater portion of his estate." This information is transmitted under the text's section on the *lex Iulia.* It has been argued, not unreasonably, that the *lex Scantinia* established criminal penalties for male sexual receptivity, possibly a fixed fine, which the *lex Iulia* modified with a sliding scale. All we can say is that from the early to the late empire the *lex Scantinia* is spoken of as a rule not quite in desuetude but never energetically applied. It was a legal *loup-garou,* haunting enough, even if verified sightings were rare.[23]

The economic punishments of the *lex Scantinia* were, in fact, probably not the most effective or worrisome legal impositions faced by men who played the passive role in sex. Men who "submitted to the female role" were stigmatized by the civil disabilities of *infamia,* official disrepute. The concept of *infamia* truly places us at the vital interface of social reputation and public order. In the early days of Rome, in an agrarian, militaristic society, it is likely that the censors who controlled access to voting and to public office could strike men guilty of sexual deviance from the ranks of the eligible. Censorian *infamia,* this primitive maintenance of the circle of honor, can be pieced together only from later clues because it disappeared, ineluctably, with the transformation of Roman society into a vast, urbanized, civilian society. But the use of *infamia* survived into the imperial period. Never a perfectly systematic concept, *infamia* entailed civil disabilities, especially limits on the ability to hold office or to access public legal remedies. If we judge simply by the legal debris that survive in the late codifications of Roman law, *infamia* appears to have relatively little bite. In fact, the only specific disability that we can be sure was applied to men who willingly submitted to sexual penetration was the ineligibility to apply to a public magistrate on *someone else's* behalf. This deprivation may have be an ominous sign of other incapacities, but it is not in itself the most insidious form of stigmatization ever contrived.[24]

The dispositions against male sexual passivity in the classical law are strikingly few and general. They reflect enormous prejudice, but it is an abstract prejudice, giving little sense of how the law might actually have impinged on the lives of its subjects. The forms of legal discrimination against men who "used their bodies like women" in the high Roman Empire have rightly been described as ad hoc. They came into play reactively, and "there were never any witch-hunts." This is not to trivialize the viciousness of social prejudice, but rather to emphasize the limits of legal technology to regulate sex. "Legislation was never the main source of social coercion in the massive institution of Roman law, which relied heavily on custom, family self-supervision based on the power of the *paterfamilias,* and civil rather than criminal process." Modern observers have been rightly curious how a man could "be *proven* to have been penetrated unless there were eye-witnesses to the act, or the man himself confessed it." The occasional, bloodless rules that we glimpse in the lofty edifice of the classical law seem abstract and distant from what happened on the ground, in the towns and villages of an empire where there abided vicious prejudices against sexual passivity.[25]

To turn away from the abstraction and formalism of the classical law, we might explore the neglected testimony of a late antique lawyer: Firmicus Maternus. Writing in Sicily during the age of Constantine, Firmicus abandoned the bar and turned to the science of astronomy. He penned a remarkable astrological treatise in Latin, the *Mathesis,* whose social assumptions offer unexpected insights into the intersection of sexual life and public order. Firmicus has occasionally been summoned to speak about the history of sexuality, but usually to testify on the question that has most consumed modern scholars: whether or not there was a concept of sexual orientation in the ancient world. Firmicus has been in fact a chief witness, because his star charts assume that the universe will compose humans with definite, and often deviant, sexual morphologies. (Indeed, *cinaedi* appear in nearly fifty astral configurations.) But Firmicus has more to offer to the student of ancient sexual life. He imagines wildly different fates befalling *cinaedi.* In no less than seven horoscopes, the *cinaedi* are *publici*—male prostitutes. The same stellar arrangement makes "public *cinaedi*" of men and "whores" of women. In three birth charts, Firmicus foresees that *cinaedi* will be branded with public *infamia.* But in five cases the stars will make *latentes cinaedi*—*cinaedi* in the closet; one chart predicts the *cinaedus* will actually attain high honors and conspicuous office. What the *Mathesis* suddenly reveals is a society where sexual privacy is a high-stakes problem. Much can be hidden behind the screen of the household, but much can be known, too. Most notable of all, the life of the *cinaedus* is frequently assimilated to prostitution or marked by *infamia.* For Firmicus, damnation to official disrepute is a real and present danger.[26]

Although Firmicus, like many of his generation, would be swept up by the winds of change and convert to Christianity, his *Mathesis* evokes a world that is distinctly late classical in its outlook and its familiar cast of sexual types. Like Firmicus, the only extant law of the Constantinian dynasty that approaches the problem of same-sex love is in fact closer to the spirit and motivation of ancient machismo than Christian moralism. An important imperial constitution of AD 342, issued by the chancery of Constantine's son Constans, is so florid that its precise content has been the object of much speculation. "When a man couples in the manner of a woman, that is, as a woman who will have granted men what they want, when sex has lost its place, when there is a crime it is best not to know, when *venus* is changed into another form, when love is sought but not seen, we command the laws to rise up and justice to be armed with an avenging sword, so that those infamous persons who are or will be guilty shall be subjected to exquisite penalties." Questions immediately arise. Does "couple" *(nubit)* here mean "marry" or does it imply the physical act of copulation? At stake is the precise aim of the law. The law of Constans has sometimes been seen as a reaction against "gay marriage." But this view is unlikely. Marriage between men, mentioned in a handful of imperial sources, received no legal recognition and entailed no legal effects, so juridically there was no legal marriage to regulate or prohibit. Instead "coupling" has been taken in a purely sexual sense, which is suggested by the parallel clauses of the law. The enactment stands as a grandiloquent, sneering attack on male sexual passivity. The measure of Constans proposes, ominously, "exquisite penalties" where the *Sentences of Paul* had envisioned a fine. The violent punishment of sexual deviance makes the law something of a landmark, if one obscured by the haze of its bilious rhetoric.[27]

The author of the comparison between Roman and Mosaic law does not mention this enactment, which he may well not have had at his disposal. It would not have helped his case anyhow, because the law is an inspired defense of old-fashioned virility. The conservative idiom of the law of Constans is the one thing truly beyond dispute. It is about the *vir,* the man, who abandons his role. The ominous penalties were directed against *infames,* men whose official reputation was impaired by their sexual deviance. If the language and categories of the law are regarded seriously, its motivation must have been the enforcement of old-fashioned sex roles. The rhetorical flourishes, the judicial savagery, the greater zeal in the direct enforcement of morality are all broadly characteristic of late antique statecraft, and not necessarily tied to religious change. In combination with the traditional hatred of male passivity, these would be sufficient to explain the outburst of Constans.[28]

The contrasts with the law of 390 are telling. The measure of Theodosius I ordering the incineration of the male prostitutes in Rome also deployed a vocabulary of Roman manhood that would have been not unfamiliar to Cicero. And though the measure of Theodosius was aimed against male prostitutes and thus might seem more narrowly constructed, there is good reason to regard it as a more portentous enactment. The immolation of male prostitutes was not a vice-squad operation. As Firmicus shows, there was a tendency to assimilate open sexual passivity, *infamia,* and prostitution. Similarly, John Chrysostom slips inadvertently between discussion of same-sex eros and same-sex prostitution. The mental association was imponderably ancient. The incineration of male prostitutes was a malevolent and symbolic act, which might be seen as something like a proxy measure against male passivity altogether, conducted within the technological means of the Roman state.[29]

With Theodosius I's enactment, a state that had refrained from "witch hunts" was now explicitly trying to eradicate the "contamination" of sexual passivity. The sense of sexual deviance as a disease threatening to infect the body politic is subtly but ominously new in the legislative domain. This sensibility rests on the assumption, not indigenous to Roman legal tradition, that the people itself risked pollution by irregular sexual practices. The law is emphatic on this point. The drafter enunciates a concern that the *plebs* will become weakened if defiled. The holocaust was meant to be executed "with the *populus* watching." This language reflects a new style of social solidarity in late antiquity, in which the sexual behavior of "the people" might be the object of imperial concern. In earlier phases of Roman history, enormous social prejudice in combination with rigid stratification of rank and citizenship allowed the state to stare past the inconsequential lives beneath its field of vision. Christianity carried with it a sense of "the people" not only as a civic category but as the human collective itself. This solidarity, in the field of sexual regulation, had unintended and at times violent consequences.

The remarkable sexual persecution of 390 was further enabled by a very real sense of sexual deviance as a *contaminatio.* The conception of grave sexual crime as a sort of pollution made it an acute public worry. John Chrysostom spoke of same-sex eros as a "grievous and incurable disease," and even more consequentially as a "plague harsher than all other plagues." The pagan Libanius, too, spoke of "love for males" as a disease, so the purchase of this idea extended beyond Christian circles in late antiquity. Christian voices uttered not only the diagnosis but also, more grimly, the need for a drastic cure. "Those who do these things are worthy of death, and not only those who do them, but also those who consent. For assent is participation. . . . Therefore Moses recalled the wicked deeds of Sodom and Gomorrah, and did not leave their end in silence, but to create fear of this thing to be avoided. Thus, this vice, this contamination of a life without decency is not allowed by one whose soul is thinking of God. There are those, to be sure, who believe that they are not guilty if they do not perform such deeds, even while they assent to their performance. But to remain quiet or to take amusement at the report of such things, when they should be condemned, amounts to assenting to them."[30]

These are the words of a Christian theologian, writing in Rome, in the years just before the constitution of Theodosius I. The linguistic overlap was not circumstantial. Only a few years after the law of Theodosius, in Rufinus's translation of Origen's commentary on Paul's Letter to the Romans, the question is posed whether more glory was accrued by those who had abstained from same-sex intercourse under the explicit command of the Mosaic Law or those who had abstained "from this contagion by the judgment of their own mind, not even letting their thoughts approach it. Would you not much prefer the one who, not because held back by the intervention of a law, still kept himself pure from the contamination of such flagitious deeds?" Only a little later still, Augustine could describe same-sex love as "against nature" and "without doubt more flagitious and disgraceful" than even sinful heterosexual conjunctions. The linguistic similarities are not just striking incidences of a shared, finite vocabulary. They represent a phase of mental rapprochement between traditional and Christian modes of prejudice, one in which Christian authors gravitated toward a traditional vocabulary, even as they infused it with a new spirit. The law of 390 was generated out of the same unstable mixture. The Christianization of public sexual morality produced new and often unpredictable harmonies, but there is no mistaking the fact that the shrillest notes came from the ecclesiastical side of the choir.[31]

Between the Theodosian crusade against male prostitution and the reign of Justinian, there are no imperial measures bearing on same-sex erotics.

But in 438 the court of Theodosius II completed the milestone of legal codification known as the Theodosian Code. Its editors were empowered to include all "general" laws promulgated since the time of Constantine, catalogued in orderly fashion, with all extraneous rhetoric excised. From January of AD 439, the laws as they stood in the code, in chronological order and whittled down to their legal core, were in force. Both the law of Constans and the law of AD 390 were included in the title of the Theodosian Code on the *lex Iulia de adulteriis.* That classification is remarkably significant. It reveals the extent to which the umbrella of the *lex Iulia* had become the utterly dominant locus of sexual regulation. More importantly, it suggests the extent to which the editors of the Code wished to maximize the scope of the law against male prostitution. Thanks to the handiwork of the Christian jurist who transmitted the law of Theodosius in the *Collatio,* we have a relatively rare opportunity to assess the legal surgery performed by the Theodosian editors. If the measure was originally about male prostitution, then it would be more accurate to describe the editors' work as a decapitation. There is no mention of the "male brothels," only the raving attack on male passivity, to be punished with "the avenging flames." The editors of the Code, intelligent Christian jurists who knew precisely what they were doing, made the law of 390 into a blustering prohibition on male passivity itself. This redaction was doubly significant, because the Theodosian Code was a fundamental source of law in the early medieval west. The editors left no doubt that men playing the passive role in intercourse risked grave physical punishments.[32]

If the Theodosian program can be described as a mix of Christian enthusiasm and novel conceptions of public contamination poured into traditional regulatory channels, it is only in the age of Justinian that a wholly transformed legal order, fully consonant with Christian sexual ideology, can be found. Two regulatory innovations are notable. First, the imponderably ancient distinction between active and passive has unceremoniously vanished as a regulatory paradigm. The *Institutes,* the textbook of Roman law issued as part of Justinian's codification, baldly declared that the *lex Iulia de adulteriis coercendis* "punished with the sword not only the violators of others' marriages but also those who dare to carry out their unspeakable libido with males." Without fuss or detail, Justinian laid down the death penalty for forms of sexual exercise that had been private and permitted since time immemorial. The attribution of the crime to an "unspeakable libido" places the law in the avant-garde of Christian thought, where the notion of a specifically deviant form of desire remained inchoate. Most of all the law represents the fulfillment of a Pauline view of same-sex love in Roman law (though there is not to be found in Justinian's legislation any awareness of female homoeroticism as a problem capable of regulation). Now the gender of the partners was the primary determinant, capable of activating the punitive machinery of the Roman state. The traditional media of Roman regulation—property transfers, judicial access, public honor—have been fully displaced by a stark willingness to dictate sexual behavior as such.[33]

The strict criminalization of same-sex love strikes us as a momentous innovation. But Justinian's regulatory ambitions outreached the technologies of surveillance, and very little in fact is heard of his blanket prohibitions on intercourse between males. Instead it was another aspect of Justinian's sexual reforms that flared into a massive public operation. In the very first years of his reign, Justinian enacted a law specifically aimed at pederasty. Details of the law, and its application, are preserved only by the historians, principally Procopius and John Malalas. Malalas relates that Justinian arrested two bishops accused of "living badly and bedding males." He identifies them by name, Isaiah of Rhodes and Alexander from Diospolis in Thrace. Tried by the prefect of Constantinople, Isaiah was "gravely tortured" and sent into exile, while Alexander was relieved of his male organ and paraded through the streets of Constantinople. According to Malalas, their behavior incited Justinian to pass a law that "those discovered in pederasty were to have their penises amputated." "At that time many men inclined toward males were rounded up and, after their members were cut off, died." Procopius, whose *Secret History* is a salacious and highly skewed memoir of Justinian's reign, describes the affair with patent disgust, as an example of Justinian's extremism. His account provides two details absent in Malalas—that the charges could be applied retroactively, and that even slaves could make an accusation—which we simply cannot check against other contemporary informants. They are in the spirit of the measure.[34]

It is worth considering why Justinian's crusade against pederasty has left traces in the historical record, whereas the criminalization of same-sex love enters the annals of jurisprudence with scarcely a whimper. In part the answer may lie in the continuing vitality of pederastic practices. In the fourth century, Libanius and John Chrysostom speak, with disgust, of pederasty as a lively contemporary institution. But they are perhaps the last observers to do so, and it is hard to imagine that pederasty—for so long legally confined to the bodies of slaves, now relentlessly attacked by ecclesiastical hectoring—had much of its old public acceptance, much less open advocacy, by the time of Justinian. But in a world that expected sexual attraction toward smooth bodies, that sequestered its women, and that nourished institutions like the schools and monasteries where male companionship was fostered, it was not an unlikely occurrence. The intense violence of Justinian's campaign reflects both the importance of pederasty as a social practice and its flagrant offensiveness to a Christian emperor, for whom it was an insufferable blazon of errant, bygone cultures. The spectacular mutilation mandated by the law presages the more lurid strains of the Byzantine penal code, and it testifies to the belief that terror could go where surveillance might not. According to Malalas, the strategy worked. "And a great fear followed among those diseased with lust for males."[35]

The violent repression of same-sex love dates to the ambitious early years of Justinian's reign. It was the dramatic and decisive policy of a zealous emperor bent on rebuilding the Roman Empire, without time or tears for those who risked the favor of God. The enterprise of reconquest, of course, was to collapse, crumbling of its own overweening ambition and the unforeseeable advent of plague. The later legislation of Justinian bears the darkened mood of political disappointment and desperate suffering. A law issued sometime in the years after the appearance of the bubonic plague reflects the utterly transformed atmosphere. The law is motivated by the fear of God, whose displeasure manifested itself in the famines, earthquakes, and pestilence that had struck so inexplicably. It is written in the language of sin and salvation. Justinian, as legislator, considered the "sins" against nature within his regulatory remit. The prefect was charged to take care lest these sins lead to the destruction of the "city and the polity." Another law, composed toward the end of Justinian's reign, represents a complete union of Christian ideology, state power, and ecclesiastical ambition. In response to terrible earthquakes, Justinian came to believe that God was angry at the sins of man, with special anger reserved for the grievous impiety of sex between men. If proof were needed, he pointed to the fires of Sodom, which smoldered "up to the present time." What God wanted, even more than the destruction of sinners, was their repentance. Justinian commanded that all guilty of such sin immediately repent. They were to take themselves to the patriarch of Constantinople, undergoing penance as a "therapy for their disease." The prefect was to encourage penitence, but any who failed to submit themselves faced "atrocious penalties." To allow sin to abide was to invite "the good God to destroy us all."[36]

The late measures of Justinian are truly the end of a late antique trajectory. In Justinian's reign the legal regime has become fully consonant with a cultural system that organized sexual morality first and foremost around the gender of the participants. The conception of same-sex desire as a disease, susceptible to ecclesiastical therapy, has come to be embodied in imperial law. Justinian's policies presume a powerful religio-juridical complex. The state, with its monopoly of violence, is used to control and enforce private morality directly. The reign of Justinian marks a terminal point where sin and salvation, rather than shame and reputation, have come to form the dominant axis of public regulation.

SANCTIFYING SEX: VIRGINITY, MARRIAGE, AND FORNICATION

At nearly the exact same moment when a Christian set out to demonstrate the essential similarities between Roman and Mosaic law, one of his coreligionists, probably in Rome, published an imaginary philosophical conversation between a pagan philosopher and a Christian. Their dialogue, spread over three days, ranged widely across the accumulated doctrine of the Christian church, and it included a long disquisition on the Christian "mode of living." The Christian speaker was an advocate of the monastic life. Within his lifetime, ascetic ideas had swept across the Mediterranean, from east to west, and in their trail came organized asceticism. The dialogue, the *Consultationes Zacchei christiani et Apollonii philosophi,* appeared at a moment of intense and fateful reckoning in the western empire; against the backdrop of the Theodosian dynasty, which gave such great impetus to mass conversion, the vogue of complete sexual renunciation was an unstable element. The *Consultationes* is a studiously moderate document. The married Christian might never hope to shine as brightly as "the most brilliant stars" in the kingdom of heaven—that is, the virgins. But the possibility of moral decency was not to be denied to the married householders who were the foundation of the church. "Honorable marriages are not displeasing to God, nor is a sober love for the dignified marriage couch in the procreation of children." The salvation of the married was not in any special doubt. As baptized Christians, they were heirs to the "promise of everlasting life." The author's language echoes the idiom of late Roman status: the ordinary married Christians were the *mediocres,* those of middling attainment, while the monks were *clarissimi,* the most brilliant. Lay householders could be fine citizens of the city of God, but those who had renounced the flesh altogether formed its spiritual aristocracy.[37]

The *Consultationes* is valuable because it is an unremarkable artifact, one of any number of late antique texts that simultaneously laud virginity while salvaging dignity for the married life. The *Consultationes* appeared at a moment that called forth some of the most remarkable reflection on the place of sex within Christian society. In the span of about two decades, western churchmen were to produce a body of literature on sex and marriage that would define the Latin Christian tradition for the next thousand years. The proximate cause of this great outpouring was the brazen doctrine of a Christian teacher named Jovinian, who began to argue, amid the spreading fashion of ascetic extremism, that virginity accrued no special merit to its practitioners, that married and virginal Christians were capable of achieving equal virtue. His teaching touched a deep nerve in Roman society, for he at once gave voice to a certain resentment against ascetic pride and threatened to undermine the core criterion of spiritual elitism at a moment of brisk change. The backlash provoked by Jovinian was fierce, immediate, and unrelenting. The western church mobilized an organized resistance, and in AD 393 Jovinian was officially condemned. But the very swiftness of Jovinian's defeat revealed the extent to which he had forced an uncomfortable issue into the foreground. The next decades saw a bitter intellectual struggle over how, exactly, virginity and marriage were to be evaluated by the increasingly dominant church. Jerome—monk, scholar, translator of the Latin Vulgate, and acrid critic—immediately issued a pointed rebuttal in his two books *Against Jovinian.* His response was so immoderate that it embarrassed his friends. He provided a reading of First Corinthians so stilted that few could follow him. Jerome took the words of the apostle to mean that marriage was a lesser evil. For the author of the *Consultationes,* virginity was the highest good, and continence right after. But this pecking order did not make marriage a lesser evil, only a lesser good. The praise of virginity "was meant to encourage that which is greater, not to damn what is an actual good."[38]

The *Consultationes* presaged Augustine's *On the Good of Marriage,* written a decade later in another attempt to lay to rest the lingering effects of Jerome's extremism. Augustine's treatment of sex and marriage was to prove definitive. But it came in the distinctive aftermath of the Jovinianist controversy, which had seen the entire eastern ascetic tradition absorbed, debated, and reformulated in the west in the compressed space of a few decades. The threefold justification of marriage—fidelity, procreation, sacred bond—that Augustine hewed out of a formless chaos was bound to ensure married laypeople an authoritative ideology of respectability. In one sense the Jovinianist controversy and the aftershocks that rumbled for the next decades were just one episode in a long history of tension between the church's commitment to the supreme ideal of virginity and the scriptural injunctions to reproduction. This same tension is embedded in Paul's epistles; it called forth the pastoral letters; it defined the battle between encratic and orthodox Christians in the second and third centuries; it would replay itself in the Protestant Reformation (which saw Luther derided as Jovinian reborn); it continues to rumble in Catholic debates over clerical celibacy. Because the problem of sex is inevitably tied to the problem of Christianity's relation to the world, it is a tension that will surface during any great readjustment in the relationship between Christianity and the world. This is what makes the reckoning of the church in the Theodosian period so significant, for these generations saw the most decisive reconciliation of the church to secular society, perhaps in all of Christian history. The fourth century saw the wild, untamed asceticism of the desert pour across the Mediterranean, only to be slowly and incompletely corralled into monastic orders; the fifth century would see the diffuse ideals of clerical celibacy harden into formal requirements of lifelong abstinence. As the Christian church and secular society gradually became coterminous, the multifarious strands of Christian asceticism were progressively institutionalized, as a spiritual elite presiding over the mass of mediocre Christians. Sexual renunciation became not so much a rejection of the world and its ruling order, as a secession from material society and its entanglements. It is against this backdrop that the less colorful, but ultimately more consequential, formulation of Christian marriage—and conjugal sexuality—must be considered.[39]

It is not infrequently assumed that married Christians formed a "silent majority" across early Christian history. The breezy assumption of a quiet core of reliable reproducers is not so much inaccurate as inattentive to the actual processes by which sexual culture became Christian. The idea of a stable base of conservative patriarchs, within the faith, renders frictionless the absorption of society by the church. Here the lingering influence of Veyne's model, in which Christianity rides deeper currents of sexual repression, is subtly felt. But the stern counsels of gloomy Stoics are hardly representative of imperial culture, which in its ebullient eroticism—within and beyond the marriage bed—defies any characterization as proto-Christian. The feeble and isolated injunctions of eccentric and usually senescent philosophers are incommensurable with the diffusion of a mass ideology, affixed to a high-stakes message about man's place in the cosmos, demanding radical austerity for all. The idea of a silent majority of Christian householders simply underestimates how important, and how dramatic, the formation of holy matrimony in the fourth and fifth centuries truly was, both for society and for the Christian church. The debris of this greater revolution are to be found not in the grandiloquent tracts on virginity but in the pedestrian sermons that preserve some of the heat generated at the combustible meeting point between pastoral ambition and mainstream habits.

There was much that Christianity, almost subconsciously, adopted from the traditional form of Greco-Roman marriage. Monogamy, as Augustine recognized, was a Roman rather than a Jewish institution, and its adoption by the early Christians was not as inevitable as the lack of attention devoted to the topic by modern historians might suggest. The ideal of marriage as the focus of one's most important private relationships, in short as "the principal affair in human life," was discreetly borrowed from mainstream beliefs. The idea of the conjugal unit as the primary axis of the family (rather than as an extension of a great clan, spanning back generations through the men of the line) was deeply ingrained in Roman society and momentously absorbed by Christianity. At the same time, Christian sexual doctrine would serve to radicalize, in unexpected ways, the married pair as the focal point of the most meaningful human bonds. In particular, two doctrines emerged as staples of Christian marriage and departures from mainstream tradition: sexual exclusivity and opposition to divorce or remarriage. All the world's diffuse erotic energy was to be cramped into one, frail, sacred union.[40]

No witness takes us with him quite so vividly into the trenches of Christianization during the crucial period as the remarkable John Chrysostom. Some thousand or so of his sermons, delivered at Antioch and Constantinople, survive. In Chrysostom's campaign to reform the morals of his congregation, we can watch one Christian leader's efforts to hector his audience, by threat, suasion, and enticement, into a modicum of sexual decency. His delicate efforts to instill Pauline values in his flock form an object lesson on the collision between Christian norms and deeply entrenched patterns of sexual conduct. Marriage, he claimed, was originally instituted for two reasons: the creation of children and sexual self-control. The passing of time had dimmed the urgency of reproduction; the earth was full, and the promise of resurrection nullified the imperative to live through future generations. Thus, Chrysostom would argue, the prime justification for marriage was sexual restraint. But here Chrysostom dropped a surprise on his audience: it was wrong, even for a man, to have sex outside of marriage. Even with prostitutes or slaves, a married man should not have sex beyond the marriage couch. "What I am saying is a paradox, but it is true!"[41]

In this sermon, Chrysostom juxtaposed Christian sexual boundaries with the ordinary rules of conduct. "I am not unaware that most think it is adultery only to violate a married woman. But *I* say that it is a wicked and licentious adultery for a man with a wife to have an affair even with a public whore, a slave girl, or any other woman without a husband." The preacher recognized that society's standards, which accepted dalliances between married men and their slaves or prostitutes, found a powerful ally in Roman law. "Do not show me the laws of the outside world, which say a woman committing adultery is to be brought to a trial, but that men with wives who do it with slave girls are not considered guilty." And if appeal to God's law was not enough, Chrysostom invoked the traditional hopes of a peaceful house. "Your wife did not come to you, and leave behind her father and mother and her entire household in order to be humiliated." The point bore repetition: "Thus we say a man commits adultery, if he sates his lust with a slave girl or a public whore while he has a wife." Marital fidelity was the Christian path. "A wife *(eleuthera)* offers at once pleasure and security and joy and honor and order and a clean conscience." John Chrysostom was not, of course, a great exponent of the gifts of physical "pleasure," so his passing praise, or at least tolerance, of it here must be written down as a rhetorical effusion in an effort to persuade the crowd of the practicability of his model of Christian marriage. It is a telling concession.[42]

Documents like Chrysostom's sermons provide some of the grittiest and most authentic reflections on the dynamics of power within the ancient marriage relationship. He claimed that "there is nothing more shameful than a fornicating husband." He bolstered his condemnation, though, with an uncomfortable depiction of the mundane conflicts within the household. "Do you want to know just how awful it is? Think of what life is like for those who suspect their wives. Food and drink become repulsive. An insidious poison seems to suffuse the whole table. Countless evils fill the house, like ruin, and they flee the home. There is no sleep, no gentle night, no commerce of lovers, no rays of sunshine. They will actually think the light is a torment, not only when the wife is seen to be an adulteress, but even once there is the slightest suspicion. So, realize that your wife suffers these very things when she hears or suspects that you have given yourself over to some whore." In Chrysostom's sermons, we see how the notion of sex as a cosmic battleground came to settle within the domestic squabbles of marriage. "If dread of hell doesn't restrain you, then fear their black magic. When you deprive yourself of God's help through your debauchery, and denude yourself of assistance from above, the whore will seize you more brazenly. Hatching plots against you and calling on her familiar demons with amulets devised for it, she will gain control over your well-being, making you a risible shame before all who live in the city." How far removed John is from the lofty pronouncements of a Clement of Alexandria is evident in the fact that public shame could be invoked as a check on the fornication of Christian men.[43]

The dire insistence on sexual exclusivity grated against the most entrenched habits of sexual life in the Roman Mediterranean. More subtle but no less consequential in its challenge to mainstream habits was the Christian opposition to divorce and remarriage. For the Christians, marriage was not only the exclusive legitimate venue for erotic experience, it was a unique bond that could not be dissolved by civil law. The Romans had one of the most liberal regimes of divorce in human history; legally, divorce could be obtained unilaterally, without cause, by either party, without cumbersome procedural obstacles; the strict separation of spousal property, and the prohibition of gifts between the husband and wife, abetted easy separation. This image must be qualified by an appreciation for the hard realities faced by the majority of families who lived along the edges of subsistence; divorce was the prerogative of the well-to-do. Nevertheless it was a discreet reserve of feminine power in Roman society. But the stark commands of Christian scripture ensured that the church would universalize a strict opposition to divorce and erode this wellspring of women's clout.[44]

The result was an inevitable slide toward patriarchy. Women were flatly prohibited from seeking divorce, and so long as their first husband was still living, they were forbidden to remarry, on pain of accusation of adultery. John Chrysostom, in the very same set of sermons that showed him sympathetic to the humble sufferings of women, could unleash a rhetoric against women that grates the modern ear. "They are like runaway slaves, who flee the master's house but drag their chains along. Women who leave their husbands carry around the condemnation of the law like a chain, and are accused of adultery. . . . For she whose husband is alive becomes an adulteress." In a society where a woman's sexual honor was the measure of her worth, those were words calculated to bruise. John knew that Christian rules ran against common practice. "It may happen that slaves change their masters, even if the master is living, but the wife can never change husbands so long as he is living. It is adultery. Don't read me the laws which have been laid down for those outside, which command that a notice of divorce be rendered and then set you free. You will not be judged by those laws on the day God has appointed, but by the law he has established." Men, too, were deprived of access to divorce, with one all-important exception: female infidelity. In late antiquity the exception clauses uttered by Jesus in the Gospel of Matthew were taken to mean that a husband could dismiss an unfaithful wife. Even John would accept it, with a little tergiversation. "An adulteress is not really even a wife." The most he could find to say for such a rule was that it prevented bloodshed in the house. But what emerges so clearly from his sermons is the way that the church forcefully sought to alleviate the *sexual* double standard while importing a new double standard in the rules of *divorce.*[45]

The homiletic corpus of the late fourth and early fifth centuries provides abundant and vivid testimony to the intense war on fornication that trailed the mainstreaming of Christianity. The sermons of Chrysostom were heard by rich and poor, powerful and powerless, free and slave, men and women. He truly hoped that he might transform Antioch or Constantinople into a Christian city through the diligent reform of one household at a time. But prostitution was a particularly formidable challenge to this agenda, even in the late empire. A fourth-century catalog of the urban amenities of Rome still included some forty-five public brothels (listed between the public grain mills and the public latrines); it is telling that prostitution remained part of the official, public face of civic life in the early phases of the Christian empire. It is not surprising, then, that prostitution became a particular preoccupation of leaders like John Chrysostom, and that through his eyes we can see the anger and despair of a Christian preacher working amid a society where prostitution remained a vibrant part of the sexual economy.[46]

Chrysostom's sermon is only the tip of the iceberg in his own extensive homiletic corpus and those of his contemporaries. In the moment of Christian triumph, the leadership of the church began to recognize that prostitution was part of an entrenched social system that encouraged the sexual use of dishonored women. The bishops of the later fourth century articulated with unprecedented clarity the structural mechanics of the Greco-Roman sexual economy. Asterius of Amasea could see that the double standard of sexual behavior was rooted in a society where property and legitimacy were transmitted through monogamy: "If men consort with many women, they do no harm to their own hearth, but if women commit sexual sin, they introduce alien heirs into their house and their line." John Chrysostom was hardly the only bishop to appreciate the role of Roman law in solidifying an alternative set of sexual norms. Augustine explicitly rejected the "law of the forum" in favor of the "law of heaven." Salvian of Marseilles summarized Greco-Roman sexual policy in the pithiest, and most accurate, formulation on record: forbidding adulteries, building brothels. Prostitution was not simply tolerated—it was viewed as a way of protecting the honor of decent women. Ambrose despaired that his Christians could visit the brothel "as though it were a law of nature." Christian leaders became desperately aware of the double standard, and the braver among them were perfectly willing to identify its origins. "The laws were made by men, and they are disposed against women." The acerbic Jerome offered a penetrating reflection on the fundamentally distinct logics of classical and Christian sexual boundaries. "Among them [the Romans], the bridles of sexual restraint are unloosed for men. The Romans condemn only *stuprum* and *adulterium,* letting lust run wild through whorehouses and slave girls, as though social status makes an offense, and not sexual desire."[47]

Although the bishops of this period recognized the place of prostitution in secular society and rejected it, they were slow to articulate an alternative social vision, and the residues of more ancient thought occasionally seeped into Christian discourse. Greeks and Romans had long held the idea that prostitution was a social necessity. It is not hard to find expressions of the idea that prostitution was like a safety valve, a safe outlet for male sexual energies. In his early tract *On Order,* Augustine provided the most lucid statement of prostitution's necessity that has survived from antiquity. "What could claim to be more filthy and more worthless, more full of shame and defilement, than prostitutes and pimps and other infections of this kind? But take whores out of human affairs, and you will overturn everything because of lusts. Put them in the place of matrons, and you will ruin honor with fallenness and disgrace." Augustine was no stranger to the world of procured sex, though he was more familiar with the sophisticated side of the flesh trade. He spent over a decade with one concubine, and when forced to dismiss her, by his engagement to a ten-year-old girl of the Roman gentry, he quickly "procured another" companion in the interim. So he had a robust appreciation for the forces that prostitution held in check. If prostitutes were to be removed from society, not just the honor of free women, "everything" would be thrown into confusion.[48]

Prostitution for Augustine was a necessary evil. The social order had to make such compromises, to allow virtue to flourish. "[Pimps and prostitutes] represent the most impure part of mankind by their habits and the most vile condition in the laws of order. Are there not in the bodies of living things certain parts that, if you tried to consider only these, you couldn't stand it? Nevertheless, the order of nature did not wish for things that are necessary to be lacking, but neither did it allow them, as they are dishonorable, to be conspicuous. Still, these imperfections, by holding their place, concede the better part to their superiors." Matrons enjoyed their place in society because prostitutes deflected dangerous lusts away from honorable women. An unfortunate passage, with a long future, it was no more than the meeting point of Augustinian pessimism and perfectly traditional ideology.[49]

If prostitution was an obstacle to Christianization, marriage was an opportunity for reformist ambitions. Chrysostom's sermons reveal an ecclesiastical ambition to control the rituals of marriage as a means of gaining control over the meaning of marriage. It is telling that, across late antiquity, the ancient *deductio in domum,* a festive march from the bride's house to the groom's, remained the ordinary marriage ritual. The endurance of joyous, erotically charged wedding ceremonies testifies to the survival, beneath the spread of religious solemnity, of a sexual sensibility that is probably closer to Achilles Tatius than anything contrived by a Christian bishop. Nothing nettled Chrysostom so much as the "diabolical pomp," which, he argued in vain, "dishonored" the marriage. The "whorish songs," the "shameful speeches," the "unrestrained laughter" were an immovable part of the rite for young men and women entering into the mysteries of conjugal love. Again, he invoked a fear of demons to accomplish through superstition what moral suasion could not. The "songs of Venus," the hired entertainers—no more than "whores and she-men"—were an open invitation to demonic possession. What irked Chrysostom was that the same couple who indulged in the frankly erotic celebrations of an ancient wedding now expected the Christian priest to drop in, on the next day, to bless the union! But the preacher knew where he stood; the inhabitants of an ancient Mediterranean town were in no mood to surrender such a precious moment of release. "I know that I will seem severe and tiresome, urging you to uproot such an ancient custom . . . but where sin dares to surface, make no mention to me of 'custom.' "[50]

Chrysostom's sermons evince a strong will to gather the loose energy of the marriage ceremony into Christian form, but it is striking how gradually and unevenly Christian rituals developed. In the east, priests slowly became part of the traditional ceremonies, blessing the couple and even participating in parts of the ceremony such as veiling, crowning, or the joining of hands. By the fifth century, clerical blessings became routine, although the wedding maintained its profane form and never became truly liturgical in late antiquity. In the west, clerical blessings in which the couple was veiled are attested in late fourth-century Italy. The rite of blessing gave the church a chance to promote its view of marriage: only first marriages were blessed, and Caesarius of Arles reports that only virgins received the honor. But Christian *rituals* developed late. Augustine, significantly, never mentioned a Christian ritual of marriage. Paulinus of Nola was the first to mention a marriage inside a church, specifically at the altar—but both spouses were the scions of episcopal families (the groom was none other than Augustine's nemesis, Julian of Eclanum). An important sacramentary, reflecting sixth-century practices, finally presents a full-fledged Christian liturgy of marriage, including a nuptial mass. It would be interesting to know at what moment in history a marriage had to occur in a church to be considered publicly legitimate: the answer is probably not until deep in the Middle Ages.[51]

The legal record provides an imperfect but revealing index of the endurance of old structures of matrimony and the volatile mixture at times produced by the synthesis of traditional patriarchy and fresh strains of sexual austerity. The reign of Constantine is significant, not so much for introducing Christian values into law as for accelerating a new, more aggressive style of imperial lawmaking. Constantine extensively reformed Roman private law, but not in ways that show particularly Christian inspiration. Rather, he was a fiercely conservative enforcer of traditional Roman values. Constantine, like Augustus, saw himself as the founder of a social order, and like Augustus he carried out a sweeping renovation of the aristocracy, complete with renewed prohibitions on the intermarriage of his aristocracy and women of "humble or low" birth. Like Augustus, too, he simultaneously reformed the adultery statute, which as ever protected decent women while consigning vulnerable women, perhaps more than ever, to systematic sexual exploitation. Constantine, for instance, was more explicit and more severe than the classical law in defining which women were beyond the pale of public respectability. Women working in taverns, who "served the wines of intemperance," were rendered "unworthy of notice by the public law" by their "lowness of life."[52]

The tenor of Constantine's rule can be judged from his procedural reforms of the adultery law. Constantine ended the Augustan tradition of public informing, which had pressed public vigilance into the cause of sexual surveillance. Constantine wished to limit eligible informants to the woman's husband or her male relatives. His outlook is informed by a sharper sense of honor and shame, and the patriarchal obligations on men to manage their own womenfolk. Constantine allowed a revealing exception: in cases where a woman, presumably a widow, was having sex with a slave. "If a woman is revealed to be having a hidden liaison with a slave, let her be sentenced to capital punishment, and the reprobate slave sent to the flames. And let everyone have the capacity to report this public crime, let it be a full duty to declare it, let even a slave have permission to make an accusation, which if it is true shall bring him freedom, though if it is false, a penalty waits." It was the first time that a Roman emperor had deigned to created a law to redress the nefarious possibility that a woman might find sexual companionship among her own domestics. What is so interesting about Constantine's law is not the disapproval of a type of sexual conjunction that had always horrified public opinion. It is the will of the emperor to regulate, directly, the sexual impropriety itself, rather than the secondary effects of such a *mésalliance.* Certainly such willingness played unintentionally into Christian designs. Slaves were ubiquitous in late ancient society, and the phobia of surreptitious female infidelity spiraled into a general paranoia. Jerome, predictably, found such suspicion amenable to his anti-erotic program. "A woman's reputation for sexual virtue is a fragile thing, like a precious flower that breaks in the soft breeze and is ruined by the light wind. It is especially vulnerable when she is of an age which allows her to fall into vice, but lacks the authority of a husband, whose shadow is the protection of a wife. What business does a widow have among a crowd of slaves? Among a herd of servants? . . . I know many women who keep their gates closed to the public, but have not avoided suspicions of disgrace with slaves. The slaves have become suspect by their fancy appearance or their noticeably well-fed bodies." But it was not just Jerome's lurid idiosyncrasy. The incubus of male slave sexuality, and its perpetual endangerment of feminine honor, haunts the late antique mind. Constantine's legislation, if was not actually a spur to paranoia, was at least consonant with a broader mood.[53]

One of the most revelatory enactments of Constantine's entire legislative package was his thunderous decree against abduction marriage. Abduction marriage, in which the girl was often a conspiring partner, was simply part of life in a world of arranged marriages. Classical Roman law had the sense to ignore the phenomenon and leave society to sort out the distinctions between rape and voluntary seizure, offering the young man a chance to persuade the girl's father to relent. Constantine preferred to impose his strict will. If the girl did not consent, the man was no more than a rapist. If she did consent, she was to be punished as harshly as her ravisher. Even the victim was punished, because the girl should have stowed herself safely at home or secured the help of neighbors by her screams. If the girl's nurse, charged to protect her, was found complicit, she was to have molten lead poured down her throat. Again, Constantine encouraged slaves to report such an egregious crime should the families attempt to cover it up. The values of the Constantinian reforms are strictly traditionalist. But the means of enforcing them are more direct, more aggressive, and more violent than in the classical dispensation.[54]

What is distinctive about late antique law, in the words of an authority, is that "it comes to reflect prevailing social morality less ambiguously than in previous centuries." This shift was subtle, and it truly accelerates in the reign of Constantine. In some sense Constantine's legal program was more radical but less Christian than much of what followed. The law of divorce is an especially revealing domain for examining the subtle dynamics of continuity and change, of vigorous moralism and traditional restraint. In 331 Constantine abolished the ancient system of unilateral divorce. He restricted the grounds for divorce to crimes that hardly qualify as ordinary domestic tensions—murder, the violation of tombs, and the manufacture of poisons. If a woman repudiated her husband for any lighter cause, she not only lost her dowry, she was deported. If a man repudiated his wife without just cause (limited to a restricted class of offenses, but including adultery), he had to return the dowry and remain unmarried. Constantine's policy was an extraordinary reversal of classical principles, but his reforms were not to endure. Julian, his apostate nephew, repealed the measure. We are informed about this development only by Ambrosiaster, who complained that Julian's law had allowed women to divorce their husbands "freely" and "constantly." Thus, the dynasty of Constantine saw a swing from a completely classical system of divorce, to a radically new and restricted regime, back to the classical model.[55]

In the fifth century, the law of divorce was the object of frequent reform. In 421 the western empire reestablished limits on unilateral divorce. This law instituted a completely new system of rules. It maintained a double standard between men and women, but now there were three categories of justification: without cause, minor cause, and grave offenses. The law established penalties for unilateral divorce, albeit much lighter ones than Constantine had decreed. Mutual divorce remained entirely permissible and was to remain the rule in the west. The eastern empire generally supported a more liberal regime. An attempt at compromise was issued in 449, with a broader list of justifications for unilateral divorce and substantially reduced penalties. The law was a milestone, for it recognized that a woman might legitimately seek divorce if her husband "has sexual congress with dishonorable women in contempt of his own house and wife, while she is looking on," or if "he has given her beatings which are unsuitable for a freeborn woman." This law hardly overturned the double standard, but the intrusion of male infidelity—even if of a particularly flagrant kind—into the public expectations of divorce law was remarkable enough.[56]

This moderately liberal approach would prevail in the east down to the reign of Justinian. Although it is tempting to ascribe the gradual constriction of divorce law to Christian currents, both the pattern and the nature of the reforms caution against this diagnosis and reveal how complex the dynamics of change truly were. The system of free divorce, characteristic of classical law, was inextricable from a property regime in which the marriage bond involved few property transfers. In the late empire, the law increasingly recognized the realities of conjugal property, and, in tandem, unilateral divorce became more difficult. The keyword is "unilateral." Late Roman law did not prohibit divorce: it prohibited one spouse from leaving the other without coming to a settlement. Certainly these rules would have insinuated themselves in petty domestic conflicts in ways that we will never be able to see. But the basic fact is that the law of divorce, from Constantine to Justinian, was primarily about property; the changed moral climate, driven by Christianity, contributed, but secondarily.[57]

Until Justinian. As with same-sex eros, so with marriage and divorce, the legislative reforms of Justinian marked a breakthrough and reveal what a legal program truly driven by Christian norms could look like. For the first time, in his reign, Christian ideas determined sexual policy irrespective of ancient, intricate patterns of relationship between state and society. "We command that everyone live as chastely as possible," the Christian legislator commanded. "Because marriage is such an honorable matter that, by the mercy of God, it has brought immortality to the human race and sustains our continual renewal so far as is possible by giving an eternal nature through the procreation of children under the auspices of matrimony, it is proper that we devote our care to it." The rules instituted by Justinian matched his rhetoric. In AD 542, Justinian revisited the law of divorce, sharply limiting the class of offenses for which divorce could be sought. The only cause of divorce that received wider scope was, revealingly, the husband's sexual malfeasance. If he kept a woman "in the very house where he lives with his wife," or even if he was guilty of "frequenting a woman in his city in another house," the wife had cause to dissolve the union. Although this rule fell far short of sexual equality, it was the closest any ancient lawgiver went. But the radicalism of Justinian's reform lay elsewhere. He proceeded to abolish divorce by mutual consent. The immemorial capacity of couples to part ways by agreement was abrogated by the Christian state. This reform marked a considerable advance of the state's tutelage over the marriage bond, and it can be explained only by a firm will to suppress divorce itself rather than to mediate the circulation of property through society and across generations. Justinian's law, in short, reveals a moral activism. It is again the middle of the sixth century that marks the terminus of a fateful passage toward the alignment of Christian morality and public power.[58]

THE TRIUMPH AND DISINTEGRATION OF THE FREE WILL

The sack of Rome by a Visigothic army in AD 410 was a profound moral and mental shock; in its aftermath, confusion and recrimination quickly followed. Among the most visceral horrors of the experience was that the immemorial adjunct of war, sexual violence against women, was visited on the eternal city. The rape of wives and virgin daughters was a bitter tragedy; the rape of nuns was, for many, unambiguous proof that the Christian God was uninterested in Roman fortunes. Such a dark insult to Roman honor demanded a reckoning. The crisis of AD 410 was the proximate cause for the composition of Augustine's magnum opus, *The City of God.* The issue of sexual violence called forth some of the most astonishing, and indelicate, passages of the entire Augustinian oeuvre. In the defense of his religion, the bishop of Hippo put on trial a whole cluster of deep and usually implicit assumptions about the nature of female sexual honor, as old as the hills of Rome. He insisted that female purity was a mental, intentional, and not an objective, physical state. "One can only assent or refuse with his mind. Who of sound sense would believe that someone who has been seized and forced to use his flesh to slake the lust of someone else has lost his sexual honor?" To console the wounded pride of Rome in the aftermath of defeat, he attacked Roman values at their core. He insisted, in short, that sin, rather than shame, provided the only real scale of sexual values.[59]

The Romans were not accustomed to blaming rape victims. For centuries the law had recognized the innocence of women subjected to sexual violence. But a primitive sensibility toward physical violation abided in ancient Mediterranean societies; rape was a social, as well as a personal, trauma. Certainly the social rehabilitation of abused bodies was something that was strictly beyond the limits of comfortable discussion. Augustine was deliberately, and brashly, scraping against some of the most primitive strata of belief about a woman's body. The lust of another, he defiantly claimed, could not "pollute" one's purity. Intent was all that hung in the scales. A woman whose body was forced into sex "but who offered no consent with her will" kept her chastity intact. With his unfailing instinct for drama, Augustine hailed before the tribunal of sexual justice the legendary Roman matron Lucretia. It was a savvy choice. In a culture that had long valued the moral *exemplum,* Lucretia was the example of examples. She preferred death over dishonor, and her suicide made her the unquestioned paragon of female honor. Lucretia was such a wrenching case precisely because of the deep tension at the heart of her story: she was innocent in mind, but voluntarily accepted the penalty of death. It was this tension that Augustine unraveled with remorseless zeal. If she was innocent in her will, then she had killed an innocent person. "If she is cleared of adultery, then she becomes guilty of murder. There is absolutely no escape when someone asks, 'If she was an adulteress, why is she praised? If she was sexually honorable, why did she have to be killed?' "[60]

It is a truism of the Western Civilization classroom that *The City of God* represents the passage across the threshold from classical to medieval civilization. It is almost accurate. Augustine's sneering prosecution of Lucretia was a cultural landmark. It represented the high-water mark of a distinctly volitional framework of sexual morality in the ancient church. Augustine could condemn Lucretia with such force because he carried with him a refined Christian model of sin that dissociated sexual behavior from its place in a network of social relationships. The first installment of *The City of God* represented the apex of Christian free will for another reason, though. It appeared at precisely the same moment when the great Pelagian controversy erupted. In the last two decades of his life, Augustine was engulfed in a doctrinal war over the nature of the human will, the repercussions of which would echo through the centuries, with momentous consequences for the history of sexuality. The Pelagian controversy, which can appear so compressed in its course and circumstantial in its substance, was an affair of such extraordinary moment because it represented Christian sexuality suddenly coming to terms with the newfound social dominance of the church. The hopeful, if naive, notions of free will, native to primitive Christianity, were washed out by the tidal wave of Augustinian pessimism—in the west.

Dark premonitions of this impending crash lurk already the first installment of *The City of God.* In his pursuit of Lucretia, Augustine compasses a murky possibility. "Perhaps she killed herself not because of her innocence but because of her guilty conscience? What if (and only she would have known), despite the fact that she was violently ravished, her libido was led astray and she consented, and she was so racked by her guilt she thought to expiate it by her death?" The sinister insinuation—from which Augustine sheepishly retreats—cannot be ascribed to prosecutorial zeal. It was part of Augustine's distinctive view of the sex drive, a view that was to receive fateful expression in the coming years. Augustine developed a view of human sexuality as something refractory, uncontrollable, mysterious. Centuries of untrammeled Christian optimism about the pliability of the sexual instinct would crash on the rocks of Augustine's doctrine of original sin. Augustine believed not only that the state of the will was the measure of morality, but also that mastery of the will was humanly impossible. Sex came to epitomize, for Augustine, the recalcitrance of the will. *The City of God,* like no other text, symbolizes the simultaneous triumph and disintegration of ancient Christian notions of the will.[61]

The century between the conversion of Constantine and the appearance of the first installment of *The City of God* was a golden age for Christian free will. Eusebius, the church historian, wrote about free will more extensively, if less creatively, than any Christian before him. In his polemic against Hierocles, Eusebius attacks pagan determinism at length, a sign that fatalism had become caught up in the sniping between pagans and Christians in the last age of persecution. The entire sixth book of his *Preparation for the Gospel* is dedicated to the defense of free will against an eclectic pagan determinism. He attacks the critic Porphyry, who cited the veracity of oracles as a manifest proof of an overarching fate. Eusebius was intent to establish the justice of divine judgment, which was incompatible with determinism. Every event had one of three causes: natural law, randomness, and human will. All evil had its origins in the "self-initiated choice of the soul." The human soul stood outside of nature and its chain of physical causes; the soul was "free, autonomous, and master of itself." What impious slanderer, for instance, would accuse God of making a man use his body "against nature"? More than any other author, Eusebius offered a defense of free will that was framed against a developed form of pagan determinism in which a Platonic cosmos and the governance of the traditional pantheon were assimilated into a compassing determinism. Over the next decades, in the wake of Christian triumph, the freedom of the will—a concept born in the competition of cosmologies of the high Roman Empire—would spread farther than ever before.[62]

What is so striking about the discourse of free will in the long fourth century is its quantity and breadth. For three or four generations the Christian understanding of the universe flourished and spread across the Mediterranean. It is remarkable how untroubled this literature is by the impending Augustinian earthquake. In the late fourth century, a Cappadocian bishop, Amphilocius of Iconium, could insert the doctrine of free will unproblematically into an exegesis of the "sinful woman" from the Gospel of Luke. His sermon is revealing on many counts, not least its total innocence of the doctrinal issues that would, within a few decades, erupt with such force. The "sinful woman" was, unsurprisingly, regarded as a prostitute. More unexpectedly, she was interpreted as a figure of Eve, the protosinner. The "sinful woman" abused the gifts of sexual love, ruining the "youth" of the city and violating their sanctified bodies. Her sins were heavy, but she was forgiven by the grace of Jesus. Like the debtor, she could never repay her debts, but God called only for repentance, which was merely an act "of free will."[63]

For most of the fourth century it was not Stoic fatalism, gnostic doctrine, or even vulgar pagan determinism that occasioned Christian preaching on free will. Rather, it was that irrepressible enemy: astrology. In the west, Ambrosiaster battled against the lively threat of astral determinism: "Nothing is so contrary to Christian doctrine." It was in Syria, in the latter half of the fourth century, that the *Clementine Recognitions* repackaged Bardaisan's voluntarism, but without so much allowance for the influence of the stars. Christian preachers of the age like Augustine and John Chrysostom regularly attack the lures of astrology. In Constantinople a sermon on the Magi led Chrysostom inexorably into a diatribe against astral determinism. "We are free and masters of our wills. . . . If human affairs were under the power of their sign, why do you lash your slave in anger? Why do you haul your adulterous wife before the courts? . . . If sins arise by necessity, why do you bear insult harshly?" Only someone who was possessed by a demon lost his "free will" and deserved pity rather than censure. Chrysostom's sermon dates to around AD 400. He speaks of "free will" with complete innocence, in a fashion not far removed from Justin, Origen, or Methodius. It was still unproblematically a cosmological, antideterminist formulation. Sex, as ever, remained the reflexive paradigm of human freedom. In the middle of the fourth century, Cyril of Jerusalem could write, in his *Catechetical Lectures,* that the devil could suggest but not compel fornication, because the soul was self-governing. "If you wish, you will receive the suggestion, and if not, you won't. For if you committed fornication by necessity, then for what reason has God prepared the hellfire?" Yet within just a few years, such untroubled absolutisms will come to seem hopelessly naive.[64]

Vivifying the tensions between freedom and determinism in the fourth century was the spread of Manichean beliefs. The strongly dualist religion offered answers to the problem of evil that were seductive in their simplicity, proposing to solve through myth some of the most impossible theological conundrums of late antiquity. It is telling that the Manichean threat called forth Augustine's tract *On the Free Choice of the Will*, a work whose principal agenda is to exonerate God by assigning the origins of evil to human will, which Augustine already in this early work, more clearly than any of his predecessors, construes as a faculty rather than a condition of being. It is equally telling that within a few years the Pelagians will attempt to throw Augustine's own arguments back in his face and accuse him of being, under the bishop's cloak, still a Manichean.[65]

The primitive embrace of free will would crumble in the generations on either side of AD 400, in the period of rapid Christianization. Two blows were to bring the edifice tumbling to the ground. Though in very different ways, both arose from the expansion of the church and the need to reconcile the religion with mainstream society. The first was the debate between Augustine and the Pelagians, a theological controversy that unraveled with astonishing force in the 410s. The polemics over original sin had little purchase in the Greek-speaking east, though Augustinian pessimism would be officially ratified as orthodox doctrine at the Council of Ephesus. But the triumph of original sin over Pelagian optimism undercut the ancient models of free will, ultimately providing a new model of "the will" as a faculty lodged in the flesh and disobedient to reason. The stakes of the debate were so high, not least because "Pelagius and Augustine were both religious geniuses. Both made unambiguous sense of a conglomerate of ideas and attitudes which men of a previous age had been content to leave undefined. Both men were revolutionaries, and the controversy which followed their disagreement, far from being a purely academic wrangle, was a crisis in which the spiritual landscape of Western Christendom can be clearly seen for the first time." In the course of the Pelagian debate, human sexuality, which had for centuries of Christian apologetics been a paradigm of human freedom, rapidly becomes, in the hands of Augustine, the paradigm of human bondage to the flesh. That Augustine was capable of rebuilding entrenched Christian assumptions out of the elements of Christian orthodoxy in so short a space of time is testimony not only to his individual genius but also to the subtly rearranged position of the church in the world.[66]

The Pelagian debates erupted unexpectedly, and at first murkily, out of a brew of unsettled questions, which guaranteed that the storm was to be a multidimensional affair. The Origenist controversy continued to reverberate in discussions about the nature and origin of the soul; the perduring tensions between ascetic elitism and ordinary piety, which flared in the Jovinianist controversy, lurked within a religion that extolled virginity as an ideal; the orthodox exegesis of Genesis, especially the nature of the Fall, remained an open question. But the spark that was to ignite the conflagration was the ideal of perfection. Pelagius argued that the very existence of divine commandment implied the capacity for complete fulfillment. At the heart of Pelagian doctrine is the optimistic idea that man is always *capable* of doing good or evil, according to his will. The capacity for total obedience to God's law was, for Pelagius, intrinsic to human nature. "Whenever it falls to me to speak about the rules of morality and the maintenance of the holy life, it is my custom to demonstrate, first of all, the power and quality of human nature and to show what it has the capacity to effect, and only then to encourage the spirit of those listening toward the face of virtue, lest it be without profit to be called to those things which might seem impossible to them." For Pelagius, each human enjoyed the same plenitude of freedom experienced by Adam and Eve in paradise, and each human reenacted the fateful choice to disobey God. The possibility of individual perfection carried high stakes: "Pelagius wanted every Christian to be a monk." Pelagius offered a particularly severe vision of how Christianity might relate to society: by transforming it. It is no coincidence that the Pelagians produced some of the most honest and acute social criticism of the late empire. The Pelagians envisioned a church that stood apart from society, pure through and through. The Pelagian movement carried within it ancient strains of Christian separatism, but in an age of Christian accommodation.[67]

The consequences of Pelagian attitudes for sexual morality are most apparent in the thought of Julian of Eclanum, the ablest exponent of Pelagian doctrines and the fiercest holdout against Augustinianism. Julian held that the very shape of morality required humans to be naturally endowed with free will. "For if justice does not lay blame unless there existed the freedom to abstain, and, before baptism, there is a necessity to do evil, because, as you have said, the will is not free to do good and therefore it cannot do anything but evil, then the will is exonerated from the disgrace of doing evil by the very necessity which it suffers." Thus, for Julian, humans were capable of obeying all of God's sexual commandments. There was nothing inherently sinful in sexual desire, when kept within its licit bounds. For Julian, the sexual drive was a natural instinct, created by God; it was only sinful if an individual chose to indulge it in *excess.* "God made the sexual desire of humans, just as he did of beasts; but God allotted an unbridled instinct to the beasts, while for man he established a limit subject to reason. The wisdom and honor that God gave to man is appropriately reflected in the fact that man wears clothing. Therefore, it is not the proper amount or the very nature of sexual desire that God deems sinful but its excess, which arises from the insolence of the free will and brings blame not on the endowment of nature but on the merit of the individual actor." Julian's sexual ideology is marked by a distinctive combination of radicalism and optimism.[68]

Augustine's response to the challenge of Pelagius and Julian would destroy ancient notions of free will by deliberately posing the radical moral autonomy advocated by his opponents as a threat to the meaning of Christianity's most sacred rituals. For Augustine, sin was a matter of inheritance, not imitation, or else the ancient practice of infant baptism was senseless. Augustine reinterpreted the Fall, which came to stand as a dark, transmissible stain on human nature, lodged deep within the recalcitrant will. In Augustine's reimagining, the prelapsarian Adam and Eve were already sexual beings. Sexual reproduction was part of the original, perfect creation. But before their sin, Adam and Eve were capable of perfectly rational sexual acts. After their disobedience, they were punished with a disease befitting their crime: a disobedient will. What was lost in the Garden was the perfect, innocent control over the flesh. "As soon as the first man transgressed the law of God he began to have another law, repugnant to his mind, in his members, and he felt the wickedness of his own disobedience when he found in the disobedience of his own flesh a punishment which he most appropriately deserved." Adam and Eve, feeling this intractable movement within their flesh, realized their nakedness, experienced shame, and covered themselves. The will itself was dislodged and placed outside man's complete control, and nothing symbolized so powerfully the defiance of the will like the uncontrollable forces of sexual desire.[69]

The debates with Julian saw Augustine, who had written so eloquently on the "Good of Marriage" against the ascetic elitism of men like Jerome, turn his focus toward the inevitable sinfulness of sexual desire, even within marriage. Augustine continued to maintain his threefold account of the goods of marriage: reproduction, mutual fidelity, and sacred bond. But in his later years he would write more energetically about the impossibility of defeating concupiscence, even within marriage. For Augustine, "concupiscence, this law of sin which abides in our members," was an intractable symptom of human nature. Concupsicence was "not to be imputed to marriage, but only to be tolerated within marriage." Procreative sex alone was not to be reckoned a sin, but even the act of procreation, in the postlapsarian world, required the mobilization of dangerous forces beyond man's complete control. "Conjugal intercourse which is had with procreative intention is not in itself a sin, because a righteous will leads the spirit which follows, and does not follow the lead of bodily pleasure; human choice is in this case not led by mastering sin, when the attack of sin is rightly redirected for the purpose of procreation." Augustine was led to articulate a model of procreationist sex that was, momentously, far more specific than anything that had preceded it. Certainly Clement of Alexandria, the most important early exponent of procreationism, had avoided backing himself into the corners where Augustine finds himself. Augustine provided a pessimistic reading of Paul's First Letter to the Corinthians. Sex within marriage was indeed a safeguard against "damnable crimes, that is fornication and adultery." But conjugal sex that served "an overpowering concupiscence" was allowed only by way of concession. The Apostle had allowed that marriage could act as a mitigating factor in the commission of sexual sin. Marriage transformed sexual acts performed out of desire into "venial sins."[70]

What is at stake in Augustine's pessimism, in the largest sense, is the ability of the church to absorb society. The impossibility of human perfection was the necessary adjunct to a vision of the church as an embracing institution, impure in its present form. Unlike Pelagius or Julian, Augustine was willing to accept that the church was far from a perfect body of holy men and women, standing apart from the world. The church was a collective where men and women strove, day by day, to be healed of their moral imperfections. "So not only all the sins, but all the evils of mankind, are in the course of being taken away by the sanctity of the Christian wash, by which Christ cleanses his church so that He might present her to Himself not in this age but in the future one, when she will have no stain or spot or anything of such a kind. For there are people who say that the church is already so, and yet they themselves are in her midst!" "Nevertheless, we ought to will not to experience these sexual desires, even if we cannot obtain this goal so long as we are in this body of death." It is a measure of the distance traveled that Augustine returns, like Epictetus, to the position that a free will is an achieved state; but what for Epictetus was achieved through the cultivation of reason, for Augustine was rehabilitated by the mysterious power of divine grace. The sacraments replaced the power of reason; mysterious rites administered by the church, rather than meditative philosophy, enabled human freedom.[71]

Both Augustine and his Pelagian opponents reworked immemorial assumptions about the body in the service of radical ideas; their dispute unfolded within an intellectual vanguard vying for the helm of a successful revolution, not unlike that between Trotsky and Stalin; this too was a struggle between a purist party and a more cunning faction. The Augustinian coup, which saw the demise of the naive psychology of early Christianity, was just one of the two breaking points for absolute free will in late antiquity. The other, which was to have greater purchase in the Greek-speaking east, was no less driven by the expansion of the church. The mainstreaming of the religion brought the Christian leadership face-to-face with the blunt reality of sexual coercion. Given the centrality of sexual exploitation in the Roman Empire, what is notable is that the early church maintained a deafening silence on the problem of sexual coercion in the centuries after the Pauline mission. Clement of Alexandria was the first to notice the "miserable creatures" sold into the flesh trade, and Lactantius evinced an empty sympathy for women forced into the brothel. The truth is that vulnerable men and women, boys and girls, probably had shown up at the doorsteps of Christian house-churches long before the problem enters our field of vision. It has been provocatively asked, given the presumptive sexual abuse of slaves, what their status was in a religious community with a deeply ritual sense of purity and pollution; had not Paul unambiguously counseled that the fornicator be cast from the body of the church? What about those who were fornicators by force? Ingenious answers have been devised, but the glaring fact is precisely that *we do not know*. As a persecuted, minority sect struggling to survive in a hostile environment, the church managed to avoid definitive answers to these questions for over three centuries. Over the fourth century, though, against the backdrop of Christian triumph, amid the Christianization of society, the problem of systemic sexual exploitation became increasingly difficult to avoid. The missionary success of the church imperiled the fragile silence. The pastoral wing of the church was forced to confront the social mechanics of sexuality in the Mediterranean. In the golden age of Christian free will, bishops came to realize that their gospel of freedom rang hollow in the face of the complex social realities of sexuality.[72]

The earliest stirrings of a new consciousness are preserved in the sermons of Basil of Caesarea. This origin is fitting, both because the homiletic context demonstrates the practical role of pastoral Christianity, and because Basil's canons demonstrate an effort toward systematic thought. Basil and his Cappadocian colleagues were avid readers of Origen, from whom they drank deeply the gospel of freedom. For Basil, experience as the leader of a vast and rapidly growing community gradually exposed him to the contradictions between his ideology and the structure of the society around him. Prostitution brought bishops face-to-face with the fact that even if sex were a matter of sin, not all sex was the outcome of free will. The clearest expression of the idea occurred in one of Basil's sermons on the Psalms, as he was explaining to his congregation the problem of pain and injustice. "If you ask why the life of the sinner is long, but the days of the just man are cut short, why the wicked prosper and the good are oppressed, why the child is snatched away before his time, where war comes from, why ships wreck, why the earth shakes, why the waters flood, or drought strikes, why afflictions were created for mankind, why this man is a slave and this man free, why this man is rich and this man poor—the difference is greater among those who commit sin and those who are righteous. For while the slave woman who was sold to a pimp is in sin by necessity, she who happens to belong to a wellborn mistress was raised with sexual modesty, and on this account the one is shown mercy, the other condemned."[73]

Without any natural impetus to use the example of prostitution, it came to mind as the coerced sin par excellence. The problem of evil was a challenge to Christian theodicy, but Basil's God was intuitively just, and he would spare the innocent. Basil simply assumed that a prostitute was a slave, sold to a pimp. She was in sin as a result, but forgiven by God. In contrast, the honorable woman had agency in her sexual immorality, and as a result her actions were damnable. Basil's notion that some prostitutes were condemned to sexual sin through coercion was by no means an incidental or passing thought. In another sermon, Basil explicitly contrasted two prostitutes. Some sins, he said, were "involuntary," others from a "wicked disposition." Here we see fully articulated the stark difference between voluntary sin and coerced sin. "One prostitute has been sold to the pimp and is in evil because of necessity, for she must provide her body for the work of her wicked master. But there is another who gives herself to sin voluntarily, because of pleasure." In a more systematic context—one of his canonical letters—Basil carried his thought to its logical conclusion. "Sexual violations that occur through necessity are to be without blame." Basil's canon represents a monumental breakdown of the traditional social and mental barriers that had insulated the church from the need to think about the material realities behind sin. Here is a not insignificant expansion of human consciousness. Basil cut through the curtain that had for centuries blocked the need to think about the moral capacity of society's most vulnerable.[74]

We might fruitfully contrast the sermon of Basil with the novel of Achilles Tatius. Achilles is aware of the ineffable strings of fate that pull human action. He walks us to the precipice and, at least for dramatic effect, asks us to contemplate the mysterious dispensation that could make Leucippe free and the prostitute an effigy of social death. But having stared at the abyss, he retreats, and takes solace in the order of a world that does allow beauty, pleasure, and existential fullness for some. Basil ponders this same mysterious dispensation, but with a conviction of its profound injustice and a confident hope for a final redemption in which all moral creatures will receive their due. The radicalism of Basil's discovery is attributable to the stark collision between an ideology of free will and an earnest form of nascent social leadership. It is no accident that Basil's brother, Gregory of Nyssa, has left the very earliest extant attack on slavery; for Gregory, slavery was an institution unjust to its very foundations, a violation of basic human rationality and moral autonomy. The takeover of society by the church opened a brief window for such radically creative social thought.[75]

Basil's idea, if it was first his, was to prove more fertile than Gregory's attack on slavery. The dichotomy between consent and coercion found its way into the Christian mind in the late fourth century. Other Greek pastors picked up the idea of consent, specifically in the context of slavery and prostitution. The idea was clearly alive in the early fifth century, when Cyril of Alexandria explained that there were two kinds of prostitutes. "See how some wish to practice shameful pollution willingly and of their own volition while some are accustomed to impress it upon others as though by force. . . . Do not some go into fornication on their own choice, women and young men voluntarily making wages off selling their youth to the disorderliness of some? Yes. What's more—some are conquered by shameful profits and prostitute out their own slave women, even some of their males to those who wish, and thus the wretched who happen to be sold must turn over a tribute?" Cyril's argument turns on the same idea, "out of necessity," to describe the prostitution of slaves, male and female, forced into venal sex. Cyril's account was, like Basil's, just as emphatic about the consent of some prostitutes. In his writings, we see the figure of the prostitute as a spectacular embodiment of sin gestating in the Christian mind.[76]

The new consciousness evinced in Basil's writings did not have an immediate impact, but Cyril's use of it—sometime in the 410s or 420s—shows that the idea was percolating decades later. Indeed, in the AD 420s the idea of prostitutes "sinning by necessity" would intersect, in one of those deeply symbolic coincidences that history sometimes provides, with the final phases of the doctrinal debates between Augustine and Julian. In 418 Pelagius and his Italian supporters were condemned to exile, and Julian of Eclanum sailed east to carry on the struggle against the Augustinian coup. Julian settled, for the better part of a decade, in Cilicia, near the figure of Theodore of Mopsuestia. His place of refuge was well chosen. Theodore was an auspicious protector who offered not only intellectual nourishment but also, quite possibly, advantageous political networks. When on December 24, 427, the archbishop of Constantinople died, Nestorius, a Syrian and a complete outsider, was elected; when he traveled to the capital in early 428, Nestorius passed through Mopsuestia to visit his old teacher, Theodore, en route. It is quite possible that Julian joined his entourage, for he too was in Constantinople later in 428. On April 10, Nestorius was installed as archbishop. He considered reopening the case against Julian and his allies, writing the pope for details about their condemnation. The polemics between Augustine and Julian—and their theological slogans about the "necessity of sinning"—reverberated throughout the eastern capital in the spring of 428. The words sat at the intersection of high theological debate and mundane social fact. It is remarkable that on April 21, just eleven days after the enthronement of Nestorius, the chancery of the emperor, Theodosius II, issued one of the most remarkable, and misunderstood, laws of the later Roman Empire. The law was suggested by Florentius, a man of Syrian origin who was then praetorian prefect of the east. The law declared: "We cannot suffer for pimps, fathers, and slave-owners who impose the necessity of sinning on their daughters or slave women to enjoy the right of power over them nor to indulge freely in such crime. Thus it pleases us that these men are subjected to such disdain that they may not be able to benefit from the right of power nor may anything be thus acquired by them. It is to be granted to the slaves and daughters and others who have hired themselves out on account of their poverty (whose humble lot has damned them), should they so will, to be relieved of every necessity of this misery by appealing to the succor of bishops, judges, or even defensors. So that, if the pimps shall think these women are to be urged on or impose the necessity of sin on those who are unwilling, they will lose not only that power which they held, but they will be proscribed by exile to the public mines, which is less of a punishment than that of a woman who is seized by a pimp and compelled to endure the filth of an intercourse that she did not will."[77]

Rarely is the translation of Christian ideology into statutory law quite so clear. The "necessity of sinning" was precisely the language of Basil and Cyril, Augustine and Julian, and the formulation undoubtedly reflects the impact of Christianity on the imperial chancery. The law of 428 was a pathbreaking act of social policy. It addressed sin as a social problem. The state took an active concern in the spiritual welfare of women forced into prostitution. The constitution of Theodosius II made a statement that the government was willing to interfere with the private powers of masters and fathers. It also offered aid to poor women who had been forced into prostitution by circumstance rather than private legal power. But there were limits to the new policy. The measure did not punish women who prostituted themselves, nor men who patronized the brothel. Prostitution remained legal. Forcible prostitution, forcible sin, even sin caused by poverty, was redressed.[78]

The nature, timing, and ideological basis of this legislative program have been broadly misunderstood. The notion of coerced sin, first outlined by Basil, was in fact at the center of Christian policy on prostitution and was to remain so down to the age of Justinian. The attempt to segregate slavery from prostitution was much more than a cosmetic reform. Ancient prostitution was enmeshed in the slave trade. The law struck, materially, at the heart of the sex industry in antiquity. Even more, it was the state's first move toward a moral realignment of the system of prostitution. Women without honor, prostitutes and slaves, were still exposed to the forces of male sexuality. But one of the most important subsets of these women, women forced into prostitution, was no longer allowed to exist with state approval. And once the Christian discourse of coercion and consent behind this law is recognized, it becomes clear that these categories remained the moral basis of state policy on prostitution for the next century.[79]

After the law of 428, all prostitution was theoretically sinful but consensual. A decade later, in 439, Theodosius II followed with another measure that confirmed the new moral posture toward prostitution. Like other trades, prostitution had been subject to an imperial tax. The tax corresponded to the acceptance of prostitution as a legitimate form of commerce. Only in 439 did the state publicly admit that collecting revenue from prostitution was indecent in a Christian empire. The language of the law implied, disingenuously, that the emperor and his officials had lately discovered this impropriety. The praetorian prefect, Florentius, "saw that the negligence of our predecessors had been exploited by the damnable shrewdness of pimps, as though having obtained the right under the payment of some tax, they were allowed to conduct the business of ruining sexual modesty. Nor did the state, in its ignorance, check this injury to itself." Florentius, "because of his respect for all people, his love of sexual propriety and chastity," suggested to the emperors that it was "an injury in our times that pimps be allowed to operate in this city, or that their vile profit seem to augment the treasury." Florentius offered to compensate the treasury from his own pocket for any lost revenue, but the actual disposition of the law was to ban pimping rather than to amend the state's fiscal policy. It seems that henceforth the tax was levied on prostitutes directly, and Florentius offered to pick up the tab on any shortfalls this reform caused. Clearly, the main business of this law was the criminalization of pimping. "If anyone hereafter should through a sacrilegious effrontery try to prostitute the bodies of slaves, be they his own or another's, or of freeborn women who have been contracted at any price, first, these most oppressed slaves are vindicated into freedom and the freeborn are freed from this unholy contract. The pimp, having been severely flogged as an example and lesson to all, shall be driven from the boundaries of this city, in which he thought his illicit abomination was to be practiced."[80]

The law of 439 was an extension of the principles laid out a decade earlier, though in the latter law the court reverted to a more traditional vocabulary of sexual morality—*pudicitia* and *pudor* rather than *peccare.* The later law was also more robust. All pimps in Constantinople were flogged and exiled. What had begun as a crusade against coercive pimping was simplified into a prohibition of pimping altogether. Above all the law of 439 is a strong indication that pimping was inherently, incurably coercive. As enacted, the measure was valid in Constantinople. The reign of Leo saw this policy extended beyond Constantinople. In an edict issued to the people, Leo decreed that "no one may hereafter act as a pimp, nor shall revenue be brought into the accounts from this source." The law thus established on an empire-wide basis the ban on pimping that Theodosius II had enacted for the capital city. Leo's law clearly proscribed pimping, not prostitution. And he banned the collection of taxes throughout the provinces from this source, pimps, not from prostitution in general. In one regard he showed a new level of precision: women could not be prostituted, even if they were actresses. Stage performance had an association with venal sex, and actresses were exempt from the penalties of *stuprum.* Acting troupes numbered prostitutes, slave and free, among their company. It is not hard to imagine that, in the wake of Theodosius II's ban on pimping, stage companies continued to run prostitution rings. Leo's law redressed that possibility and highlighted the state's eagerness to combat sexual procurement in any form. Only in AD 498, in the reign of Anastasius, with the abolition of the commercial tax altogether, did the Roman state completely extract itself from the sordid revenues of the sex trade. The emperor was specially lauded for this moral dimension, at best secondary, of his fiscal policy.[81]

These changes lie in the background of the efforts of Justinian to address prostitution as a public policy concern. Early in his reign, Justinian chartered an investigation into the status quo of prostitution in Constantinople. The results of his commission were recorded in the preamble to a new law. Justinian announced that the "name and deeds of pimps were detestable to the ancient laws and emperors." He claimed that he had already passed legislation to increase the penalties against pimps, and he tried to maintain a vigilant policy against them. His investigation, which resulted in the legislation of 535, uncovered a seething underworld of violent and fraudulent procurement. In sixth-century Constantinople, where all prostitution was nominally independent, voluntary, and untaxed, the old system of coercive prostitution was thriving.[82]

The preamble of Justinian's law provides remarkable insight into the state of affairs in sixth-century Constantinople. Justinian found that some pimps "went around the provinces and many places deceiving pitiful young girls, promising them food and clothing." They brought these girls to the capital, where they were kept in miserable conditions. "The pimps offer them out to the perversion of any who wish and take the entire filthy profit that comes from prostituting the girls. The pimps have even made the girls sign written agreements stipulating that they will fulfill the impious and unholy service for the pimps as long as the pimps see fit." Girls as young as ten were being forced into prostitution, and if anyone wanted to redeem one of the victims, the pimps extorted enormous sums. When Justinian went to examine the world of prostitution in sixth-century Constantinople, he found the ancient slave trade in every regard, except the state's approval. Pimps were using classic means of obtaining slaves: defrauding the young and kidnapping them. The young age of the girls brought into prostitution is suggestive of the sheer violence of the system. Kept in squalid brothels, given none of the profits and only enough to survive, the young women were victims of the sort of forcible prostitution that had been illegal for a century.[83]

The law of Justinian showed particular displeasure for the fact that many pimps papered their activities with the trappings of legality. Pimps used written agreements with the prostitutes and "even sought securities for some of the women." Justinian recognized that the contracts between pimps and prostitutes were intrinsically coercive and little more than an effort to lend a modicum of legality and legitimacy to their practice: it is even possible that pimps extracted consent waivers in response to the legislation of Theodosius II and Leo that forbade coercive pimping and then pimping altogether. Justinian's remedy was the most sweeping action yet undertaken by the Roman state. The law prohibited anyone from "leading women into perversion by guile, deceit, or coercion." Justinian decreed even further that "there will henceforth be no allowance given to pimping, keeping women in brothels, offering women for public perversion, or trafficking such women by any other means." The emperor came down hard on the sex trade. He was specific and exhaustive. Whereas the law of Leo had, in terse language, enjoined "let no one be a pimp," Justinian's law forbade pimping, brothel-keeping, prostituting, or any other means of acting as a vendor of sex.[84]

For both Theodosius II and Justinian, the two great Christian codifiers of the law, prostitution was a particular fixation. Under Justinian, prostitution was the target of a policy even wider than his campaign against sexual procurement. Justinian and Theodora founded a convent for reformed prostitutes. This refuge was to be a means of escape for women trapped in the life of the brothel. Named "Repentance," the convent advertised the possibility of inner change for the prostitute and established a reformatory on Christian terms. As we will see in Chapter 4, the idea of the penitent prostitute is exactly contemporaneous, and ideologically correlated, with the legal program against coercion in the sex industry. As with the regulation of same-sex eros, the state's intervention in the sex trade reached its pitch of ideological fervor in the reign of Justinian, and once again relied on a religio-juridical complex. In his *Secret History,* Procopius cynically reported that the emperor and empress *forced* prostitutes who did not want to convert, against their will, to enter the monastery. He claimed that these prostitutes threw themselves off the walls of the convent as their only means of resistance. The very language, "forced to convert," showed a close familiarity with the moral and intellectual foundations of Christian policy between Theodosius II and Justinian. Procopius inverted the dynamics of consent and coercion to create a malicious send-up of the Christian approach to prostitution.[85]

The policy initiated in 428 and fulfilled in the age of Justinian represented a momentous crack in the foundations of an ancient institutional order. What requires emphasis, though, and what proves revealing for the larger question of the Christianization of law, is the extent to which this was not destined to be one Christian sexual policy among others. It was *the* front edge of Christian legislative intervention in the sexual economy. Rules against homoerotic acts were explosive but exceedingly rare; the statutes against adultery already on the books were sufficient; the direct repression of prostitution was inconceivable. So the Christian state, from Theodosius II to Justinian, the two great codifiers, made sexual coercion *the* signal reform issue. Over a crucial century, in which other examples of Christian sexual legislation are virtually nonexistent, the problem of coerced prostitution generated a string of enactments whose evolving scope reflects the earnest ambitions of lawmakers. At its core this campaign against coerced prostitution is an expression of a new model of human solidarity. In the name of suppressing sin, the campaign brought the most morally invisible bodies inside the horizons of public solicitude. The state, so long accustomed to limiting its prerogatives to the regulation of property, status, and rank, could no longer remain absolutely indifferent to the exploitation of those bodies beyond *civic* claim to honor; it is no huge exaggeration to say that this policy marks the passing of an age.

CONCLUSION: RHYTHMS OF CHANGE IN LATE ANTIQUITY

Beneath the extreme surface contingency of the changes that unfolded in the later Roman empire, a certain deep pattern seems to emerge. The Constantinian conversion triggered a massive surge toward Christian sexual culture, but one that was still highly uncertain in terms of its outcome and its potential relation to the public order. The era of the Theodosian dynasty appears as the crux of change, when the influence of Christian sexual morality begins to find some uncertain expression in public law, when the leadership of the church was forced to confront a broader array of social realities in the wake of mass conversion, and when a thoroughly ascetic sexual morality made its decisive reckoning with the institution of marriage. It is perhaps not immaterial that the culture of erotic lamps, that humble domestic instrument, experiences a decisive decline in the decades around AD 400; a jarring change pulses through the Mediterranean world in these years. But only in the age of Justinian do we find a more complete, more confident assimilation of Christian sexuality and the public order of law and culture. Any historian is unwise to bet against complexity, against the deeper continuities that abide beyond the reach of ecclesiastical power or prerogative. The historian of eros most of all must remember that talk is merely talk, and that no moral ideology can control such quixotic, individual, human forces as shame or desire. We are not positing, nor would it be possible to posit, a sea change in human behavior. But it is worth risking the obvious dangers of overstatement, if the opposite tendency, of failing to emerge from the thicket of Christian disagreements, threatens to obscure the truth that the Theodosian generations witnessed one of the great revolutions in the history of public sexual morality. Perhaps it would be safer to hedge bets and call the transition of these years an inflection point in a longer, slower, and highly circumstantial passage from classical to Christian values. In the case of same-sex eros, ideals of marriage, and concepts of sexual agency alike, the victory of Christianity drove an epochal reorganization of the substance of sexual morality and its place in the order of the ancient city. As Chapter 4 will show, imaginative literature was called upon to represent this new order of relationships between individual, society, and cosmos, and it was particularly suited for doing so.

CHAPTER FOUR

Revolutionizing Romance in the Late Classical World

SELF, SOCIETY, AND LITERARY SYMBOLS

In the days leading up to his execution, with confrontation hanging over the atmosphere like a leaden sky, Jesus relayed to the priests of the Temple in Jerusalem the startling message that they would be preceded into the kingdom of heaven by tax-collectors and prostitutes. The charismatic Galilean rabbi had earned a reputation for his charitable attitude toward society's outcasts, and it was known on solid authority that he went so far as to share a table with them. Almost four centuries later the radical benevolence of Jesus had lost none of its original charge, in part because he had chosen his outcasts so well. In the words of the Antiochene preacher John Chrysostom, "These two represent the highest sins, born each of a grievous passion, lust for the body and lust for coin." God, in the dispensation of forgiveness, was not a respecter of persons, and nothing symbolized the limitless potential of grace like the moral rehabilitation of a prostitute. Because of her penitence, there was hope for all. She proved that "it is easy to rise from the very depths of wickedness." But John Chrysostom did not have to rely on ancient scriptures to find an example of such extraordinary transformation.

> Have you not heard how that prostitute, who once surpassed all in her wanton immorality, now overshadows all in her moral scruple? I am not talking about the prostitute in the gospels, but the one in our own time, hailing from the most lawless city of Phoenicia. For she was at one time a prostitute among us, in fact holding pride of place in the theater, and her name was famous everywhere, not just in our city but as far as Cilicia and Cappadocia. She emptied many an estate, conquered many an orphan. Not a few even accused her of sorcery, saying that she ensnared not just by her physical charms but also by the use of potions. This whore at one time held the brother of the empress under her spell, so great was her tyranny.

The conversion of such a celebrity, from the most insalubrious quarters of ancient society, furnished an irresistible opportunity for a crusader like Chrysostom to make a point about the quality of divine mercy. The woman—a stage actress and quite possibly a courtesan, for the two professions shaded into one another in law, ideology, and reality—had attained a reputation stretching across the eastern Mediterranean. We need not doubt the ability of an exquisitely beautiful woman, in a world where respectability meant seclusion, to capture the public mind. But this nameless actress walked away from her fame. If Chrysostom is to be believed, her retirement caused such resentment that the governor was prodded to force her back on stage, going so far as to dispatch armed soldiers for the purpose. But having received the purifying waters of baptism, she could not be dislodged from the virgins who had received her.[1]

Some people, their every movement full of mysterious resonance, are destined to become symbols. This star of the stage who repented and retired among the virgins was to launch a thousand legends. Her story was ready-made for literary adaptation, and not only because of the sheer arc of her conversion. Her legend was born at an opportune moment. She lived in the age of mass conversion, during a generation that saw the ranks of the baptized grow at a startling pace. The waters of baptism flowed over men and women who brought into the church different depths of spiritual commitment. As society trudged listlessly into the Christian church, the entry of the penitent prostitute offered crystalline sharpness. Her story of repentance struck a chord. The female body was a symbol beyond time and circumstance. Across ancient literature, the woman's body stood as a cipher, capable of expressing the most intensely felt beliefs about the order of the world. The stark *opposition* between purity and pollution, between honor and shame, was endlessly reworked in the literary imagination. But the *transition* from one pole to the other, from purity to corruption or vice versa, was almost never compassed, precisely because the woman's body was an objective correlative for an entire state of being. The passage of a prostitute's body from prurience to penitence handed Christian authors a figure that not only resonated in an ancient arcade of symbols. Quite inadvertently, the penitent prostitute transcended the very logic of an immemorial symbolic architecture.[2]

Here we will trace the embodiment of shame and sin in prose narratives spanning the high and late empires. The claims made are, at one level, literary. While it has been recognized that early Christian literature is related to the Greek romance, the depth of Christian engagement with the dynamics of female honor in pre-Christian fiction remains to be fully explored. The subgenre of literature that grew up around the figure of the penitent prostitute not only demands to be read in light of ancient fictional traditions; the narrative possibilities opened by the story of sexual transformation suddenly illuminate the inner logic of the old literature. In other words, penitent prostitutes are good to read with. But the claims of this chapter go beyond the literary. Literature, in the words of Stephen Greenblatt, is "an exceptionally sensitive register of the complex struggles and harmonies of culture." The romances—Greek novels and Christian legends alike—are artifacts of a shared, public system of values. Even a mode of literature as formal and fantastic as the romance reflects the expectations and experiences of the society that produced it. The transformation of female honor in prose fiction recapitulates the profound revolution in sexual morality in the late classical world. The ancient novels are stories of eros in which honorable female sexuality is inviolable, because sexual morality itself is lodged in a social order whose logic provides the syntax of the romance. The early Christian literature adopts this form but directly inverts it, preserving the heroine's corporal integrity but doing so eternally, so that her perpetual chastity becomes, like the apostle's martyrdom, a rejection of society and society's claim to represent the constitutive grounds of the self. Early Christian romance is the literature of a persecuted minority; the heroine's integrity is a renunciation of the dominant order and a submission to the grander, invisible, cosmic order. But in the wake of the Constantinian revolution, as Christianity absorbed society, the secular order could no longer serve as an anti-Christian backdrop. The symbolism of female sexual honor shifted accordingly. The penitent prostitute emerged as a new archetype. The penitent prostitute violated, in the most explosive form, the deep, unifying convention of romance—the heroine's chastity. The salvation of the prostitute, by offering redemption to the figure whose claim to social honor was most impossible, symbolized the supremacy of a divine scale of sexual morality. The arrival of this new archetype—whose birth depended on the enduring vitality of the ancient array of character types—was a cultural moment of the greatest significance. The heroines of fiction were transformed from "damsels in distress" at the mercy of fate into empowered sexual agents who determine their own destiny. The rise of this new type symbolized not just a new set of sexual norms or values, but a new, Christian order of sexual morality.[3]

VIRGINITY IMPERILED IN THE ANCIENT ROMANCE

The *Ephesian Tale,* an imperial romance authored by an otherwise unknown bearer of the name Xenophon, has seemed so abrupt and artless that it is uncertain whether what we have is the original text or a mere summary. Regardless, romance, even at its best, is a genre made of conventions, and the author of the *Ephesian Tale* as we possess it has made strikingly little effort to conceal the dependence of his narrative on prefabricated parts. The heroine, Anthia, is a superlative beauty who suffers an utterly predictable sequence of threats to her chastity. "Oh dangerous charm, oh ill-starred beauty, why do you persecute me, why do you cause me such evil? Were the tombs and murders, the chains of slavery and the lawlessness of pirates not enough?" Having survived all this, the final threat to Anthia's corporal integrity was to be the most trying, as well as the most melodramatic. "Now I will be placed in a house of ill-repute, and a pimp will *compel* me to lose the chastity which I have guarded up to now for Habrocomes." When she learns that it is her lot to be sold into prostitution, she asks the slave who is the instrument of her fate to kill her. Anthia's experience of the brothel, and her eventual escape from it, is not only the climactic episode of the *Ephesian Tale.* It is, in its utter conventionality, a paradigm of the romance, of the genre's most basic assumptions about the body and society.[4]

Despite her pitiful death wish, Anthia ended up in the clutches of a brothel keeper in Tarentum, Italy. He *compelled* her to be placed in front of the brothel, and she lamented that she was *compelled* to play the harlot. But her despair quickly turned to resolve. "Why do I bewail my fate instead of finding some contrivance [*mēchanē*] by which I might preserve the chastity which I have safeguarded up to now?" As the crowd of lustful customers jostled to pay for her services, Anthia, "without any recourse [*amēchanē*] from this evil, nevertheless found a device for her escape." She threw herself to the ground and feigned the violent convulsions of an epileptic fit. The dumbstruck crowd felt "pity and fear," and their erotic aspirations were, temporarily, dampened. The pimp took her home to recover, and she wove an elaborate story to convince him that she was truly afflicted with the disease. Her feint succeeded in creating just enough delay to let the universe resolve itself happily. She remained inviolate, and when she eventually rejoined her husband, she could boast to him, "I remain pure for you, having contrived every device [*mēchanē*] for the preservation of chastity." He, too, protested his unimpeachable fidelity, and they "easily persuaded each other, since that was what they wanted."[5]

Anthia's escape from the brothel is a paradigm of the heroine's chastity in the romance. Parallel endangerments from pimps and pirates, slave owners and other ruffians, recur throughout the entire genre. The most direct parallel, and the only rival to the *Ephesian Tale* in the transparency of its conventionality, survives in the popular *History of Apollonius, King of Tyre.* The *History of Apollonius* is a family romance rather than an erotic romance, but the pattern of separation, endurance, and reunion is structurally parallel. In this story, which survives in Latin, it is the protagonist's daughter, Tarsia, who has been cast on the cruel winds of fate and endures lurid threats to her virginal purity. In the climactic scene of the *History,* Tarsia, like Anthia, is placed for sale in a slave market. The prince of the city and the town's most notorious procurer enter a bidding war for the beautiful girl, with equally prurient interests. As the price escalates, the prince reckons that the purchase of this one creature would force him to sell off a number of his other slaves. With the dispassionate logic of a cost-cutting accountant, he reasons that he can let the pimp buy her, then pay to be the first customer for just a fraction of the girl's sale price. "I'll go in first and snatch the knot of her virginity at a low price and it will be the same as if I had bought her." The deep material and ideological connection between the flesh trade and the sex trade was rarely exposed to such direct view. The demand for sex was a major impetus behind the circulation of human chattel in the Roman world.[6]

The pimp in this story, a monochromatic villain, ignores Tarsia's pleas for compassion. "Don't you know that supplications and tears have no force with pimps and executioners?" Like the executioner, the pimp is an agent of death. He sends her to the brothel. The prince, with his face covered, entered first. Tarsia prostrated herself at his feet and in the most desperate terms begged for his pity. "Listen to the misfortune that brought me to this unhappy state, weigh the fact of my respectable ancestry." The prince was startled into compassion. He, too, had a virgin daughter, for whom he might fear a similar fate. He abandoned his lustful intentions and told Tarsia to implore future customers with the same sad recital, until she had earned enough to buy her own freedom. A train of suitors follows, and all are so moved by Tarsia's story that they refrained from impairing her chastity. She endured, inviolate, until she was reunited with her father, who promised Tarsia to the noble prince as a bride (and incited the people of Mytilene to burn the merciless pimp alive). Tarsia's preservation of her chastity was less elaborately contrived than Anthia's. She relied on the bare compassion of strangers. But the underlying assumptions about the order of the universe were the same.[7]

The inviolability of the heroine's sexual integrity is the deep premise of the ancient romance. Leucippe was said to have endured "every indignity and outrage against her body, except one." It went without saying what single disgrace she had been spared. The physical integrity of the female protagonist was *the* convention, in a genre of conventions. The great literary critic Northup Frye has observed of the genre, that "with romance it is much harder to avoid the feeling of convention, that the story is one of a family of similar stories. Hence in the criticism of romance we are led very quickly from what the individual work says to what the entire convention it belongs to is saying through the work." The insight is crucial, but it requires an important amendment. Frye simply underestimated the sophistication of some ancient romances. To compare, for example, naive texts like the *Ephesian Tale* with more artful confections like *Leucippe and Clitophon,* without recognizing the entirely different literary registers of the texts, is to miss the supreme command of the medium that authors like Achilles Tatius display. The *Ephesian Tale* and *Leucippe and Clitophon* use the same set of conventions but use them to vastly different effect. What they share is a generic syntax, out of which the meaning of the individual work is created.[8]

The ancient romances are stories of eros, a consuming physical passion that binds two beautiful lovers, a young man and young woman, in mutual attraction. The protagonists are unfailingly of high birth, born into the civic aristocracies of a broadly Hellenic Mediterranean. The stories are set against the backdrop of a physically familiar but temporally irreal Greek past, what Bakhtin called "adventure time." Eros is the driving force of the story: a force of nature that, unbeckoned, guides human destiny. The novels celebrate eros as a gift of nature; they ponder the stark mystery that replenishing the city with new generations should also be a source of the greatest pleasure. The romances are unhesitantly carnal: eros is the ecstatic joy of bodily friction. At the same time the eros they admire is a force that has been safely caged in matrimony—if just barely. The novels are conservative, but hardly frigid. The novels unabashedly celebrate sex itself. The romances are idealizing. The lovers are noble in blood and mien, their passion is pure and true. Even the men are usually faithful, physically; emotionally, it is imperative that they remain committed. The mutual attraction between two lovers, married or about to be so, represented a new space for literate cultural idealism around domestic bliss and private fulfillment. The social and moral logic that underwrites the genre is shared between texts, even if the individual authors regard it with different levels of reverence. The social logic of the romances transcends the genre; the raw material of the romance is preliterary, essentially folkloric.[9]

Structurally the romances are stories of adversity and adventure that resolve happily in marriage. In the prelude to the final book of his romance, Chariton signaled the shift from misadventure to resolution in revealing terms: "No longer shall we have piracy and slavery, trials and battles, grisly suicide, war or captivity, but righteous passions and legitimate marriages." Throughout the narrative the heroine faces grave dangers that call into question her status. The heroine of romance is a recognizable social type; her essence precedes her individuality. She is beautiful, of free and noble birth, and in the prime of her marriageable years. Preferably the heroine is superlatively beautiful and impeccably wellborn. Callirhoe, for instance, was the daughter of the leading citizen of Syracuse, and she was the "glory of all Sicily," with a "beauty that was not human but divine." Anthia, at fourteen, was "in the very bloom of her body's beauty," a beauty that "was an astonishment, far beyond all the other virgins." In *Leucippe and Clitophon,* we first encounter Leucippe through the eyes of her lover, Clitophon, who dilates on the experience of such superhuman beauty. In *Daphnis and Chloe,* the drama revolves around the fact that the protagonists were exposed as infants and raised by simple peasants; Chloe, even as a sheepherder, is supremely if naively charming, but it is only in the very last sequence of the story that her true identity, as a daughter of the town's gentry, was revealed. In fact, once she was literally scrubbed of her rural grime and properly dressed, it was indisputably obvious that her rustic parents did not in reality produce "such a maiden as that."[10]

The heroine is free, but her status is not merely an external attribute describing her current condition. Though the heroine is routinely subjected to enslavement, she retains her free nature. The heroine's freedom is objective, a quality of her being that is apparent even to other characters in the romance. When tomb raiders abducted Callirhoe, they were worried that it would be obvious from her appearance that they had kidnapped a free person. "Her beauty isn't human and won't go unnoticed. Will we say, 'She's a slave'—who would believe that once they've seen her?" The man who buys her immediately perceives her true status. "It is impossible for anybody who is not free by nature to be beautiful." In the *Ephesian Tale,* Anthia's master gives her to a fellow slave, a goatherd, but she manages to convince him to pity her "good birth." When Leucippe is enslaved in Ephesus, she throws herself at the feet of her mistress, Melite, who instantly recognized, despite her tattered appearance, that the girl was not really a slave. "Even among such travails your beauty proclaims your good birth." In *The Ethiopian Tale,* status is such an objective quality that, after a battle, the victors ransom the free captives and keep the slaves in slavery![11]

Because the heroine's identity partakes in the mysterious essence of her freedom, to lose that freedom would be a sort of death. The romantic heroine must be, volubly, willing to die. Callirhoe would expressly rather be dead than be a slave. Anthia tells the slave about to sell her, "Just kill me yourself." Slavery, and with it presumptive sexual shame, is a sort of social death. For the heroine to lose her physical purity would be, in effect, to cease to exist. The sentiment receives arch expression in *The Ethiopian Tale.* The heroine, Charicleia, reflects on her willingness to commit suicide rather than experience defloration. "If it is a death achieved without violation, sweet will be my end . . . chastity is a glorious winding sheet." The line between honor and shame, freedom and slavery, chastity and violation, was considered a threshold between life and death. This conception fuels one of the more stunning tropes of the romance, the apparent death and resurrection of the heroine. Clitophon repeatedly believes that Leucippe has suffered a gruesome death, but each time she is "reborn," in that she reappears in the story unharmed—alive and virginal.[12]

Characterization in the romance is based on sharply drawn types. In the social logic that assigns meaning to each role, slavery is encoded as the opposite of the heroine. The logic is often exposed in highly contrived judicial dramas, which are a stock element of the genre. The civil law in the Greek romance is like the backdrop of the urbanized Mediterranean: recognizable, slightly irreal, and bent to suit the author's purposes as needed. The law is an expression of a sort of universal social grammar. A character in Chariton's romance, for instance, defended himself against charges of adultery by alleging that Callirhoe was a slave: "The law of adultery does not protect slaves." The trial scene in *Leucippe and Clitophon* is an elaborately rendered judicial set piece. The law, especially as it bears on sexual rights and prohibitions, is a cipher for the social system. In the trial of Melite for adultery, the prosecutor outlines the thoroughly social matrix of the rules governing sexual contact. "If her husband was dead, the guilt would be removed, for there is no one to suffer the injury of adultery. A marriage lacking a husband cannot be outraged. But if the husband lives, the marriage has not been abolished, and he who has so thoroughly violated the lawfully wedded wife of another man has become an outlaw."[13]

The shared plot of these stories, in which an archetype of the beautiful, noble, free virgin is subjected to a series of stock threats to her physical integrity, belongs to the deep structure of romance. In his interpretation of romance, Frye distinguished between the structure of realist narrative and the structure of romance by observing that realism is generally "horizontal"—it uses "a technique of causality in which the characters are prior to the plot, in which the problem is normally 'given these characters, what will happen?'" Romance, by contrast, is vertical, "sensational," moving "[from] one discontinuous episode to another, describing things that happen to characters, for the most part, externally." Realism presents a "hence" narrative, romance an "and then" narrative. This analysis generally holds true for the ancient examples of the genre. The characters are presented, but they do not develop. Heroes and villains are highly stereotyped, and the "moral facts," at the surface level, are greatly simplified.[14]

The discontinuous episodic structure that was the skeleton of ancient romance was closely related to the undercurrents of popular fatalism that run through the genre. Fortune is omnipresent in the novels. To her capricious will all the twists of the plot are attributed. In *Leucippe and Clitophon,* some form of *tuch-* is used 142 times, that is, several times on each page. The Fortune of the imperial romances is not an orderly theological concept; her very nature is mysterious and arbitrary, but ultimately benevolent. She subjects the protagonists to fearsome travails, but she rescues them too. This uncanny mixture of whim and providence, of flux and order, is within the mainstream of religious currents in the high empire. The Fortune of the novels is no mere literary ornamentation. She is the same awesome divinity who was worshipped, in cult, across the Mediterranean, like never before in the Roman Empire—a syncretistic, cosmological goddess in a syncretistic, cosmological age. The romances were, like the temples where Fortune was worshipped, monuments built in awe of her supervenient power over human affairs.[15]

The Fortune who presides over the romances is a literary spirit. Over and over again, Fortune is said to be a dramatist. One character tells Chareas, "Fortune loves invention, and you have been cast in an unhappy drama." Not just the authors of romance, but also the characters are aware that their lives have the shape of literature. Clitophon launches on his story with the reflection, "I was nineteen years of age when Fortune began her drama." Later he laments yet another bad turn. "Fortune as usual has set upon me and contrived a new drama." In *The Ethiopian Tale* the characters experience the "ceaseless turning of the human lot, full of twists." In despair Theagenes wonders if he and Charicleia should not just submit to the "destiny that everywhere chased" them by surrendering. The gods' vendetta was "making us into playthings, as though our affairs were a drama on a stage." Charicleia, by contrast, counsels resistance. In the final scenes, the king and his people alike marvel at the "theatrics of Fortune." The literary pretensions of Fortune are part of the high-pitched aesthetic self-awareness of the romances. But given the real place of Fortune in the imperial pantheon, it would be misleading to dismiss these comparisons as empty authorial self-aggrandizement.[16]

The canny allusions to life as literature manifest themselves in a revealing metaphor that recurs across the romances. When Anthia is enslaved in the brothel, she laments her fate, but she steels her resolve and decides to find "some contrivance" for protecting her chastity: the feigned fit of epilepsy. After she survives and is reunited with her lover, she attributes her chastity to the fact that she contrived "every device" for the protection of virtue. Similarly, in *The Ethiopian Tale,* the protagonist can rely, in the most hopeless of circumstances, on "some contrivance" that will allow escape. The word for "contrivance," *mēchanē,* is a rich word, alluding broadly to man-made devices that illustrate human resourcefulness. But *mēchanē* can also have the more narrow sense of a stage device, a theatrical machine especially used to produce sudden apparitions of the gods. The ploys of the girls whose chastity is threatened are not only desperate and incredible ploys; they are, self-consciously, stage devices. The girls who preserve their chastity do so simply by playing their role, by compelling the drama somehow to go on, so that the story can unfold according to its logic which, of course, will preserve their bodies inviolate.[17]

The more sophisticated specimens of ancient romance, especially the works of Achilles Tatius and Heliodorus, are in such total command of the tradition that it is illuminating to consider how they exploit the tensions inherent in the standard repertoire of the genre. *Leucippe and Clitophon* is an arch melodrama, a wry, winking, sensational elaboration of the erotic romance. Its most notable idiosyncrasies form carefully wrought statements on the conventions of romantic literature. For example, the first two books of the novel are conducted according to the rules of classical pederasty, as Clitophon is tutored in seduction by his expert cousin Clinias. Achilles Tatius exploits the rich possibilities offered by this conceit. It allows him to burlesque Plato, and it serves as a kind of valediction to same-sex eros before the heterosexual romance is able to proceed. But the first two books of *Leucippe and Clitophon* are also a deliberate manipulation of the rules of the romantic genre, especially the delicate protocols of feminine respectability.

The scenes of Clitophon's tutelage in the arts of seduction call into question the distinction between volition and coercion, a distinction that is a foundational prop of the romantic genre. The classical model of pederasty, which institutionalized a certain amount of bluff and ambiguity around the question of the boy's consent, provided a ready contrast to the strident unwillingness of the romantic heroine to consent to anything but marriage.

Clinias tells Clitophon that "when you have a tacit understanding that the next step is the big deed, even those who are ready to surrender prefer the appearance of compulsion, to let the façade of force deflect the shame of consent." If the girl's resistance is "hearty," Clinias warns not to use "force, because she is not yet persuaded." But "as soon as her will begins to weaken, act your role in this play, lest your drama fail to reach its conclusion." The theatrical metaphor is clever, for the astute reader will realize that Clinias does not know exactly what sort of drama he has been cast in. His assumptions about the will—as a murky and pliable thing—contradict the social grammar of female respectability and of the romance in general.[18]

Before the first two books are finished, Achilles Tatius offers even more smirking reflections on the protocols of romantic virginity. When Leucippe proved willing to submit to the sexual advances of Clitophon, her virginity was saved, as it were, against her will, through the last-minute intervention of her mother, who was alerted by a dream. On discovering her daughter in a compromising situation, Leucippe's mother offers a doleful speech. She regrets leaving a war zone to come to Tyre, because Leucippe seemed ready to lose her chastity willfully. "Would that you had been outraged by a conquering Thracian, for at least corruption by coercion carries no shame!" This, of course, is not true, at least not in romance, which is a whole genre built on the need of respectable women to preserve their physical integrity against violent incursions. Leucippe strikes back against her mother's diatribe with a canny defense that makes equally dubious use of romantic protocols. "Impugn not my virginity, mother . . . for this I know is true: no one has done dishonor to my maidenhood." In defense of herself Leucippe turns the deepest premise of the romance, the heroine's chastity, into a mere technicality. Achilles has inverted the basic tension between internal purity and external endangerment to create a heroine who is internally compromised but externally safeguarded. Leucippe states her wish that there was some sort of virginity test to prove her innocence—a wish that is fulfilled at the novel's climax.[19]

After the failed seduction, Leucippe's virginal resolve is steeled, and she even refuses future opportunities to sleep with Clitophon. Leucippe does not so much develop as a character, as the story itself returns to conventional order. She becomes a romantic heroine to fit. The romance builds toward the final and gravest threat to her chastity, the gruesome scene in which her master, Thersander, attempts to rape her. Although the setting is a private encounter between a master and his slave, the elements of the scene are perfectly homologous with the escapes of Anthia and Tarsia from the public brothel. This scene is extremely conscious of itself and its place in the economy of romance. The villainy of Thersander is compounded by his brash refusal to believe that Leucippe has maintained her virginity through such arduous trials; thus he refused to believe in the romance as a package of happy conceits. His unwillingness to suspend disbelief, to allow this sort of literature to exist, is for the author almost as wicked as his eagerness to rape Leucippe. Leucippe, in this scene, at last becomes fully aware of her status as a romantic heroine; she taunts Thersander with the fact that his threats will only bestow greater glory on her, which would be a strange thing for a slave to say, after all, unless she knew she was a romantic heroine. She warns Thersander that her *eleutheria,* her freedom, will protect her. Achilles has contrived a brilliant scene in which *eleutheria* refers precisely to the heroine's objective status rather than to her autonomy. For no coherent reason whatsoever, this claim deters Thersander from his malicious designs. Or rather, for no reason other than the bare logic of the romantic genre itself, in which the honorable protagonist will remain inviolate, does she retain her purity. Whereas Thersander refuses to believe in the rules of romance, Achilles Tatius asks the reader to believe *solely* out of convention rather than narrative plausibility. Leucippe's *mēchanē,* her device of escape, is simultaneously the least convincing, and the most self-aware, of any in the genre.[20]

Achilles Tatius exposes the internal logic of the genre and tests whether the reader will believe in it simply because it is good theater. He is willing to lay bare the purely artificial, literary substance animating his characters. Leucippe's sudden and inexplicable transformation from a willing young girl curious about eros into a romantic heroine capable of the most soaring defenses of chastity is an example. More darkly, the creation of a doppelgänger for Leucippe, an "ill-starred" prostitute who is beheaded in Leucippe's place, is an accomplishment without equal in the ancient romances. In the riddle of the severed head, which hangs, unexplained, over much of the narrative, Achilles confronts the reader with the mysterious dispensations of fate. The brilliance of this creation ensures us that the arch tone Achilles maintains across his romance is not postmodern camp before its time, but instead a serious engagement with the deepest social and cosmological assumptions of romance. The manipulation of romantic protocols is a sincere way of questioning the Fortune that presides over the order of romance—in fact, over the world. This story, with its intricate knowingness, promises the ability to confront the theodicy that underlies literature, *through* literature.[21]

The Ethiopian Tale of Heliodorus makes equally canny use of the generic conventions underlying the inviolability of the heroine's body. *The Ethiopian Tale* is as self-aware as *Leucippe and Clitophon,* but the effect achieved by the author's consciousness is an air of baroque grandeur rather than keen lightness. *The Ethiopian Tale* is the latest of the erotic romances that survive, and there are compelling reasons to place it sometime in the second half of the fourth century. *The Ethiopian Tale* deliberately builds an aura of latest and greatest. All of the conventional themes are allowed to unravel, in stately fashion. By far the longest of the erotic romances, it is unique in weaving two story patterns into a single narrative. At one level it is the story of Theagenes and Charicleia, their separation and endurance, their eventual union. *The Ethiopian Tale* is also a homeward journey for Charicleia, who gradually discovers her true identity as the princess of Ethiopia. In the sophistication of its narrative architecture, *The Ethiopian Tale* is without peer among the ancient novels. But it is also distinctive in its fixation on male bodily purity, and in general its chilly tone toward the pleasures of the flesh. *The Ethiopian Tale* very consciously redeploys the traditional armory of the erotic romance, but in the service of a hieratic vision of human life.[22]

Heliodorus reworks the conventions of romance to serve his own purposes. Theagenes and Charicleia find themselves enslaved at the palace of a Persian satrap, whose wife has sensual designs on Theagenes. Threats to the hero are not uncommon in romance, but this scene is far removed from its direct parallel in *Leucippe and Clitophon,* which has Clitophon indulge the harmless desires of his seductress, Melite. For Heliodorus, the bodily purity of Theagenes is supremely important. Earlier in the story he has sworn that he is innocent of experience with a woman. At the end of the story, he too will undergo a virginity test (in fact, a test to ensure that he is pure, so that he can be the victim of a human sacrifice!). The language of physical and ritual purity, usually reserved for female bodies, is applied to Theagenes. He faces the threat of seduction as a threat not to his romantic fidelity but rather to his corporal integrity. He is distraught lest he, "without any experience of Charicleia, will be polluted by unlawful intercourse with another woman."[23]

Heliodorus has constructed a scene where the male hero faces the dangers that conventionally threaten a heroine's chastity. In these desperate straits Charicleia offers counsel to her lover. "If you have in mind to go all the way through with this deed, I have no place to argue. For indeed our very salvation and survival may depend upon it." But, of course, she hopes he will resolve not to submit. Charicleia tells him that he should feign assent and string out the plot, deluding the woman in her hopes and desires. "Surely in the space of time that you create it will be the will of the gods somehow to effect our deliverance." She tells him to create a *mēchanē,* a device to protect his virtue in an impossible situation. Charicleia, in short, teaches Theagenes how to be a romantic heroine. She simultaneously gives voice to the theodicy of romance. The will of the gods is inscrutable, but at the very least the shape of the story they create promises deliverance—in the form of chastity and marriage—to the protagonists.[24]

The authorial insistence on the hero's physical integrity is unusual, and it is symptomatic of the skepticism toward carnal pleasure that animates this novel. *The Ethiopian Tale* is an erotic romance in form but not in spirit. It is quite as far removed from the earthy sensuality of the earlier romances as is Christian fiction. The story is missing all the wry glances toward physical pleasure that the genre usually allows. It is impossible to imagine the pallid Charicleia as an erotic enthusiast. In the world of Heliodorus, the priestly race condemns the common *aphrodisia* and descends to intercourse "not for the use of pleasure but for the succession of generations." In the penultimate scene, as Charicleia and Theagenes are married, the high priest pronounces them solemnly wed by the law of procreation. In the final scene the two are invested as priest and priestess and march into the city to perform even "more sacred" mysteries. In any other ancient novel, such an allusion would clearly be to the rites of the nuptial couch, but here there is no hint of sex. Gone is the warm eroticism of carnal friction, in its place an obsession with purity that is sacerdotal in its tone and timbre.[25]

The fifth-century church historian Socrates reported, in the fifth book of his ecclesiastical history, that the same Heliodorus who wrote *The Ethiopian Tale* in his youth became a Christian bishop in Thessaly. Unlike later Byzantine tales which have Achilles Tatius converting to the faith, this biographical note is not so far removed in time and it is not an obvious specimen of literary wish fulfillment. The report deserves credence, as does the detail, added by Socrates, that Heliodorus introduced strict clerical continence in his church. That the author of this final romance, so frigid in its erotic outlook, enjoined sexual abstinence on even the married members of his clergy, is entirely consonant with the hieratic fixation on purity and pollution in *The Ethiopian Tale.* Heliodorus lived against the backdrop of mass conversion to Christianity and became a leader in the movement at a particularly consequential moment. He may well have found the sexual austerity of the religion congenial and familiar. But what he would have quickly discovered, on the entry to his new faith, was its will to impose rigorous codes of corporal purity on all its adherents, not just a priestly race, set apart, with special privileges of divine communication. The Christians would soon develop a literature adequate to such an ambitious project, and it would entail reworking the conventions of romance so thoroughly that we cannot but wonder if a nostalgic spirit like Heliodorus would have been enthused or scandalized. He lived on the cusp of a tremendous literary revolution. But this revolution was only possible because, from very early on, the conventions of romance—above all the charged symbolism of female purity—had fully entered the bloodstream of Christian fiction.[26]

THE CHRISTIAN ACTS AND THE INVERSION OF ROMANCE

Our most complete version of the diffuse lore that attached to the Christian apostle Andrew survives as a Latin epitome composed by the sixth-century bishop Gregory of Tours. In the preface to his summary of Andrew's legend, Gregory concedes that some critics considered the stories of Andrew apocryphal, "on account of their excessive prolixity." His avowed purpose in writing was to extract the miraculous pulp and to discard the unnecessary husk of the narrative. The story is none the better for Gregory's literary surgery. But we can be grateful to have, in however brusque and artless an outline, the shape of this ancient apostolic legend in full profile. From Gregory's bare summary we can reconstruct a rather elaborate episode built around a narrative trope that must have seemed deeply familiar to the original audience of the Acts. The apostle, shortly after arriving in the Roman province of Achaea, converts the proconsul Lesbius to the Christian faith. Then a slave, Trophima, the former concubine of the proconsul, turned to the apostle's teaching and the sexual rigors that accompanied it. Her current lover, discomfited by the loss of his sexual companion, designed a plot to undo her. He went to the slave's mistress, the proconsul's wife, reporting, "Trophima has returned to harlotry, which she used to practice with my lord the proconsul, to whom she has again joined herself." It was a well-laid trap, because to the proconsul's wife this news seemed like a revelation: "No wonder my husband has left me behind and for six months now refused our marital rites, for he loves his slave!" So the wife did what any archvillain in a romance would have done: she had Trophima, newly converted to the Christian faith, condemned to the brothel.[27]

Trophima—slave, concubine—was no romantic heroine of the ordinary build, but she nevertheless found herself in the archetypal testing grounds of feminine respectability. In the brothel, she prayed continuously, and when eager customers came to her, she clutched a copy of the gospel to her chest. One day an unusually insistent client entered, and, while resisting, Trophima dropped the gospel. She cried out to heaven, "Keep me from suffering this pollution, Lord, in whose name I esteem chastity!" An angel appeared and struck the youth dead. Then Trophima, for what reason Gregory has omitted to relate, resurrected the dead young man, a sight "the whole city" rushed to see. The proconsul's wife was killed by a demon in the public bath, a penalty for her persecution of Trophima. Nevertheless, a distraught nurse prevailed upon Andrew to resurrect the proconsul's wife, which, in the very public atmosphere of the governor's headquarters, he did. All were reconciled, miracles reported far and wide, newfound chastity saved.[28]

The romantic elements, even in the eviscerated version of the Acts that has come down to us through Gregory, are unmistakable. The *Acts of Andrew* were hardly alone. In a freestanding episode in the fifth-century *Lausiac History,* the Christian adaptation of the romantic repertoire is even more evident. In a "very old book ascribed to Hippolytus," Palladius found a story about a "certain maiden, most noble and extremely beautiful, in the city of the Corinthians, who was practicing the life of virginity." In an age of persecution, she was denounced to the governor as a Christian. The "woman-mad" governor had his own designs on her, and he "tried every device [*mēchanē*]" but "could not persuade the girl." He ordered her sentenced to a brothel, where she was subjected to the usual threats. She deflected her suitors with a ruse of her own. "I have this festering sore in a hidden place, which emits the most foul stench, and I fear it will make you hate me. Hold off from me for a few days, then make your use of me, for free." She prayed. God, seeing her chastity, sent a young man in the employ of the Roman secret service to be the instrument of her salvation. He paid the guard for a night with the girl, went in, and gave her his clothes. She escaped in disguise, "inviolate and unpolluted." The next day "the drama was known, the agent was seized and thrown to the beasts." He was a martyr twice over, both for his own sake and for "the blessed girl."[29]

In this story, the recalibration of romance for Christian ends is so transparent that it affords an opportunity to peer directly inside the artifice of fiction. The social grammar is directly taken over from romance: the girl's high birth and good looks are in the exaggerated style of the romantic heroine. If the Christian maiden's "device of chastity" is slightly less appealing than the equally desperate contrivances of Anthia or Tarsia, it is nevertheless structurally identical. The providential rescue of the girl's chastity is familiar, as is the high-pitched self-awareness of the episode as a "drama." The atmospherics of the story deliberately arouse the expectations of a romance, so the departures from the traditional script are all the more resonant. In the Christian version, the story is not set against a timeless Mediterranean but a distinctly recognizable Roman Empire. The heroine relies not on the implicit order of the fictional cosmos to rescue her but on the Christian God. Her chastity is saved, but not as a precondition for marriage. Instead, it is an end in itself. And her rescuer suffers the ultimate penalty for securing her salvation. The Christian story ends not with marriage and regeneration but with the double martyrdom of virginity and death. The spirit of eros has been evicted, replaced by a grim sexual austerity that dictates the shape of the narrative quite as much as the fervent sensuality of the classical romance ever did.[30]

These stories of Christian girls who escaped from the brothel are minor but revealing marks of a closely shared imaginative space, and they point to the central place of sex in the fictional economy of both traditions. The writings known, somewhat unhappily, under the moniker of the apocryphal *Acts* of the apostles, bear a telling family resemblance to contemporary Greek novelistic writing. The apocryphal *Acts* are the primary vehicle of early Christian romance. The apostles, the wandering heroes of early Christianity, were an endlessly fertile source of Christian legend. Close to the divine presence, the aura of the miraculous clung to them. The institutional church claimed descent from them. The canonical scriptures testified to their historicity but left ample room to the imagination. An enormous body of Christian legend, continuously reshaped, came to attach to the heroic generation. The *Acts* are adventure stories, but unlike the pagan novels the *Acts* are historical romances, set against a backdrop recognizable as the Roman Empire of the first century. As in the pagan romance, travel and serial endangerments hold together the structure, which is episodic, sensational. The apostles are miracle workers, endowed above all with the wondrous ability to resurrect the dead. They are also preachers who come to be arrested by the Roman authorities. The apocryphal *Acts*, like the romances but to an even greater degree, are forensic dramas. The gathering tension between apostolic missionizing and the Roman order inevitably resolves into a judicial conflict. The apostle, in the end, is martyred, so that death substitutes for marriage as the common ending of the apostle's story. Between the travel, miracle working, and martyrdom of the apostles, sex continually juts into the foreground of the stories. Sex functions as a primary symbolic code in the world of Christian legend, but in a radically reformulated sense. Christian romances not only preach a new model of proper sexual conduct, they also discovered a way of expressing a strikingly original romance of the eternal soul, in which this world of flux and regeneration is a façade and the reunion with God, through purity and death, is the ultimate consummation. "Nothing of yours endures, but all things, right down to human conventions, are transient."[31]

As in the pagan romances, the *Acts* reveal deep generic similarities in the treatment of sex, so that there is a sense in which the genre speaks collectively, or at least uses a shared syntax of conventions and symbols. Even in the apostolic traditions that rely least on the manipulation of sexual protocols, certain formulas recur. The *Acts of Peter* focus principally on the rivalry between the apostle Peter and the mountebank ur-heretic, Simon Magus. Sexual tropes are not, in the Petrine legends as we have them, a dominant thread. But they do suddenly play a commanding role when the story turns abruptly from the rivalry with Simon Magus toward the death of Peter. The fatal sequence begins when four concubines of the prefect Agrippa hear the "teaching about purity, and all the teachings of the Lord" and withdraw their sexual favors from the powerful official. Peter's next triumph is a "a superlative beauty," Xanthippe, the wife of a powerful man. Finally, "many other women" left their husbands, and husbands their wives, in the name of sexual purity. With so many marriage beds abandoned, Peter has put Rome in an epic stir of erotic frustration. Peter sneaks out of the city in disguise but, in a touching scene, encounters Christ and famously asks him, "Whither goest thou?" Peter marches back through the gates to his certain death. The apostle's preaching on sexual chastity is the proximate cause of the most famous scene in apocryphal literature and the most hallowed martyrdom in Christian history (save one).[32]

In the *Acts of Peter,* the "word of purity" that leads to the apostle's death is abrupt and almost mechanical in its exaggerated predictability. In the *Acts of Thomas,* the pattern of events is identical, although the drama is more elaborately developed. To the figure of Thomas stuck the most exotic legends of the early church. His *Acts* describe his mission to India, where he converts an aristocratic woman, Mygdonia, to the gospel. He teaches her that "the reputation that comes from your high rank, the authority of this world, and the disgusting intercourse with your husband will avail you not at all if you are without the union of truth . . . for the union that brings the production of children passes away, and is even worthy of contempt." Her husband, close kin to the king, is predictably befuddled by her newfound commitment to sexual abstention, not to mention the truculence with which she disobeys him. "I am your husband from the time of your virginity, by the gods and by the laws given the right to rule over you." Thomas is arrested, but his arraignment only provides a platform to spread the message that salvation comes to those who are "delivered from all bodily pleasures." The king's efforts backfire when his own wife, then his son and heir, take up chastity. The king has Thomas killed. As a postscript to his martyrdom, we are told that the king and his relative Charisius "tried very much to force their wives" but "could not persuade them to abandon their will."[33]

Whatever else may be said of them, the sexual doctrines presented by the heroes of apostolic legend are consistently extreme. Thomas denigrates married intercourse as "filthy," and he leaves no room for ambiguity. In the *Acts of Andrew,* the apostle's primary convert, Maximilla, calls sex with her husband a "defiling intercourse." When Peter preaches the "word of purity," it is a gospel of complete continence. The *Acts of Paul* have the great missionary coming into the city of Iconium proclaiming, "Blessed are those who refrain from sex altogether, for God will speak to them. Blessed are those who stand in array for something beyond the present cosmos, for they will be pleasing to God." Here the only Christian apostle whose views we actually know through his own writings, and who was so cautious that he would not upset a single marriage through the unwanted abstinence of a spouse, has been attributed a radical doctrine of chastity capable of overturning entire cities![34]

The preaching is unrelentingly shrill. But it has been perceptively observed that, in comparison with the abundant ascetic literature of late antiquity, the sexual doctrine of the apocryphal *Acts* is shallow. It is stylized rather than substantive, a symbol for something deeper and even more demanding. In other words, sexual renunciation in the corpus of apostolic legend is more rhetorical than doctrinal. The rejection of sexual experience is a direct ideological twin of the apostles' martyrdom at the hands of the temporal authorities. It is not happenstance that the *Acts of Paul* praise virginity in the same breath as they urge the Christian disciple to be "arrayed" for a cosmos beyond the present order. Andrew calls his converts to "abandon this life altogether" and to seek "life beyond time, beyond law, beyond speech, beyond body." To abandon sex—especially the congress of the marriage bed, which symbolized continuity and regeneration of this life—was a searing denunciation of the present order. The pagan romances present an enchanting vision of life as a mysterious experience, somewhere just beyond our conscious control but overseen by benevolent fates that ensure the resolution of the individual's story in marriage and reproduction. The *Acts* are romances whose protagonists are messengers of another order, a divine order, that is fundamentally at odds with the present age, its authorities, and its patterns of reproduction.[35]

In two of the *Acts* that survive completely enough to permit judgment, the *Acts of Andrew* and the *Acts of Paul*, the manipulation of romantic themes is so essential to the structure of the text that we may consider these works to be virtually inverted romances. Besides Gregory of Tour's summary of Andrew's miracles, two Greek manuscripts preserve substantial parts of his legend. In the Greek fragments, which reveal how much Gregory has chopped from the story, we meet Andrew on mission in Achaea, where Andrew's spiritual seduction of the proconsul's wife, Maximilla, leads to his demise. The proconsul, Aegeates, goes on a long trip and returns to find his wife steeled against his amorous intentions. To ward off his desires, she contrives a ruse worthy of any romantic heroine, and perhaps a little unexpected in a Christian one: "she summoned an utterly gorgeous slave-girl named Euclia who was naturally dissolute." Euclia consents to the scheme and becomes the substitute bedmate for Aegeates, who for eight months copulates unwittingly with a surrogate wife! Only the moral economy of romance allows the

Christian story to sacrifice, without apparent compunction, the sexual honesty of a slave, in the name of salvaging the chastity of a heroine. Needless to say, this detail did not survive the literary scalpel of Gregory, who makes no mention of the scam.[36]

The slave Euclia enjoys her temporary promotion, but she is undone by her pride. Tired of her airs, the fellow slaves reveal the plot to their master. Infuriated, he has Euclia's tongue cut out and her body mutilated. Rather pitifully, he goes to Maximilla in his distress and reiterates his love for her. She rebukes him in a malicious double entendre that served to fuel rather than allay his suspicions. "I love, Aegeates, I do love, but what I love is not of this world. . . . Let me have my intercourse with this love and take solace only in it." When Aegeates identifies Andrew as the cause of his troubles, he has the apostle arrested. The proconsul tempts his wife to return to bed by threatening to visit inconceivable torment on Andrew's body. In the *Acts of Andrew* the lawful husband, the image of Roman order, has become the villain, and the bond between the apostle and the heroine—a purely chaste bond—is subjected to awful trials. Strengthened by Andrew's preaching, Maximilla stands firm against Aegeates, and Andrew, after preaching from the gallows, is crucified. This artful romance, then, ends not with the mysterious pleasures of union that regenerate the world but with suffering and separation and hope for a final reunion with God.[37]

No piece of the apostolic cycle is so exquisitely framed as a romance as the legend known as the *Acts of Paul and Thecla*. The story of Paul and Thecla was a detachable part of the larger body of legends that accumulated around the figure of Paul. The *Acts of Paul and Thecla* are already, in their focus on Thecla as a protagonist, more reminiscent of romance than most apostolic lore. Thecla is directly modeled on the heroines of romance. She is a virgin, the daughter of Theoclia, citizen of Iconium. She is just of marriageable age, engaged to the leading young man of the city, Thamyris. When Thecla overhears Paul's preaching through a window, she is enraptured by his words. She sat day and night at the window and listened to his gospel of virginity. Thecla's mother, equal in her connivance to Leucippe's, is astonished and alarmed at the enthusiasm of her daughter, who is attached to the window "like a spider." Thecla's mother sounds the alarm to her daughter's fiancé, Thamyris, about the stranger whose teachings threaten to convulse the city of the Iconians. He and the other men of the city plot against Paul and have him arraigned before the governor, who exiles Paul but orders Thecla burned alive. She miraculously escapes and rejoins her apostle on the road. They travel to Antioch, where the sequence of events replays itself: a malignant suitor sets his mind on Thecla, she resists, she faces trial and execution, but she is miraculously rescued. Finally she and Paul part ways, and she journeys to Seleucia, her final resting place.[38]

The apocryphal legends are a powerful expression of early Christian sexual morality, the sexual gospel of a minority movement, when the religion and its followers stood apart from mainstream society. The Christian romances reflect a configuration of sexual morality and society in which Christian austerity represented a radical freedom from the demands of the world. The stories of wandering apostles and the eager female adherents who hear the gospel of chastity were produced by the same imagination that reconceived the problem of free will around the capacity to act without encumbrance from fate or from social expectation. This body of early Christian literature adopts, wholesale, the romantic trope of feminine inviolability. But the heroine's chastity is reoriented toward otherworldly ends rather than the reproduction of life here beneath the moon. There is something flat, compressed, about the presentation of sex in the apocryphal literature. There is a juvenile absolutism about its place in human life. No character wrestles with desire, confronts temptation, or experiences confliction. Sex is a symbol of the world, and all the more simplified by that fact. Only a religious movement that had so completely resolved to live apart from the order of society could package sex as a compact and tractable symptom of ordinary life, with its dull cycles of survival and reproduction, in contrast to the shimmering promises of an invisible order. It was a vision of sex and its pervasive role in life that the Christian authors found, with a wholly opposite purpose, in the contemporary genre of romance.[39]

THE VIRGIN IN THE BROTHEL, THE TORAH IN THE WORLD

The pervasiveness of romantic conventions, and the shared symbolic vocabulary of late classical literature, is underscored by the appearance of familiar novelistic tropes in Jewish legend. Like the Christians, the Jews of the Roman Empire developed a body of legend that both drew from and subverted the models of contemporary romance. Like the Christians, the Jews of the Roman Empire liked to imagine their heroes as defiant victims of Roman power. Among these heroes was Rabbi Hanina ben Teradion, a *Tanna* of the third generation, martyred by the Roman authorities at the apex of Roman hegemony in the second century. He was canonized as one of the Ten Martyrs. The most complete account of his martyrdom is preserved in the tractate *Avodah Zarah* of the Babylonian Talmud. *Avodah Zarah,* "foreign worship," was, simply by virtue of the domain of life it regulated, ideally suited to become a storehouse of rabbinic memory about the interaction between Jews and their idolatrous rulers. According to the tradition, Haninah was sentenced to death, his wife was condemned to exile, and his virgin daughter was assigned to penal prostitution. The Hebrew virgin in the Roman brothel, recounted in the Talmud, wrests us from the dry struggles of halakhic interpretation and thrusts us into the atmosphere of Greek romance. Like Christian romance, the Jewish story takes eternal archetypes of noble innocents and sets them against the concrete historical backdrop of Roman power. This Jewish legend, like Christian apostolic lore, is an indissoluble fusion of history and romance.[40]

Hanina's daughter was sent to the "tent of prostitution." Fortunately the girl had a sister, Beruriah, who could not bear the shame of seeing her kin in the brothel. This is the famous Beruriah, wife of Rabbi Meir, who is only in this passage identified as the daughter of Haninah—part of the Babylonian Talmud's overarching tendency to create webs of interrelationship among the *Tannaim* and their families. Beruriah induces her husband to sneak into the brothel to bribe the guard into releasing the girl. Her husband, Rabbi Meir, reckons to himself, "If she has not been subjected to anything wrong, a miracle will be wrought for her, but if she has committed anything wrong, no miracle will happen to her." If she has not been *subjected* to violence, then she will be saved. But if she has *committed* anything wrong, she is then damned to prostitution. It may appear illogical or at least unsatisfying to construe the enslaved girl's deeds as acts of commission. But this *aporia,* this surface disjuncture, is resolved at a deeper level of narrative logic, which the redactors of this story have borrowed from the assumptions of romance.[41]

When Rabbi Meir reaches the brothel, in disguise as a Roman soldier, he tests his sister-in-law's virtue by trying to hire her. In the Talmudic story, the brothel is a state institution. Whereas the pirates and pimps who threaten girls in the Greek romance are part of a mythical anti-state, beyond the legitimate social order, in the Christian and Jewish stories the Romans are the villains, the menace to the sexual integrity of the heroine. Rabbi Meir must go in disguise as part of the ruling order to rescue the girl's honor. When he approaches, she resists by telling him that "the manner of woman is upon her." We should recognize in this ruse the parallels with the "devices of virtue" in the romance—the epileptic fit, the uncontrolled weeping, the malodorous complaint that will save the girl's honor. This escape mechanism explains the logic of the disjuncture between shame and sin; the story still operates along the conventional gears of the Greek romance, but within the moral logic of Judaism, of sin and Torah. The Talmud employs the characterization of a Greek romance—character is essence and will be revealed in the crucible of danger—but sets the story within the moral architecture of Judaism. Rabbi Meir, a patient customer, offers to wait for her menstrual cycle to finish, but she redirects him to other women in the brothel. He reasons that she has acted thus with all her customers and therefore merits salvation. He bribes the guard and secures her release.[42]

The narratives of the Babylonian Talmud are beguilingly complex literary creations, none more so than this deposit of Greek literature in the very tractate dedicated to maintaining lines of separation between Jewish and gentile cultures. The punishment of Rabbi Haninah ben Teradion and his family was deeply embedded in rabbinic tradition. The story exists in kernel in other sources, including the *Sifre to* Deuteronomy. In the Talmud, the substratum of rabbinic legend has been reshaped into the form of a Greek romantic trope. The appropriation of romance for a Talmudic story would be striking enough in itself, but the true richness of the story emerges only when the episode is understood in its redactional context, in its place within a complex series of stories in *Avodah Zarah.* The tractate is principally concerned with idolatry, especially forms of commercial interaction that might have brought Jews too close to the taint of idolatry. The anonymous virgin's escape from the brothel actually sits at the end of an especially long and complex sequence that presents, in dreamlike succession, a stream of memories about rabbis brought face-to-face with the Roman authorities. The surreal quality of the memories conceals the fact that this *sugya* has an exquisitely careful design, in which a sequence of symbolically interrelated stories unfolds once, and then again. This artful doubling allows the redactors to juxtapose stories, to contrast characters, and to invert meanings. Within this grander structure the brothel scene acquires an even deeper significance.[43]

The sequence opens with the arrest and acquittal of Rabbi Eliezer, who is mistakenly charged with *minuth*—Christian heresy. This accusation, even though false, perturbs him. He remembers a conversation with a follower of Jesus that may have led to the confusion. The conversation involved the citation of three verses on fornication, on harlotry. The Talmud puts into mind both the literal meaning, prostitution, and the metaphorical meaning, spiritual promiscuity, idolatry. These passages prompt reflection on the nature of sin and evoke the question whether the literal commission of fornication is as damning as its metaphorical twin, idolatry or heresy. The editors tell the story of Rabbi Eleazar ben Dordia, a fallen rabbi who had sex with no less than every prostitute in the world. When a prostitute warned him that he was lost, he was suddenly struck to his core with remorse for his sins. He begged God for forgiveness. A heavenly voice announced his redemption, whereupon he immediately died. His sin of sexual fornication was so vast that it was like *minuth,* heresy. When Rabbi Judah ha Nasi heard this story, he wept and exclaimed, "One may acquire eternal life after many years, or in an hour!" The first half of the sequence then closes with a story that recapitulates all the themes of the preceding discussion. Rabbi Hanina and Rabbi Jonathan are walking and reach a fork in the road, and they must pass either a temple of idolatry or a brothel. They opt for the brothel. Not only does this imply that idolatry is worse than literal fornication, the rabbis hope to earn merit for overcoming their desires. As they walk past the brothel, the prostitutes scramble inside, out of their presence. Significantly, in the concluding words the anonymous of the Babylonian tells us, "Against these things the Torah will watch over thee."[44]

It is against this story that, thematically, the escape from the brothel must be understood. The text launches into another stream of memories, narrating a sequence of events which step-by-step mirrors the first series. The second panel begins with an arrest—two arrests, in fact, one of which is the arrest of Haninah ben Teradion for studying the Torah. He is executed by fire. He has with him a scroll of the Torah that he was studying, and as he expires he experiences a vision of the letters of the Torah ascending to heaven, even as the parchment burned. The executioner is moved by the scene and repents of his sins. In the first sequence, a rabbi repents of literal harlotry; in the second, a gentile repents of metaphorical harlotry. The executioner leaps into the fire, where he is consumed with the rabbi. A heavenly voice announces that the executioner has been admitted to eternal life, and again we hear the reaction of Rabbi, in identical words, that one may earn salvation in a single, wrenching moment of heartfelt repentance.[45]

After the death of Haninah comes his daughter's escape from the brothel, and this episode is surely to be read in light of all that has preceded it in this intricate, contrapuntal structure. The arrangement suggests two insights. First, harlotry is a metaphor for idolatry. Second, in the parallel episode, the rabbis learn that the Torah will save them from iniquity. When Rabbi Meir comes to test the chastity of his sister-in-law, she tells him that the "manner of women is upon her." Obviously this ruse compares to the epileptic fits or fictitious diseases of the other heroines—the "devices of virtue" that are the heroine's only defense. But this device is something more specific, more resonant. The virgin tells her prospective customer that she is menstruating. She evades him, in other words, by trying to observe *niddah,* the ritual separation of a woman commanded by the Torah. Elsewhere in the Talmudim, women use this prohibition to their advantage, even postponing the *mikveh* to avoid sex. The daughter of Haninah here uses her claim to ritual impurity as her device of virtue. She obeys the Torah, and just as the Torah came to the rescue of the rabbis walking *past* the brothel, the Torah will watch over her, *in* the brothel. Rabbi Meir is convinced of her purity, and he effects her release. The Bavli this time does not proclaim openly that the Torah will protect its adherents—perhaps because its parchment has been symbolically burned—but it is efficacious nonetheless.

This story ends with a twist. Rabbi Meir rescues his sister-in-law, and then the Romans begin to hunt for him. Walking down the street, he met Romans in hot pursuit. With nowhere else to escape, the Talmud reports, he darted into a nearby brothel, because no one would suspect Rabbi Meir of entering a brothel. Or, the Talmud relates, according to an alternative account, he saw pagans cooking food, dipped a finger in it, and pretended to eat. In this epilogue, a farrago of all that has preceded, it is the pretense of harlotry, both literal and metaphorical, that has secured his salvation from the Romans. It is possible to flirt with sin, or rather to be encompassed about by it, and yet to follow the Torah and enter the next life. That is the whole message of the tractate *Avodah Zarah*—how the faithful may endure in the midst of a hostile culture. The creative spirits who wove this tale from such varied threads refashioned the symbols of romance—the virgin's body and the haunt of shame—into a statement about the boundaries between their community and the contaminations of the outside world. Structurally the

Jewish virgin in the brothel is a direct parallel of the girls of early Christian fiction. But by the time the Talmud was redacted, Christian authors were embarking on even more daring reconfigurations of these ancient conventions.[46]

FROM SHAME TO SIN: THE PENITENT PROSTITUTES

The famous actress whose stunning conversion is memorialized in an impromptu aside of John Chrysostom was not the only woman of her time to seek a repentance that was destined to reverberate in the collective imagination of Christians. Sometime around AD 400, far from the glamours of the Antiochene stage, another woman, Taïsia, made a spiritual turn that was just as stark, if less immediately celebrated. Her story is related with brief but brutal realism in one of the most primitive documents of monastic wisdom, *The Sayings of the Desert Fathers.* Orphaned in her youth, Taïsia turned her home into a guesthouse along the fringes of the settled world, in the pioneer country of Egyptian monasticism, at the desert outpost of Scetis. Known for her generosity with the brothers, her stores were gradually exhausted, and in desperate seasons she did what many ancient women, faced by the mundane brutalities of a subsistence order, might have done. She profited with her body. The *Sayings* add no drama, subtract no shame from this bare fact: "She was led to prostitution." But the mere act of narrating a woman's passage from respectable poverty to sexual humiliation was an epochal novelty. In nearly a thousand years of the written word, there is little to match the simple authenticity of this humble lapse. More dramatic still, Taïsia was to find an escape from prostitution, no less miraculous than the "devices of virtue" that saved the heroines of romance. But unlike the imaginary girls of romance, Taïsia's body was not spared that "one single abuse" whose avoidance was the deepest convention of romance.[47]

In the small world of frontier monasticism, rumors of the girl's plight quickly spread. The brothers were distraught by her fall. They appointed the sturdiest among them, a monk known as John the Dwarf, to go to her and "set her affairs in order." His mission met resentment as soon as he reached the door, whose guardian chided him. "From the beginning you have devoured her stores, and now she is destitute." Nevertheless, Taïsia grants John entry, reasoning to herself, "Those monks are always roving about the

Red Sea and finding pearls." She readied herself on the bed, and he sat next to her. Staring into her face, he reproached her, "Why do you have such contempt for Jesus, that you come to this? . . . I see Satan toying on your face." Stirred, she asked him, "Is there repentance?" She repented and left, immediately, without even arranging her affairs. The monk and the penitent trekked into the desert. When night fell, John made her a pillow of sand, marked with a cross. He camped some distance apart. In the middle of the night, under the clear desert sky, he awoke to see a luminous path, stretching from heaven down to Taïsia. He went to her lifeless body and pricked her foot, knowing she was dead. But he heard a voice affirm, "After one hour of repentance, she will be received before those who repent for great lengths of time without showing such fervor as did she."[48]

The salvation of Taïsia is the kernel of a literary type that was to triumph with irresistible force in the fifth century. Along with Chrysostom's actress, Taïsia belongs to the earliest stratum of a new legend, and there is no reason to doubt the reality of her existence. Here is the chance to watch the birth of an archetype. The story of Taïsia, as we have it, already bears traces of artistic touch. Taïsia's internal reflections about the monks and the pearls of the Red Sea are, surely, a contrivance. We sense but cannot grasp some distant connection with the famous actress of Antioch, whose legend was fermenting in the same hothouse of spiritual imagination, and whose stage name was none other than Margarito, pearl. But the story of Taïsia hits with the thud of simple reality. Her material desperation and loss of respectability had no literary parallel. Her story is very early and little stylized, and if we cannot disentangle the authentic core from the light embellishments of time and imagination, the story of Taïsia contains a stronger dose of authenticity than will soon be found in the highly artificial morality tales of penitent women.

The tale of Taïsia's repentance is handed down among the chain of traditions about the earliest generations of monks, principally from the site of Scetis. The *Sayings of the Desert Fathers* preserve a number of memories about the colorful ascetic John the Dwarf, who flourished in the last decades of the fourth century and the first decade of the fifth. Most of the stories and sayings focus on monastic pioneers from the mid-fourth to the early fifth century. In the earliest days these memories were transmitted orally, and characteristic traces of oral transmission remain in the collections. The story of Taïsia passed through only a few generations of oral transmission before its redaction in the *Sayings,* which seems to have taken shape as a text in the second half of the fifth century, probably in Palestine. A Palestinian origin for the redaction would add poignancy to the humbling finale of Taïsia's story. The heavenly voice that affirms her salvation reminds us of nothing so much as an aphorism of Rabbi Judah ha Nasi that recurs throughout *Avodah Zarah,* uttered after the repentance of the most condign sinners. "One may acquire eternal life after many years, another in one hour!"[49]

In the desert, "the air is more pure, the heavens are more open, and God is nearer." The figure of the penitent prostitute first took shape in the sands of Egypt, in the earliest monastic traditions, because she so radically condensed the cosmic possibilities of repentance, *metanoia.* In the pioneer phases of Egyptian monasticism, fallen women begin to populate the landscape as avatars of temptation and repentance. Taïsia belongs to this most primitive stratum. The trials and ecstasies she experienced were not hers alone. In another early legend an anonymous monk discovers that his sister has fallen into prostitution. He leads her to repentance, and as they walk into the desert, she expires. In the tale that was destined to have the most extravagant afterlife, a monk named Serapion passes through a "village of Egypt" and sees "a prostitute standing in her cell." When dusk falls, he goes in with her. He chanted the psalms and prayed to God that she would "repent and be saved." The prostitute realizes that he has come to save her soul. She cries and asks Serapion to lead her away. When they arrive at a monastery of virgins, he gives the abbess instructions to be gentle with her. After a few days, the former prostitute told the abbess, "I am a sinner. I want to eat every two days." Then, again, she said, "I am a sinner. I want to eat every four days." Finally, she asked the abbess to wall her in a cell with only a little opening to pass through bread. "Thus for the rest of her life she was pleasing to God." The story begins in a cell *(kellion)* of dishonor and death, ends in a cell *(kellion)* of repentance and life. The living sepulture of the penitent prostitute symbolized both the radical possibilities, and the suffocating limits, of a purely spiritual redemption.[50]

The Egyptian desert, in late antiquity, was to prove the birthplace of new archetypes of human spirituality. With its barren horizons, the simple ecology of life on the edges of civilization provided a rarefied backdrop. Here men—and some women—wrestled with sin, stared down the devil, and sought internal transformation. In the desert tales of penitent prostitutes, the features of the moral landscape are simple. The women themselves are sketched in little detail. The focus of the brief encounter is the father—his steadfastness, his grace. The tales are monastic from start to finish; even in the prostitute's lair, the monk brings with him the whiff of the desert. The chief elements of the drama are sin and repentance. We are in a world where sin is inextricable from the machinations of the devil and his demons. In this setting, the significance of the girl's prostitution is not that it places her outside of respectable society. It is, rather, that it arrays her with the forces of evil. Her repentance is not just the recovery of a most abandoned sinner. A victory over fornication is a defeat over Satan's legions. The monks who induce the conversion of the prostitute are like a modern sports team that courts away its rival's most valuable player. The desert tales of penitent prostitutes are allegories of sin and salvation, played out against the grander cosmic battle between good and evil.

The literary side is only one half of her story, for in the same period, in the late fourth and then more explosively in the fifth century, the penitent prostitute, modeled on the "sinful woman" in the Gospel of Luke, becomes a popular subject for Christian preachers. Her tearful repentance proved congenial to homilists in an age of mass conversion. The currency of these legends, already in the late fourth century, is also confirmed in a most unlikely source: the rhetorical handbook of the pagan sophist of Antioch, Libanius. In one of his training exercises, Libanius creates a penitent *pagan* prostitute. She represents the cross-pollination of Christianity and philosophical paganism in the fourth century. The word "repentance" is glaringly absent (instead she "becomes chaste"), but the mood is entirely Christian. "I purify my mind. I flee Aphrodite, I prefer the clemency of Athena." The speech spoke of prostitution in terms of "pollution," and there was a clear religious subtext to the speech: the prostitute fled Aphrodite, preferring chaste Athena. Even so, Libanius could not resist insinuating that Aphrodite was wrongfully accused of perversion. The prostitute wanted to set up a law telling women in prostitution that they had the capacity to become pure and to flee—a full generation before Theodosius II would actually do so. The speech was a fictional school exercise, to be sure, but nevertheless represents a remarkable statement from a late pagan intellectual eager to defend the sexual integrity of his religion. The speech might be considered a pagan apology, written in response to the avant-garde of Christian sexuality.[51]

In short order the literary potential of the penitent prostitute was recognized and elaborated, and she was translated from the desert to the city, where she could be made to bear heavier symbolic associations. She was transformed into a figure capable of symbolizing the fundamental truths of sin and salvation, but of doing so in familiar and deeply resonant literary terms. Almost as soon as dramatic stories about the salvation of society's lowest began circulating in the Christian empire, the penitent prostitute was reworked, as a literary figure, into a romantic antiheroine. In late antiquity no less than four penitent prostitutes would become major literary stars, destined for fame and popularity across the Middle Ages and into the modern world. The impresarios of the Christian imagination realized that in the figure of the penitent prostitute they had not only the raw material for a Christian allegory but a plot that could express the brave new order of sexual morality. The lives of the penitent prostitutes were worked into antiromances, inverting a rich fictional tradition to express an entirely new logic of sexual morality, a new relationship between the sexual self and society.

In one case we possess both the early and the more developed version of the same story, which allows us to take measure of the literary makeover accomplished by late antique authors equally conversant with the wisdom literature of the desert and the conventions of ancient romance. The prostitute converted by Serapion and enclosed in a cell was bound to enjoy a most extravagant afterlife. Thus far we have refrained from calling her Thais. The legend of Thais is a tangled web of sensational identifications and implausible embellishments that continued right into the twentieth century. She enjoyed the longest posterity of any of the penitent prostitutes, her celebrity briefly revived in the late nineteenth century when she became the subject of a novel by Anatole France and an opera by Jules Massanet. In 1901 the French archaeologist Albert Gayet discovered the mummy of a woman named Thais in a late antique cemetery he excavated at Antinoe. Elsewhere in the same graveyard was found the body of a male mummy, buried with an iron belt, along with a potsherd that identified him as Serapion. The museum of Gayet's patron, Émile Étienne Guimet, was eager to accommodate imaginative connections with the Thais and Serapion of legend. In short order the exhumed mummies of Thais and Serapion were displayed together in a glass case at the museum. In the sweltering summer heat of 1902, in a last burst of fame for the penitent prostitutes, Thais was the sensation of Paris.[52]

The identification of the mummy as the Thais of literary legend might have faded like any other instance of archaeological exuberance, had not an eminent scholar of Syriac Christianity, l'Abbé François Nau, intervened at this juncture with a discovery that seemed not only to support the identification but to clinch it by the addition of a relationship between Thais and Serapion. This was more than Gayet had dreamed of. In the popular version of the Thais legend, best known through the Latin translation in the *Vitae Patrum* and adapted by Anatole France, Thais is led to repentance by a monk named Paphnutius. But Nau discovered an unedited Greek version of the life of Thais, preserved in a handful of European manuscripts, that presents a monk called Serapion the Sindonite as the instrument of her salvation. Nau's discovery of a Greek version of the life—noteworthy enough apart from Gayet and his mummies—came at a fortuitous moment, and it was quickly published . . . in the *Annales du Musée Guimet.* Nau made a significant discovery that was coincidentally useful to others, though he entertained sensational identifications that deserved more than a half measure of scholarly skepticism. Nau's willingness to identify Thais the mummy with the Thais of hagiography has obscured, in the glare of misspent erudition, what is a real opportunity to witness the transformation of an early monastic legend into refined literature. He treats the story of Serapion in the *Sayings of the Fathers* as the prime source for the *Life* or *Repentance of Thais*—without any reckoning of just how little is shared between the primitive and literary versions of the story.[53]

The primitive legend and the literary version of the *Life of Thais* in fact share only two details. In both cases the name of the monk is Serapion (a name widely shared by early Christian monks in Egypt, leading to no small confusion of personages with the name in the manuscript tradition). Moreover, in both the early and later versions of the story the penitent woman ends her reformation by enclosing herself in a cell featuring a small passage communicating with the outside world. This memorably grim detail is probably the principal point of connection between the earlier and more elaborate forms of the narrative. In other words, the more elaborate form of the prostitute's legend was motivated precisely by the memorably gruesome form that her penance took.[54]

The *Life,* which Nau dated to the fifth or sixth century, includes a brief prologue laying out the agenda of the story: to help those "who have fallen into the mire of sin and wish to repent." In the first line we meet the protagonist, who is now the prostitute rather than the monk. "There was in Alexandria a certain maiden named Thais, exceedingly beautiful, with a beauty that in fact surpassed all those who were ever admired for their physical charm." The spare canvas of the Egyptian desert has been replaced by a fictional landscape crowded with meanings. The supremely beautiful maiden is an artifice of the romantic imagination. Alexandria, the city par excellence, has ousted the "village of Egypt" as the home of the prostitute. And she is given a name: Thais. Nowhere in the manuscripts of the *Sayings of the Desert Fathers* is the prostitute rescued by Serapion given a name. Indeed, the name Thais is as likely as any other element of the story to be a pure concoction of the hagiographer's fancy. More profoundly, the tale of desert wisdom could leave the woman nameless, because she was simply an avatar of sin. In the *Life,* she becomes a character, and symbolic associations will rapidly grow around her.[55]

The girl's mother was an unscrupulous and worldly woman who placed her daughter in "the workshop of the devil," where the beauty of Thais could be "sold to all who wish to violate her shamefully." Men came from far and wide; they lost all self-control, dissipated their property, even turned to brigandage to subsidize their lust. The hero Serapion heard of this diabolical temptress and hastened to respond. The author of the *Life* mobilized what is surely one of the least felicitous metaphors in the library of Greek literature: "Like a wise fisherman, ready with a baiting device, he hunts after the lamb to snatch her soul from the maws of the devil." In the *Life* it is Serapion's mission to find her, and he must go to the city to do so. The monk disguises himself in "worldly apparel" and goes to her. In early Christian and Jewish adaptations of the romance, the rescuer invading the brothel must dress as a Roman soldier; in those legends, to pass into the brothel is figuratively to step into the secular world, a world identified with the ruling power. In the age of Serapion, there was no clear-cut divide between the social order and the Christian church. There was only the city—symbol of sin and civilization—and the ascetic who entered it as an outsider. And unlike the chaste girls of romance whose corporal integrity is miraculously preserved in the brothel, Thais has, quite flagrantly, long since lost her physical purity.[56]

When Serapion meets Thais, he sees a bed and out of shame inquires about finding another, less visible place for their assignation. She assures him that the bed is secluded and adds, "If it is God you fear, the one who knows our secrets will see us wherever we go." The monk is struck and asks if she knows of God. She confesses that she was baptized as a child but she never learned Christian teaching. She fell at the monk's feet. "I know there

Table 1 Serapion and Thais

	Early Version	Elaborated Version
Includes prologue	No	Yes
Thais	Not named	Named
Place	Village of Egypt	Alexandria
Cause of prostitution	Unstated	Mother prostituted her
Encounter	Fortuitous	Inspired by divine foresight to find her
Prompt to penance	Hears prayers	Believes in God and shamed
Includes Antony?	No	Yes
Ending	Immured	Immured, in grim detail

is repentance for sinners, but by my wickedness I have exceeded the measure of forgiveness which can be offered." He assures her that there is salvation, even for her. She gathered her worldly wealth and burned it "in the middle of the city." Thais symbolizes a society superficially baptized but not reordered to strive for God—a reasonable likeness of the post-Theodosian world.[57]

As in the primitive version of the tale, Serapion leads the penitent prostitute to a female monastery. Thais is immured in a small cell with a hole just wide enough for food to be passed in. But in the refined version, the bare details of her enclosure and penance have become a grotesque portrait of human debasement. The cell is dark. Serapion seals it with lead himself. When Thais asks him where she is to discharge her bodily necessities, he answers, "Do what you must in the cell. You have luxuriated in sweet oils and perfumes, now let a fetid stench work its good on you." She spent three years in darkness, as if in a tomb. Serapion went to Anthony—the father of Egyptian monasticism, who has been invited into this dark spiritual antiromance—to ask about the poor woman. Anthony's disciple, Paul, dreams of a heavenly bed, attended by three virgins carrying lamps, with a crown upon it. A voice tells him that the bed is for Thais, the whore. Serapion goes to tell her that she is forgiven, and he finds her body so wasted away from penance that her skeleton is visible through her skin. Just days after coming out of her cell, Thais dies.[58]

The story of Thais is dominated by its heroine's debasement. Though her life is said to have fulfilled the dictum "The prostitutes and publicans will precede you into the kingdom of heaven," the gospel expression retains none of its original compassion for society's outcasts. The *Life of Thais* is valuable because it allows us to watch the translation of a primitive monastic tale into the symbolic world of classical fiction. It already reveals the way that new configurations of religion, society, and the body fueled the literary imagination. Because the *Life of Thais* is aesthetically clumsy, its author's handiwork is nakedly obvious. The other three examples of the subgenre are more artful, and they reveal a deeper mastery of the medium and its potential. Among the earliest competitors to the *Life of Thais* is the story of Pelagia, a prostitute and actress of Antioch. Thanks only to the brief aside in the sermon of Chrysostom do we know that there is a kernel of historicity in the story of a glamorous celebrity who converted to the ascetic life. We cannot say how far legendary material had accreted around her by the time the author of the life, sometime in the fifth century, elaborated the written version that survives. We can only say that the author, who purports to be a deacon named Jacob, was a highly literate spirit, one of those soldiers of Christian culture who remade the ancient tradition in a Christian mold.[59]

The *Life of Pelagia* is highly conscious of its status as an antiromance. It counterposes its hero, an ascetic bishop named Nonnos, and its heroine, the redoubtable Pelagia, in the symmetrical fashion of the Greek novel. The story begins as Nonnos and other bishops have gathered at Antioch at the behest of the bishop of the great city. One day the visitors were sitting together outside the shrine of the martyr Julian when Pelagia, "first lady of the Antiochene stage," rode by with her cortege. No detail of the fantasia is omitted. Pelagia rides on a donkey, head uncovered, attended by a great throng of slaves, all of whom are bedecked with gold, gems, and pearls. The aromatics of her passing entourage could stun the unwary soul. The bishops avert their gaze, except for Nonnos, who holds her in his mind with his eyes. He is struck by her beauty, but his interest is not prurient. He is fired with envy by the care she takes to make herself pleasing to men; he wishes he could take such care to prepare his soul for God. Her glorious physical charms, in good Platonic fashion, remind Nonnos of the "inconceivable beauty" *(to amēchanon kallos)* at which even the cherubim dare not gaze, which the Christian will find in heaven![60]

This first encounter between Nonnos and Pelagia is layered with meaning. As has been noticed, it mimics the scenes of love at first sight between the heroes and heroines of romance. Carnal eros has been displaced by spiritual yearning. Nonnos's anguish and weeping are drawn directly from the stock of romantic tropes. By the time the *Life* was written, stylized encounters between holy men and prostitutes had become a regular part of the fictional repertoire. The true holy man—monks like John the Dwarf or Serapion, even rabbis like Hanina and Meir—could stand face-to-face with the prostitute, unfazed by her charm. These scenes assume, and defy, the serious physics of the gaze that are essential to romance. In *Leucippe and Clitophon,* beauty comes in at the eye; its ray of particulates enters and enervates the soul. An even richer *comparandum* is the scene in Heliodorus's *Ethiopian Tale* in which the priest Kalasiris fled his native town because a courtesan of unparalleled beauty appeared in his city; there was no escape from the "dragnet of erotic charm" that emanated from her eyes. So Kalasiris fled to Greece! Kalasiris, a richly characterized holy man who plays a central role in the narrative, is closer to late antique fiction than to erotic romance, but because *The Ethiopian Tale* is still a romance, it obeys the erotics of the gaze. Simple indifference or moral superiority to the power of beauty would offend the conventions of the genre, so to preserve his purity Kalasiris must emigrate. The Christian ascetic, by contrast, has attained a spiritual power that transcends the physics of beauty, and the scenes of encounter between holy men and whores dramatize their impassibility.[61]

The bishop Nonnos plays the role of Pelagia's lover. He groans, prays, and fasts for her. Soon he is the recipient of a nocturnal dream, a surreal vision of himself praying at the altar, while a dove, befouled with mud, hovered over him. As he left the sanctuary, the dove flitted above him, and he snatched it, plunging it into the nearest basin of water. The grime was washed away, the stench disappeared, and the beautiful white bird fluttered off over the horizon. As in romance, the dream is both a harbinger of things to come and a soft assurance to the characters and the reader alike that the story is wrapped in divine providence. When Sunday comes, the bishops attend services at the great church of Antioch, and Nonnos is asked to preach. His sermon is true fire and brimstone, describing the torments reserved for the wicked. Unexpectedly, Pelagia had stepped into church that day and heard his homily. The words of Nonnos lanced her spirit. She sobbed, inconsolably, with her sins before her eyes. The crowd stirred at the sight of the famous actress in tears. She has to leave when the mysteries begin, but two of her slaves find Nonnos and deliver a letter from their mistress in wax. She pours out her remorse and begs for an audience with Nonnos. Nonnos agrees to see her, in the relative safety of a small conclave of bishops. She groveled before them, grasping the feet of Nonnos, soaking them with her tears, like the sinner in the gospels. Her confession is a tsunami of self-loathing guilt: "I am a sea of sins. I am an abyss of wickedness." Pelagia asks Nonnos himself to be her sponsor in baptism, as she exchanges her whorish garb for the robes of purification. The two will be united in her spiritual rebirth.[62]

When she is baptized, she reveals that the name by which she was famous throughout Antioch, "Margarito," "Pearl," was merely a stage name. In fact her parents had named her Pelagia. Under her true name she is baptized and receives the holy mysteries. As the assembly rejoices, Satan himself appears, glowering at the baptismal party. He berates Nonnos and then Pelagia herself. He takes the guise of a jilted lover, humiliated by Pelagia's betrayal. Pelagia, whose bridehood is now vouchsafed to Christ, crosses herself and turns away her old companion. He tempts her again, by night, but she resists and confesses her allegiance to her heavenly marriage chamber. The scenes do not generate much compelling spiritual drama, but as a transposition of romantic tropes they are at least clever. Pelagia bequeaths her estate to Nonnos, who instructs the church's steward, following Mosaic law, not to allow the wages of the prostitute to cross the threshold of the church. Instead the money is distributed directly to orphans and widows. Pelagia manumits her slaves, urging them to free themselves from "slavery to the sin of this world." The crowds marvel at her very public transformation, and many of her fellow prostitutes are inspired to follow her example.[63]

Pelagia's days of public fame are behind her. She takes a hair shirt and woolen robe from Nonnos, and by night, dressed as a man, she leaves the city. No one saw her depart. Three years later the author of the life, Jacob, went to Jerusalem on pilgrimage. Nonnos told him to find a monk named Pelagius, a eunuch. Jacob finds him living in a cell on the Mount of Olives, wasted by asceticism, with cavernous eyes. Jacob does not recognize the shell of skin and bones before him as the once-famous actress. Pelagius has achieved, through gruesome self-mortification, a state beyond biological sex, transcending male or female. When Pelagius dies, crowds gather for the burial of the recluse. Anointing the body, the clergy of Jerusalem realize that Pelagius was a woman. She is buried on the Mount of Olives. Indeed, the sepulture of Pelagia provides a reminder that the stories of penitent prostitutes do not simply belong to a closed world of monastic literature. In the 570s a western pilgrim visiting the holy land reported, among the other sights encountered on his journey, the tomb of Pelagia. Her memory belonged to a vibrant world of popular Christian imagination. Indeed, a tomb of Pelagia can still be visited in Jerusalem today, a numinous site sacred to Jews, Christians, and Muslims alike. A custom is remembered at the site, by which a curious penitent may try to step through a cramped passage in the tomb, to test whether forgiveness for one's sins has been granted. The deep symbolism of these folk traditions is almost too perfect: just as the penitent prostitutes replaced the virgins of romance, the tomb of Pelagia has replaced the cave of Pan—and as a test of penance rather than purity.[64]

Pelagia inhabited the vibrantly bilingual world of late antique Syria. The legends of the penitent prostitutes passed easily between the interconnected worlds of Greek and Syriac. At least one of the legends of a penitent prostitute, Mary the niece of Abraham, was originally composed in Syriac. The tale of her repentance belonged to a longer cycle of narratives about her uncle, the hermit Abraham of Qidun. The *Life of Abraham* is an early text, preserved in a manuscript as old as the fifth century. Thus, the legend of Mary is almost exactly contemporary with the spread of the *Sayings of the Fathers* beyond Egypt and the elaboration of the story of Pelagia. Although her story was written in Syriac, the narrative betrays an intimate familiarity with Greek fiction—indeed, the text depends as much on its inversions of romance as do the lives of Thais and Pelagia. Unsurprisingly, the text was translated into Greek and Latin, and like the other legends of the penitent prostitutes, it was popular across the Mediterranean.[65]

Mary was an only child, orphaned by her parents and left in the charge of her uncle, Abraham, a monk in a village near Edessa. For the first twenty years of her life she imitated her uncle and lived "like a chaste lamb, like a spotless dove." Then she became the target of a satanic plot: she was seduced by a devious monk. Having lost her purity, Mary is distraught, but her distress is that of a romantic heroine subjected to the unthinkable. Unchastity is a sort of death. "I am now as good as dead." Darkened by guilt, she cannot so much as look on her uncle's face, and she exiles herself, trading her ascetic habits for life in a tavern. Mary is the perfect opposite of the romantic heroine. At the first, slight assault on her virginity, she caves. Rather than being taken to a brothel by force, she deposits herself in a den of ill repute, a self-imposed sentence that represents a willful submission to the rules of romance: the girl without honor belongs in the house of shame.[66]

Abraham failed to notice Mary's absence. When he receives a "fearful vivid dream" of a huge snake devouring a dove, he still fails to understand this premonition of lost virginity (which reminds us of Leucippe's mother's dream). Two days later, he has another dream. This time the snake returns to Abraham's house, and out of its belly flies the dove, unharmed. Finally the dreams become sensible to Abraham. After two years Abraham discovers where his niece is hiding. He disguises himself as a soldier, a costume familiar from such rescue operations. Abraham finds the tavern and asks the keeper to arrange a conjunction with the "pretty lass" who worked there. When he sees Mary "dolled up and dressed like a prostitute," he nearly loses his composure, but he maintains his poise. She serves him, caresses him, kisses his neck—one feels to a degree slightly exceeding strict literary necessity. As she arouses him, "the smell of asceticism that issued from the blessed man's body hit her," but she does not yet recognize her uncle. They dine and prepare for venery. When they retire to a private room, the monk removes his helmet. She sees the face of her uncle and goes stiff with terror. "I cannot bring myself to look upon you, sir, seeing what a shameful thing I have done. How can I pray to God, now that I have befouled myself in this stench and mud?" He convinces her that God will forgive her *sin,* and she repents. They return to their former life together, in austere holiness, and passersby would come at night to hear her sobbing prayers of penitence.[67]

The author of Mary's story has summoned the atmospherics of romance throughout this tale of sin and redemption. The romantic elements are not mere "motifs," decorative ornaments to impress the author's erudition upon his audience. They are integral to the meaning of the story and add considerably to the psychological drama. Mary is created in the image of a romantic heroine, to accentuate the fact that she experiences the one cataclysm that cannot befall a romantic heroine. Moreover, the most distinctive element in the story is Mary's self-relegation to a brothel. Her flight is a psychologically compelling reaction to the blunt paralysis of sexual shame. By willfully submitting to the life of prostitution as a penalty for her sexual delinquency, Mary is acting under the traditional rules of honor and shame. Her uncle, Abraham, resurrects her from this social death by presenting a supervenient logic of sexual morality organized around sin and righteousness.

The subgenre culminates in what is indisputably its finest expression, the *Life of Mary of Egypt.* Her story is the latest of the four main examples, having its origins around AD 600. It was destined to become the most popular scion of the family. It is, aesthetically, the most accomplished of the penance narratives, and it is no exaggeration to say that this *Life* is a real measure of the distance traveled in the passage from a classical to a Christian sexual culture. The *Life of Mary of Egypt* is, like *Leucippe and Clitophon,* a quintessential text, a mature and representative expression of a wider culture, filled with its "struggles and harmonies." Mary's story is set within the frame narrative of a monk from Jerusalem, Zosimas. This monk experiences an overly satisfied spiritual pride—until he meets Mary. As he treks the desert beyond the River Jordan, he glimpses a "shadowy image of the human body," a naked woman blackened by the sun who runs from him. It is Mary. Mary of Egypt, when we meet her through the eyes of Zosimas, is a spectral figure. She constantly insists on her sinful nature and prays, in mysterious tongues, toward the east. Zosimas is entranced by her strange sanctity and begs for her story. Much like Achilles Tatius, the author of this *Life* has contrived to deliver the core of the narrative in the first person and uses the perspective to artful effect: confession as a form of narrative.[68]

Mary is the consummate antiheroine. "My homeland was Egypt. When I turned twelve, with my parents still alive, I spurned this filial affection and took myself to Alexandria. I am ashamed to recall how I first ruined my virginity, and what an unmitigated and insatiable lust for sex I had." Her sexual depravity cannot be excused by extenuating circumstances—no orphan is she. Nor can plain moral weakness explain her fall. When she reached the first threshold of sexual maturity—twelve, the legal minimum for marriage—she willingly fled her loving family. And she did so for one purpose, defined with crystalline precision: lust. For seventeen years, she so loved pleasure that she was a blazing inferno of sexual dissolution. "And not for the sake of money, to tell the truth. Often men wanted to pay something and I would not accept. I figured that I could make more men come to me if I made a free gift of my abandonment. Do not think that I refused such emoluments because I was rich. I survived by begging, or sometimes spinning flax. My unslakable passion and boundless desire was to wallow in such foul mire. Such was my life, and my consuming purpose—to rape my nature."[69]

Mary is no damsel afloat the winds of fate. The romantic heroine is a passive character, actively suffering the whims of Fortune. Mary is lust incarnate, the driving force in her own destiny. When she reaches the age at which a respectable girl might be contemplating the marriage market, she careens headfirst into a life of sexual abandonment. Most ancient literature emphasizes the lust of the male customer. The *Life of Mary* foregrounds the sexual aggression of this antiheroine. The story deliberately isolates Mary's will as the true agent of her sexual depravity. She says she was poor—making barely enough to survive by selling the flax she could spin. (And with the mention of spinning, Mary evokes a symbol of female chastity as old as Penelope.) Despite her generosity, Mary is a prostitute. In the ancient Mediterranean, promiscuity—sexual availability, dishonor—was the essence of prostitution. The Roman lawyer Ulpian, in a legal definition of prostitution, claimed that sexual promiscuity was the decisive criterion of the prostitute, even more fundamental than venality. There is no reason to believe that the author of this *Life* had read his Ulpian; rather, both are pushing the definition of prostitution by imagining the liminal case of a woman who did not accept payment. For Ulpian shame and prostitution merge at the horizon of his conservative worldview; for the Christian author, prostitution becomes, in the figure of Mary, pure sin.[70]

While Mary is living her debased life in Alexandria, she sees a crowd of Libyan and Egyptian men running toward the sea. They are destined for Jerusalem, travelers to a holy feast. She has an urge to go with them but lacks money for the fare. Her motives are less than pure. "I wanted to go away with them in order to have a great many lovers, ready to serve my passions." Mary throws down her distaff and approaches a group of youths who seem a likely mark for her ambitions. Waiting to board, she unlooses a torrent of shameless words that communicate her intentions. "Tongue cannot speak, ear cannot hear the things that happened on the journey, what acts I forced upon the wretched youths, against their will." She stows on board, confident of passage: "I have a body, and they will take that as my sailing fare." What could be a clearer inversion of the romance? All the romances are tales of travel, of movement at sea; the heroine of the romance is moved by the force of necessity, taken captive by pirates against her will. Mary has set sail willingly, and corrupted herself with the crew out of her own lust. She has coerced men into sin. What the heroine of romance suffered unwillingly as a test of her chastity, for Mary is an event that she engineered and during which her shamelessness reached new depths. Mary is the pirate.[71]

In Jerusalem Mary's debauchery continues blazing its path. As the pilgrims gather for the feast, Mary hunts fresh prey. She brazenly goes to the Church of the True Cross, and even tries to enter, but she is repelled by some invisible force. Standing in the courtyard of the church, she senses that her own deeds are preventing her entrance. When she looks up, she sees an icon of the Mother of God. She prays to the chaste, pure, and undefiled virgin. "I have heard that the God who became man did so on this account, that he might call sinners to repent. Help me, for I am alone, and I have none to help me." Mary promises that she will not only abandon her life of shame, she will renounce this world altogether if she can only see the wood of the true cross. The Mother of God extends God's grace upon Mary the prostitute, and she is saved. Whereas Thais, Pelagia, and the niece of Abraham are shepherded to repentance through the guidance of a holy man, Mary of Egypt finds unmediated salvation. She falls into sin of her own volition, and she finds redemption without an intermediary between her and the archetypal virgin whose name she shared.[72]

When Zosimas finds Mary, she has lived alone in the desert for forty-seven years. In that time she has eaten a total of three loaves of bread. She has wrestled with temptations, with the thoughts of fornication that constantly pricked the mind of the male monk. For seventeen years, the span of time she lived in wantonness in Alexandria, she suffered and struggled, as her withering body paid for her crimes. Then she spent thirty years in ascetic tranquility. She instructs Zosimas not to repeat her tale while she lives, but to return to Jerusalem and to visit her in a year with the bread and wine of the Eucharist. He comes to her again in the desert and she takes communion. Again she instructs him to return in a year. He begs her to pray, "for the church, for the empire, and for him." When Zosimas returns the next year, he finds Mary, dead, her corpse turned to the east. He weeps over her, soaking *her* feet with *his* tears, inverting the biblical trope. In the sand he finds a message from her, revealing her name and asking for burial. A lion appears and helps dig the grave. Zosimas cries, prays, and returns to his monastery, where at last he relates the story that Mary conveyed to him, a story that was handed down by the monks through the generations. Finally the author's voice breaks in, claiming to have inscribed the unwritten truth at the command of God: like the artful confections of the sophistic romance, the *Life of Mary* makes the reader aware of the frames within which the narrative is stored.[73]

It is hard to suppress a mixed reaction to the story. In the *Life of Mary* all the features of the subgenre, both attractive and disturbing, are refined to the highest degree. The blunt, unquestioning grace offered to the sinner finds its most poignant expression in Mary's encounter with the mother of God. Because this is an allegory of sin and repentance, the scale of Mary's depravity is a measure of the infinite grace she can receive. At the same time, in Mary's story the toll of such forgiveness is plain to see. Mortification, self-abasement, death unto this world—such are the adjuncts of redemption. The penitent prostitute is walled into a cell, she surrenders her beauty, she sobs eternally. In Mary's case, she suffers hauntingly until her evils have evaporated along with her body. She becomes a phantasm, a pure, pitiful creature whose body has been wasted to virtual nothingness. The body, its existence in the world, its participation in the mysterious cycles of regeneration, offer no truth, no pleasure, no redemption. In structure and in spirit, the *Life of Mary* is the quintessential antiromance.

CONCLUSION: MYTHICAL IMPERIALISM IN LATE ANTIQUITY

In the eighth century, a mischievous Byzantine author wrote a hagiographical romance that begins where the novel of Achilles Tatius ends. Clitophon and Leucippe—whose name has been apathetically disguised as "Gleucippe"—are married and living in Emesa. Gleucippe is infertile, and Clitophon is a wife-beater. She regularly beseeches Artemis (her savior in the romance) to allow her to have a child, without issue. Not until she converts to Christianity does she bear a son, Galaktion, who will become the chaste, Christian hero of the story. The saint's life proves that hagiographers, even at this date, simply could not live without the imaginary world created by the authors of romance. The grotesque story of Gleucippe and Clitophon is probably the least subliminal instance of what Frye called "mythical imperialism." The invention of the penitent prostitutes was only one campaign in a massive cultural conquest that sprawled across the entire continent of ancient literature. But this new archetype, born from the warm embers of imperial romance, reflects an especially meaningful encounter in the transition to a Christian culture. The stories of the penitent prostitutes, as a subgenre, mirror the coming of age of Christianity as a dominant public ideology. The woman's body was a potent symbol, a shorthand for the order of society. At the deepest level, the redemption of a prostitute's corrupted flesh stood for the ability of the church to absorb society and through baptism to cleanse it. The prostitute's sins are only an exaggerated and especially condensed symbol of the sins of the world. The prostitute is everyman.[74]

The reach of these stories underscores their place as part of a broad cultural transformation. So, too, does the manifest correspondence between the growth of this literary legend and the legal program of the Christian state. The remarkable attack on coerced prostitution that was launched under Theodosius II and would reach its climax in the age of Justinian was coterminous with the period of the penitent prostitute's gestation and florescence. Just as Christian lawmakers, suddenly anxious about the "necessity of sin," broke with immemorial tradition and extended succor to society's most vulnerable, Christian litterateurs created stories in which sexual dishonor is the product of sin rather than circumstance, choice rather than destiny. The Justinianic monastery "Repentance," offered as a refuge for former prostitutes, was part of a much deeper reorientation of state and society around the logic of a sexual morality grounded on the idea of sin.[75]

Narrative literature proved such a rich medium for exploring the relation between sexual morality and the individual experience across the ancient world because stories are naturally suited for dramatizing the tension between freedom and fate. In antiquity this tension, as we have seen, was an endlessly fertile source of speculation about the nature, purpose, and limits of moral claims on the body's sexual potential. The Greek romances seem, in their very form, structurally derived from pagan fatalism; yet the authors who most completely sense this equation of form and fate—Achilles Tatius and Heliodorus—are the ones who create characters that stridently accept their moral responsibility in the face of an overwhelming destiny. This powerful sense of sweeping external motion bearing down on the individual offers a satisfying concession to the mysterious fact that the self is part of nature. The Christian authors, by contrast, recreate from the pieces of classical romance stories in which the characters determine their own destiny. In the early period, the characters they imagine are little more than symbols of moral liberty, standing apart from the dark forces of the world in their absolute purity, within a narrative arc that ends in death rather than rebirth. In the period of the church's triumph, the bright division between the protagonist and the *saeculum* becomes blurred, and the individual's freedom consists precisely in the action of turning away from the world and separating herself from it. So a literature in which honorable girls were preserved inviolate by the dispensations of fate or providence becomes a literature in which girls choose to stain themselves and then choose to become righteous, of their own volition, by accepting the grace of divine pardon.

Stories have a claim, just as much as formal philosophical literature, to a privileged place in the history of sexuality. The narrative literature of the late classical world proved capable, like no other medium, of representing the pattern and experience of sexual morality, measured against the shape of life. The collective body of texts, and the literary syntax shared between them, seems to speak to us directly—*especially* in the hands of the authors who understood the mechanics and conventionality of their stories most profoundly. In the late classical world, the shared syntax of narrative changed. The structural transformation that enabled the creation of characters like Pelagia and Mary traces the deeper reordering of the form and logic of sexual morality. A romance like *Leucippe and Clitophon* was possible because—even if the author is smirking or sneering—ultimately the romance belonged to a world where individual sexual morality was locked within and subordinate to systems of valuation that were external, objective, and social. The self, with its uncanny eroticism, was constituted by its place in the harmonious synthesis of nature and society that the ancient city had achieved. A romance like the *Life of Mary of Egypt* was possible because sexual morality was now a troublesome inheritance of the flesh, in a universe whose true scale of values lay in the hope of the spirit to transcend its embodiment.

CONCLUSION

Sex and the Twilight of Antiquity

IN THE COLORFUL treasury of monastic tales known as *The Spiritual Meadow,* written down sometime around AD 600, we meet two brothers following the ascetic life who have sworn never to be separated from each other. One of them sensed himself falling victim to the lures of the flesh and asked his partner to release him from their oath of spiritual camaraderie. "I am being dragged into fornication, and I want to return to the world." His brother would not release him from their bond but instead accompanied him "into the city," standing right outside the door of the "den of fornication." After his assignation, the fallen brother refused to return to the desert; "I will remain in the world." Still his faithful companion refused to depart from him, and so they continued living in the city, Jerusalem, earning wages as day laborers, the one brother living in complete abandonment, the other in continual penance for his brother's sins. Eventually the sinner was brought to repent of his transgressions and asked his holy brother, in contrition, to take him back "into the wilderness, so that I may be saved." They took up residence in a cave, where they would live out their days in fulfillment of their oath. In this moralizing vignette we see, through the eyes of monks, the lines between sexual sin and bodily restraint laid out across the landscape. The "world," the "city," was virtually synonymous with the submission to the flesh. The wilderness, in its barren, craggy recesses, was a retreat from the corruption of the civilized order. In the stark figures of monastic imagination, the world remained, as ever, in the grip of demonic eros.[1]

By the time John Moschus composed *The Spiritual Meadow,* it has become harder for us to see the "world" from the inside than from the distant and stilted view of monastic retreat. Such a perspective makes us wonder to what extent the effort to reform the sexual habits of the ancient city had, simply, failed to take more than superficially. But it is important not to be seduced by the alarmist fables of monastic lore, composed by writers who were not as far removed from the life of the world and its cities as they wished to project. The two brothers in the tale of Moschus were shepherded back to holiness under the guidance of Abraham, an ambitious monastery builder from the age of Justinian who lived in the highest imperial circles and eventually became archbishop of Ephesus. John Moschus himself was an ascetic journeyman who moved easily across a Mediterranean Sea that had endured the first, devastating rounds of bubonic plague and still tied Italy and the Aegean into the vibrant societies of the Levant; Moschus, who died in Rome, would dedicate his collection of monastic stories to Sophronius, who possibly authored the *Life of Mary of Egypt* and who witnessed firsthand the fall of Palestine to the armies of Islam. As their broad horizons suggest, authors like John Moschus and Sophronius are more rightly considered the last spokesmen of antiquity than harbingers of an incipient medieval era. But in some ways the Mediterranean-Levantine society in which they moved was, by their time, the vital remnant of a classical world that was already reduced in scope and complexity. What this means is that the revolution in sexual morality that we have traced in these pages, far from simplistically ushering in the Christian Middle Ages, belonged to an ancient thought-world that very slowly crumbled in upon itself. The intellectual assumptions that undergird Augustinian theology, or the patterns of state and society that are presumed by Justinianic law, are in important ways closer to the philosophers and legislators of the second century, where we began, than to the monks and kings who would inherit the ruins of the Roman Empire; even though the values of an Augustine or a Justinian, we have emphasized, were radically novel, the intellectual and political architecture of their thought recognizably belongs to the ancient world. Thus the Christianization of sexual morality is an episode of late classical history, rather than one chapter in a seamless transition to the Christian Middle Ages.

The crisis that swept across the former territories of Roman rule, progressing from northwest to southeast, carried in its train unpredictable consequences for erotic life. Perhaps the reverberations of the crisis were least felt inside the monastery, which possessed the cultural resources to maintain ancient styles of moral philosophy indifferent to the transformations of the external world. In the ascetic literature we find an ethics of the sexual body that, despite its novelty, seems to extend backward in time across the centuries. Here we encounter the vital legends of the monastic fathers, like Paphnutius, who once believed that he had vanquished the demonic impulses that tempted his flesh. His pride earned him a visitation from an angel of the Lord, who warned him how incomplete his spiritual transformation remained. "Go, take a most beautiful naked virgin, and if holding her you feel that the tranquility of your heart remains undisturbed and your peace is untouched by fleshly burnings," then only might he vaunt his spiritual accomplishment. If this was an unusual proposal for an angel to make, we are quickly informed that it worked its effects without having to be tried literally, as the humility of Paphnutius was restored. In stories like these we see how intimately the array of cosmic beings had settled into ancient conversations about sexual desires; but the psychological assumptions and moral imagination of such lore draws on centuries of tradition. We remember that Epictetus had imagined a philosopher confronted with the temptations of a willing girl; the Stoic imagined victory in such a scenario as a rational decision to discount the impulses of pleasure. Epictetus frankly admitted that you could cut off the penis but never cut out desire. In the ascetic literature of late antiquity, we see the fulfillment of the trajectory promised already by Clement of Alexandria, that Christian sexual morality, in its purest expression, would not conquer desire but eliminate it.[2]

We meet the story of Paphnutius and the virgin in the *Conferences* of John Cassian, a later contemporary of Augustine who did more than anyone to translate the lessons of eastern asceticism into a western tradition of cenobitic monasticism. Although Foucault's work on ancient Christianity was cut short by his death, it is evident from the published fragments that he intended to treat Cassian's thought as the quintessence of late antique sexual morality. This would have been both a canny and an idiosyncratic choice. Cassian outlines, with the prescriptive clarity of an institutional founder, the place of sexual austerity within a communal monastic regimen. For Cassian, chastity was one element in a complex of interrelated virtues through which the monk sought extraordinary personal transformation. The pursuit of chastity entailed a demanding regimen to control both "the heat of the body" and the "motion of the soul." For Cassian, the monk could transcend sexual desire only by reaching a state of exalted love for his own purity; to resist pleasure was mere abstinence, but to rebuild the self as a creature untouched by its temptations was true chastity. Cassian outlined six degrees of chastity through which the monk might, with the infusion of divine grace, seek perfection: first, not to be struck down by carnal sin; second, not to let his mind dilate on thoughts of pleasure; third, not to let the sight of a woman move him to lust; fourth, not to suffer a "little movement of the flesh" while awake; fifth, when some occasion for thought of human generation occurred, such as a suggestive passage of the reading, not to give the "slightest assent" to sensual thoughts; and finally, not to be tormented by seductive visions of women while sleeping. For Cassian, a concern with nocturnal emissions that had quietly percolated in ecclesiastical and monastic circles for centuries suddenly lurches into the foreground, as the supreme test of having transcended physical desire. For Cassian, involuntary discharges were not a matter of purity and pollution, in any physical sense. Rather, they were a sign of the monk's interior state, a privileged window into the murkiness of the self in an intense system of self-scrutiny.[3]

What captivated Foucault was not simply the repressive agenda of this monastic founder but the sense in which sexuality has become a deep and only semiconscious source of the self, something that must be sought and controlled through an elaborate technology of surveillance. Cassian prescribed an encompassing regime of transformation, physical and spiritual. It entailed diet and meditation. It specified grids of evaluation that seem extraordinarily detailed: three emissions a year was a modest goal for the monk earnestly in pursuit of chastity. It required forceful modes of introspection that could be achieved in dialogue between the monk and his superior. Here Cassian's model of chastity foreshadows the confessional, a place where the deepest recesses of the self were to be searched with the sure guidance of an experienced master. The goals of this spiritual exercise were tranquility and transparency. The healed patient could hope to reach a state where "he is found to be the same in the night as in the day, whether reading or praying, when solitary or surrounded by the crowd, so that he never sees himself in secret in such a way that he would blush to be seen by others, and finally so that the eye from which there is no flight will never catch him in anything which he would wish to be hidden from human sight." Here the notion of the sexual being, constantly before the face of God, receives its purest expression. It might seem a fair measure of the distance traveled, that we have departed from a civilization whose prime virtue was the wondrously indeterminate command of moderation and have arrived in a civilization where the frequency of involuntary discharge has become a matter of punctilious surveillance.[4]

The sedimentation of ascetic energy into monastic rules and institutions is, to be sure, one legacy of Christian sexual morality. But this is only one trajectory in the tumultuous final centuries of late antiquity. Around the time the two ascetics of the *Spiritual Meadow* left the civilized "world" to escape its temptations, a man in the Frankish territories of northern Gaul was succumbing to the power of eros. In the telling of Gregory of Tours, this man, a priest, was "much too attached to the life of luxury, a lover of women, abandoned to gluttony, fornication, and every iniquity." He eventually fell in love with a certain woman and "often copulated with her, in the manner of a whore." He cropped her hair, dressed her as a man, and led her to another town where they could live "without suspicion of adultery." But she was "a freeborn woman, descended from honorable stock. When, after some time, her relations discovered what had passed, they rushed forth to avenge the dishonor brought upon their line. They found the priest and clamped him in irons, but the woman they flayed alive." A bishop named Aetherius pitied the priest and ransomed him from their custody, employing him in the cathedral school and sponsoring his moral rehabilitation. But like a "dog to his vomit," the priest returned to his sin and tried to seduce the mother of a boy under his tutelage. She, "being a woman of sexual modesty," informed her husband, whose clan promptly subjected the priest "to excruciating torments" and would have killed him but for the intervention once more of the compassionate bishop. Such tales thrust us into a world that is far less familiar than the settled landscape of cities and ascetic retreats of the eastern Mediterranean. What is so conspicuously absent from the dramas reported by Gregory of Tours is any strong sense of the state, of a public power that acts as the communal arbiter of legitimate violence in the sexual arena. To be sure, private force had always played a role in the mechanics of sexual regulation, but only within the terms established by the public authorities, whose criminalization of adultery was the foundation of an ancient political economy of sex. In Gregory's world, those authorities have lost a little of their precarious hold on the circulation of sexual honor.[5]

The expansion of private force at the expense of public power was gradational, but no less dramatic for that fact. Already in the reign of Theoderic in Italy, generally one of the most traditional of the successor kingdoms, we find the king excusing justifiable homicide in the case of adultery on the grounds that it was simply a law of nature for men to defend their wives with the same violence that "bulls," "rams," and "stallions" controlled their mates, whereas the failure to do so would "redound to a man's eternal shame"! Here, in early sixth-century Italy, was a society that still possessed a relatively strong apparatus of public law. A generation later, during the regency of Theoderic's grandson, an edict was issued in the name of defending *civilitas,* civility. It compasses a number of sexual regulations. A man convicted of adultery was deprived of all rights of legitimate marriage himself; if rich, he lost half his property, and if poor, he was exiled. No man was to be joined to two wives at the same time, which was lust or cupidity, and in either case was to cost a man all of his property. If a man dishonored his marriage by being joined to a concubine, the woman was punished. A freeborn concubine was to be yoked to the slavery of the man's wife; a slave who engaged in such disgrace was subjected to a penalty of the mistress's choosing, "excepting the penalty of blood." What is notable about this promulgation is not the headlong intrusion of moralism into lawgiving, but the subtle disappearance of old modes of regulation, in which status above all framed the dynamics of power between state and society. A century later, in the Visigothic kingdom of Spain, the mix of Christian moralizing and public pronouncement had continue to progress. Men who "lie with men" were to be castrated and placed under ecclesiastical supervision. For the first time we hear that a woman who "plays the role of a prostitute" was condemned to three hundred lashes and exiled from her city; so serious was the lawmaker that judges who were negligent in the enforcement of these measures were themselves to receive one hundred lashes and a fine of thirty gold coins. In the Byzantine world, older frameworks organized around status maintained their strength even in the Justinianic dispensation, and only in the *Ecloga* of the eighth century do we find a total breakdown of the old order.

Gone is the ancient rubric of the *lex Iulia.* All extramarital sex is punished. Men are lashed for "fornication," twice as harshly if they are married when they commit the offense; sex with one's own slave is subject to public penalties. In these early medieval law codes, both eastern and western, we find Christian values fully expressed within the scaffolding of a new public order, one that owes less than might be imagined to ancient traditions even in so conservative a domain as juristic culture.[6]

The trajectory we can only wonder about, though, because it is virtually invisible to us, is the erotic tradition, in both life and literature. On occasion its embers flare, even into the fifth or sixth century. It was perhaps around the court of Justinian that an erudite litterateur named Aristaenetus composed a fictive book of love letters that are charming tales steeped in the ancient erotic tradition, affirming the enigmatic force of the sex drive in human life. In a historian of the same period we are struck to read a hostile portrait of a Justinianic official whose debauched entertainments with sex servers, both male and female, were described in calculated detail; what is striking is not that exaggerated sexual invective remained a potent form of insult but that the terms of the criticism would have been familiar to Lucian, or for that matter an Athenian of the classical age; the official's crime was immoderation, in the consumption of unmixed wine and dainty fish plates as in the more carnal pleasures. We recall, too, that someone, after all, copied by hand the erotic novels and epigrams that still serve to offer us precious windows into the ways humans in the distant past thought about sex, but these texts become, as time passes, safely stowed in the storehouse of cultural memory. Inexorably the visible monuments of eros fade, and the celebrations of its power become faint. We can strain to hear men and women who resisted cold counsels and continued to celebrate, in their forgotten wedding songs and in their lost tales that escaped the permanence of writing, the uncanny, earthy power of eros in human life. But in the early Middle Ages, strident affirmations of joy are hard to hear, because they have lost their place in public forms of expression, and that in itself is a true change, both in the experience of sexual culture and, more selfishly, in the ways that we can know the past.[7]

The changes that unfolded in the sixth and seventh centuries marked the end of an ancient Mediterranean world, as the collapse of transmarine connections cut apart the sea, as the great urban monuments became testaments of ruin, as a classical way of life—with its rhythms, its modes of expression—was quietly silted up like the valley settlements the ancients had hewn out of the lowlands. If the Christian revolution in sexual morality brings us toward a world that seems somehow more familiar, the revolution itself was defined by terms and preoccupations that were resolutely ancient. It played out against debates over the nature of society's claims on the body and the question of whether those claims were to be a matter of fate or freedom. Some of the fatalism of the old order was lost forever, and with it an indifference toward the brutalities accepted in the name of destiny, but also, perhaps, some of the enchantment that comes with the belief that eros makes us part of nature and constitutes a mysterious source of the self. In the freedom of the new order, we recognize how potent was the idea that claims of moral dignity might cut across all accidents of circumstance to the core of the individual's being. But it is one of history's true paradoxes that such a model of freedom was harnessed to a movement that was anti-erotic to its very foundations, and that this concept of freedom enabled a model of responsibility that would promote unprecedented accumulations of power in the regulation of sexual acts. These paradoxes are part of our cultural history, and it has been the hope of this book that, by exploring them, we might gain a better understanding of the inheritance fate has delivered to us.

Abbreviations

The following list offers the full forms of the authors and titles of works cited in the Endnotes. To locate the editions used, the reader may consult, for classical sources, S. Hornblower and A. Spawforth, eds., *The Oxford Classical Dictionary*, 4th ed. (Oxford, 2012), and for Christian sources in Greek and Latin, respectively, M. Geerard et al., eds., *Clavis patrum graecorum* (Turnhout, 1974–87) and E. Dekkers, ed., *Clavis patrum latinorum*, 3rd ed. (Turnhout, 1995).

PRIMARY SOURCES

Ach. Tat.	Achilles Tatius
Ps.-Acro	Pseudo-Acro
Act. Andr. gr.	*Acts of Andrew*, Greek version
Act. Paul. et Thec.	*Acts of Paul and Thecla*
Act. Thom.	*Acts of Thomas*
Adamantius	
Physiog.	*Physiognomy*
Alciph.	Alciphron
Ep.	*Epistulae*

Alex. Aphr.	Alexander of Aphrodisias
De fat.	*De fato*
Ambr.	Ambrose of Milan
Abr.	*De Abraham*
De virg.	*De virginitate*
Ep.	*Epistulae*
Ambrosiast.	Ambrosiaster
Comm. Ep. I Cor.	*Commentarius in xiii epistulas Paulinas, ad I Cor.*
Comm. Ep. I Tim.	*Commentarius in xiii epistulas Paulinas, ad I Tim.*
Comm. Rom.	*Commentarius in xiii epistulas Paulinas, ad Rom.*
Quaest. vet. et nov. test.	*Quaestiones Veteris et Novi Testamenti*
Amphil. Icon.	Amphilocius of Iconium
Or. in mul. pecc.	*Oratio in mulierem peccatricem*
Anth. Gr.	*The Greek Anthology*
Anth. Pal.	*The Palatine Anthology*
Anton. Plac.	Antoninus of Piacenza
Itin.	*Itinerarium*
Apoc. Pet.	*Apocalypse of Peter*
Apophth. patr., coll. alph.	*Sayings of the Fathers, alphabetic collection*
Aristaen.	Aristaenetus
Ep.	*Epistulae*
Artem.	Artemidorus
On.	*Oneirocritica*
Aster. Amas.	Asterius of Amasea
Hom.	*Homiliae*
Athan.	Athanasius
Contra gent.	*Contra gentes*
Athen.	Athenaeus
Athenag.	*Athenagoras*
Leg.	*Legatio*
Aug.	Augustine of Hippo
Civ.	*De civitate Dei*
Conf.	*Confessiones*
Contr. Iul. op. imp.	*Contra Iulianum opus imperfectum*
De bon. coniug.	*De bono coniugali*
De lib. arb.	*De libero arbitrio*

De nupt. et concup.	*De nuptiis et concupiscentia*
De ord.	*De ordine*
Psalm.	*Enarrationes in Psalmos*
Retr.	*Retractationes*
Serm.	*Sermones*
Serm. nov.	*Sermones novissimi*
Aul. Gell.	Aulus Gellius
Aur. Vict.	Aurelius Victor
Caes.	*De Caesaribus*
Auson.	Ausonius
Epig.	*Epigrammata*
Bard.	Bardaisan
Lib. leg. reg.	*Liber legum regionum*
Bas.	Basil of Caesarea
Ep.	*Epistulae*
En. proph. Isaiah	*Enarratio in prophetam Isaiam*
Hom. prov.	*Homilia in principium proverbiorum*
Hom. psalm.	*Homiliae super Psalmos*
Bas. Anc.	Basil of Ancyra
Ps.-Bas. Seleuc.	Pseudo-Basil of Seleucia
Vit. mir. Thecl.	*De vita et miraculis Theclae*
BGU	*Aegyptische Urkunden aus den Königlichen Museen zu Berlin*
Cael. Aur.	Caelius Aurelianus
Tard. pass.	*Tardae passiones*
Caes. Arel.	Caesarius of Arles
Serm.	*Sermones*
Cass. Dio	Cassius Dio
Cedren.	Cedrenus
Hist. comp.	*Compendium historiarum*
Chariton	Chariton of Aphrodisias
Choric. Gaz.	Choricius of Gaza
Or.	*Orationes*
Cic.	Cicero
Cael.	*Pro Caelio*

CIG	*Corpus Inscriptionum Graecarum*
CIL	*Corpus Inscriptionum Latinarum*
Clem. Alex.	Clement of Alexandria
Paid.	*Paidogogos*
Protrep.	*Protrepticus*
Str.	*Stromata*
Ps.-Clem.	Pseudo-Clement
Rec.	*Recognitiones*
CJ	*Codex Justinianus*
Coll. leg. mos. rom.	*Collatio legum mosaicarum et romanarum*
Conc. Illib.	*Council of Elvira*
Const. apost.	*Constitutiones apostolorum*
Consult. Zacc. et Apoll.	*Consultationes Zacchei christiani et Apollonii philosophi*
CT	*Codex Theodosianus*
Cyr. Alex.	*Cyril of Alexandria*
De ador.	*De adoratione et cultu in spiritu et veritate*
Cyr. Hier.	Cyril of Jerusalem
Cathec.	*Catecheses ad illuminandos*
Dig.	*Digesta*
Dio	Dio Chrysostom
Or.	*Orationes*
Ps.-Dio	Pseudo-Dio Chrysostom
Donat.	Donatus
Vit. Verg.	*Vita Vergilii*
Ep. Barn.	*Epistulae Barnabae*
Ep. Clem. ad Jac.	*Epistula Clementis ad Jacobum*
Epict.	Epictetus
Diss.	*Dissertationes*
Enchir.	*Enchiridion*
Fr.	*Fragmenta*
Eus.	Eusebius of Caesarea
Hist. eccl.	*Historia ecclesiastica*
Praep. evan.	*Praeparatio evangelica*

Eutrop.	Eutropius
Brev.	*Breviarium*
Evag.	Evagrius
Hist. eccl.	*Historia ecclesiastica*
Exc. Theod.	*Excerpta ex Theodoto*
Firm. Matern.	Firmicus Maternus
Math.	*Mathesis*
Gal.	Galen
Loc. aff.	*De locis affectis*
San. tu.	*De sanitate tuenda*
Sem.	*De semine*
Simplic. med. temp.	*De simplicium medicamentorum temperamentis ac facultatibus*
Greg. Naz.	Gregory of Nazianzus
Or.	*Orationes*
Greg. Nys.	Gregory of Nyssa
Ep. can. ad Let.	*Epistula canonica ad Letoium*
Hom. in Eccl.	*In Ecclesiasten*
Greg. Tur.	Gregory of Tours
Hist.	*Libri historiarum*
Mir. Andr.	*Miracula Andreae*
Hel.	*Heliodorus*
Aeth.	*Aethiopica*
Hier.	Jerome
Comm. in Isaiam	*Commentarius in Isaiam*
Comm. Tit.	*Commentarius in epistulam ad Titum*
Ep.	*Epistulae*
Hippol.	Hippolytus
Fr. in Prov.	*Fragmenta in Proverbia*
Hist. Apoll. reg. Tyr.	*Historia Apollonii Regis Tyri*
Hor.	Horace
Serm.	*Sermones*
Inst.	*Institutiones* (*Corpus iuris civilis*)
Ioh. Cass.	John Cassian
Coll.	*Collationes*
Inst.	*Institutiones*

Ioh. Chrys.	John Chrysostom
Ad Theod.	*Ad Theodorum lapsum*
Ad vid. iun.	*Ad viduam iuniorem*
Adv. oppug.	*Adversus oppugnatores vitae monasticae*
Hom. hab. Goth.	*Homilia habita postquam presbyter Gothus concionatus fuerat*
In Hebr.	*In epistulam ad Hebraeos*
In Matt.	*In Matthaeum*
In Rom.	*In epistulam ad Romanos*
Lib. repud.	*De libello repudii*
Propt. forn.	*In illud: Propter fornicationes*
Ioh. Lyd.	John Lydus
De magis.	*De magistratibus populi Romani*
Ioh. Malal.	John Malalas
Chron.	*Chronographia*
Ioh. Mosch.	John Moschus
Prat. spir.	*Pratum spirituale*
Ios. et Asen.	*Joseph and Aseneth*
ILS	*Inscriptiones latinae selectae*
Iren.	Irenaeus
Adv. her.	*Adversus haereses*
Iul. Ecl.	Julian of Eclanum
See Aug. Contr. Iul. op. imp.	
Iust.	Justin Martyr
Apol.	*Apologia*
Dial. Tryph.	*Dialogus cum Tryphone*
Iustin.	Justinian
Nov.	*Novellae*
Juv.	Juvenal
Sat.	*Saturae*
Lact.	Lactantius
Epit. inst.	*Epitome divinarum institutionum*
Inst.	*Divinae institutionum*
Lib.	Libanius
Decl.	*Declamationes*
Or.	*Orationes*
Prog.	*Progymnasmata*

Luc.	Lucian
Adv. indoct.	*Adversus indoctum*
Alex.	*Alexander*
Bacc.	*Bacchus*
Catap.	*Cataplus*
De merc. cond.	*De mercede conductis potentium familiaribus*
De mort. Peregr.	*De morte Peregrini*
Demonax	*Demonax*
Dial. meretr.	*Dialogi meretricii*
Imag.	*Imagines*
Jupp. trag.	*Juppiter tragoedus*
Pseudolog.	*Pseudologista*
Rhet. praecept.	*Rhetorum praeceptor*
Saturn.	*Saturnalia*
Symp.	*Symposium*
Ver. Hist.	*Verae historiae*
Ps.-Luc.	Pseudo-Lucian
Amor.	*Amores*
Ps.-Mac.	Pseudo-Macarius
Hom. spirit.	*Homiliae spirituales*
Marc.	Marcellus Empiricus
De medic.	*De medicamentis*
Marc. Aur.	Marcus Aurelius
Med.	*Meditationes*
Mart.	Martial
Ep.	*Epigrammata*
Mart. Agap. Iren. et Chion.	*Martyrium Agapae, Irenae, Chionae et sodalium*
Mart. Petr.	*Martyrium Petri*
Mart. Pion.	*Martyrium Pionii*
Meth.	Methodius
Conv.	*Convivium decem virginum*
Lib. arb.	*De libero arbitrio*
Muson. Ruf.	Musonius Rufus
Diss.	*Dissertationes*
Nemesianus	Nemesianus
Ecl.	*Eclogae*
Niceph. Callist.	Nicephorus Callistus
Hist. eccl.	*Historia ecclesiastica*

Nov. Theod.	*Novellae Theodosii II*
Orig.	Origen
Comm. in 1 Cor.	*Fragmenta ex commentariis in epistulam i ad Corinthios*
De princ.	*De principiis*
Hom. in Luc.	*Homiliae in Lucam*
In Rom.	*Commentarii in epistulam ad Romanos*
Ovid	Ovid
Ars am.	*Ars Amatoria*
Her.	*Heroides*
P. Ant.	*The Antinoopolis Papyri*
P. Herm. Rees	*Papyri from Hermopolis and Other Documents of the Byzantine Period*
P. Oxy.	*The Oxyrhynchus Papyri*
Pall.	Palladius
Laus. Hist.	*Historia Lausiaca*
Pass. Andr. gr.	*Passio Andreae graeca*
Pass. Artem.	*Passio Artemii*
Paulin. Nol.	Paulinus of Nola
Carm.	*Carmina*
Paus.	Pausanias
Pelag.	Pelagius
Ep. ad Demet.	*Epistula ad Demetriadem*
PGM	*Papyri graecae magicae*
Phaedr.	Phaedrus
Fab.	*Fabulae*
Philo	Philo
De vit. cont.	*De vita contemplativa*
Ios.	*De Josepho*
Spec. leg.	*De specialibus legibus*
Philostrat.	Philostratus
Ep.	*Epistulae*
Vit. soph.	*Vitae sophistarum*
Plaut.	Plautus
Cist.	*Cistellaria*

Plin.	*Pliny the Younger*
Ep.	*Epistulae*
Pan.	*Panegyricus*
Plut.	Plutarch
Amat.	*Amatorius*
Conj. Pr.	*Conjugalia praecepta*
Polemo	Polemo
Physiogn.	*Physiognomica*
Procop.	Procopius of Caesarea
De aedif.	*De aedificiis*
Hist. Arc.	*Historia arcana*
Procop. Gaz.	Procopius of Gaza
Panegyr.	*Panegyricus in Anastasium imperatorem*
Prudent.	Prudentius
Peristeph.	*Peristephanon*
PS	*Pauli sententiae*
PSI	*Papiri greci e latini*
Ptol.	Ptolemy
Tetr.	*Tetrabiblos*
RSV	Revised Standard Version
1 Cor.	1 Corinthians
1 Tim.	1 Timothy
Act. apost.	Acts of the Apostles
Apoc.	Revelation
Matt.	Gospel of Matthew
Rom.	Letter to the Romans
Rufinus	
trans.	See Origen
Salv.	Salvian
Gub.	*De gubernatione Dei*
Sen.	Seneca the Elder
Contr.	*Controversiae*
Sen.	Seneca the Younger
Cons. Helv.	*Consolatio ad Helviam matrem*
Ep.	*Epistulae*

SHA	*Scriptores historiae augustae*
Comm.	*Commodus*
Marcus	*Marcus*
Sifr. Deut.	*Sifre to Deuteronomy*
Siric.	Siricius
Ep.	*Epistulae*
Socr.	Socrates
Hist. eccl.	*Historia ecclesiastica*
Soran.	Soranus
Gyn.	*Gynaeciorum libri*
Stat.	Statius
Silv.	*Silvae*
Strabo	Strabo
Geog.	*Geographica*
Suet.	Suetonius
Ner.	*Nero*
Tib.	*Tiberius*
Syn.	Synesius of Cyrene
Ep.	*Epistulae*
T. Bavli	*The Babylonian Talmud*
A.Z.	*Avodah Zarah*
Gitt.	*Gittin*
Kidd.	*Kiddushin*
Nidd.	*Niddah*
Tac.	Tacitus
Ann.	*Annales*
Tat.	Tatian
Or.	*Oratio ad Graecos*
Tert.	Tertullian
Ad nat.	*Ad nationes*
Test.	*Testament of the Twelve Patriarchs*
Levi	*Testament of Levi*
Sim.	*Testament of Simeon*
Theoph.	Theophilus
Aut.	*Ad Autolycum*
Theophan.	Theophanes
Chron.	*Chronographia*

Tri. Trac.	*Tripartite Tractate*
Ulp. Reg.	*Tituli ex corpore Ulpiani*
Val. Max.	Valerius Maximus
Vit. Mar. (nept. Abr.)	*Vita Mariae meretricis (neptis Abrahae)*
Vit. Mar. Aeg.	*Vita Mariae aegyptiacae*
Vit. Pelag.	*Vita Pelagiae*
Xen. Eph.	Xenophon of Ephesus
Zonar.	Zonaras
Zosim.	Zosimus
Hist. nov.	*Historia nova*

JOURNALS AND REFERENCE MATERIALS

AARC	*Atti dell'Accademia romanistica costantiniana*
ACO	*Acta conciliorum oecumenicorum*
AJA	*American Journal of Archaeology*
AJP	*American Journal of Philology*
Annales ESC	*Annales. Économies, Sociétés, Civilisations*
BDAG	*Greek-English Lexicon of the New Testament*
BHG	*Bibliotheca Hagiographica Graeca*
BHO	*Bibliotheca Hagiographica Orientalis*
BMCR	*Bryn Mawr Classical Review*
CP	*Classical Philology*
CQ	*Classical Quarterly*
HTR	*Harvard Theological Review*
JBL	*Journal of Biblical Literature*
JECS	*Journal of Early Christian Studies*
JRA	*Journal of Roman Archaeology*
JRS	*Journal of Roman Studies*
JTS	*Journal of Theological Studies*

OLD	*Oxford Latin Dictionary*
Lampe PGL	*Patristic Greek Lexicon*
PG	*Patrologiae cursus completus . . . series graecae*
PL	*Patrologiae cursus completus . . . series . . . ecclesiae latinae*
PLRE	*Prosopography of the Later Roman Empire*
RAC	*Reallexikon für Antike und Christentum*
TAPA	*Transactions of the American Philological Association*
TDNT	*Theological Dictionary of the New Testament*
TDOT	*Theological Dictionary of the Old Testament*
ZPE	*Zeitschrift für Papyrologie und Epigraphik*
ZRG	*Zeitschrift der Savigny-Stiftung für Rechtsgeschichte. Romanistische Abteilung*

Notes

INTRODUCTION

1. Kenneth J. Dover, *Greek Homosexuality,* rev. and updated ed. (Cambridge, Mass., 1989 [1978]); Paul Veyne, "La famille et l'amour sous le haut-empire romain," *Annales ESC* 33 (1978): 35–63. See now Paul Veyne, *Sexe et pouvoir à Rome* (Paris, 2007); Michel Foucault, *Histoire de la sexualité,* vol. 2, *L'usage des plaisirs* (Paris, 1984); and Foucault, *Histoire de la sexualité,* vol. 3, *Le souci de soi* (Paris, 1984). For the fragments of Foucault's arguments on Christianity, see Jeremy Carrette, ed., *Religion and Culture: Michel Foucault* (New York, 1999), esp. 153–197; Daniel Boyarin, Elizabeth Castelli, "Introduction: Foucault's *The History of Sexuality:* The Fourth Volume, or, A Field Left Fallow for Others to Till," *Journal of the History of Sexuality* 10 (2001): 357–374; Peter Brown, *The Body and Society: Men, Women, and Sexual Renunciation in Early Christianity* (New York, 1988). For recent syntheses, see Mark Golden and Peter Toohey, *A Cultural History of Sexuality in the Classical World* (Oxford, 2011); and Marilyn B. Skinner, *Sexuality in Greek and Roman Culture* (Malden, 2005). For a reflection on the state of the field, see Amy Richlin, "What We Need to Know Right Now," *Journal of Women's History* 22 (2010): 268–281.

2. Same-sex eros: Danilo Dalla, *Ubi Venus Mutatur: Omosessualità e diritto nel mondo romano* (Milan, 1987). On prostitution, Thomas McGinn, *Prostitution,*

Sexuality, and the Law (New York, 1998), and McGinn, *The Economy of Prostitution in the Roman World: A Study of Social History and the Brothel* (Ann Arbor, 2004), are fundamental; the only dedicated study of late antique prostitution is Stavroula Leontsini, *Die Prostitutione im frühen Byzanz* (Vienna, 1989). Charles Chauvin, *Les chrétiens et la prostitution* (Paris, 1983), has little to offer for our period.

3. For a learned overview of sin in the New Testament, see E. P. Sanders, "Sin, Sinners (NT)," *Anchor Bible Dictionary* (New York, 1992), 6:40–47; for *pudicitia* and *impudicitia,* see Rebecca Langlands, *Sexual Morality in Ancient Rome* (Cambridge, 2006), 19–32; on *infamia,* see A. H. J. Greenridge, *Infamia: Its Place in Roman Public and Private Law* (Oxford, 1894); on the close connection between *impudicitia* and *infamia,* see, e.g., Dig. 47.10.1.2; on *sōphrosynē* as self-control, see, e.g., Dio Or. 3.10; as respectability, Dio Or. 75.8; Ach. Tat. 8.7.1; see further Chapter 1; on *aidōs,* see Douglas Cairns, *Aidōs: The Psychology and Ethics of Honour and Shame in Ancient Greek Literature* (Oxford, 1993); on *pudor,* Robert Kaster, "The Shame of the Romans," *TAPA* 127 (1997): 1–19; Dio Or. 7.139; compare Muson. Ruf. Diss. 2; e.g., Ioh. Chrys. Ad Theod. 19; on the Christian use of "shame" more generally, see Elizabeth A. Clark, "Sex, Shame, and Rhetoric: En-Gendering Early Christian Ethics," *Journal of the American Academy of Religion* 59 (1991): 221–245.

4. For the moral substance of shame in classical Greece, see Bernard Williams, *Shame and Necessity* (Berkeley, 1993); Kaster, "Shame of the Romans," 4; Aul. Gell. 19.6.3: *timor iustae reprehensionis . . . αἰσχύνη ἐστὶν φόβος δικαίου ψόγου.*

5. "Slaves had": see Kaster, "Shame of the Romans," 9; for some limited exceptions, see Langlands, *Sexual Morality in Ancient Rome,* 22; on the role of slavery in sharpening attitudes toward honor and shame in Roman society, see Kyle Harper, *Slavery in the Late Roman World, AD 275–425* (Cambridge, 2011), esp. 326–348.

6. On *pudicitia* as both a bodily condition and a moral quality, see Langlands, *Sexual Morality in Ancient Rome,* 49; see esp. Chapter 1 for the literature that juxtaposes the subjective and objective grounds of honorable behavior.

7. Friedrich Nietzsche, *Die vier grossen Irrthümer,* 7, in *Götzen-Dämmerung* (orig. Leipzig, 1889).

8. Study of the ancient novel begins with Erwin Rohde, *Der griechische Roman und seine Vorläufer* (Leipzig, 1876); in the last generation, the reputation of the ancient romance has been fully rehabilitated, and the bibliography is now vast: selectively, Ben Perry, *The Ancient Romances: A Literary-Historical Account of Their Origins* (Berkeley, 1967); Tomas Hägg, *The Novel in Antiquity* (Oxford, 1983); Graham Anderson, *Ancient Fiction: The Novel in the Graeco-Roman World* (London, 1984); Shadi Bartsch, *Decoding the Ancient Novel: The Reader and the Role of Description in Heliodorus and Achilles Tatius* (Princeton, 1989); Massimo Fusillo, *Il romanzo greco: Polifonia ed eros* (Venice, 1989); J. R. Morgan and R. Stoneman, eds.,

Greek Fiction: The Greek Novel in Context (New York, 1994); James Tatum, ed., *The Search for the Ancient Novel* (Baltimore, 1994); Gareth Schmeling, ed., *The Novel in the Ancient World,* rev. ed. (Leiden, 2003); Tim Whitmarsh, ed., *The Cambridge Companion to the Greek and Roman Novel* (Cambridge, 2008), esp. Helen Morales, "The History of Sexuality," 39–55. For the purposes of this book, four contributions have been indispensable: David Konstan, *Sexual Symmetry: Love in the Ancient Novel and Related Genres* (Princeton, 1994); Glen Bowersock, *Fiction as History: Nero to Julian* (Berkeley, 1994); Simon Goldhill, *Foucault's Virginity: Ancient Erotic Fiction and the History of Sexuality* (New York, 1995); and Helen Morales, *Vision and Narrative in Achilles Tatius' Leucippe and Clitophon* (Cambridge, 2004). Finally, it is imperative to note that throughout this book, when I speak of "the genre of romance" I am referring to the set of Greek romances that happen to be extant (principally the novels of Achilles Tatius, Heliodorus, Xenophon of Ephesus, Longus, and Chariton); these are sometimes described as the "idealizing" romances, even though an author like Achilles Tatius was (at best) a sardonic idealizer. We possess a significant number of fragments that make it plain that what happens to survive is only a particular subset of novelistic literature (and that Achilles would not have been the most sensationalist if the others had survived). For reflections on the genre, see Helen Morales, "Challenging Some Orthodoxies: The Politics of Genre and the Ancient Greek Novel," in *Fiction on the Fringe: Novelistic Writing in the Post-Classical Age,* ed. Grammatiki Karla (Leiden, 2009), 1–12; Tim Whitmarsh, "The Greek Novel: Titles and Genre," *AJP* 126 (2005): 587–611; Niklas Holzberg, *The Ancient Novel: An Introduction* (New York, 1995 [1985]), 1–27. For the fragments of other novels, see Susan Stephens and John Winkler, eds., *Ancient Greek Novels: The Fragments* (Princeton, 1995). On the dating of the novels, again from a massive bibliography, see Ewen Bowie, "The Chronology of the Earlier Greek Novels since B. E. Perry: Revisions and Precisions," *Ancient Narrative* 2 (2002): 47–63; and Albert Henrichs, "Missing Pages: Papyrology, Genre, and the Greek Novel," in *Culture in Pieces: Essays on Ancient Texts in Honour of Peter Parsons,* ed. Dirk Obbink and Richard Rutherford (Oxford, 2011), 302–322, at 303–305.

9. For the totalizing ambitions of Christian ideology, see Averil Cameron, *Christianity and the Rhetoric of Empire: The Development of Christian Discourse* (Berkeley, 1991).

10. See Chapter 1.

11. Kyle Harper, "*Porneia:* The Making of a Christian Sexual Norm," *JBL* 131 (2012): 365–385.

12. Rom. 1:26–27 (RSV); see esp. B. Brooten, *Love between Women: Early Christian Responses to Female Homoeroticism* (Chicago, 1996).

13. E.g., Jennifer A. Glancy, "Obstacles to Slaves' Participation in the Corinthian Church," *JBL* 117 (1998): 481–501; Carolyn Osiek, "Female Slaves, *Porneia,* and the Limits of Obedience," in *Early Christian Families in Context: An*

Interdisciplinary Dialogue, ed. David L. Balch and Carolyn Osiek (Grand Rapids, 2003), 255–274.

14. Jennifer Wright Knust, *Abandoned to Lust: Sexual Slander and Ancient Christianity* (New York, 2006); Kathy Gaca, *The Making of Fornication: Eros, Ethics, and Political Reform in Greek Philosophy and Early Christianity* (Berkeley, 2003); on the diversity of early Christianity, see the recent treatment in David Brakke, *The Gnostics: Myth, Ritual, and Diversity in Early Christianity* (Cambridge, Mass., 2010).

15. Inst. 4.18.4; Procop. Hist. Arc. 11.34–36; see Chapter 3.

16. On the formation of marriage, prostitution, and same-sex eros in the archaic and classical Greek period, see Carola Reinsberg, *Ehe, Hetärentum und Knabenliebe im antiken Griechenland* (Munich, 1989).

17. See esp. Kate Cooper, *The Virgin and the Bride: Idealized Womanhood in Late Antiquity* (Cambridge, Mass., 1996).

1. THE MORALITIES OF SEX IN THE ROMAN EMPIRE

1. Unless otherwise noted, all translations are my own.
Ach. Tat. 6.18–21, esp. 6.20.1–3; on the date of Achilles Tatius, see most recently Henrichs, "Missing Pages," 308–309, arguing on the basis of P. Oxy. 56.3836 that the novel belongs even to the first half of the second century; following Guglielmo Cavallo, *Il calamo e il papiro: La scrittura greca dall'età ellenistica ai primi secoli di Bisanzio* (Florence, 2005), at 225–257; on the tone of Achilles, see B. P. Reardon, "Achilles Tatius and Ego-Narrative," in *Oxford Readings in the Greek Novel,* ed. Simon Swain (Oxford, 1999), 243–258; Morales, *Vision and Narrative,* 83–84, on Thersander's unwillingness to believe in the conventions of romance.

2. Ach. Tat. 6.22.4; on the language of *eleutheria,* see Harper, *Slavery in the Late Roman World,* 306; for the great antiquity of this idiom, see Rosanna Omitowoju, *Rape and the Politics of Consent in Classical Athens* (Cambridge, 2002), 88, 101, 206–207.

3. For the discursive connections between Stoicism and romance, see esp. Judith Perkins, *The Suffering Self: Pain and Narrative Representation in the Early Christian Era* (New York, 1995), 77–103, though I would maintain that Achilles Tatius and the Stoics give very different answers to some of the same questions: see below; Morales, *Vision and Narrative,* 57–60, is convincing; Goldhill, *Foucault's Virginity,* 91–102, on Achilles Tatius and philosophy generally; Stoic fate: Susanne Bobzien, *Determinism and Freedom in Stoic Philosophy* (Oxford, 1998); Michael Frede, *A Free Will: Origins of the Notion in Ancient Thought* (Berkeley, 2011); more generally, Jörn Müller und Roberto Hofmeister Pich, eds., *Wille und Handlung in der Philosophie der Kaiserzeit und Spätantike* (Berlin, 2010); Richard Sorabji, "The Concept of the Will from Plato to Maximus the Confessor," in *The Will and*

Human Action: From Antiquity to the Present Day, ed. Thomas Pink and M. W. F. Stone (London, 2004), 6–28; Albrecht Dihle, *The Theory of Will in Classical Antiquity* (Berkeley, 1972).

4. Ach. Tat. 1.10.6.

5. Veyne, "La famille et l'amour," 50; "current fashion": Ach. Tat. 2.35.2; orgasm: Act. Tat. 2.37; Plut. Amat. 769a; on these contests, which cluster in the high empire, see James Jope, "Interpretation and Authenticity of the Lucianic *Erotes,*" *Helios* 38 (2011): 103–120 (though not fully convincing in arguing for the Lucianic authorship of the *Erotes*); Goldhill, *Foucault's Virginity,* 102–111; Marcelle Laplace, *Le roman d'Achille Tatios: "Discours panégyrique" et imaginaire romanesque* (Bern, 2007), 261–278; on the authorship of the *Erotes,* see still Robert Bloch, *De pseudo-luciani amoribus* (Strasbourg, 1907).

6. Ach. Tat. 2.36, 2.38; on Roman pederasty in general, the best treatment is Christian Laes, *Children in the Roman Empire: Outsiders Within* (Cambridge, 2011), 222–277.

7. Foucault, *Care of the Self,* 229, 189, 192.

8. "Lofty formulations": Foucault, *The Care of the Self,* 189; compare Luc. Demonax 24.

9. "Did you never": Epict. Diss. 4.1.15; Luc. Ver. Hist. 2.18; Virgil: Donat. Vit. Verg. 9; Nemesianus Ecl. 4; Marc. Aur. Med. 1.16.2 and 1.17.6; Anth. Gr. 5.65 *(adesp.)* ll.3–4.

10. "Short season": Anth. Gr. 5.12 (Rufinus); compare Athen. 6.620E; Luc. Alex. 6; Philostr. Ep. 13; courtesan: Athen. 13.605D; "time": Anth. Gr. 12.10 (Strato); Anth. Gr. 12.22 (Strato); compare Dio Or. 36.8; age list: Anth. Gr. 12.4 (Strato); alternating: Ps.-Luc. Amor. 26; Luc. Ver. Hist. 1.22; on the context and dates of Strato and Rufinus, see Alan Cameron, "Strato and Rufinus," *CQ* 32 (1982): 162–173.

11. Aristocratic: Thomas Hubbard, "Popular Perceptions of Elite Homosexuality in Classical Athens," *Arion* 6 (1998): 48–78; law: David Cohen, *Law, Sexuality, and Society: The Enforcement of Morals in Classical Athens* (Cambridge, 1991); Veyne, "La famille et l'amour," 50–51; Ramsay MacMullen, "Roman Attitudes to Greek Love," *Historia* 31 (1982): 484–502; Saara Lilja, *Homosexuality in Republican and Augustan Rome* (Helsinki, 1983); Eva Cantarella, *Secondo natura: La bisessualità nel mondo antico* (Rome, 1988); Craig Williams, "Greek Love at Rome," CQ 45 (1995): 517–539, and Williams, *Roman Homosexuality;* Hans Peter Obermayer, *Martial und der Diskurs über männliche "Homosexualität" in der Literatur der frühen Kaiserzeit* (Tübingen, 1998); on the law, see below and Chapter 3.

12. On Roman slavery, Jerzy Kolendo, "L'esclavage et la vie sexuelle des hommes libres à Rome," *Index* 10 (1981): 288–297; Marguerite Garrido-Hory, *Martial et l'esclavage* (Paris, 1981); Keith Bradley, *Slaves and Masters in the Roman Empire: A Study in Social Control* (New York, 1987); Moses Finley, *Ancient Slavery*

and Modern Ideology (Princeton, 1998, [1980]); Williams, *Roman Homosexuality,* 15–40; Laes, *Children in the Roman Empire;* Harper, *Slavery in the Late Roman World;* on the Warren Cup, see Clarke, *Roman Sex,* 78–91; I have followed the compelling analysis of James Butrica, "Some Myths and Anomalies in the Study of Early Roman Sexuality," *Journal of Homosexuality* 49 (2005): 209–269, at 236–238, for the interpretation of the scenes.

13. Ovid Ars. Am. 2.683–684; Roman slave sources and numbers: Walter Scheidel, "Quantifying the Sources of Slaves in the Early Roman Empire," *JRS* 87 (1997): 156–169; Scheidel, "The Slave Population of Roman Italy: Speculation and Constraints," *Topoi Orient-Occident* 9 (1999): 129–144; Scheidel, "Human Mobility in Roman Italy, II: The Slave Population," *JRS* 95 (2005): 64–79; relegating to farms: Ps.-Luc. Amor. 10; sub-elite slave ownership: Roger Bagnall and Bruce Frier, *The Demography of Roman Egypt* (Cambridge, 1994), 48, 70; Harper, *Slavery,* also tries to call attention to the pervasiveness of "bourgeois" slaveholders; swollen: Hor. Serm. 1.2.116–119; dream: Artem. On. 1.78 ll.70–72; compare Mart. Ep. 2.43.

14. Edward Gibbon, *History of the Decline and Fall of the Roman Empire,* vol. 1 (New York, Modern Library Edition, 1995 [1776]), 59; Tiberius: Suet. Tib. 43–45; Nero: Suet. Ner. 28–29; Cass. Dio 63.13; Domitian: Mart. Ep. 9.11–13, 16–17, 36; Stat. Silv. 3.4; Commodus: SHA, Comm. 11; on the sex lives of the emperors, Caroline Vout, *Power and Eroticism in Imperial Rome* (Cambridge, 2007); Catherine Edwards, *The Politics of Immorality in Ancient Rome* (Cambridge, 1993); on eunuchs in antiquity generally, Peter Guyot, *Eunuchen als Sklaven und Freigelassene in der griechisch-römischen Antike* (Stuttgart, 1980); Walter Stevenson, "The Rise of Eunuchs in Greco-Roman Antiquity," *Journal of the History of Sexuality* 5 (1995): 495–511; Mathew Kuefler, *The Manly Eunuch: Masculinity, Gender Ambiguity, and Christian Ideology in Late Antiquity* (Chicago, 2001); Sean Tougher, ed., *Eunuchs in Antiquity and Beyond* (London, 2002).

15. See, in general, Hugo Meyer, *Antinoos: Die archäologischen Denkmäler unter Einbeziehung des numismatischen und epigraphischen Materials sowie der literarischen Nachrichten* (Munich, 1991); Vout, *Power and Eroticism,* 52–135; and Christopher P. Jones, *New Heroes in Antiquity: From Achilles to Antinoos* (Cambridge, Mass., 2010), 75–83. The primary literary sources are numerous, but especially important are Paus. 8.9.7–8; Cass. Dio 69.11; Athen. 677D. As Jones, *New Heroes,* 82, points out, the earliest sources are ambiguous about the exact nature of the relationship between Hadrian and Antinous. Pausanius says that he was "exceedingly favored" by the emperor (*οὗτος ἐσπουδάσθη περισσῶς δή τι ὑπὸ βασιλέως* Ἀδριανοῦ), which is at least suggestive of amorous attachment (see, for example, a sexual sense in Luc. Adv. indoct. 25 and Cass. Dio 68.7.4, quoted below); Iust. I Apol. 29.4, written under Hadrian's successor, need not be entirely discounted simply because it is a Christian source—the apology is (formally) addressed to Antoninus Pius and is not luridly worded. He says that Antinous was worshipped "although people knew what

he was and where he came from"; more fulsome Christian invective against Antinous can be found at Clem. Protrep. 4.49; Tert. Ad nat. 2.10.1; Athan. Contra gent. 9.

16. Trajan: Cass. Dio 68.7.4; Herodes: Philostr. Vit. soph. 558; Walter Ameling, *Herodes Atticus,* 2 vols. (Hildesheim, 1983), 113; on Polydeucion, Aul. Gell. Noct. Att. 19.12 and Louis Robert, "Deux inscriptions de l'époque imperiale en Attique," *AJP* 100 (1979): 153–165; "no doubt acquiesced": Sarah Pomeroy, *The Murder of Regilla: A Case of Domestic Violence in Antiquity* (Cambridge, Mass., 2007), 53–65; Anth. Gr. 12.175, 194, 199 (Strato); Luc. Symp. 15; Alex. 50; Saturn. 24; Artem. On. 1.78 ll.43–44.

17. Dio: Or. 7.139; Or. 7.149; Or. 75.8; Roman law: PS 2.26.12–14 with Dalla, *Ubi venus mutatur,* and Chapter 3; as Dalla notes (at 126) in a significant analysis, it is probable that the jurisdiction of Roman governors to punish acts classified as *iniuria* or *crimen vis* gradually absorbed the regulation of pederasty; PS 5.4.4 and 5.4.14 are tremendously important; the example in Lucian would strongly support his interpretation: Luc. De mort. Pereg. 9; compare Luc. Catap. 26; Luc. Jupp. trag. 52. Trial: P. Oxy. 3.471 (2C), re-edited with commentary, Herbert Musurillo, *The Acts of the Pagan Martyrs: Acta Alexandrinorum* (Oxford, 1954), 33–43; with Dominic Montserrat, *Sex and Society in Græco-Roman Egypt* (New York, 1996), 151–153; Vout, *Power and Eroticism,* 141f.

18. On the worries around school, Richlin, "Not before Homosexuality," 538; bribes: Dio Or. 66.11. Philosophers: Clem. Str. 2.23.138; compare Lucian Vit. auct. 15 and De mort. Pereg. 43; assenting: Anth. Gr. 12.200 (Strato); the now: Anth. Gr. 12.228 (Strato).

19. Plut. Amat. 4.751B; "that central text in the history of desire": Goldhill, *Foucault's Virginity,* 112.

20. Conjugal friendship: Plut. Amat. 5.751C and 23.769A; consent: Plut. Amat. 5.751D; Aphrodite: Plut. Amat. 5.752A; Frederick Brenk, "Plutarch's *Erotikos:* The Drag Down Pulled Up," *Illinois Classical Studies* 13 (1988): 457–471.

21. Plutarch on male passives: Plut. Amat. 23.768E; muscular lads: Luc. Adv. indoct. 25; male prostitute: Luc. Adv. indoct. 25; Polyphemus: Luc. Pseudolog. 27; for graffiti, see Antonio Varone, *Erotica pompeiana: Iscrizioni d'amore sui muri di Pompei* (Rome, 1994), and most recently Sarah Levin-Richardson, "*Facilis hic futuit:* Graffiti and Masculinity in Pompeii's 'Purpose-Built' Brothel," *Helios* 38 (2011): 59–78.

22. Ptol. Tetr. 3.14; in general, Tamsyn S. Barton, *Power and Knowledge: Astrology, Physiognomics, and Medicine under the Roman Empire* (Ann Arbor, 1994); Brooten, *Love between Women,* 140–142.

23. Ptol. Tetr. 3.14.171–172; for the relative lack of sources on lesbianism (esp. in Latin), see Butrica, "Some Myths and Anomalies," 261.

24. Born to be penetrated: Sen. Ep. 95.21; Luc. Adv. indoct. 23; Rhet. praecept. 11; appearance and deviance: Adamantius, Physiog. A4; Simon Swain, ed., *Seeing the Face, Seeing the Soul: Polemon's* Physiognomy *from Classical*

Antiquity to Medieval Islam (Oxford, 2007), 496–497; "knowledge of the internal constitution": Istanbul Polemon, fo. 40, trans. Antonella Ghersetti, in Swain, *Seeing the Face,* p. 481; "easily outed": Adamantius, Physiog. B38, in Swain, *Seeing the Face,* p. 536.

25. Phaedr. Fab. 4.16.

26. Richlin, "Not before Homosexuality," 530; Taylor, "Two Pathic Subcultures," 319–371; Bruce Frier, "Review of Craig A. Williams, *Roman Homosexuality: Ideologies of Masculinity in Classical Antiquity,*" *BMCR,* Nov. 5, 1999; Butrica, "Some Myths and Anomalies," 236.

27. Ptol. Tetr. 3.14.172.

28. Nero: Suet. Nero 28; Tac. Ann. 15.370; Elagabulus: Cass. Dio 79–80; Xen. Eph. 5.15; Mart. Ep. 7.58; 12.42; 1.24; Juv. Sat. 2.47; John Boswell, *Same-Sex Unions in Premodern Europe* (New York, 1994), 53–107, is a useful assemblage of evidence.

29. Ptol. Tetr. 3.14.171; instrument: Ps.-Luc. Amor. 28; wives: Ptol. Tetr. 3.14.172; Clem. Paid. 3.3.21.3; Luc. Dial. meretr. 5; for the *dextrarum iunctio,* and in general by far the most reliable treatment, Brooten, *Love between Women,* 59; Boswell, *Christianity, Social Tolerance, and Homosexuality,* 83, part of broader changes in the emotional value of marriage.

30. Boat chase: Ach. Tat. 5.7; severed head: 8.15.4; ill-starred: 8.16.1.

31. McGinn, *Prostitution, Sexuality, and the Law,* on the polarization of female sexual honor; Langlands, *Sexual Morality in Ancient Rome,* on female norms in general.

32. Plaut. Cist. 78–81, with Langlands, *Sexual Morality in Ancient Rome,* 207; Cic. Cael. 49; Theodor Mommsen, *Römisches strafrecht* (Leipzig, 1899), 691; in general, Riccardo Astolfi, *La Lex Iulia et Papia* (Padua, 1970); David Cohen, "The Augustan Law on Adultery: The Social and Cultural Context," in *The Family in Italy from Antiquity to the Present,* ed. David Kertzer and Richard Saller (New Haven, 1991), 109–126; see esp. McGinn, *Prostitution, Sexuality, and the Law.*

33. Behavior: Dig. 50.16.46; vestments: Dig. 47.10.15.15; on the language of *mater familias,* see McGinn, *Prostitution, Sexuality, and the Law,* 9, 153.

34. Age structures: Brent Shaw, "Latin Funerary Epigraphy and Family Life in the Later Roman Empire," *Historia: Zeitschrift für alte Geschichte* 33 (1984): 457–497; Brent Shaw, "The Age of Roman Girls at Marriage: Some Reconsiderations," *JRS* 77 (1987): 30–46; Bagnall and Frier, *Demography of Roman Egypt,* 111–118; Walter Scheidel, "Progress and Problems in Roman Demography," in *Debating Roman Demography,* ed. Walter Scheidel (Leiden, 2001), 1–81; Walter Scheidel, "Roman Age Structure: Evidence and Models," *JRS* 91 (2001): 1–26; Scheidel, "Roman Funerary Commemoration and the Age of First Marriage," *CP* 102 (2007): 389–402; on widows: Jens-Uwe Krause, *Witwen und Waisen in römischen Reich,* 4 vols. (Stuttgart, 1994–1995); Thomas McGinn, "Widows, Orphans, and Social History," *JRA* 12 (1999): 617–632.

35. Judaism and virginity: Michael L. Satlow, *Jewish Marriage in Antiquity* (Princeton, 2001), 118–119; Shulamit Valler, *Women and Womanhood in the Talmud,* trans. Betty Sigler Rozen (Atlanta, 1999), 29–50; on virginity in general: Giulia Sissa, *Greek Virginity,* trans. Arthur Goldhammer (Cambridge, Mass., 1990); for a second-century medical view: Soran. Gyn. 1.3.16–17; nurses: Aristaen. Ep. 1.6; songs: Dio Or. 7.142; "wounding": Plut. Amat. 24.769E; Villa Farnesina: Clarke, *Looking at Lovemaking,* 103.

36. In general, Langlands, *Sexual Morality in Ancient Rome;* Carlos Noreña, "Hadrian's Chastity," *Phoenix* 61 (2007): 296–317; Helen North, *Sophrosyne: Self-Knowledge and Self-Restraint in Greek Literature* (Ithaca, 1966), focused on the early period, as is Adriaan Rademaker, Sophrosyne *and the Rhetoric of Self-Restraint: Polysemy and Persuasive Use of an Ancient Greek Value Term* (Leiden, 2005); "ornament": Sen. Cons. Helv. 16.4; fertility and *pudicitia:* Val. Max. 7.1.1; slaves: Langlands, *Sexual Morality in Ancient Rome,* 22; Dig. 47.10.9.4–10; Dig. 1.6.2; *sōphrosynē* in the romances: Dimitri Kasprzyk, "Sur la notion de ΣΩΦΡΟΣΥΝΗ chez Achille Tatius," in *Passion, vertus et vices dans l'ancien roman,* ed. Bernard Pouderon and Cécile Bost-Pouderon (Lyon, 2009), 97–115.

37. Be and seem: Sen. Contr. 2.7.9; precious flower: Hier. Ep. 79.8; signs: Sen. Contr. 2.7.4; only protection: Sen. Contr. 2.7.9; blush: Sen. Contr. 2.7.3.

38. Coins: Langlands, *Sexual Morality in Ancient Rome,* 69; Plut. Conj. Pr. 9.139C; city without walls: Ioh. Chrys. Ad vid. iun. 2.79–85; slave chaperones: Harper, *Slavery in the Late Roman World,* 342–343; Ramsay MacMullen, *Changes in the Roman Empire: Essays in the Ordinary* (Princeton, 1990), 162–168; danger: Philostr. Ep. 30; Dio Or. 7.140; bathing: Garrett Fagan, *Bathing in Public in the Roman World* (Ann Arbor, 1999), esp. 26–29; Fikret Yegül, *Bathing in the Roman World* (Cambridge, 2010).

39. Rare: Ovid Her. 17.41; age of Saturn: Juv. Sat. 6.1; Plato: Epict. Fr. 15; philosopher interrupted: Luc. De merc. cond. 36; on the popularity of adultery motifs in mime: Ruth Webb, *Demons and Dancers: Performance in Late Antiquity* (Cambridge, Mass., 2008), 95–115; "all women": Anth. Gr. 5.41 (Rufinus); adultery trials: Cass. Dio 76.16.

40. Cass. Dio 76.16; toga: McGinn, *Prostitution, Sexuality, and the Law,* 156–171, doubting the realities of enforcement.

41. On rape in general, Susan Deacy and Karen Peirce, eds., *Rape in Antiquity: Sexual Violence in the Greek and Roman Worlds* (London, 1997); Angeliki Laiou, ed., *Consent and Coercion to Sex and Marriage in Ancient and Medieval Societies* (Washington, D.C., 1993); see further Chapter 3; disaster: Ach. Tat. 2.24.3.

42. Ach. Tat. 5.27.2–3; prosecution of Melite: Ach. Tat. 8.10.12.

43. Jane Gardner, *Women in Roman Law & Society* (London, 1986); for late antiquity, Joëlle Beaucamp, *Le statut de la femme à Byzance,* 2 vols. (Paris, 1990–1992).

44. Plut. Conj. pr. 16.140B; domestic violence: Leslie Dossey, "Wife Beating and Manliness in Late Antiquity," *Past & Present* 199 (2008): 3–40, suggesting that the western Mediterranean was more violent than the east.

45. "Bathetic": Goldhill, *Foucault's Virginity,* 81; Leucippe's mother: Ach. Tat. 2.24.4; statues: Juv. Sat. 6.165.

46. Sexual exploitation of slaves in general: Harper, *Slavery in the Late Roman World,* 281–325; "morals of the mistress": Hier. Ep. 79.9; Leucippe as field slave: Ach. Tat. 5.17.3–9; slave marriages: Ulp. Reg. 5.5; Dig. 38.10.10.5; Hier. Ep. 107.11; Querolus, ed. Randstrand, p. 74; slave fathers: see T. Bavli, Kidd. 69a, for an especially clear formulation, if from beyond Roman frontiers; Aug. Serm. nov. (Dolbeau) 2.13; P. Herm. Rees 18 (AD 323); Keith R. Bradley, "The Age at Time of Sale of Female Slaves," *Arethusa* 11 (1978): 243–252.

47. Most impure part: Aug. De ord. 2.4.12; in general, see esp. McGinn, *Prostitution, Sexuality, and the Law,* and McGinn, *Economy of Prostitution;* Rebecca Fleming, "*Quae corpore quaestum facit:* The Sexual Economy of Female Prostitution in the Roman Empire," *JRS* 89 (1999): 38–61.

48. Toleration and degradation: McGinn, *Prostitution, Sexuality, and the Law,* 347; Cato: Hor. Sat. 1.2 and Ps.-Acro. 1.2; necessity: Artem. 1.45; Dio: Or. 7.139–140; public good, like baths: Alciph. Ep. 3.22; Lais: Lib. Decl. 25; forbidding adulteries: Salv. Gub. 7.22; further, Harper, *Slavery in the Late Roman World,* 311–313; on the antiquity of these ideas, Frank Frost, "Solon Pornoboskos and Aphrodite Pandemos," *Syllecta Classica* 13 (2002): 34–46.

49. "Visible everywhere": Dio Or. 7.133–134; papyri: PSI 9.1055; the identification of brothels at Pompeii has occasioned a significant amount of commentary with widely disparate interpretations; only the famous Purpose-built Brothel can be identified with certainty, but this should not be taken to imply that there was any sort of moral zoning practiced; for this discussion, see Andrew Wallace-Hadrill, "Public Honour and Private Shame: The Urban Texture of Pompeii," in *Urban Society in Roman Italy,* ed. T. J. Cornell and K. Lomas (New York, 1995), 39–62; Ray Laurence, *Roman Pompeii: Space and Society* (London, 1994); McGinn, *Economy of Prostitution,* 78–111, 182–219.

50. Laura McClure, *Courtesans at Table: Gender and Greek Literary Culture in Athenaeus* (New York, 2003), on Athenaeus in particular; for the earlier period, James Davidson, *Courtesans & Fishcakes: The Consuming Passions of Classical Athens* (New York, 1998); Leslie Kurke, *Coins, Bodies, Games and Gold: The Politics of Meaning in Archaic Greece* (Princeton, 1999); and the essays in Christopher Faraone and Laura McClure, eds., *Prostitutes and Courtesans in the Ancient World* (Madison, 2006).

51. "No trivial": Luc. Imag. 22; disabilities of stage performers: Dig. 23.2.44; CT 4.6.3; Ulp. Reg. 13.1; with McGinn, *Prostitution, Sexuality, and the Law,* 91–2; these prohibitions on the marriage of actresses were overturned in the reign of Justin, of course: CJ 5.4.23; see further Chapter 4; prostitution and slavery: Harper,

Slavery and the Late Roman World, 304–310, with abundant evidence and cautions about the limits of the evidence; McGinn, *Economy of Prostitution,* 74; Flemming, *"Quae corpore,"* 58; poor: e.g., Artem. On. 1.56; Dio Or. 7.133.

52. Collar: ILS 9455; papyrus: PSI 9.1055; man who buys girls: Aug. Psalm. 128.6; slavery or brothel: Lact. Inst. 6.20; covenants: McGinn, *Prostitution, Sexuality, and the Law,* 288–319.

53. Art in brothels: Clarke, *Looking at Lovemaking,* 202–204; price: McGinn, *Economy of Prostitution,* 40–55, is the most comprehensive discussion, and see p. 43–44 for fellatio; corpse: BGU 4.1024.

54. Aug. Civ. 2.20; patronized by slaves: Ioh. Chrys. In Hebr. 15.3; Clarke, *Looking at Lovemaking,* 196; McGinn, *Economy of Prostitution,* 71–72.

55. *Bios:* Alciph. Ep. 3.22; "that was that": Peter Garnsey, "Introduction: The Hellenistic and Roman Periods," in *The Cambridge History of Greek and Roman Political Thought,* ed. C. Rowe and M. Schofield (Cambridge, 2000), 401–414, at 407.

56. Sen. Contr. 1.2; see Langlands, *Sexual Morality in Ancient Rome,* 258–259; Amy Richlin, "Gender and Rhetoric: Producing Manhood in the Schools," in *Roman Eloquence: Rhetoric in Society and Literature,* ed. W. J. Dominik (London, 1997), 90–110.

57. Ach. Tat. 8.7.1.

58. On Regilla in general, see now Pomeroy, *The Murder of Regilla;* for the inscription, Ameling, *Herodes,* no. 100, p. 120–121; this translation is from Pomeroy, p. 107.

59. Mimicked: Ach. Tat. 5.20.5; "philosophers": Ach. Tat. 8.5.7; on "sexual symmetry" in the novel, see esp. Konstan, *Sexual Symmetry.*

60. See, in general, Christian Laes, "Male Virgins in Latin Inscriptions from Rome," in *Religion and Socialisation in Antiquity and the Middle Ages,* ed. K. Mustakallio, S. Katajala-Peltomaa, and V. Vuolanto (Rome, 2013), forthcoming, and Kirk Ormand, "Testing Virginity in Achilles Tatius and Heliodorus," *Ramus* 39 (2010): 160–197; RSV Apoc. 14.4; Ios. et. Asen. 4.9; 8.1; in the *Symposium* of Methodius, Christ is called the *archiparthenos* (10.3 and 10.5); but for the rarity, see Lampe PGL s.v. *parthenos,* II (p. 1038); for *virgo* used of males, OLD has only CIL 13.2036; compare the late fourth-century Marc. De medic. 7.15, 8.126, 21.11, and 26.107; Ioh. Cass. Inst. 6.19; a handful of other instances in A. Blaise, *Dictionnaire latin-français des auteurs chrétiens* (Turnhout, 1954), s.v. *virgo;* Athenag. Leg. 33.3; compare Hippol. Fr. in Prov. 62; Treggiari, *Roman Marriage,* 234; for *sōphrosynē* as the pure status of a woman's body, see, e.g., Hel. Aeth. 1.8.3; for its application to male sexual self-control, Mus. Ruf. Diss. 12; Dio Or. 3.10.

61. Drachma (i.e., proverbially cheap): Plut. Amat. 16.759E; compare Anth. Gr. 5.109 (Antipater); "first and most fitting": Athen. 1.8E; "follow me": Clem. Paid. 2.11.116; Simon Goldhill, "The Erotic Eye: Visual Stimulation and Cultural Conflict," in *Being Greek under Rome: Cultural Identity, the Second Sophistic and the*

Development of Empire, ed. Simon Goldhill (Cambridge, 2001), 154–194; Laura Nasrallah, *Christian Responses to Roman Art and Architecture: The Second-Century Church amid the Spaces of Empire* (Cambridge, 2010).

62. I. Kajanto, "Balnea, Vina, Venus," in *Hommages à Marcel Renard*, vol. 2, ed. J. Bibauw (Brussels, 1969), 357–367; see esp. Foucault, *Care of the Self*, for models of male restraint.

63. Age at marriage: see above; rite of passage: Laes, *Childhood in the Roman Empire*, 279–280; Philo, Ios. 43.

64. Ptol. Tetr. 4.10.205; "slippery time": Sen. Contr. 2.6.4; Mar. Aur. Med. 1.17.2; erotic passions: Mar. Aur. Med. 1.17.7.

65. Mirth, law of youth: Sen. Contr. 2.6.11; gloominess: Sen. Contr. 2.6.10; "required training": Sen. Contr. 2.6.11; "violence of youth": Ach. Tat. 8.18.2; Val. Max. 7.3.10.

66. For a deep history of Mediterranean adultery: Eva Cantarella, "Homicides of Honor: The Development of Italian Adultery Law over Two Millennia," in Kertzer and Saller, *Family in Italy*, 229–244; for the connotations of *moecheia*, see Harper, *"Porneia,"* 367; the democratic aura of the brothel went back to classical Athens: Halperin, *One Hundred Years of Homosexuality*, 88–112; tyranny and adultery: Ach. Tat. 6.20.3; Dio Or. 47.24; "sense of shame": Epict. Diss. 2.10.18; P. Ant. 1.36 (AD 326).

67. Aggressive masculinity: Amy Richlin, *The Garden of Priapus: Sexuality and Aggression in Roman Humor*, rev. ed. (New York, 1992); pleasure and softness: Holt N. Parker, "Love's Body Anatomized: The Ancient Erotic Handbooks and the Rhetoric of Sexuality," in *Pornography and Representation in Greece and Rome*, ed. Amy Richlin (Princeton, 1992), 90–111; Dale Martin, *Sex and the Single Savior: Gender and Sexuality in Biblical Interpretation* (Louisville, 2006), 44; "he who cannot bridle his anger": Dio Or. 3.34.

68. "Harmony": Gal. San. tu. 1.5; young and old: Gal. Loc. aff. 3.6; sex: Gal. San. tu. 3.11, 6.4, 6.14; Aline Rousselle, *Porneia: On Desire and the Body in Antiquity* (Oxford, 1988), who, however, stresses the anti-erotic side of medicine.

69. Heat of young: Gal. San. tu. 1.1, 2.2; food: Gal. Loc. aff. 6.5; and Teresa Shaw, *The Burden of the Flesh: Fasting and Sexuality in Early Christianity* (Minneapolis, 1998), 99; semen: Gal. Sem. 16.25, 16.30; widower: Gal. Loc. aff. 6.5.

70. Wine in the Roman world: Nicholas Purcell, "Wine and Wealth in Ancient Italy," *JRS* 75 (1985): 1–19; André Tchernia, *Le vin de l'Italie romaine: Essai d'histoire économique d'après les amphores* (Rome, 1986); Dionysus: Ach. Tat. 2.3.3; regulation of consumption: Gal. San. tu. 1.11, 5.5; accelerant: Plut. Mor. 701F; Aphrodite's milk: Athen. 10.444d; sex fuel: Ach. Tat. 2.3.3.

71. Dance: Gal. Sem. 16.28; entire body: Gal. Sem. 16.25; *pneuma:* Gal. Sem. 16.30.

72. Abstention: Gal. Loc. aff. 6.5.

73. Diogenes: ibid.

74. See esp. Gal. San. tu. 5.1, on the possibility of health for the "free" man.

75. Festivals: Montserrat, *Sex and Society in Graeco-Roman Egypt,* 128; schools: Epict. Diss. 2.8.15; rich youth: Alciph. Ep. 1.16.2; households: Aul. Gell. Noct. att. 1.2.2; Salv. Gub. 7.3–4 is later but evocative; "what happens": Luc. Bacc. 7; symposia: Dio. Or. 27.1; on masturbation, see esp. Thomas W. Laqueur, *Solitary Sex: A Cultural History of Masturbation* (New York, 2004), 106.

76. Plin. Pan. 82.

77. Anth. Pal. 9.203 with Francesco Tissoni, "Anthologia Palatina IX 203: Fozio, Leone il Filosofo e Achillo Tazio moralizzato," *Medioevo greco* 2 (2002): 261–270; for a reading emphasizing the narratives as vehicles of subversion, Goldhill, *Foucault's Virginity;* for readings emphasizing the romances' conservatism, Cooper, *Virgin and the Bride,* and Konstan, *Sexual Symmetry.*

78. The definitive study of marriage in the Roman Empire is Susan Treggiari, *Roman Marriage:* Iusti Coniuges *from the Time of Cicero to the Time of Ulpian* (Oxford, 1991); on the conjugalization of pleasure, Foucault, *Care of the Self,* remains provocative.

79. On the sentimental family generally, see Steven Ozment, *Ancestors: The Loving Family in Old Europe* (Cambridge, Mass., 2001); in republican Rome: Suzanne Dixon, *The Roman Family* (Baltimore, 1992); now for Plautus: Helen Barber, *Plautus and the Sentimental Ideal of the Roman Family* (PhD thesis, Durham University, 2011); Juv. Sat. 6.287, a classic contrast of past and present; wine: Val. Max. 2.1.5; Aul. Gell. Noct. att. 10.23; no divorce: Val. Max. 2.1.4; Aul. Gell. Noct. att. 4.3.1; on patterns of aristocratic subjectivity, Veyne, "La famille et l'amour."

80. Treggiari, *Roman Marriage,* 83–160; Soran. Gyn. 1.9.34, in Owsei Temkin, trans., *Soranus' Gynecology* (Baltimore, 1956), 32.

81. Dio Or. 7.80; Plin. Ep. 1.14.

82. Polemo Physiogn. 69 (Leiden version, ed. and trans. R. Hoyland, in Swain, *Seeing the Face*); on abduction marriages generally, Judith Evans Grubbs, "Abduction Marriage in Antiquity: A Law of Constantine (CTh IX.4.1) and Its Social Context," *JRS* 79 (1989): 59–83.

83. In general, Andrew Wallace-Hadrill, "Houses and Households: Sampling Pompeii and Herculaneum," in *Marriage, Divorce, and Children in Ancient Rome,* ed. B. Rawson (Oxford, 1991), 191–227; slaves watching sex has turned up mostly in Jewish sources: T. Bavli Nidd. 17a; Gitt. 58a.

84. In general, Jane Gardner, *Family and* Familia *in Roman Law and Life* (Oxford, 1998), 209–267; Treggiari, *Roman Marriage;* Keith Bradley, *Discovering the Roman Family: Studies in Roman Social History* (New York, 1991); the essays in Beryl Rawson and Paul Weaver, eds., *The Roman Family in Italy: Status, Sentiment, Space* (Oxford, 1997), esp. Richard Saller, "Roman Kinship: Structure and Sentiment," 7–34.

85. Dig. 23.2.1 (Modestinus); romance: Statius Silv. 1.2.26–30; *philia:* Plut. Amat. 5.751C and 19.767C; Plin. Ep. 7.5, compare 6.4 and 6.7; *homonoia:* Dio Or. 38.15; Artem. 1.56; Plut. Conj. pr. 43; "circling dance": Dio Or. 40.39; see Mary T. Boatwright, "Women and Gender in the Forum Romanum," *TAPA* 141 (2011): 105–141, esp. 135.

86. "Where does eros": Muson. Ruf. 13A; conjugal Aphrodite: Plut. Conj. pr. 1.138C; modesty: Plut. Conj. pr. 10.139C; "school": Plut. Conj. pr. 47.145A (the Loeb's rather unforgettable rendering).

87. Pessimism: Veyne, "Roman Empire," 202; John R. Clarke, *Roman Sex: 100 BC–AD 250* (New York, 2003), 155, captures the universality of sexual art in the Roman Empire, and 31–35 for the villa of Iucundus.

88. Clarke, *Looking at Lovemaking,* 269–274; Clem. Protrep. 4.60.1 on erotic art in late second-century Alexandria; Rachel Kousser, "Mythological Group Portraits in Antonine Rome: The Performance of Myth," *AJA* 111 (2007): 673–691, esp. 685–686.

89. In general, Clarke, *Looking at Lovemaking,* 250–254; on the popularity of erotic themes, see, e.g., Donald M. Bailey, *A Catalogue of Lamps in the British Museum,* vol. 2 (London, 1980), 64; Annalis Leibundgut, *Die römischen Lampen in der Schweiz: Eine Kultur- und handelsgeschichtliche Studie* (Bern, 1977), for a focused study; for the *relative* rarity of same-sex conjunctions and oral sex, see Bailey, *Catalogue,* 64–65.

90. For the Athenian lamps, see Arja Karivieri, *The Athenian Lamp Industry in Late Antiquity* (Helsinki, 1996), 46 on Pireithos, 48, 95, 110, 123; Judith Perlzweig, *Lamps from the Athenian Agora* (Princeton, 1963), 34–36, 47–48, 122; Corinth: Kathleen Slane, *The Sanctuary of Demeter and Kore: The Roman Pottery and Lamps* (Princeton, 1990), 17, nos. 32, 35, 44–46.

91. "Whorish": PGM 26.142; *mulier equitans:* Clarke, *Looking at Lovemaking,* 217.

92. Mouth pollution: e.g., Aul. Gell. Noct. att. 1.5.1; Luc. Rhet. praec. 23; Artemid. On. 4.59; Anth. Gr. 6.17 (Lucian); prostitutes: see Clarke, *Looking at Lovemaking,* 226; possibilities unknown: Bas. Anc. 61–62 can easily be construed as a misinterpretation; Gal. Simplic. medic. temp. 249 (Kühn 12); compare Luc. Pseudolog. 28; Ovid Ars. Am. 2.683–684; Ps.-Luc. Amor. 27; Ach. Tat. 2.37.6; clarification on the basic meaning of many ancient sexual acts began with A. E. Housman, "Praefanda," *Hermes* 66 (1931): 402–412; see, more generally, J. N. Adams, *The Latin Sexual Vocabulary* (Baltimore, 1982); Butrica, "Some Myths and Anomalies."

93. On the setting, see Morales, *Vision and Narrative,* 57–60.

94. To abstain: Ach. Tat. 5.16.7, 6.21.3, 8.5.7; to wax eloquent: Ach. Tat. 1.12.1, 5.27.1; to suffer: Ach. Tat. 5.23.7; see Goldhill, *Foucault's Virginity,* 98–100.

95. Marc. Aur. Med. 1.8; in general, Malcolm Schofield, "Stoic Ethics," in *The Cambridge Companion to the Stoics,* ed. Brad Inwood (Cambridge, 2003), 233–256;

Richard Sorabji, *Emotion and Peace of Mind: From Stoic Agitation to Christian Temptation* (Oxford, 2000), 169–180.

96. Bobzien, *Determinism and Freedom in Stoic Philosophy;* Frede, *A Free Will;* Roberto Hofmeister Pich, "*Προαίρεσις* und Freiheit bei Epiktet: Ein Beitrag zu philosophischen Geschichte des Willenbegriffs," in *Wille und Handlung in der Philosophie der Kaiserzeit und Spätantike,* ed. Jörn Müller and R. M. Pich (Berlin, 2010), 95–127.

97. See Epict. Diss. 2.11.19–20; it is important to recognize that although the early Stoa propagated radical sexual doctrines, already from Antipater of Tarsus (a student of the great Chrysippus) Stoicism evinces conservative views toward marriage, so that more conservative views had been at home in Stoicism long before the Roman Stoics thrived; Gaca, *Making of Fornication,* 82; Ilaria Ramelli, *Hierocles the Stoic,* Elements of Ethics, *Fragments, and Excerpts,* trans. David Konstan (Leiden, 2009), 108–112.

98. Mus. Ruf. Diss. 12.

99. Ibid. 19.

100. Dio Or. 7; J. Samuel Houser, "*Eros* and *Aphrodisia* in the Works of Dio Chrysostom," *Classical Antiquity* 17 (1998): 235–258.

101. "Sexual-restraint drug": Dio Or. 7.140; "open, dishonorable": Dio 7.139.

102. "Women and boys": Dio Or. 7.133.

103. In the scales: Epict. Diss. 2.11.20; "citizenship, marriage": Epict. Diss. 3.7.26–28; "if you see": Epict. Diss. 3.2.8; "if a girl": Epict. Diss. 2.18.15–18.

104. Penis: Epict. Diss. 2.20.19; "learn to use": Epict. Diss. 3.12.11; "remain as pure": Epict. Enchir. 33.8.

105. "Cheap": Marc. Aur. Med. 2.12; a point: Marc. Aur. Med. 2.17, 4.3, 5.23; "commotion": Marc. Aur. Med. 6.13.1; "meditate": Marc. Aur. Med. 4.32; concubine: SHA Marcus 29.10.

106. "Peculiar quality": Marc. Aur. Med. 3.16, compare 7.57; "gods do exist": Marc. Aur. Med. 2.11.

107. "Mystic fire": Ach. Tat. 5.15.6.

108. On Achilles Tatius and Christianity, see Bowersock, *Fiction as History,* 125–128; Morales, *Vision and Narrative,* 203–205.

2. THE WILL AND THE WORLD IN EARLY CHRISTIAN SEXUALITY

1. Great, marvelous: Meth. Conv. 1.1; "vales of immortality": Meth. Conv. 8.2; on Methodius generally, L. G. Patterson, *Methodius of Olympus: Divine Sovereignty, Human Freedom, and Life in Christ* (Washington, D.C., 1997).

2. Meth. Conv. 2.1.

3. "Rapids": Meth. Conv. 4.3; "horns of the devil": Meth. Conv. 8.13.

4. "Greatest evil": Meth. Conv. 8.13; "self-ruling": Meth. Conv. 8.13; on Stoic fate, see Chapter 1; on the importance of astrology in early Christianity, see Tim Hegedus, *Early Christianity and Ancient Astrology* (New York, 2007).

5. Timothy Barnes, "Methodius, Maximus, and Valentinus," *JTS* 30 (1979): 47–55.

6. See esp. Jennifer Wright Knust, *Abandoned to Lust: Sexual Slander and Ancient Christianity* (New York, 2006).

7. On Clement's sexual ideology, see Henny Fiskå Hägg, "Continence and Marriage: The Concept of *Enkrateia* in Clement of Alexandria," *Symbolae Osloenses* 81 (2006): 126–143; Brown, *Body and Society,* 122–139; Gaca, *Making of Fornication,* 247–272; on his cultural context, see Nasrallah, *Christian Responses to Roman Art and Architecture,* 249–295; on his thought in general, see Eric Osborn, *Clement of Alexandria* (Cambridge, 2005).

8. On *porneia* and same-sex eros, see below; "above all else": Ep. Clem. ad Jac. 8.1.

9. "Weakness": 1 Cor. 2:3 (RSV); temples: Strabo Geog. 8.6.20; Paus. 2.5.1; useful is J. Murphy-O'Connor, *St. Paul's Corinth: Texts and Archaeology* (Wilmington, 1983); Joseph A. Fitzmeyer, *First Corinthians: A New Translation with Introduction and Commentary* (New Haven, 2008); "do you": 1 Cor. 6:19 (RSV).

10. Corinth and Aphrodite: Ps.-Dio [Favorinus] Or. 37.34.

11. "All things": 1 Cor. 6:12 (RSV); "it is good": 1 Cor. 7.1 (RSV); on the sexual doctrine of 1 Corinthians, from a massive bibliography, I have found most helpful Dale Martin, *The Corinthian Body* (New Haven, 1995); Will Deming, *Paul on Marriage and Celibacy: The Hellenistic Background of 1 Corinthians 7* (Cambridge, 1995); Renate Kirchhoff, *Die Sünde gegen den eigenen Leib: Studien zu πόρνη und πορνεία in 1 Kor 6, 12–20 und dem sozio-kulturellen Kontext der paulinischen Adressaten* (Göttingen, 1994).

12. For this argument, see Harper, *"Porneia;"* F. Hauck and S. Schulz, "*πόρνη, κτλ,*" *TDNT* 6:579–595; *BDAG,* "*πορνεία,*" 854–855; Fitzmeyer, *First Corinthians,* 233, 255, 279; Deming, *Paul on Marriage and Celibacy,* 13; Gaca, *Making of Fornication;* Osiek, "Female Slaves, *Porneia,* and the Limits of Obedience"; Glancy, "Obstacles to Slaves' Participation in the Corinthian Church"; Martin, *Corinthian Body,* 169; Kirchhoff, *Die Sünde gegen den eigenen Leib;* Peter J. Tomson, *Paul and the Jewish Law: Halakha in the Letters of the Apostle to the Gentiles* (Minneapolis, 1990), 97–103; Gerhard Dautzenberg, "*Φεύγετε τὴν πορνείαν* (1 Kor 6,18): Eine Fallstudie zur paulinishen Sexualethik in ihrem Verhältnis zur Sexualethik des Frühjudentums," in *Neues Testament und Ethik: Für Rudolf Schnackenburg,* ed. Helmut Merklein (Freiberg, 1989), 271–298; Joseph Jensen, "Does Porneia Mean Fornication? A Critique of Bruce Malina," *Novum Testamentum* 20 (1978): 161–184; Bruce Malina, "Does Porneia Mean Fornication?" *Novum Testamentum* 14 (1972): 10–17; Hanz Conzelmann, *1 Corinthians: A Commentary on the First*

Epistle to the Corinthians (Philadelphia, 1975), 95–96; C. K. Barrett, *A Commentary on the First Epistle to the Corinthians* (New York, 1968): 121–122; Heinrich Baltensweiler, *Die Ehe im Neuen Testament: Exegetische Untersuchungen über Ehe, Ehelosigkeit und Ehescheidung* (Stuttgart, 1967), 197–202; on the Latin, J. N. Adams, "Words for 'Prostitute' in Latin," *Rheinische Museum für Philologie* 126 (1983): 321–358, at 337–338.

13. S. Erlandsson, "zānāh," *TDOT* 4: 99–104; Phyllis Bird, "'To Play the Harlot': An Inquiry into an Old Testament Metaphor," in *Gender and Difference in Ancient Israel,* ed. Peggy Day (Minneapolis, 1989), 75–94; Phyllis Bird, "Prostitution in the Social World and the Religious Rhetoric of Ancient Israel," in *Prostitutes and Courtesans in the Ancient World,* ed. C. Faraone and L. McClure (Madison, 2006), 40–58.

14. This fact, along with the inability to sustain the preferred meaning ("exogamy") in close readings of specific passages, are among the obstacles to accepting the reconstruction of Gaca, *Making of Fornication.*

15. "Mother": Test. Sim. 5.3; "polity": Philo Spec. leg. 3.51; *miasma:* Philo Spec. leg. 3.51; on Philo's sexual ideology generally, see David Winston, "Philo and the Rabbis on Sex and the Body," *Poetics Today* 19 (1998): 41–62.

16. Various NT meanings, see Harper, *"Porneia"*; apostolic decree: RSV Act. apost. 15:20, 15:29, 21:25; Joseph A. Fitzmeyer, *The Acts of the Apostles: A New Translation with Introduction and Commentary* (New York, 1998), 557; Terrance Callan, "The Background of the Apostolic Decree (Acts 15:20, 29; 21:25)," *Catholic Biblical Quarterly* 55 (1993): 284–297; S. G. Wilson, *Luke and the Law* (Cambridge, 1983), 84–94; A. J. M. Wedderburn, "The 'Apostolic Decree': Tradition and Redaction," *Novum Testamentum* 35 (1993): 362–389; Peder Borgen, "Catalogues of Vices, the Apostolic Decree, and the Jerusalem Meeting," in *The Social World of Formative Christianity and Judaism,* ed. Jacob Neusner et al. (Philadelphia, 1988), 126–141.

17. "A kind of *porneia*": 1 Cor. 5.1 (adapted from RSV); "I wrote": 1 Cor. 5:9 (adapted from RSV); for the motif of a man in love with his father's wife, see William Adler, "Apion's 'Encomium of Adultery': A Jewish Satire of Greek Paideia in the Pseudo-Clementine *Homilies,*" *Hebrew Union College Annual* 64 (1993): 15–35.

18. 1 Cor. 6:12–20 (adapted from RSV); with esp. Martin, *Corinthian Body.*

19. 1 Cor. 7:1–9 (adapted from RSV).

20. "Not of this age": 1 Cor. 2:6 (RSV); "everything created": 1 Tim. 4:4 (RSV).

21. Rom. 1:20–32 (RSV); by far the best treatment is Brooten, *Love between Women,* 195–302; Dale Martin, *Sex and the Single Savior: Gender and Sexuality in Biblical Interpretation* (Louisville, 2006), 51–64, on the traditions of interpretation surrounding the passage.

22. Rom. 1:20, 26–27, 32 (RSV).

23. "Boasted of": Philo Spec. leg. 3.37; "desires themselves": Philo De vit. cont. 59; "against nature": Philo Spec. leg. 3.39.

24. "Not one ember": Philo Spec. leg. 3.37; on same-sex preference as an acquired characteristic, compare Soranus apud Cael. Aur. Tard. pass. 4.9, where it is debated; androgyne: Philo De vit. cont. 60; "debasing": Philo Spec. leg. 3.38.

25. 1 Cor. 6:9; 1 Tim. 1:10; with Martin, *Sex and the Single Savior,* 40–41.

26. "Sharp and scalding": Dio Or. 4.102; softness and sexual submission: Plut. Amat. 5.751D; with women specifically, Plut. Amat. 4.751B.

27. John W. Martens, "'Do Not Sexually Abuse Children': The Language of Early Christian Sexual Ethics," in *Children in Late Ancient Christianity,* ed. C. B. Horn and R. R. Phenix (Tübingen, 2009), 227–254; early Christian uses include Didache 2.2; Ep. Barn. 19.4, 10.6; Theoph. Auto. 3.27; Iust. Dial. Tryph. 95.1; for Clement of Alexandria, see below; the only pre-Christian candidate is Test. Levi 17.11, which could be an interpolation or may again demonstrate the dependence of early Christian sexual norms on Hellenic Judaism; as Martens rightly notes, *paides* could include slave or free, male or female victims.

28. For other early Christian uses of *arsenokoitēs,* see Martin, *Sex and the Single Savior,* 37–50; "pollute their own bodies": Apoc. Pet. 31; with Brooten, *Love between Women,* 306–307.

29. The one exception is Clement, discussed below.

30. Tert. Ad nat. 1.16.7; in general, Knust, *Abandoned to Lust.*

31. Tert. Ad nat. 1.16.12; on Christian conceptions of the *gens,* see Denise Kimber Buell, *Why This New Race: Ethnic Reasoning in Early Christianity* (New York, 2005).

32. Tertullian, Ad nat. 1.16.14–20.

33. Apology: Nasrallah, *Christian Responses;* the essays in Mark Edwards, Martin Goodman, and Simon Price, eds., *Apologetics in the Roman Empire: Pagans, Jews, and Christians* (Oxford, 1999); *L'apologétique chrétienne gréco-latine à l'époque prénicénienne,* Entretiens sur l'Antiquité classique, Fondation Hardt (Geneva, 2005).

34. "Once reveled": Iust. Apol. 1.14.2; "we see": Iust. Apol. 1.27.1–2.

35. "Our principle": Iust. Apol. 1.29.1.

36. "They set up": Athenag. Leg. 34.1–3; slaves: Athenag. Leg. 35.3; "since we have a hope": Athenag. Leg. 33.1–2.

37. "They set up a marketplace": Athenag. Leg. 34.2; "since we have a hope": Athenag. Leg. 33.1–2.

38. "I hate": Tat. Or. 11; "pederasty": Tat. Or. 28; "effeminates": Tat. Or. 29; "those who marry": Tat. Or. 8; on Tatian's sexual ideology, see Gaca, *Making of Fornication,* 221–246.

39. Hier. Comm. Tit. pr.: *Tatianus encratitarum patriarches;* for Clement, see below.

40. On the symbolic value of the renunciation of sex, see esp. Cooper, *Virgin and the Bride;* "open text": David Konstan, "Acts of Love: A Narrative Pattern in the Apocryphal Acts," *JECS* 6 (1998): 15–36; Christine M. Thomas, "Stories without Texts and without Authors: The Problem of Fluidity in Ancient Novelistic Texts and Early Christian Literature," in *Ancient Fiction and Early Christian Narrative,* ed. Ronald Hock, Bradley Chance, and Judith Perkins (Atlanta, 1998), 273–291.

41. Citations: Osborne, *Clement,* 2ff.; "accursed sophists": Clem. Str. 1.3.22; "use the wisdom": 1.5.29; "doctrine of the Greeks": Clem. Str. 1.2.19; on Clement among the apologists, see Annewies van den Hoek, "Apologetic and Protreptic Discourse in Clement of Alexandria," in *L'apologétique chrétienne gréco-latine à l'époque prénicénienne* (Geneva, 2005), 69–93.

42. "True tradition": Clem. Str. 1.1.11; for portraits of Clement's sexual outlook, see Brown, *Body and Society,* 122–139; Gaca, *Making of Fornication,* 247–272; Harry Maier, "Clement of Alexandria and the Care of the Self," *Journal of the American Academy of Religion* 62 (1994): 719–745; J. P. Broudéhoux, *Mariage et famille chez Clément d'Alexandrie* (Paris, 1970).

43. "Very roots": Clem. Paid. 2.6.51.

44. Encratism: esp. Clem. Str. 3.6.49; "sacrilege against creation": Clem. Str. 3.6.45; "polluted": Clem. Str. 3.6.46; "vaunt that they apprehend": Clem. Str. 3.6.49; against Tatian's exegesis: Clem. Str. 3.12.81; "passions of the devil": Clem. Str. 3.12.81; "distance" Clem. Str. 3.12.84.4.

45. "Taken together": Clem. Str. 3.12.86; "harmonies": Clem. Str. 3.12.81.

46. "Generally advisable": Clem. Str. 2.23.140; "scripture counsels": Clem. Str. 2.23.145; "co-worker in creation": Clem. Paid. 2.10.83 and Str. 3.9.66.

47. "Aim": Clem. Paid. 2.10.83; "stony places": Clem. Paid. 2.10.83; "proper moments": Clem. Paid. 2.23.143; "shortly to be human": Clem. Paid. 2.10.92; "not exclusively": Clem. Paid. 2.18.88; hare or hyena: Clem. Paid. 2.10.83–88; "rape of nature": Clem. Paid. 2.10.95.

48. "Concord according to the Word": Clem. Str. 2.23.143; "love of pleasure": Clem. Paid. 2.10.92; "more uncontrolled than beasts": Clem. Str. 2.23.139; "as in the case of food": Clem. Paid. 2.10.90; exemption from desire: Clem. Str. 3.9.67; "do nothing from desire": Clem. Str. 3.7.58.

49. "Physical impulse": Clem. Str. 3.11.71; "completely destroyed": Clem. Str. 3.9.63; "not to experience desire at all": Clem. Str. 3.7.57.

50. "Antagonists": Clem. Str. 2.20.120; not for daytime: Clem. Paid. 2.10.97; advice for symposia: Clem. Paid. 2.7.54–55.

51. "Wine": Clem. Paid. 2.2.20; "food": Clem. Paid. 2.2.29; in general, on contextualizing Clement's advice in terms of contemporary medicine, see Maier, "Clement of Alexandria."

52. Eunuchs: Clem. Paid. 3.4.26; art: Clem. Protrep. 4.60.1–2; "adultery with the eyes": Clem. Paid. 3.11.70; comparing Clement and Achilles, Goldhill, "Erotic

Eye"; Goldhill, *Foucault's Virginity,* 76; compare Shadi Bartsch, *The Mirror of the Self: Sexuality, Self-Knowledge, and the Gaze in the Early Roman Empire* (Chicago, 2006), 68–69.

53. "Corruption of children": Clem. Paid. 2.10.88–89, Paid. 3.12.89; Protrep. 10.108; Str. 3.4.36; body parts: Clem. Paid. 2.10.85–86; procreationism: Clem. Paid. 2.10.86.

54. Zeus, Dionysus: Clem. Protrep. 2.15; 2.34; "disease": Clem. Paid. 3.3.20; depilation: Clem. Paid. 3.3.20; "by night": Clem. Paid. 3.3.20; compare Gleason, "The Semiotics of Gender," 405; "she-men": Clem. Paid. 3.3.15, 3.4.29; *kinaidos:* Clem. Paid. 3.11.69.

55. "Such complete lasciviousness" etc.: Clem. Paid. 3.3.21; "fornication like wine or grain": Clem. Paid. 3.3.22; "whole earth": Clem. Paid. 3.3.22.

56. "Holy procreation": Orig. Comm. in 1 Cor. Fr. 35; gift of God: Orig. Comm. in 1 Cor. Fr. 29; following 1 Cor. 7: Orig. Comm. in 1 Cor. Fr. 33; different forms of grace: Orig. Comm. in 1 Cor. Fr. 29; "in the mud": Orig. Comm. in 1 Cor. Fr. 13; "corrupts the temple": Orig. Comm. in 1 Cor. Fr. 16; "quantity and quality": Orig. Comm. in 1 Cor. Fr. 23; sins to the bishop: Orig. Comm. in 1 Cor. Fr. 26; "not mocked": Orig. Comm. in 1 Cor. Fr. 27; on Origen generally, see Brown, *Body and Society,* 160–177; Henri Crouzel, *Virginité et mariage selon Origène* (Paris, 1963).

57. On Origen's understanding of demons, see Gregory Smith, "How Thin Is a Demon?," *JECS* 16 (2008): 479–512.

58. Iust. Mart. Apol. 1.43.1–8: *προαιρέσει ἐλευθέρᾳ*; with Bobzien, *Freedom and Determinism,* 344–345.

59. Tat. Or. 7; on the topic, see Frede, *A Free Will;* Jörn Müller und Roberto Hofmeister Pich, "Auf dem Weg zum Willen? Eine problemgeschichtliche Hinführung zur Genese des philosophischen Willensbegriffs in Kaiserzeit und Spätantike," in *Wille und Handlung in der Philosophie der Kaiserzeit und Spätantike,* ed. Müller and Pich (Berlin, 2010), 1–22; Dihle, *Theory of Will.*

60. In general, see Brakke, *The Gnostics,* 72–74, 116; Karen King, *What Is Gnosticism?* (Cambridge, Mass., 2003), 206–207; Dihle, *Theory of Will,* 150–157; Elaine Pagels, "The Valentinian Claim to Esoteric Exegesis of Romans as Basis for Anthropological Theory," *Vigiliae Christianae* 26 (1972): 241–258; Louise Schottroff, "*Animae naturaliter salvandae:* Zum Problem der himmlischen Herkunft des Gnostikers," in *Christentum und Gnosis,* ed. W. Eltester (Berlin, 1969), 65–97; on the "elect seed" in Sethianism, see the (hostile) Epiphanius Pan. 39, but with Brakke, *The Gnostics,* 73–74; on Valentinianism, see Ismo Dunderberg, *Beyond Gnosticism: Myth, Lifestyle, and Society in the School of Valentinus* (New York, 2008); on the claimed pedigree of Valentinius, Clem. Str. 7.17; for the tripartite division, see Tri. Trac. 118–119; see Exc. Theod. 56, 61 for deterministic views (in 56 it is expressly stated that the animate, in distinction to the spiritual and the material,

are beings with free will); for orthodox responses, see, e.g., Iren. Adv. her. 1.6.1–4; Clem. Strom. 2.3.10–11; Method. Lib. arb. is probably framed as an argument against Valentinus's doctrines; "these heretics": Orig. De princ. 3.1.8.

61. Frede, *A Free Will,* 44–48; on Stoic determinism, see esp. Bobzien, *Determinism and Freedom;* Zeus: Epict. Diss. 1.12.25; "not under": Epict. Diss. 1.22.10.

62. "Leg you can fetter": Epict. Diss. 1.1.23; "withdraws from external things": Epict. Diss. 1.4.18; Frede, *A Free Will,* 77.

63. On Origen, Frede, *A Free Will,* 102–124; compare Matthias Perkams, "Ethischer Intellektualismus und Willensbegriff: Handlungstheorie beim griechischen und lateinischen Origenes," in Müller and Pich, *Wille und Handlung,* 239–258.

64. "Nothing at all": Ps.-Clem. Rec. 1.3; Iust. Apol. 2.7.4–5; Epict. Diss. 4.7.15; one must be hesitant to criticize a posthumous publication, but as published, Frede, *A Free Will,* is inadequate in many respects, especially with regard to anything bearing on Christian philosophers (for instance, Tatian rather than Justin is credited as the first person to use the notion of "free will," Clement is said to be a student of Origen, Origen, rather than Bardaisan, is said to be the first Christian to treat free will systematically, and indeed the author seems completely unaware of Bardaisan).

65. On Philopator, see Bobzien, *Freedom and Determinism,* 370; every school: ibid., 4.

66. Alexander Jones, "The Place of Astronomy in Roman Egypt," in *The Sciences in Greco-Roman Society,* ed. T. D. Barnes (Edmonton, 1995), 25–51; Alexander Jones, "The Astrologers of Oxyrhynchus and Their Astronomy," in *Oxyrhynchus: A City and Its Texts,* ed. A. Bowman, R. Coles, N. Gones, D. Obbink, and P. Parsons (London, 2007), 307–314; on the foundations of Ptolemy's science, see A. A. Long, "Astrology: Arguments Pro and Contra," in *Science and Speculation: Studies in Hellenistic Theory and Practice,* ed. Jonathan Barnes et al. (Cambridge, 1982), 165–192; outdated in many respects but still evocative, Franz Cumont, *Astrology and Religion among the Greeks and Romans* (New York, 1912); finally, it is a testimony to the cultural power of astrology that someone like Origen was so well informed in his criticism of it: see Alan Scott, *Origen and the Life of the Stars: A History of an Idea* (Oxford, 1991), 119–120.

67. Act. Tat. 1.2–3; I have learned much from David Carlisle, *καὶ ὄναρ καὶ ὕπαρ: Dreaming in the Ancient Novel* (PhD thesis, University of North Carolina, 2009).

68. Ptol. Tetr. 1.3.11; at this point it is worth recalling that the *Suda,* a tenth-century Byzantine encyclopedia, credits Achilles Tatius not only with the authorship of *Leucippe and Clitophon* but also with an etymology and an astronomical work *On the Spheres.* A trio of astronomical texts—*On the Universe,* a *Life of Aratus,* and an *Introduction* to Aratus—have survived under the name of Achilles,

but these texts date to the third century and thus almost certainly cannot be from the pen of the romance's author. It is just possible that the confusion, as in the intractable case of multiple generations of Philostratoi, arises from a family relationship. See, in general, Georgius Di Maria, *Achilles quae feruntur astronomica et in aratum opuscula* (Palermo, 1996), x–xii; on the idea that Achilles intentionally proposes "contrary readings," see Tim Whitmarsh, "Reading for Pleasure: Narrative, Irony, and Erotics in Achilles Tatius," in *The Ancient Novel and Beyond,* ed. Stelios Panayotakis, Maaike Zimmerman, and Wytse Keulen (Leiden, 2003), 191–205.

69. Porphyry: see Cristiano Castellati, *Porfirio, Sullo Stigo* (Milan, 2006), 270–278; Jan Bremmer, "Achilles Tatius and Heliodorus in Christian East Syria," in *All Those Nations: Cultural Encounters within and with the Near East,* ed., H. L. J. Vanstiphout (Groningen, 1999), 22–24; Ilaria Ramelli, *Bardaisan of Edessa: A Reassessment of the Evidence and a New Interpretation* (Piscataway, 2009), 110–111, arguing that Achilles used Bardaisan, which is impossible on chronological grounds; Goldhill, *Foucault's Virginity,* 121, on the effects of Achilles's juxtaposition.

70. "Stars in heaven": Hel. Aeth. 2.24–25; "fate's stage management": Hel. Aeth. 10.16.3; "by decree": Hel. Aeth. 10.40.2; it is worth noting another intertextual echo: the courtesan who startles Kalasiris is named Rhodopis, which is also the name of the maiden who, according to Achilles Tatius, betrayed Artemis; see further Chapter 4.

71. Clem. Str. 1.17.83.

72. Eus. Hist. eccl. 4.30.2; Alex. Aph. De fat. 1 (164); see R. W. Sharples, "Alexander of Aphrodisias, *De Fato:* Some Parallels," *CQ* 28 (1978): 243–266, for its context; Cass. Dio 78.2; "man's natural": Bard. Lib. leg. reg. (trans. Drivjers) p. 23; "there are people": Bard. Lib. leg. reg. (trans. Drivjers) p. 25; see Nicole Kelley, *Knowledge and Religious Authority in the Pseudo-Clementines: Situating the Recognitions in Fourth-Century Syria* (Tübingen, 2006), 115–116; Hans J. W. Drijvers, "Bardaisan's Doctrine of Free Will, the Pseudo-Clementines, and Marcionism in Syria," in *Liberté chrétienne et libre arbitre,* ed. G. Bedouelle et al. (Fribourg, 1994), 13–30; on the cultural setting of Bardaisan, see G. W. Bowersock, *Hellenism in Late Antiquity* (Ann Arbor, 1990), 31–34.

73. "Chaldeans": Bard. Lib. leg. reg. (trans. Drivjers) p. 31; Seres: ibid., p. 41.

74. Ibid., p. 43–49.

75. "Problem": Orig. De princ. 3.1.1; "ecclesiastical preaching": Orig. De princ. 3.1.1; "if a woman": Orig. De princ. 3.1.4; Epict. Diss. 2.18.15–18.

76. Method. Conv. 8.13–16; Method. De lib. arb.; Patterson, *Methodius of Olympus,* 60–63; see Elizabeth A. Clark, *The Origenist Controversy: The Cultural Construction of an Early Christian Debate* (Princeton, 1992), 194–197.

77. See esp. F. Stanley Jones, "Eros and Astrology in the *Περίοδοι Πὲτρου*: The Sense of the Pseudo-Clementine Novel," *Apocrypha* 12 (2001): 53–78; Kelley,

Knowledge and Religious Authority; Annette Yoshiko Reed, "'Jewish Christianity' as Counterhistory? The Apostolic Past in Eusebius' *Ecclesiastical History* and the Pseudo-Clementine *Homilies,*" in *Antiquity in Antiquity: Jewish and Christian Pasts in the Greco-Roman World,* ed. Gregg Gardner and Kevin Osterloh (Tübingen, 2008), 173–216; Mark Edwards, "The *Clementina:* A Christian Response to the Pagan Novel," *CQ* 42 (1992): 459–474; Christoph Jedan, "Philosophy Superseded? The Doctrine of Free Will in the Pseudo-Clementine Recognitions," in *The Pseudo-Clementines,* ed. Jan Bremmer (Louvain, 2010), 200–216; on the date and place of composition of the *Recognitions,* see Jan Bremmer, "*Pseudo-Clementines:* Texts, Dates, Places, Authors and Magic," in Bremmer, *The Pseudo-Clementines,* 1–23; and esp. Kate Cooper, "Matthidia's Wish: Division, Reunion, and the Early Christian Family in the Pseudo-Clementine *Recognitions,*" in *Narrativity in Biblical and Related Texts*=La narrativité dans la bible et les textes apparentés, ed. G. J. Brooke and J.-D. Kaestli (Louvain, 2000), 243–264, on the *Recognitions* as a family romance that use the form of the *Apocryphal Acts* for a socially conservative rather than encratic message.

78. "I have learned": Ps.-Clem. Rec. 9.16.3–4; "leads women": Ps.-Clem. Rec. 9.32.5; "attribute to the course": Ps.-Clem. Rec. 9.6.4; "a chaste mind": Ps.-Clem. Rec. 9.34.3; Meinolf Vielberg, *Klemens in den pseudoklementinischen Rekognitionen: Studien zur literarischen Form des spätantiken Romans* (Berlin, 2000), 106–109; other novels have astrological frameworks as well: see Chapter 4 and G. A. A. Kortekaas, "The *Historia Apollonii regis Tyri* and Ancient Astrology: A Possible Link between Apollonius and *κατοχή,*" *ZPE* 85 (1991): 71–85.

3. CHURCH, SOCIETY, AND SEX IN THE AGE OF TRIUMPH

1. Conversion of Constantine: see, reliably and recently, Noel Lenski, "The Reign of Constantine," in *The Cambridge Companion to the Age of Constantine,* ed. Noel Lenski (Cambridge, 2006), 59–90; Peter Weiss, "The Vision of Constantine," *JRA* 16 (2003): 237–259; Bruno Bleckmann, *Konstantin der Grosse* (Rowohlt, 1996); Timothy D. Barnes, *Constantine and Eusebius* (Cambridge, Mass., 1981); older, canonical treatments: A. H. M. Jones, *Constantine and the Conversion of Europe* (Toronto, 1978); Norman H. Baynes, *Constantine the Great and the Christian Church* (London, 1929); Jacob Burckhardt, *The Age of Constantine the Great* (New York, 1967 [1853]); Aphrodite expelled by the Christians (in this case, by Thecla) "like a debauched slave-girl": Ps.-Bas. Seleuc. *Vit. mir. Thec.* 3.1, see *Miracle Tales from Byzantium,* trans. Alice-Mary Talbot and Scott Johnson, *Dumbarton Oaks Medieval Library,* no. 12 (Cambridge, Mass., 2012).

2. "Doomed": 1 Cor. 2.6 (RSV).

3. "Severely repressed": Lact. Inst. div. 6.23.1; "so that no one": Lact. Inst. div. 6.23.7; "he joined": Lact. Inst. div. 6.23.8; "among them": Lact. Inst. div.

6.23.10; on Lactantius's context, see Elizabeth DePalma Digeser, *The Making of a Christian Empire: Lactantius and Rome* (Ithaca, 2000).

4. "Let no one desert": Lact. Inst. 6.24.1; "difficult for man": Lact. Epit. inst. 67; on Elvira: Samuel Laeuchli, *Power and Sexuality: The Emergence of Canon Law at the Synod of Elvira* (Philadelphia, 1972).

5. For one of the best attempts to recover the appropriation of Christian values by lay householders, see Kate Cooper, *The Fall of the Roman Household* (Cambridge, 2007); on desert monasticism, from an immense bibliography, see Douglas Burton-Christie, *The Word in the Desert: Scripture and the Quest for Holiness in Early Christian Monasticism* (New York, 1993); Brown, *Body and Society,* 213–240.

6. On preaching, see esp. Jaclyn Maxwell, *Christianization and Communication in Late Antiquity: John Chrysostom and His Congregation* (Cambridge, 2006); Wendy Mayer, "Homiletics," in *The Oxford Handbook of Early Christian Studies,* ed. Susan Ashbrook Harvey and David Hunter (Oxford, 2008), 565–583; M. Sachot, "Homilie," *RAC* 16 (1994): 148–175; Alexandre Olivar, *La predicación cristiana antigua* (Barcelona, 1991); Jean Bernardi, *La prédication des pères cappadociens: Le prédicateur et son auditoire* (Paris, 1968); on the relationship between Christianity and late Roman law, see Kyle Harper, "Marriage and Family in Late Antiquity," in *The Oxford Handbook of Late Antiquity,* ed. Scott Johnson (Oxford, 2012), 667–714; Antti Arjava, *Women and Law in Late Antiquity* (Oxford, 1996); Judith Evans Grubbs, *Law and Family in Late Antiquity: The Emperor Constantine's Marriage Legislation* (Oxford, 1995); Beaucamp, *Le statut de la femme à Byzance;* Jean Gaudemet, *Sociétés et mariage* (Strasbourg, 1980); Manlio Sargenti, *Il diritto privato nella legislazione di Costantino: Persone e famiglia* (Milan, 1938).

7. For free will in the golden age, see Theo Kobusch, "Der Begriff des Willens in der christlichen Philosophie vor Augustinus," in *Wille und Handlung in der Philosophie der Kaiserzeit und Spätantike,* ed. Jörn Müller und Roberto Hofmeister Pich (Berlin, 2010), 277–300.

8. Coll. leg. mos. rom. 5.1.1, on the Mosaic rule; Coll. leg. mos. rom. 5.2.1–2 for the Roman rules; on the text, and for its Christian authorship, see now Robert M. Frakes, *Compiling the* Collatio legum Mosaicarum et Romanarum *in Late Antiquity* (Oxford, 2011), 59, for a date of around 392–395; for an alternative view, see Leonard Rutgers, *The Jews in Late Ancient Rome: Evidence of Cultural Interaction in the Roman Diaspora* (Leiden, 1995).

9. Coll. leg. mos. rom. 5.3.1, with Frakes, *Compiling the* Collatio, 168, for the text.

10. Far and away the most reliable discussion of this law, and the late antique legislation on same-sex eros in general, is Dalla, *Ubi Venus mutatur,* here 71–99; Eva Cantarella, *Bisexuality in the Ancient World,* 2nd ed. (New Haven, 2002 [1988]), 177–180; for the identification of Virius Nicomachus Flavianus as the author of the constitution, see Tony Honoré, *Law in the Crisis of Empire, 379–455*

AD: The Theodosian Dynasty and Its Quaestors, with a Palingenesia of Laws of the Dynasty (Oxford, 1998), 59–70.

11. It is worth noting that this was not the first measure aimed at male prostitution; Philip the Arab, in the third century, was said to have banned male prostitution, when, after a failed sacrifice, he saw a prostitute resembling his son: Aur. Vict. Caes. 28.6–7; Jerome (Hier. Comm. in Isaiam 1.2.5–6) credited Constantine with abolishing the practice of prostituting boys at the entrances to public theaters; the law has left no trace in the legal record, though such a policy is not implausible; at the same time, we should not follow Jerome in attributing it to Constantine's "Christianity" so much as to his streak of puritanical conservatism (see below); the different degree of violence evident in the measure of 390 is telling.

12. Conc. Illib. 71.

13. "Do not violate": Const. apost. 7.2; "sin of the Sodomites": Const. apost. 6.28; "doer of unspeakable deeds": Const. apost. 8.32; "scrutinized": Const. apost. 8.32; "hard to wash out": Const. apost. 8.32: *δυσέκνιπτος γὰρ ἡ κακία.*

14. Basil: Bas. Ep. 188.7 and 217.62; Gregory: Greg. Nys. Ep. can. ad Let. (PG 45: 228–289).

15. "Adulteration of nature": Greg. Nys. Ep. can. ad Let. (PG 45: 228); the configuration of body parts was the primary determination of what was natural, and it is not possible to accuse someone like Augustine of a failure of nerve to carry the thought to its logical conclusion: "But for that part of the body which has not been installed for generative purposes, if it is used sexually, even within marriage, is against nature and flagitious": Aug. De nupt. et concup. 2.20.35; consider that a search of all texts in the *Thesaurus Linguae Graecae* from the fourth through the sixth centuries produces 64 instances of the root *kinaid-*, 45 of *arsenokoit-*, 2,193 of *porne-*, 909 of *Sodom-*, and 2,509 of *para phusin;* the word *kinaidos* never disappeared: see Ioh. Malal. Chron. 7.12, and Ioh. Lyd. De magis. 3.62 (Bandy p. 234), for late usages; in general Mathew Keufler, *The Manly Eunuch: Masculinity, Gender Ambiguity, and Christian Ideology in Late Antiquity* (Chicago, 2001), 166–167.

16. Artem. On. 1.78–80; Musonius: Mus. Ruf. Diss. 12.11: *αἱ πρὸς ἄρρενας τοῖς ἄρρεσιν, ὅτι παρὰ φύσιν τὸ τόλμημα.*

17. Ioh. Chrys. In Rom. 4 (PG 60: 417).

18. Ibid. (PG 60: 417–419).

19. Dio Or. 33.63–64; on the interconnection of gender deviance and sexual deviance in pre-Christian thought, see Gleason, "The Semiotics of Gender," esp. 411–412.

20. *Stuprum* against a male, see esp. PS 2.26.12 and 5.4.14; sexual passivity: PS 2.26.13; on the *lex Scantinia,* see esp. Dalla, *Ubi Venus mutatur,* 107–109, 117, 126.

21. Prudent. Peristeph. 10.201ff.; PLRE 1 Aurelius Prudentius Clemens 4; see McGinn, *Prostitution, Sexuality and the Law,* 141, for the conclusion that the *lex Iulia* did not originally regulate *stuprum* with freeborn boys but saw such offenses

come within its ambit either by juristic construction or later legislation; compare Dalla, *Ubi venus mutatur,* 107; Dig. 48.5.9(8).pr (Marcianus) and Dig. 48.5.35(34).1 (Modestinus) treat *stuprum cum puero* under the *lex Iulia;* Dig. 48.5.6 (Papinianus) suggests that *stuprum* was principally committed against females.

22. PS 5.4.1, 4, and 14; with Dalla, *Ubi Venus mutatur,* 117, 126; on the text, see Detlef Liebs, "Roman Vulgar Law in Late Antiquity," in *Aspects of Law in Late Antiquity: Dedicated to A. M. Honoré on the Occasion of the Sixtieth Year of His Teaching in Oxford,* ed. A. J. B. Sirks (Oxford, 2008), 35–53; and Liebs, *Römische Jurisprudenz in Afrika: Mit Studien zu den pseudopaulinischen Sentenzen* (Berlin, 1993); on *iniuria,* see Dig. 47.10, esp. 47.10.45 (Hermogenianus).

23. Juv. Sat. 2.43–44; Auson. Epig. 99; PS 2.26.13; from set penalties to sliding scale: Dalla, *Ubi Venus mutatur,* 109.

24. On the importance of *infamia* in the social discrimination against sexual minorities, see esp. Richlin, "Not before Homosexuality," 555–561; on *infamia* generally, A. H. J. Greenridge, *Infamia: Its Place in Roman Public and Private Law* (Oxford, 1894), and Max Kaser, "Infamia und ignominia in den römischen Rechtsquellen," *ZRG* 73 (1956): 220–278; ineligibility to apply on someone else's behalf: Dig. 3.1.1.6.

25. Ad hoc: Richlin, "Not before Homosexuality," 560; never witch-hunts: Williams, *Roman Homosexuality,* 216; legislation was never: Richlin, "Not before Homosexuality," 554; "be proven?" Williams, *Roman Homosexuality,* 215.

26. *Publici:* Firm. Matern. Math. 6.31.5, 7.16.2, 7.25.13, 7.25.15, 7.25.20, 7.25.21, 8.19.7; *infamia:* Firm. Matern. Math. 8.20.2, 8.25.4, 8.27.8; *latentes:* Firm. Matern. Math. 7.25.7, 7.25.12, 7.25.19, 7.25.23, 8.29.7; high honors: Firm. Matern. Math. 7.25.22.

27. CT 9.7.3; see Dalla, *Ubi Venus mutatur,* 167–170, who suggests the measure may have been restricted to male prostitutes, which is possible but not warranted by any information at our disposal; Cantarella, *Bisexuality in the Ancient World,* 175–176.

28. It cannot pass unremarked that a number of ancient authorities, not far removed from the reign of Constans, attribute a highly irregular sex life to the emperor, and in fact attribute his downfall to a spiral of debauchery: Aur. Vict. Caes. 41.24; Zosim. Hist. nov. 2.42.1; Pass. Artem. 10; Zonar. 13.5.15; Eutrop. Brev. 10.9.

29. Ioh. Chrysos. In Rom. 4 (PG 60: 420); Hesychius, too defines *κιναιδία* as *πορνικὴ ἀσχημοσύνη*.

30. "Grievous and incurable": Ioh. Chrysos. Adv. oppug. 3.88 (PG 47: 360); Lib. Or. 53.10; Ambrosiast. Comm. Rom. 1.32.

31. Rufinus, trans. Origen In Rom. 4.4; Aug. Contr. Iul. op. imp. 5.17 (PL 45: 1450).

32. On the composition of the *Codex Theodosianus,* and especially the editors' role, see Kyle Harper, "The *Senatus Consultum Claudianum* in the *Codex Theodosia-*

nus: Social History and Legal Texts," *CQ* 60 (2010): 610–638; A. J. B. Sirks, *The Theodosian Code: A Study* (Friedrichsdorf, 2007); John Matthews, *Laying Down the Law: A Study of the Theodosian Code* (New Haven, 2000).

33. Inst. 4.18.4. compare CJ 9.9.30(31) = CT 9.7.3.

34. Ioh. Mal. Chron. 18.167–168; Procop. Hist. Arc. 11.34–36, 16.18–22; compare Theophan. Chron. (PG 108: col. 408) and Cedren. Hist. comp. 368 (PG 121: 704).

35. Lib. Or. 53.8; Ioh. Chrysos. Adv. oppug. 3.88 (PG 47:360); with A. J. Festugière, *Antioche païenne et chrétienne: Libanius, Chrysostome et les moines de Syrie* (Paris, 1959), 192–210; Ioh. Mal. Chron. 18.168; for anxieties about same-sex desire in monastic settings, see the sources gathered by Derek Krueger, "Between Monks: Tales of Monastic Companionship in Early Byzantium," *Journal of the History of Sexuality* 20 (2011): 28–61, esp. 51.

36. Iustin. Nov. 77 (540s); Iust. Nov. 141 (559).

37. Consult. Zacc. et Apoll. 3.1.5 (mode of life), 3.1.16 *(clarissima sidera)*, 3.1.13 (honorable marriages); 3.1.16 (promise of eternal life); on the date, see M. A. Claussen, "Pagan Rebellion and Christian Apologetics in Fourth-Century Rome: The *Consultationes Zacchei et Apollonii*," *Journal of Ecclesiastical History* 46 (1995): 589–614; for its context in the aftermath of the Jovinianist controversy, see David G. Hunter, *Marriage, Celibacy, and Heresy in Ancient Christianity: The Jovinianist Controversy* (Oxford, 2007), 250–256.

38. On Jerome's response, see Hunter, *Marriage, Celibacy, and Heresy*, 230–242; "meant to encourage": Consult. Zacc. et Apoll. 3.5.8.

39. On the development of clerical celibacy, Hunter, *Marriage, Celibacy, and Heresy*, 213–219; Roger Gryson, *Les origines du célibat ecclésiastique du premier au septième siècle* (Gembloux, 1970), and Gryson, "Dix ans de recherches sur les origins du célibat ecclésiastique: Reflexions sur les publications des années 1970–1979," *Revue théologique de Louvain* 11 (1980): 157–185; rules of clerical celibacy remained only modestly effective throughout late antiquity and the early Middle Ages: James Brundage, *Law, Sex, and Christian Society in Medieval Europe* (Chicago, 1987), 150.

40. In general, see Harper, "Family in Late Antiquity"; Judith Evans Grubbs, "Pagan and Christian Marriage: The State of the Question," *JECS* 2 (1994): 361–412; Manlio Sargenti, "Matrimonio cristiano e società pagana: Spunti per una ricera," *Studia et documenta historiae et iuris* 51 (1985): 367–391; on monogamy: Aug. De bon. coniug. 7.7; compare CJ 1.9.7 (393); for Jewish polygamy, see Michael Satlow, *Jewish Marriage in Antiquity* (Princeton, 2001), 188–192; Tal Ilan, *Jewish Women in Greco-Roman Palestine* (Tübingen, 1996); "principal affair": Aster. Amas. Hom. 5.2.3; on monogamy, see Walter Scheidel, "A Peculiar Institution? Greco-Roman Monogamy in Global Context," *History of the Family* 14 (2009): 280–291.

41. On Chrysostom's corpus generally, see Wendy Mayer, *The Homilies of St. John Chrysostom, Provenance: Reshaping the Foundations* (Rome, 2005); on the

context of his pastoral efforts, see Maxwell, *Christianization and communication;* Brown, *Body and Society,* 305–322; Ioh. Chrys. Propt. forn. 1.4 (PG 51: 213).

42. Ioh. Chrys. Propt. forn. 1.4–5 (PG 51: 213–217).

43. Ibid., 1.5 (PG 51: 213–216).

44. On Roman divorce, see Treggiari, *Roman Marriage,* 350–356; on the development of a standard Christian model, still under way in the fourth and fifth centuries, see Philip Reynolds, *Marriage in the Western Church: The Christianization of Marriage during the Patristic and Early Medieval Periods* (Leiden, 1994), 173–226.

45. Ioh. Chrys. Lib. repud. 1–3 (PG 51: 218–221).

46. For the fourth-century brothels of Rome, *Libellus de regionibus urbis Romae* (Nordh p. 105); with McGinn, *Economy of Prostitution,* 167–169; on Chrysostom's audience, see Harper, *Slavery in the Late Roman World,* 51–52; Maxwell, *Christianization and Communication,* esp. 65–87; Wendy Mayer, "Who Came to Hear John Chrysostom Preach? Recovering a Late Fourth-Century Preacher's Audience," *Ephemerides theologicae Lovanienses* 76 (2000): 73–87; for an alternative view, see Ramsay MacMullen, "The Preacher and His Audience (AD 350–400)," *JTS* 40 (1989): 503–511, now refined and bolstered in MacMullen, *The Second Church: Popular Christianity* A.D. 200–400 (Atlanta, 2009).

47. In general, see Harper, *Late Roman Slavery,* 281–325; Aster. Amas. Hom. 5.11; Aug. Serm. 153.6 (PL 38: 828); Salv. Gub. 7.22; Ambr. Abr. 2.11.78; "laws were made by men": Greg. Naz. Or. 37.6 (PG 36: 289); Hier. Ep. 77.3.

48. On prostitution as a necessity, see Chapter 1; Aug. De ord. 2.4.12; "procured another": Aug. Conf. 6.15.

49. Aug. De ord. 2.4.12; see McGinn, *Economy of Prostitution,* 99–105, though the suggestion that Augustine is advocating a sort of moral zoning within the city is unlikely; compare Harper, *Slavery in the Late Roman World,* 313, n. 217; in the abundant late antique record, there is simply no trace of the notion of deliberate moral zoning.

50. Ioh. Chrys. Propt. forn. 1.2 (PG 51: 210–211); Lucien Anné, *Les rites des fiançailles et la donation pour cause de mariage sous le Bas–Empire* (Louvain, 1941), 156; Marcel Metzger, "Apports de l'histoire de la liturgie à la théologie du mariage," *Revue de droit canonique* 42 (1992): 215–236.

51. On the development of Christian marriage rituals generally, see Korbinian Ritzer, *Le mariage dans les églises chrétiennes du Ier au XIe siècle* (Paris, 1970) esp. 134–141, 223–225; David Hunter, "Sexuality, Marriage, and the Family," in *The Cambridge History of Christianity,* vol. 2: *Constantine to c. 600,* ed. A. Casiday and F. Norris (Cambridge, 2007), 585–600, at 590–592; veiling: Ambrosiast. Comm. ep. I Tim., 3.13; Ambrosiast. Comm. ep. I Corinth., 7.40; Caes. Arel. Serm. 42.5; Siric. Ep. 1.4.5 (PL 13: 1136); Ambr. Ep. 19.7; and Reynolds, *Marriage in the Western Church,* 321–322; Augustine: David Hunter, "Augustine and the

Making of Marriage in Roman North Africa," *JECS* 11 (2003): 63–85; Paulinus: Paulin. Nol. Carm. 25, ll. 199–232; with Henri Crouzel, *L'Église primitive face au divorce, du premier au cinquième siècle* (Paris, 1971); Verona Sacramentary: Ritzer, *Le mariage*, 238–246; for the late triumph of Christian marriage ceremonies: Pierre Daudet, *L'Établissement de la compétence de l'Église en matière de divorce & de consanguinité, France, Xème–XIIème siècles* (Paris, 1941); Georges Duby, *Medieval Marriage: Two Models from Twelfth-Century France* (Baltimore, 1978); and esp. Pierre Toubert, "L'institution du mariage chrétien, de l'antiquité tardive à l'an mil," in *Morfologie sociali e culturali in Europa fra tarda antichità e alto Medioevo: 3–9 aprile 1997* (Spoleto, 1998), 503–553.

52. For Constantine's social legislation, including the intermarriage prohibitions (reflected but not instituted by CT 4.6.3), see Harper, *Slavery in the Late Roman World*, 443–455; Thomas McGinn, "The Social Policy of the Emperor Constantine in *Codex Theodosianus* 4.6.3," *Tijdschrift voor rechtsgeschiedenis* 67 (1999): 57–73; "wines of intemperance": CT 9.7.1 (326); on Constantine's reforms of family law, see Evans Grubbs, *Law and Family in Late Antiquity*.

53. Reforms to adultery law: CT 9.7.2 (326) with Evans Grubbs, *Law and Family*, 205–216; a woman and her own slave: CT 9.9.1 with Harper, *Slavery in the Late Roman World*, 438–441; G. Bassanelli Sommariva, "Brevi considerazioni su CTh. 9, 7, 1," *AARC* 14 (2003): 197–239, at 226–269; Beaucamp, *Le statut*, 1:141–145; Hier. Ep. 79.8; broader anxieties about women and slaves: Harper, *Slavery in the Late Roman World*, 335–340.

54. CT 9.24.1 (326); Judith Evans Grubbs, "Abduction Marriage in Antiquity"; Cam Grey, "Two Young Lovers: An Abduction Marriage and Its Consequences in Fifth-Century Gaul," *CQ* 58 (2008): 286–302.

55. "Comes to reflect": McGinn, "Social Policy," 69; Constantine on divorce: CT 3.16.1 with Evans Grubbs, *Law and Family*, 228–232; Julian: Ambrosiast. Quaest. vet. et nov. test. 115.12, with Antti Arjava, "Divorce in Later Roman Law," *Arctos* 22 (1988): 5–21, esp. 9–13.

56. New limits in the west: CT 3.16.2; in 448, with the adoption of Theodosius II's novels, the east's more liberal standard temporarily became law in the west, but in 452 Valentinian III returned again to the restrictive standard, which would remain the last word of Roman law on divorce in the west: Nov. Val. 35.11; Michael Memmer, "Die Ehescheidung im 4. und 5. Jahrhundert n. Chr," in *Iurisprudentia universalis: Festschrift für Theo Mayer-Maly zum 70. Geburtstag*, ed. M. Schermaier et al. (Cologne, 2000), 489–510; compromise: CJ 5.17.8.

57. Harper, "The Family"; Joëlle Beaucamp, "L'Égypte byzantine: Biens des parents, biens du couple?," in *Eherecht und Familiengut in Antike und Mittelalter*, ed. D. Simon (Munich, 1989), 61–76; Roger Bagnall, "Church, State, and Divorce in Late Roman Egypt," in *Florilegium Columbianum: Essays in Honor of Paul Oskar Kristeller*, ed. Karl-Ludwig Selig and Robert Somerville (New York, 1987), 41–61.

58. "Live as chastely": Iustin. Nov. 14 (535); "marriage is such an honorable": Iustin. Nov. 22 (536); restriction of divorce: Iustin. Nov. 117.8–10 (542), overturned after his reign by Justin II in Nov. 140 (566); Franco Casavola, "Sessualità e matrimonio nelle *Novelle* giustinianee," in *Mondo classico e cristianesimo* (Rome, 1982), 183–190.

59. Aug. Civ. 1.16–20, here 1.19; see Dennis Trout, "Re-Textualizing Lucretia: Cultural Subversion in the *City of God*," *JECS* 2 (1994): 53–70.

60. Aug. Civ. 1.18–19; see Diana C. Moses, "Livy's Lucretia and the Validity of Coerced Consent in Roman Law," in *Consent and Coercion to Sex and Marriage in Ancient and Medieval Societies*, ed. Angeliki Laiou (Washington, D.C., 1993), 39–81.

61. Aug. Civ. 1.19.

62. "Self-initiated": Eus. Praep. evan. 6.6.47; "free, autonomous": Eus. Praep. evan. 6.6.48; impious slanderer: Eus. Praep. evan. 6.6.49.

63. Amphil. Icon. Or. in mul. pecc. 4.10.

64. Ambrosiast. Quaest. vet. et nov. 115; for Augustine's relentless attacks on astrology, see F. Van der Meer, *Augustine the Bishop: The Life and Work of a Father of the Church*, trans. B. Battershaw and G. Lamb (London, 1978 [1947]), 60–67; Ioh. Chrys. Hom. hab. Goth. 6 (PG 63:509); Cyr. Hier. Catech. 4.21; Clark, *The Origenist Controversy*, 198–207.

65. On the anti-Manichean context of De lib. arb., Aug. Retr. 1.9; see in general Clark, *Origenist Controversy*, esp. 218, on Julian's attacks on Augustine; Paula Fredriksen, *Sin: The Early History of an Idea* (Princeton, 2012), 124–125; Pier Franco Beatrice, *Tradux peccati: Alle fonti della dottrina agostiniana del peccato originale*, 60–63; Dihle, *Theory of Will*, 123–144, stressing the novelty of Augustine's view of the will; see more recently S. Harrison, *Augustine's Way into the Will: The Theological and Philosophical Significance of* De libero arbitrio (Oxford, 2006).

66. "Both religious geniuses": Brown, *Body and Society*, 370.

67. "Whenever it falls to me": Pelag. Ep. ad Demet. 2; "Pelagius wanted": Peter Brown, *Augustine of Hippo: A Biography*, rev. ed. (Berkeley, 2000), 348; see Clark, *The Origenist Controversy*, 197, noting that the Pelagian controversy revolved around problems "left over from the dissolution of the Origenist scheme."

68. On Julian in general, see Brown, *Augustine of Hippo*, 383–399; Josef Lössl, *Julian von Aeclanum: Studien zu seinem Leben, seinem Werk, seiner Lehre und ihrer Überlieferung* (Leiden, 2001); "for if justice": Iul. Ecl. apud Aug. Contr. Iul. op. imp. 1.105; "God made the sexual desire": Iul. Ecl. apud Aug. Contr. Iul. op. imp. 4.41.

69. Aug. De nupt. et conc. 1.6.7; generally, Brown, *Body and Society*, 387–427; Augustine thus rejects the ancient Christian criterion of the ability to act otherwise as a condition of "free will." Augustine defends a model of free will that rejects any exterior determination of action but not causes internal to the subject; in the

process, the will as a faculty becomes a much clearer entity; see, in general, Eleonore Stump, "Augustine on Free Will," in *The Cambridge Companion to Augustine,* ed. E. Stump and N. Kretzmann (Cambridge, 2001), 124–147.

70. "Conjugal intercourse": Aug. De nupt. et conc. 1.12.13; "this law of sin": Aug. De nupt. et conc. 1.23.25; "not to be imputed" Aug. De nupt. et conc. 1.17.19; "damnable crimes": Aug. De nupt. et conc. 1.14.16; "venial sins": Aug. De nupt. et conc. 1.15.17.

71. "So not only": Aug. De nupt. et conc. 1.34.39; "nevertheless": Aug. De nupt. et conc. 1.27.30; Dihle, *Theory of Will,* 123–144.

72. For the early period, see Glancy, "Obstacles to Slaves' Participation in the Corinthian Church"; Clem. Alex. Paid. 3.3.21; Lact. Inst. 6.23.7.

73. Angeliki Laiou, "Sex, Consent, and Coercion in Byzantium," in Laiou, *Consent and Coercion,* 109–221, though focused on the later period, is the only treatment to recognize the importance of Basil; "if you ask": Bas. Hom. psalm. 32.5 (PG 29: 336); Bernardi, *La prédication des pères cappadociens,* 27, places the sermon sometime after AD 372.

74. "One prostitute": Bas. Hom. prov. 9 (PG 31: 404); "sexual violations": Bas. Ep. 199.49, which explicitly covers the slave woman violated by her master.

75. On Gregory's opposition to slavery, Greg. Nys. Hom. in Eccl. 4.1; see Harper, *Slavery in the Late Roman World,* 345–347; Peter Garnsey, *Ideas of Slavery from Aristotle to Augustine* (Cambridge, 1996), 81–82.

76. Other sermons: Bas. (dub.) En. proph. Isaiah 5.158 (PG 30: 376–377); Ps.-Mac. Hom. spirit. 27.2; Cyr. Alex. De ador. 14 (PG 68: 905).

77. On Julian's exile, see esp. Lionel Wickham, "Pelagianism in the East," in *The Making of Orthodoxy: Essays in Honour of Henry Chadwick,* ed. R. Williams (Cambridge, 2002), 200–213; CT 15.8.2; significantly, the drafter of the law was none other than Antiochus Chuzon, the prime mover behind the creation of the Theodosian Code: Honoré, *Law in the Crisis of Empire,* 112–118.

78. The phrase *necessitas peccandi* is completely alien to Roman law, and in Latin nearly all occurrences appear in the Pelagian debates, especially in the polemics between Augustine and Julian, which reverberated in Constantinople in 428; what precedent there was for the policy lay in a series of late fourth-century constitutions concerning women of the stage. By 371 the emperors exempted Christian women from being forced on stage. This was a problematic form of coercion, because stage performance could be defined as a public obligation and thus enforced by the state. Policy would waver, especially when performers were scarce, but these laws foreshadowed the state's approach to prostitution: CT 15.7.1 (371); CT 15.7.2 (371); CT 15.7.4 (380); CT 15.7.8 (381); with Ruth Webb, "Female Performers in Late Antiquity," in *Greek and Roman Actors: Aspects of an Ancient Profession,* ed. P. Easterling and E. Hall (Cambridge, 2002), 282–303; and Richard Lim, "Converting the Un-Christianizable: The Baptism of Stage Performers in Late Antiquity," in

Conversion in Late Antiquity and the Early Middle Ages: Seeing and Believing, ed. K. Mills and A. Grafton (Rochester, 2003), 84–126; compare Cornelia B. Horn, "The Martyrdom of the Mimes," *The Harp* 18 (2005): 55–69; CT 15.8.1 (AD 342) was not in fact a precedent (though the inclusion in the same title of the Theodosian Code is something of an optical illusion that makes it appear so); that law belongs to the struggle between paganism and Christianity that raged intermittently in the decades after Constantine and reveals an ugly, private dimension to the conflict in which pagan masters, in "a sort of mockery," might deliberately sell into prostitution Christian slaves who refused the master's religion.

79. E.g., Amalia Sicari, *Prostituzione e tutela giuridica della schiava: Un problema di politica legislativa nell'impero romano* (Bari, 1991), the only dedicated treatment of the laws, is unaware of the Christian discourse lying behind the new policy; Valerio Neri, *I marginali nell'occidente tardoantico: Poveri, "infames" e criminali nella nascente società cristiana* (Bari, 1993), at 223, argues that the church ignored the social causes of prostitution.

80. On the taxation of prostitution, see McGinn, *Prostitution, Sexuality, and the Law,* 248–287; Nov. Theod. 18.

81. On the limitation to Constantinople, Beaucamp, *Le statut de la femme à Byzance, 4e–7e siècle,* 1:125; Neri, *I marginali,* 217–219; Leo: CJ 11.41.7 + CJ 1.4.14 (457–468); on the relation between the stage and the sex industry, Neri, *I marginali,* 233–250; the connection was controversial but real: Lib. Or. 64.38, arguing in defense of theater, has to contend that not *all* performers were prostitutes; compare Choric. Gaz. Or. 32.7 and 32.29; Syn. Ep. 110; on the abolition of the *chrysargyron,* see McGinn, *Prostitution, Sexuality, and the Law,* 273; Evag. Hist. eccl. 3.39 offers a breathless account of Anastasius's virtue in eliminating the tax; Procop. Gaz. Panegyr. 13 (PG 87c: 2812–2813); on the context of the panegyric, see Alain Chauvot, *Procope de Gaza, Priscien de Césarée, Panégyriques de l'empereur Anastase Ier* (Bonn, 1986), 97.

82. Iustin. Nov. 14 (535); already CJ 6.4.4.2 (531) reaffirmed the prohibition on coerced prostitution; Johannes Irmscher, "Die Bewertung der Prostitution im byzantinischen Recht," in *Gesellschaft und Recht im griechisch-römischen Altertum: Eine Aufsatzsammlung,* vol. 2, ed. Mihail Andreev (Berlin, 1969), 77–94 at 79; Beaucamp, *Le statut de la femme à Byzance, 4e–7e siècle,* 1:127; compare Iustin. Nov. 51 (537); in CJ 5.4.23, Justin legalized intermarriage between senators and former actresses; see David Daube, "The Marriage of Justinian and Theodora: Legal and Theological Reflections," *Catholic University Law Review* 16 (1966–1967): 380–399; this measure was obviously instituted to suit the personal needs of Justinian and Theodora, but the century of background behind the policy of Nov. 14 obviates the need to explain it in speculative terms centered on the personal psychology of the imperial couple.

83. Iustin. Nov. 14.

84. Ibid.

85. Procop. De aedif. 1.9; Procop. Hist. arc. 17.5–6.

4. REVOLUTIONIZING ROMANCE IN THE LATE CLASSICAL WORLD

1. RSV Matt. 21:31; Ioh. Chrys. In Matt. 67:3–4 (PG 58: col. 636); the sermon obviously belongs to John's Antiochene days, and possibly sometime around the year 390: see Mayer, *The Homilies of St. John Chrysostom, Provenance,* 178; for the interregional fame of an actress, see the third-century inscription: CIG 14.2324.

2. General treatments of the subgenre include Benedicta Ward, *Harlots of the Desert: A Study of Repentance in Early Monastic Sources* (London, 1987); Lynda Coon, *Sacred Fictions: Holy Women and Hagiography in Late Antiquity* (Philadelphia, 1997), 71–94; Patricia Cox Miller, "Is There a Harlot in This Text? Hagiography and the Grotesque," *Journal of Medieval and Early Modern Studies* 33 (2003): 419–435; Virginia Burrus, *The Sex Lives of Saints: An Erotics of Ancient Hagiography* (Philadelphia, 2004), 128–159.

3. Stephen Greenblatt, *Renaissance Self-Fashioning: From More to Shakespeare* (Chicago, 1980), 5.

4. Xen Eph. 5.5.5.

5. "Why do I bewail": Xen. Eph. 5.7.2; "without recourse": Xen. Eph. 5.7.4; "I remain": Xen. Eph. 5.14.2; "easily persuaded": Xen. Eph. 5.15.1.

6. Hist. Apoll. reg. Tyr. 33; on the text generally, see G. A. A. Kortekaas, *Commentary on the Historia Apollonii Regis Tyri* (Leiden, 2007); David Konstan, "*Apollonius, King of Tyre* and the Greek Novel," in *The Search for the Ancient Novel,* ed. James Tatum (Baltimore, 1994), 173–182.

7. "Don't you know": Hist. Apoll. reg. Tyr. 33; "Listen to": Hist. Apoll. reg. Tyr. 34.

8. "Every indignity": Ach. Tat. 8.5.5; Northup Frye, *The Secular Scripture: A Study of the Structure of Romance* (Cambridge, Mass., 1976), 60.

9. Mikhail Bakhtin, *The Dialogic Imagination: Four Essays,* ed. Michael Holquist (Austin, 1981), 87–91; on the importance of mutual commitment, see Konstan, *Sexual Symmetry.*

10. "No longer": Chariton 8.1.4; "glory": Chariton 1.1.1; "an astonishment": Xen. Eph. 1.2.5; "such a maiden": Longus 4.32.1–2.

11. "Her beauty": Chariton 1.10.7; "it is impossible": Chariton 2.1.5; it is a sentiment shared by the author, too: Chariton 2.3.10; Anthia: Xen. Eph. 2.9.4; "even among": Ach. Tat. 5.17.4; Hel. Aeth. 9.26.1, compare 1.19.5, 7.4.3.

12. Callirhoe: Chariton 1.11; 2.8.1; Anthia: Xen. Eph. 5.5.6; "if it is a death": Hel. Aeth. 1.8.3; Ach. Tat. 3.17.4, 5.19.2.

13. "The law of adultery": Chariton 5.7.3; "if her husband": Ach. Tat. 8.10.12.

14. Frye, *Secular Scripture,* 47; the complication of the "moral facts" in a story like *Leucippe and Clitophon* makes it hard to classify, just as Achilles Tatius would have wanted it.

15. A survey of Tychē in the Roman period is overdue: Fernand Allègre, *Étude sur la déesse grecque Tyché: Sa signification religieuse et morale* (Paris, 1899), is focused on the earlier period; Charles Edwards, "Tyche at Corinth," *Journal of the American School of Classical Studies at Athens* 59 (1990): 529–542.

16. "Fortune loves invention": Chariton 4.4.2; "I was nineteen": Ach. Tat. 1.3.3; "Fortune as usual": Ach. Tat. 6.3.1; "ceaseless turning": Hel. Aeth. 6.7.3; "destiny that everywhere chased": 5.6.2; "making us into playthings": Hel. Aeth. 5.6.3; "theatrics": Hel. Aeth. 10.16.3; in general, Karl Kerényi, *Die griechisch-orientalische romanliteratur in religionsgeschichtlicher Beleuchtung: Ein Versuch mit Nachbetrachtungen* (Tübingen, 1927), 11–15.

17. Hel. Aeth. 7.25.6; 6.9.7.

18. "When you have": Ach. Tat. 1.10.6; "hearty": Ach. Tat. 1.10.7; "as soon as her will": Ach. Tat. 1.10.7.

19. "Would that": Ach. Tat. 2.24.3; "Impugn": Ach. Tat. 2.25.1–2.

20. Morales, *Vision and Narrative,* 83–84.

21. Leucippe as *kakodaimon:* Ach. Tat. 6.20.1; prostitute: Ach. Tat. 8.16.1; this reading of the prostitute is rather different from that given by Judith Perkins in "Fictive *Scheintod* and Christian Resurrection," *Religion and Theology* 13 (2006): 396–418, at 404–405, for whom Leucippe's sacrifice is expressive of "the resilient identity of the Greek elite in the context of Roman hegemony."

22. A new era in the interpretation of Heliodorus was opened in 1982 by the appearance of J. R. Morgan, "History, Romance, and Realism in the *Aithiopika* of Heliodorus," *Classical Antiquity* 1 (1982): 221–265, and J. J. Winkler, "The Mendacity of Kalasiris and the Narrative Strategy of Heliodoros' *Aithiopika,*" *Yale Classical Studies* 27 (1982): 93–158; see esp. Ken Dowden, "Heliodoros: Serious Intentions," *CQ* 46 (1996): 267–285, whose reading of the story is similar to the one offered here in that it posits religious intentions behind the clever narrative structure of the novel; Heliodorus closest to Christian virginity: Ilaria Ramelli, "Les vertus de la chasteté et de la piété dans les romans grecs et les vertus des chrétiens: Le cas d'Achille Tatius et d'Héliodore dans les romans grecs," in *Passion, vertus et vices,* ed. Pouderon and Bost-Pouderon, 149–168; on the date, Bowersock, *Fiction as History,* 149–160, remains convincing.

23. Swears he is inexperienced: Hel. Aeth. 3.17.4; pure: Hel. Aeth. 10.9.1; "will be polluted": Hel. Aeth. 7.25.7.

24. "If you have": Hel. Aeth. 7.21.3; "surely": Hel. Aeth. 7.21.4.

25. "Not for the use": Hel. Aeth. 1.19.7; solemnly wed: Hel. Aeth. 10.40.2; on the ending, Goldhill, *Foucault's Virginity,* 120–121; J. R. Morgan, "A Sense of the Ending: The Conclusion of Heliodoros' *Aithiopika,*" *TAPA* 119 (1989): 299–320.

26. Socr. Hist. eccl. 5.22.51.

27. Prolixity: Greg. Tur. Mir. Andr. pr.; "returned to harlotry": Greg. Tur. Mir. Andr. 23; "no wonder": Greg. Tur. Mir. Andr. 23; in general, Dennis MacDonald, *The Acts of Andrew and the Acts of Andrew and Matthias in the City of the Cannibals* (Atlanta, 1990): Gregory's epitome "tendentious and frequently garbled"; on this episode, see Tamás Adamik, "Eroticism in the *Liber de miraculis,*" in *The Apocryphal Acts of Andrew,* ed. Jan Bremmer (Leuven, 2000), 35–46.

28. Greg Tur. Mir. Andr. 23.

29. Pall. Laus. Hist. 65.1–6; although Palladius attributes the story to a *βιβλίῳ παλαιοτάτῳ ἐπιγεγραμμάένῳ* *Ἱππολύτου*, the agent of the girl's salvation is described as *ὁ μαγιστριανὸς*, a late antique title; the story appears in Niceph. Callist. Hist. eccl. 7.13, perhaps derived from Palladius; see the commentary of G. J. M. Bartelink in *Palladio, La storia Lausiaca,* ed. Christine Mohrmann, G. J. M. Bartelink, and Marino Barchiesi (Milan, 1974), 398–399; for what it is worth, the Romans seem actually to have practiced penal prostitution against Christians: from many examples, see Mart. Pion. 7; Giovanni Crescenti, *La condonna allo stupro delle vergini cristiane durante le persecuzioni dell'impero romano* (Palermo, 1966); for still more Christian girls rescued from sexual endangerment, see Mart. Agap. Iren. et Chion. 5–6; Ambr. De virginibus, 2.4; Prudent. Peristeph. 14.

30. The reading of the apocryphal literature offered here assumes that the five extant Greek romances rely on a sufficiently coherent generic structure that the Christian authors could respond to and manipulate it: for a defense of this position, see David Konstan, "Reunion and Regeneration: Narrative Patterns in Ancient Greek Novels and Christian Acts," in *Fiction on the Fringe: Novelistic Writing in the Post-Classical Age,* ed. Grammatiki Karla (Leiden, 2009), 105–120.

31. Pass. Andr. gr. 47; on the "apostolic period" as a site for Christian memory, see Reed, "'Jewish Christianity' as Counterhistory?"; on the relation of Christian narrative to Greek fiction, see Scott Johnson, "Apocrypha and the Literary Past in Late Antiquity," in *From Rome to Constantinople: Studies in Honour of Averil Cameron,* ed. H. Amirav and Bas ter Haar Romeny (Leuven, 2007), 47–66; the essays in *Ancient Fiction: The Matrix of Early Christian and Jewish Narrative,* ed. Jo-Ann Brant, Charles Hedrick, and Chris Shea (Leiden, 2005); Scott Johnson, "Late Antique Narrative Fiction: Apocryphal Acta and the Greek Novel in the Fifth-Century *Life and Miracles of Thekla,*" in *Greek Literature in Late Antiquity: Dynamism, Didacticism, Classicism,* ed. Scott Johnson (Burlington, 2006), 189–207; William Robins, "Romance and Renunciation at the Turn of the Fifth Century," *JECS* 8 (2000): 531–557; Bowersock, *Fiction as History,* esp. 119; Richard Pervo, *Profit with Delight: The Literary Genre of the Acts of the Apostles* (Philadelphia, 1987); Tomas Hägg, *The Novel in Antiquity* (Berkeley, 1983), 154–165; Rosa Söder, *Die apokryphen Apostelgeschichten und die romanhafte Literatur der Antike* (Stuttgart,

1932); Perkins, *Suffering Self*; above all, this discussion is indebted to Cooper, *The Virgin and the Bride* ; on the *Apocryphal Acts* generally, see Hans-Josef Klauck, *The Apocryphal Acts of the Apostles: An Introduction* (Waco, 2008 [2005]), and the bibliography cited for the individual texts below.

32. Mart. Petr. 4–6 (Lipsius, vol. 1, p. 84–88); on the text in general, see Jan Bremmer, "Aspects of the *Acts of Peter:* Women, Magic, Place and Date," in *The Apocryphal Acts of Peter: Magic, Miracles and Gnosticism,* ed. Jan Bremmer (Leuven, 1998), 1–20.

33. "The reputation": Act. Thom. 88 (Lipsius vol. 2.1, p. 203); "I am your husband": Act. Thom. 114 (Lipsius vol. 2.1, p. 225); "delivered": Act. Thom. 126 (Lipsius vol. 2.1, p. 235); "tried very much": Act. Thom. 169 (Lipsius vol. 2.1, p. 283).

34. Act. Paul. et Thec. 5 (Lipsius vol. 1, p. 238).

35. Act. Andr. gr. 57 (Prieur); see esp. Cooper, *The Virgin and the Bride.*

36. "She summoned": Act. Andr. gr. 17 (Prieur).

37. Act. Andr. gr. 23 (Prieur).

38. Act. Paul. et Thec. (Lipsius vol. 1, p. 235ff.); on the *Acts of Paul and Thecla* and ancient fiction, see Melissa Aubin, "Reversing Romance? *The Acts of Thecla* and the Ancient Novel," in *Ancient Fiction and Early Christian Narrative,* ed. Ronald Hock, Bradley Chance, and Judith Perkins (Atlanta, 1998), 257–272.

39. Charles Altman, "Two Types of Opposition and the Structure of Latin Saints' Lives," *Medievalia et Humanistica* 6 (1975): 1–11.

40. See Jeffrey Rubenstein, introduction to *Creation and Composition: The Contribution of the Bavli Redactors (Stammaim) to the Aggada,* ed. Jeffrey Rubenstein (Tübingen, 2005), 1–20; and Alyssa Gray, "The Power Conferred by Distance from Power: Redaction and Meaning in b. A.Z. 10a–11a," in Rubenstein, *Creation and Composition,* 23–69, on the roles of the Bavli editors.

41. T. Bavli, A.Z. 18a, trans. A. Mishcon, *The Babylonian Talmud,* Nezikin VII, ed. I. Epstein (London 1935), 93.

42. T. Bavli, A.Z. 18a, trans. Mishcon, 93; Daniel Boyarin, *Dying for God: Martyrdom and the Making of Christianity and Judaism* (Stanford, 1999), 67–73; Daniel Boyarin, "Virgins in Brothels: Gender and Religious Ecotypification," *Estudios de literatura oral* 5 (1999): 195–217; Rachel Adler, "The Virgin in the Brothel and Other Anomalies: Character and Context in the Legend of Beruriah," *Tikkun* 3 (1988): 28–32, 102–105; compare her strategy of avoidance with Ach. Tat. 4.7.7.

43. I have especially benefited from the interpretive example of Jeffrey Rubenstein, *Talmudic Stories: Narrative Art, Composition, and Culture* (Baltimore, 1999); for a rich discussion of Greco-Roman narratives adapted by rabbinic literature (though missing our scene in the brothel!), see David Stern, "The Captive Woman: Hellenization, Greco-Roman Erotic Narrative, and Rabbinic Literature,"

Poetics Today 19 (1998): 91–127; Sifr. Deut. 307, *Sifre to Deuteronomy: An Analytical Translation,* vol. 2, ed. Jacob Neusner (Atlanta, 1987), 320; for the transmission of Greco-Roman folklore and romance into Jewish literature, Joshua Levinson, "The Tragedy of Romance: A Case of Literary Exile," *HTR* 89 (1996): 227–244, has many insightful comments.

44. T. Bavli, A.Z. 17a–b, trans. Mishcon, 87–88.

45. T. Bavli, A.Z. 18a, trans. Mishcon, 92.

46. T. Bavli, A.Z. 18b, trans. Mishcon, 94; on Beruriah, see Daniel Boyarin, *Carnal Israel: Reading Sex in Talmudic Culture* (Berkeley, 1993), 186–196.

47. Apophth. patr., coll. alph., John the Dwarf, 40; see the important discussion of Lucien Regnault, *Les Pères du désert: À travers leurs apophtegmes* (Sablé-sur-Sarthe, 1987), 47–51; as Regnault notes, the story is not included in some of the early witnessess to the tradition (most importantly the sixth-century Latin translation), but this is not evidence against the story's early circulation; Regnault accepts the historicity of the incident.

48. "One hour": Apophth. patr., coll. alph., John the Dwarf, 40.

49. T. Bavli, A.Z. 10b, 17a, trans. Mischon, 54, 88; on the *Apophthegmata patrum* and their transmission, see William Harmless, *Desert Christians: An Introduction to the Literature of Early Monasticism* (Oxford, 2004); Frances M. Young with Andrew Teal, *From Nicaea to Chalcedon: A Guide to the Literature and Its Background,* 2nd ed. (Grand Rapids, 2010), 83–91; Derwas Chitty, "The Books of the Old Men," *Eastern Churches Review* 6 (1974): 15–21; Jean-Claude Guy, *Recherches sur la tradition grecque des Apophthegmata Patrum* (Brussells, 1962); Regnault, *Les Pères du désert,* 57–83; Burton-Christie, *The Word in the Desert,* 76–79.

50. "Air is more pure": Orig. Hom. in Luc. 11.4; other prostitutes in the primitive strata include Apophth. patr., coll. alph., Ephrem 3; John the Dwarf 16; John of the Cells 1; Timotheus 1; coll. anon. 43 (gruesome but important, which Regnault, *Les Pères du désert,* 48–49, sees as a sanitized version of the tale in John the Dwarf 40) at François Nau, "Histoires des solitaires Égyptiens," *Revue de l'Orient chrétien* 12 (1907): 174; Serapion and the prostitute: Apophth. patr., coll. alph., Serapion 1.

51. Repentance of the sinful woman in Christian homilies: e.g., Amphil. Icon. Or. in mul. pecc. 4, discussed in Chapter 3; see also Hannah Hunt, "Sexuality and Penitence in Syriac Commentaries on Luke's Sinful Woman," *Studia Patristica* 44 (2010): 189–194; Scott Johnson, "The Sinful Woman: A *memra* by Jacob of Serug," *Sobornost* 24 (2002): 56–88; Sebastian Brock, "The Sinful Woman and Satan: Two Syriac Dialogue Poems," *Oriens Christianus* 72 (1988): 21–62; François Graffin, "Homélies anonymes sur la pécheresse," *L'Orient Syrien* 7 (1962): 175–222; Lib. Prog. 11.18; with Craig A. Gibson, *Libanius's* Progymnasmata: *Model Exercises in Greek Prose Composition and Rhetoric* (Atlanta, 2008), 402–405.

52. Albert Gayet, *Antinoë et les sépultures de Thaïs et Sérapion* (Paris, 1902); Florence Calament, *La révélation d'Antinoé par Albert Gayet: Histoire, archéologie, muséographie,* 2 vols. (Cairo, 2005), has brilliantly reconstructed the archaeologist's work, esp. 125; Nancyt Arthur Hoskins, *The Coptic Tapestry Albums and the Archaeologists of Antinoé, Albert Gayet* (Seattle, 2004), 10–11.

53. François Nau, *Histoire de Thaïs: Publication des textes grecs et de divers autres textes et versions* (Paris, 1903).

54. To make matters more complicated, at least by the seventh century Syriac versions of the story credited Bessarion with her rescue! See E. A. Wallis Budge, *The Sayings and Stories of the Christian Fathers of Egypt: The Paradise of the Holy Fathers,* vol. 1 (London, 2002 [1904]), 140–142.

55. BHG 1695–1697; although Nau's date is not unreasonable, and likely correct, it rested on nothing more than Nau's instincts about the style and spirit of the work. The only hard *terminus ante quem* is the eleventh-century manuscript at Paris that preserves the *Life of Thais;* but a fifth- or sixth-century date secured the priority of Serapion as the monk who saved Thais and thus bolstered the possibility of a connection with the mummies of Antinoe and the legendary saints.

56. Nau, *Histoire de Thaïs,* 40.

57. Ibid., 42–48.

58. Ibid., 50–62.

59. On Pelagia, BHG 1478; Hippolyte Delehaye, *The Legends of the Saints: An Introduction to Hagiography* (Whitefish, 2006 [1905]), 197–204; for the Greek text, see Bernard Flusin, "Les textes grecs," in *Pélagie la pénitente: Métamorphoses d'une légende,* 2 vols., ed. Pierre Petitmengin (Paris, 1981–1984); for the Syriac, BHO 919; Sebastian Brock and Susan Ashbrook Harvey, *Holy Women of the Syrian Orient* (Berkeley, 1987), 40–62.

60. "First lady": Vit. Pelag. 4; see Lim, "Converting the Un-Christianizable," 94–98.

61. Hel. Aeth. 2.25.1; on the romantic elements in the *Life of Pelagia,* see esp. Z. Pavlovskis, "The Life of St. Pelagia the Harlot: Hagiographic Adaptation of Pagan Romance," *Classical Folia* 30 (1976): 138–149.

62. Vit. Pelag. 24.

63. Ibid., 38.

64. Pilgrim: Anton. Plac. Itin. 16; on the tomb, Ora Limor, "The Tomb of Pelagia: Sin, Repentance, and Salvation on the Mount of Olives," *Cathedra* [Hebrew] 118 (2006): 13–40; Ora Limor, "Sharing Sacred Space: Holy Places in Jerusalem between Christianity, Judaism and Islam," in *In Laudem Hierosolymitani: Studies in Crusades and Medieval Culture in Honour of Benjamin Z. Kedar,* ed. Iris Shagrir, Ronnie Ellenblum, and Jonathan Riley-Smith (Aldershot, 2007), 219–231; on the literary afterlife of Pelagia, see Andrew Beresford, *The Legends of the Holy Harlots: Thaïs and Pelagia in Medieval Spanish Literature* (Rochester, 2007).

65. BHG 5–8; BHO 16–17; I have used the translation of Brock and Harvey, *Holy Women of the Syrian Orient*, 27–39.

66. Vit. Mar. (nept. Abr.) 17; Burrus, *Sex Lives of Saints*, 134.

67. Vit. Mar. (nept. Abr.) 19–29.

68. BHG 1041–1044; for the Vit. Mar. Aeg., I have used the Greek text in PG 87; on the narrative, and its antecedents, see esp. Maria Kouli, "Life of St. Mary of Egypt," in *Holy Women of Byzantium: Ten Saints' Lives in English Translation*, ed. Alice-Mary Talbot (Washington, D.C., 1996), 65–93; in the manuscripts, the Vit. Mar. Aeg. is attributed to Sophronius (AD 560–638), patriarch of Jerusalem; the attribution is possible: Paul B. Harvey, "'A Traveler from an Antique Land': Sources, Context, and Dissemination of the Hagiography of Mary the Egyptian," in *Egypt, Israel, and the Ancient Mediterranean World: Studies in Honor of Donald B. Redford*, ed. Gary Knoppers and Antoine Hirsch (Leiden, 2004), 479–499, is brilliant on the antecedents to the Life, though without discussion of the family of similar penitent prostitutes; F. Delmas, "Remarques sur la Vie de Sainte Marie l'Égyptienne," *Échos d' Orient* 4 (1900): 35–42; on the afterlife of the story, see, e.g., Silvia Brusamolino, *La Leggenda di Santa Maria Egiziaca: Nella redazione pavese di Arpino Broda* (Milaon, 1992); Erich Poppe and Bianca Ross, eds., *The Legend of Mary of Egypt in Medieval Insular Hagiography* (Dublin, 1996); Peter Dembowski, ed., *La Vie de sainte Marie l'Égyptienne: Versions en ancien et en moyen français* (Geneva, 1977); Konrad Kunze, *Studien zur Legende der heiligen Maria Aegyptiaca im deutschen Sprachgebiet* (Berlin, 1967).

69. Vit. Mar. Aeg. 18 (PG 87: col. 3709–3712).

70. Compare Cox Miller, "Is There a Harlot in This Text?"

71. Vit. Mar. Aeg. 19–21 (PG 87: col. 3712).

72. Vit. Mar. Aeg. 22–23 (PG 87: col. 3712–3713).

73. Vit. Mar. Aeg. 36 (PG 87: col. 3721–3714).

74. For the text, Anne Alwis, *Celibate Marriages in Late Antique and Byzantine Hagiography: The Lives of Saints Julian and Basilissa, Andronikos and Athanasia, and Galaktion and Episteme* (London, 2011); Frye, *Secular Scripture*, 13.

75. Further evidence that penitent prostitutes were a live issue in the first half of the sixth century survives in the eastern conciliar collections of the period, which show that they were a controversial element in ecclesiastical politics: see *Collectio Sabbaitica contra acephalos et origeniastas destinata* 5 (ACO 3.1) 96 and 107.

CONCLUSION

1. Ioh. Mosch. Prat. spir. 97; compare Ioh. Mosch. Prat. spir. 14.

2. Ioh. Cass. Coll. 15.10.

3. Foucault's thoughts can be found, e.g., in Carrette, *Religion and Culture*, 188–197; in general see Elizabeth A. Clark, "Foucault, the Fathers, and Sex," *Journal of*

the American Academy of Religion 56 (1988): 619–641; "heat of the body": Ioh. Cass. Coll. 12.6; degrees of chastity: Ioh. Cass. Coll. 12.7–8; on the Christian discourse of nocturnal emissions, see esp. David Brakke, "The Problematization of Nocturnal Emissions in Eary Christian Syria, Egypt, and Gaul," *JECS* 3 (1995): 419–460.

4. Frequency of emissions: Ioh. Cass. Coll. 2.23; compare Inst. 6.20; inspection by monastic elders: Ioh. Cass. Coll. 2.10; "he is found": Ioh. Cass. Coll. 12.8; chastity vs. abstinence: e.g., Ioh. Cass. Coll. 12.10.

5. Greg. Tur. Hist. 6.36.

6. Justifiable homicide: Cass. Var. 1.37 (AD 507/511); Athalaric's edict: Cass. Var. 9.18 (AD 533/4); prostitutes in Visigothic law: Lex. Vis. 3.4.17; sex between men: Lex. Vis. 3.5.4; Byzantine law: Eclog. 17.19–21; with Angeliki Laiou, "Sex, Consent, and Coercion in Byzantium," in *Consent and Coercion,* ed. Laiou, 109–221, at 117–126.

7. Aristaenetus: Ep., see Anna T. Drago, *Aristeneto: Lettere d'amore* (Lecce, 2007); Ioh. Lyd. De magis. 3.62 (Bandy 230).

Acknowledgments

I would like to express my gratitude to the many friends, teachers, and colleagues who have contributed to the completion of this book. Over the years, generous audiences at Harvard University, Dumbarton Oaks, Cambridge University, the University of Missouri, Princeton University, and the Society of Biblical Literature have heard parts of this argument and provided valuable feedback. My friends Scott Johnson and Greg Smith have been continuous sources of ideas and inspiration. Christian Laes has always shared his work and his ideas, much to my benefit. I am eternally in the debt of my teachers, Rufus Fears, Michael McCormick, and Christopher Jones, all of whom will recognize, I hope, their influence in whatever is valuable in this book.

In numerous ways my alma mater and employer, the University of Oklahoma, has made this book possible. Audiences in Classics, Judaic Studies, and Modern Languages and Literature have listened to various parts of the book and offered stimulating conversation. I would like to thank Jordan Shuart and Jill Chance for very capable research assistance and the Honors College for enabling such assistance. The staff at Bizzell Library—especially in circulation and interlibrary loan—have been astonishingly generous with a difficult patron. My Department and its chairman, Sam Huskey, have offered unwavering support, as has the entire administration, most of all President David Boren. To my friends who make the University of Oklahoma an intellectually lively place, especially on Fridays, I am grateful—Kevin Butterfield, Rangar Cline, Don Maletz, Jason Houston, Justin Wert, Luis Cortest, David Anderson, Kermyt Anderson, Jonathan Havercroft, Erik Braun, David Chappell, Eric Lomazoff, Amber Rose, Janet Ward, Dustin Gish, Jane Wickersham, David Wrobel, and Andrew Porwancher.

It has been a pleasure working with Sharmila Sen and the staff of Harvard University Press. I am grateful to the anonymous reader who made a number of invaluable suggestions. Above all, I would like to express my gratitude to Glen Bowersock, whose thoughtful guidance has made this a much better book; I have learned much from him about late antiquity in general and literature in particular. It is an honor to be included in the Revealing Antiquity series. Of course, all remaining infelicities and errors are my own stubborn fault.

Lastly, I thank my family for their continuous support. Mom, Haley, and Lance are always there for me. My daughter Sylvie is perfect, and she has taught me so much already. The book is dedicated to my amazing wife Michelle, *τὸ κάλλος οὐκ ἀνθρώπινον ἀλλὰ θεῖον*. Without her love and support it could never have been written.

Index

REVEALING ANTIQUITY

G. W. BOWERSOCK, GENERAL EDITOR

1. *Dionysos at Large,* by Marcel Detienne, translated by Arthur Goldhammer
2. *Unruly Eloquence: Lucian and the Comedy of Traditions,* by R. Bracht Branham
3. *Greek Virginity,* by Giulia Sissa, translated by Arthur Goldhammer
4. *A Chronicle of the Last Pagans,* by Pierre Chuvin, translated by B. A. Archer
5. *The Orientalizing Revolution: Near Eastern Influence on Greek Culture in the Early Archaic Age,* by Walter Burkert, translated by Margaret E. Pinder and Walter Burkert
6. *Actors in the Audience: Theatricality and Doublespeak from Nero to Hadrian,* by Shadi Bartsch
7. *Prophets and Emperors: Human and Divine Authority from Augustus to Theodosius,* by David Potter
8. *Hypatia of Alexandria,* by Maria Dzielska
9. *The Craft of Zeus: Myths of Weaving and Fabric,* by John Scheid and Jesper Svenbro
10. *Magic in the Ancient World,* by Fritz Graf, translation by Franklin Philip
11. *Pompeii: Public and Private Life,* by Paul Zanker, translated by Deborah Lucas Schneider
12. *Kinship Diplomacy in the Ancient World,* by Christopher P. Jones
13. *The End of the Past,* by Aldo Schiavone, translated by Margery J. Schneider
14. *The Invention of Jane Harrison,* by Mary Beard
15. *Ruling the Later Roman Empire,* by Christopher Kelly
16. *Mosaics as History: The Near East from Late Antiquity to Islam,* by G. W. Bowersock
17. *Histoires Grecques: Snapshots from Antiquity,* by Maurice Sartre, translated by Catherine Porter
18. *New Heroes in Antiquity: From Achilles to Antinoos,* by Christopher P. Jones
19. *Spartacus,* by Aldo Schiavone, translated by Jeremy Carden